Linux Kernel Development

Linux Kernel Development

Robert Love

DEVELOPER'S
LIBRARY

Sams Publishing, 800 East 96th Street, Indianapolis, Indiana 46240

Linux Kernel Development

International Standard Book Number: 0-672-32512-8

Library of Congress Catalog Card Number: 2002115935

Printed in the United States of America

First Printing: August 2003

06   05   04   03   4   3   2   1

Trademarks

All terms mentioned in this book that are known to be trademarks or service marks have been appropriately capitalized. Sams Publishing cannot attest to the accuracy of this information. Use of a term in this book should not be regarded as affecting the validity of any trademark or service mark.

Warning and Disclaimer

Every effort has been made to make this book as complete and as accurate as possible, but no warranty or fitness is implied. The information provided is on an "as is" basis. The author and the publisher shall have neither liability nor responsibility to any person or entity with respect to any loss or damages arising from the information contained in this book.

Bulk Sales

Sams offers excellent discounts on this book when ordered in quantity for bulk purchases or special sales. For more information, please contact

> U.S. Corporate and Government Sales
> 1-800-382-3419
> corpsales@pearsontechgroup.com

For sales outside of the U.S., please contact

> International Sales
> 1-317-581-3793
> international@pearsontechgroup.com

Acquisitions Editor
Kathryn Mohr

Development Editor
Scott Meyers

Managing Editor
Charlotte Clapp

Project Editor
George E. Nedeff

Copy Editor
Chip Gardner

Indexer
Rebecca Salerno

Proofreader
Tracy Donhardt

Technical Editor
Zack Brown

Team Coordinator
Vanessa Evans

Multimedia Developer
Dan Scherf

Interior Designer
Gary Adair

Cover Designer
Alan Clements

Page Layout

❖

To my parents, for everything.

❖

Plan-it Publishing

Contents at a Glance

Appendixes

Table of Contents

About the Author

Robert Love has used Linux since the early days and is active in the open source community. Currently, he is employed as a software engineer at MontaVista Software, where he hacks on the Linux kernel.

His kernel projects include the process scheduler, the preemptive kernel, the VM, and multiprocessing enhancements. His other open source projects include *schedutils* and *procps*, both of which he maintains. He has given several talks on the kernel and he is a Contributing Editor for *Linux Journal*. He currently lives in Gainesville, Florida and enjoys photography and good food.

About the Technical Editor

Zack Brown is the author and creator of the popular weekly newsletter, *Kernel Traffic*, which he has written since 1999, and which follows events on the Linux kernel development mailing list. He regularly produces the "diff -u" feature for *Linux Journal* and "Zack's Kernel News" for Germany's *Linux Magazin*. He lives and works in San Francisco, and enjoys Perl programming, playing chess, folding origami, and stroking a wonderful, longhaired guinea pig named Marmut.

Acknowledgements

Like most authors, I did not write this book in a cave and consequently many hearts and minds contributed to the completion of this manuscript. While no list would be complete, it is my pleasure to acknowledge the assistance of many friends and colleagues who provided encouragement, knowledge, and constructive criticism.

First, I would like to acknowledge and thank my editor at Sams, Kathryn Mohr, for her support and guidance. She convinced me to write this book and guided me through the process from conception to completion. Another big "thank you" to the rest of the team at Sams for their invaluable assistance: Chip Gardner, Scott Meyers, and George Nedeff.

Extra thanks to my technical editor, Zack Brown, who provided invaluable comments and correction. Zack's insight proved crucial on many occasions. Despite his good work, however, any remaining errors are solely my own fault.

Many fellow kernel developers answered questions, provided support, or simply wrote code interesting enough on which to write a book. They are Alan Cox, Greg Kroah-Hartman, William Irwin, Daniel Phillips, David Miller, Patrick Mochel, Ingo Molnar, Andrew Morton, Rik van Riel, and Linus Torvalds.

A number of people provided encouragement and support at some point in my life that culminated in this book. They are Paul Amici, Richard Erickson, Dustin Hall, Jack Handy, Joyce Hawkins, Doris Love, Jonathan Love, Linda Love, Dustin Mounce, Randy O'Dowd, Salvatore Ribaudo and his wonderful mother, Chris Rivera, Larry Rivero, Jeremy VanDoren and family, Steve Weisberg, and Helen Whisnant.

I am gracious to my employer, MontaVista Software, and my colleagues there, especially Scott Anderson and Mark Orvek, for their support.

Special thanks to Marlena, without whom I could never have succeeded.

Finally, thank you to my parents, for their love.

Happy hacking.

Robert Love
Gainesville, Florida

We Want to Hear from You!

As the reader of this book, *you* are our most important critic and commentator. We value your opinion and want to know what we're doing right, what we could do better, what areas you'd like to see us publish in, and any other words of wisdom you're willing to pass our way.

You can email or write me directly to let me know what you did or didn't like about this book—as well as what we can do to make our books stronger.

Please note that I cannot help you with technical problems related to the topic of this book, and that due to the high volume of mail I receive, I might not be able to reply to every message.

When you write, please be sure to include this book's title and author as well as your name and phone or email address. I will carefully review your comments and share them with the author and editors who worked on the book.

Email: opensource@samspublishing.com
Mail: Mark Taber
            Associate Publisher
            Sams Publishing
            800 East 96th Street
            Indianapolis, Indiana 46240 USA

Reader Services

For more information about this book or others from Sams Publishing, visit our Web site at www.samspublishing.com. Type the ISBN (excluding hyphens) or the title of the book in the Search box to find the book you're looking for.

Foreword

As the Linux kernel and the applications that use it become more widely used, we are seeing an increasing number of system software developers who want to become involved in the development and maintenance of Linux. Some of these engineers are motivated purely by personal interest, some work for Linux companies, some work for hardware manufacturers, and some are involved with in-house development projects.

But all face a common problem: The learning curve for the kernel is getting longer and steeper. The system is becoming increasingly complex, and it is very large. And as the years pass, the current members of the kernel development team gain deeper and broader knowledge of the kernel's internals, which widens the gap between them and newcomers.

I believe that this declining accessibility of the Linux source base is already a problem for the quality of the kernel, and it will become more serious over time. Those who care for Linux clearly have an interest in increasing the number of developers who can contribute to the kernel.

One approach to this problem is to keep the code clean: sensible interfaces, consistent layout, "do one thing, do it well," and so on. This is Linus Torvalds' solution.

The approach that I counsel is to liberally apply commentary to the code: words that the reader can use to understand what the coder intended to achieve at the time. (The process of identifying divergences between the intent and the implementation is known as *debugging*. It is hard to do this if the intent is not known.)

But even code commentary does not provide the broad-sweep view of what major subsystems are intended to do, and how their developers set about doing them.

This, the starting point of understanding, is what the written word serves best.

Robert Love's contribution provides a means by which experienced developers can gain that essential view of what services the kernel subsystems are supposed to provide, and how they set about providing them. This will be sufficient knowledge for many people: the curious, the application developers, those who want to evaluate the kernel's design, and others.

But the book is also a stepping stone to take aspiring kernel developers to the next stage, which is making alterations to the kernel to achieve some defined objective. I would encourage aspiring developers to get their hands dirty: The best way to understand a part of the kernel is to make changes to it. Making a change forces the developer to a level of understanding that merely reading the code does not provide.

The serious kernel developer will join the development mailing lists and interact with other developers. This is the primary means by which kernel contributors learn and stay abreast. Robert covers the mechanics and culture of this important part of kernel life well.

Please enjoy and learn from Robert's book. And should you decide to take the next step and become a member of the kernel development community, consider yourself welcomed in advance. We value and measure people by the value of their contributions, and when you contribute to Linux, you do so in the knowledge that your work is of small but immediate benefit to tens or even hundreds of millions of human beings. This is a most enjoyable privilege and responsibility.

Andrew Morton
Digeo Interactive, Palo Alto
July 2003

Preface

When I was first approached about converting my experiences with the Linux kernel into a book, I was unsure how to proceed. I did not want to simply write yet another kernel book. Sure, there are not that many books on the subject, but I still desired something to make my approach unique. What would place my book at the top of its subject? I thought hard about how my book could be special.

I then realized that I could offer quite a unique approach to the topic. My job is hacking the kernel. My hobby is hacking the kernel. My love is the kernel. Over the years, I have surely accumulated interesting anecdotes and important tips. With my experiences, I could write a book on how to hack the kernel and how *not* to hack the kernel. Primarily, this is a book about the design and implementation of the Linux kernel. The book's approach differs, however, in that the information is given with a slant to learning enough to actually get work done—and getting it done right.

I hope that readers can walk away from this book with a better understanding of the rules (written and unwritten) of the kernel. I hope readers, fresh from reading this book and the kernel source code, can jump in and start writing useful, correct, clean kernel code. Of course, you can read this book just for fun, too.

Whatever your intentions with Linux, I hope you enjoy this book.

Author's Introduction

Developing code in the kernel does not require genius, magic, or a bushy Unix-hacker beard. The kernel, although having some interesting rules of its own, is not much different from any other big software project. There is much to learn as with any large project, but there is not too much more sacred or confusing about the kernel than any other software endeavor.

It is very important that you read the source. The open availability of the source code for the Linux system is a rarity that you must not take for granted. It is not sufficient *only* to read the source, however. You need to dig in and change some code. Find a bug and fix it. Improve the drivers for your hardware. Find an itch and scratch it! Only by *writing* code will it all come together.

Audience

This book targets software developers who are interested in understanding the Linux kernel. It is *not* a line-by-line commentary of the kernel source. Nor is it a guide to developing drivers or a reference on the kernel API (as if there even was a formal kernel API). Instead, the goal of this book is to provide enough information on the design and implementation of the Linux kernel that a sufficiently accomplished programmer can begin developing code in the kernel. Kernel development can be fun and rewarding, and I want to introduce the reader to that world as readily as possible. This book, however, in discussing both theory and application, should appeal to readers of either interest. I have always been of the mind that one needs to understand the theory to understand the application, but I do not feel this book leans too far in either direction. I hope that whatever your motivations for understanding the Linux kernel, this book will explain the design and implementation sufficiently for your needs.

Thus, this book covers both the usage of core kernel systems and their design and implementation. I think this is important, and deserves a moment's discussion. A good example is Chapter 6, "Bottom Halves and Deferring Work," which covers bottom halves. In that chapter, I discuss both the design and implementation of the kernel's bottom-half mechanisms (which a core kernel developer might find interesting) and how to actually use the exported interfaces to implement your own bottom half (which a device driver developer might find interesting). In fact, I believe both parties should find both discussions relevant. The core kernel developer, who certainly needs to understand the inner workings of the kernel, should have a good understanding of how the interfaces are actually used. At the same time, a device driver writer will benefit from a good understanding of the implementation behind the interface.

This is akin to learning some library's API versus studying the actual implementation of the library. At first glance, an application programmer needs only to understand the API—it is often taught to treat interfaces as a black box, in fact. Likewise, a library developer is concerned only with the library's design and implementation. I believe, however, both parties should invest time in learning the other half. An application programmer who better understands the underlying operating system can make much greater use of it. Similarly, the library developer should not grow out of touch with the reality and practicality of the applications that use the library. Consequently, I discuss both the design and usage of kernel subsystems, not only in the hope that this book is useful to either party, but in the hope that the *whole* book is useful to both parties.

I assume the reader knows the C programming language and is familiar with Linux. Some experience with operating system design and other computer science concepts is beneficial, but I try to explain concepts as much as possible—if not, there are some excellent books on operating system design referenced in the bibliography.

This book is appropriate for an undergraduate course introducing operating system design as the *applied* text, if an introductory book on theory accompanies it. It should fair well either in an advanced undergraduate course or in a graduate-level course without ancillary material. I encourage potential instructors to contact me; I am eager to help.

Organization of Material

This book is designed to be read from start to finish; that is, each chapter builds off the previous as much as possible to provide a linear presentation of the material. That is not to say, however, that it is impossible to visit random chapters for reference. To the contrary, I have tried to make each chapter sufficiently self-contained for one who is already familiar with the material in general, but is seeking reference on a specific topic.

Chapter 1 introduces operating systems, kernels, Unix, and ultimately Linux itself.

Someone who has previously read a book on Unix, Linux, or operating systems should find the material familiar. Chapter 2 discusses the kernel abstraction of the process and how processes are created, destroyed, and otherwise managed. Because the point of the operating system is ultimately to allow the user to run programs, this is a fundamental chapter. Continuing with the concept of processes, Chapter 3 discusses process scheduling. In preemptive multitasking operating systems such as Linux, the kernel is responsible for scheduling process execution. The Chapter begins with an overview of scheduling design and eventually goes over the Linux scheduler in detail. Chapter 4 covers system calls, which are the standard mechanism applications use to interface with the kernel. The chapter discusses the philosophy of system calls, the design of the system call handler, and how to implement new system calls. Chapter 5 covers interrupts and interrupt handlers and Chapter 6 covers bottom halves and other methods of deferring work. These concepts are instrumental in writing device drivers and managing hardware. I broke synchronization and locking into two chapters. First, Chapter 7 discusses the issues of synchronization and concurrency, including race conditions and deadlocks. The chapter suggests solutions to these problems, such as locking, and discusses related issues, such as deadlocks. Then, Chapter 8 introduces the actual kernel interfaces, such as spin locks and semaphores, which maintain synchronization inside the kernel. After Chapter 7 provides the essentials, Chapter 8 acts as a good reference to the kernel's locking interfaces. Chapter 9 is on the flow of time inside the kernel. This chapter discusses the meaning and representation of time to an operating system and how the kernel manages time for the system. The chapter then discusses both the implementation and use of kernel timers. Chapter 10 discusses memory management and how to allocate memory inside the kernel. Chapter 11 talks about the Virtual Filesystem (VFS), which provides a common filesystem interface to user-space. The VFS is the glue layer between hardware, filesystems, and user-space. The block I/O layer, the subsystem of the kernel responsible for managing devices such as hard drives, is discussed in Chapter 12. The block I/O layer is an important part of the kernel due to the performance sensitivity of block devices. Chapter 13, in turn, considers the process address space and the virtualization of memory provided to processes. Chapter 14 discusses the page cache and how the kernel carries out page writeback. The page cache is the primary memory cache in Linux. Memory caches are used to improve system performance by reducing the amount of disk access. Chapter 15 considers the art of debugging the kernel. Debugging the kernel is often cited as the largest difficulty in programming the kernel over user-space, as the kernel is not afforded the same luxuries that user-space applications are. This chapter discusses the basic methods of debugging the kernel, some of the add-on kernel debuggers available (alas, there is no standard debugger!), and some debugging tricks that might help you out of a tough spot. Chapter 16 discusses portability and the quirks of various system architectures that you must keep in mind to write code that can run on any architecture that Linux supports. Portability is an interesting topic because it sheds light on architectural design differences. It is also a very important consideration in writing good kernel code because Linux is a portable operating system and, thus, runs on many different architectures. Finally, Chapter 17 discusses issues such as generating and using patches and working in the Linux kernel community. Four appendixes and a bibliography wrap up the book. The appendixes cover the kernel linked list implementation, the per-processor allocation interface, the kernel random number generator, and algorithmic complexity, respectively. The bibliography provides a recommended reading list on a handful of related topics.

Book Web Site

I maintain a Web site at `http://tech9.net/rml/kernel_book/` that contains information pertaining to the book, including errata, expanded and revised topics, and information on future printings and editions. I encourage readers to check it out.

1

Introduction to the Linux Kernel

Aﬀer three decades of use, the Unix operating system is still regarded as one of
the most powerful and elegant systems in existence. Since the creation of Unix in 1969,
the brainchild of Dennis Ritchie and Ken Thompson has become a creature of legends, a
system whose design has withstood the test of time with few bruises to its name.

Unix grew out of Multics, a failed Bell Laboratories multiuser operating system project. With the Multics project terminated, members of Bell Laboratories' Computer
Sciences Research Center were left without a capable interactive operating system. In
the summer of 1969, Bell Lab programmers sketched out a file system design that ultimately evolved into Unix. Thompson implemented the new system on an otherwise idle
PDP-7. In 1971, Unix was ported to the PDP-11, and in 1973 the operating system was
rewritten in C, an unprecedented step at the time, but one that paved the way for future
portability. The first Unix widely used outside of Bell Labs was Unix System, Sixth
Edition, more commonly called V6.

Other companies ported Unix to new machines. Accompanying these ports were
enhancements that resulted in several variants of the operating system. In 1977, Bell Labs
released a combination of these variants into a single system, Unix System III; in 1982,
AT&T released System V[1].

The simplicity of Unix's design, and the fact that it was distributed with source code,
led to further development at outside organizations. The most influential of these contributors was the University of California at Berkeley. Variants of Unix from Berkeley are
called Berkeley Software Distributions (BSD). The first Berkeley Unix was 3BSD in
1981. A series of 4BSD releases, 4.0BSD, 4.1BSD, 4.2BSD, and 4.3BSD, followed 3BSD.
These versions of Unix added virtual memory, demand paging, and TCP/IP. In 1993, the
final official Berkeley Unix, featuring a rewritten VM, was released as 4.4BSD. Today,
development of BSD continues with the FreeBSD, NetBSD, and OpenBSD systems.
In the 1980s and 1990s, multiple workstation and server companies introduced their
own commercial version of Unix. These systems were typically based on either an AT&T

---

[1]What about System IV? The rumor is it was an internal development version.

or Berkeley release and supported high-end features developed for their particular architecture. Among these systems were Digital's Tru64, Hewlett Packard's HP-UX, IBM's AIX, Sequent's DYNIX/ptx, SGI's IRIX, and Sun's Solaris.

The original elegant design of the Unix system, coupled with the years of innovation and evolutionary improvement that followed, has made Unix a powerful, robust, and stable operating system. A handful of characteristics of Unix are responsible for its resilience. First, Unix is simple; whereas some operating systems implement thousands of system calls and have unclear design goals, Unix systems typically implement only hundreds of system calls and have a very clear design. Second, in Unix, *everything is a file*[2]. This simplifies the manipulation of data and devices into a set of simple system calls: `open()`, `read()`, `write()`, `ioctl()`, and `close()`. Third, the Unix kernel and related system utilities are written in C—a property that gives Unix its amazing portability and accessibility to a wide range of developers.

Next, Unix has fast process creation time and the unique `fork()` system call. Finally, Unix provides simple yet robust interprocess communication primitives that, when coupled with the fast process creation time, allow for the creation of simple utilities that *do one thing and do it well,* which can be strung together to accomplish more complicated tasks.

Today, Unix is a modern operating system supporting multitasking, multithreading, virtual memory, demand paging, shared libraries with demand loading, and TCP/IP networking. Many Unix variants scale to hundreds of processors, whereas other Unix systems run on small, embedded devices. Although Unix is no longer a research project, implementations continue to benefit from advances in operating system design, yet remain a practical and general-purpose operating system.

Unix owes its success to the simplicity and elegance of its design. Its strength today lies in the early decisions that Dennis Ritchie, Ken Thompson, and other early developers made; choices that have endowed Unix with the capability to evolve without compromising itself.

Introduction to Linux

Linux was developed by Linus Torvalds in 1991 as an operating system for computers using the Intel 80386 microprocessor, which was new at the time. Today, Linux is a full-fledged operating system also running on AMD x86-64, ARM, Compaq Alpha, CRIS, DEC VAX, H8/300, Hitachi SuperH, HP PA-RISC, IBM S/390, Intel IA-64, MIPS, Motorola 68000, PowerPC, SPARC, UltraSPARC, and v850. It runs on systems as small as a watch to as large as super-computer clusters. Today, commercial interest in Linux is strong. Both new Linux-specific corporations, as well as old mainstays, are providing Linux-based solutions for embedded, desktop, and server needs.

---

[2]Well, OK, not everything—but much is represented as a file. Modern operating systems, such as Unix's successor Plan9, implement nearly everything as a file.

Linux is a Unix clone, but it is not Unix. That is, although Linux borrows many ideas from Unix and implements the Unix API (as defined by POSIX and the Single Unix Specification) it is not a direct decedent of the Unix source code like other Unix systems. Where desired, it has deviated from the path taken by other implementations, but it has not compromised the general design goals of Unix or broken the application interfaces.

One of Linux's most interesting features is that it is not a commercial product; instead, it is a collaborative project developed over the Internet. Although Linus remains the creator of Linux and the *maintainer* of the kernel, work continues through a loose-knit group of developers. In fact, anyone can contribute to Linux. The Linux kernel, as with much of the system, is *free* or *open source* software[3]. Specifically, the Linux kernel is licensed under the GNU General Public License (GPL) version 2.0. Consequently, you are free to download the source code and make any modifications you want. The only caveat is that if you distribute your changes, you must continue to provide the recipients with the same rights you enjoyed, including the availability of the source code[4].

Linux is many things to many people. The basics of a Linux system are the kernel, C library, compiler, toolchain, and basic system utilities, such as a login process and shell. A Linux system can also include a modern X Window System implementation including a full-featured desktop environment, such as GNOME. Thousands of free and commercial applications exist for Linux. In this book, when I say *Linux* I typically mean the *Linux kernel*. Where it is ambiguous, I try explicitly to point out whether I am referring to *Linux* as a full system or just the kernel proper. Strictly speaking, after all, the term *Linux* only refers to the kernel.

Because the Linux source code is available, it follows that you are able to configure the kernel before compiling it. It is possible to compile support for just the drivers and features you need. This capability is controlled via configure options of the form `CONFIG_FEATURE`. For example, symmetrical multiprocessing (SMP) support is configured via `CONFIG_SMP`. If it is set, SMP support is enabled. If it is not set, SMP support is disabled. These options are stored in the `.config` file in the root of your kernel tree and set via one of the configure programs, for example `make xconfig`. The configure options are used both to decide which files to compile during a build and to manipulate the build via preprocessor directives.

Overview of Operating Systems and Kernels

Thanks to some modern commercial operating systems, the notion of an operating system is vague. Many users consider what they see on the screen the operating system.

---

[3] I will leave the *free* vs. *open* debate to those who care. See `http://www.fsf.org` and `http://www.opensource.org`.

[4] You should probably read the GNU GPL if you have not. There is a copy in the file COPYING in your kernel source tree. You can also find it online at `http://www.fsf.org`.

Generally, and in this book, the operating system is considered to be the parts of the system responsible for basic use and administration. This includes the kernel and device drivers, boot loader, command shell or other user interface, and basic file and system utilities. The stuff you *need*. The term *system* refers to the operating system and all the applications running on top of it.

Of course, the topic of this book is the *kernel*. Whereas the user interface is the outermost portion of the operating system, the kernel is the innermost. It is the core internals; the software that provides basic services for all other parts of the system, manages hardware, and distributes system resources. The kernel is sometimes referred to as the *supervisor* or *core* of the operating system. Typical components of a kernel are interrupt handlers to service interrupt requests, a scheduler to share processor time among multiple processes, a memory management system to manage process address spaces, and system services such as networking and interprocess communication. On modern systems with protected memory management units, the kernel typically resides in an elevated system state compared to normal user applications. This includes a protected memory space and full access to the hardware. This system state and memory space is collectively called *kernel-space*. Conversely, user applications execute in *user-space*. They see a subset of the machine's available resources and are unable to perform certain system functions, directly access hardware, or otherwise misbehave. When executing the kernel, the system is in kernel-space as opposed to normal user execution in *user-space*.

Applications running on the system communicate with the kernel via *system call* (see Figure 1.1). An application typically calls functions in a library—for example, the C *library*—that in turn relies on the system call interface to instruct the kernel to carry out tasks on their behalf. Some library calls provide many features not found in the system call, and thus, calling into the kernel is just one-step in an otherwise large function. For example, consider the familiar `printf()` function. It provides formatting and buffering of the data and only eventually calls `write()` to write the data to the console. Conversely, some library calls have a one-to-one relationship with the kernel. For example, the `open()` library function does nothing except call the `open()` system call. Still other C library functions, such as `strcpy()`, hopefully make no use of the kernel at all. When an application executes a system call, it is said that the *kernel is executing on behalf of the application*. Furthermore, the application is said to be *executing a system call in kernel-space,* and the kernel is running in *process context*. This relationship—that applications *call into* the kernel via the system call interface—is the fundamental manner in which applications get work done.

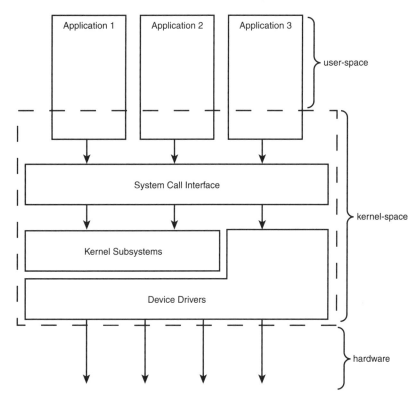

Figure 1.1 Relationship between applications, the kernel, and hardware.

Kernels also manage the system's hardware. Nearly all architectures, including all systems that Linux supports, provide the concept of *interrupts*. When hardware wants to communicate with the system, it issues an interrupt that asynchronously interrupts the kernel. Interrupts generally are associated with a number. The kernel uses the number to execute a specific *interrupt handler* to process and respond to the interrupt. For example, as you type, the keyboard controller issues an interrupt to let the system know there is data in the keyboard buffer. The kernel notes the interrupt number being issued and executes the correct interrupt handler. The interrupt handler processes the keyboard data and lets the keyboard controller know it is ready for more data. To provide synchronization, the kernel can usually disable interrupts—either all interrupts or just one specific interrupt number. In many operating systems, the interrupt handlers do not run in a process context. Instead, they run in a special *interrupt context* that is not associated with any process. This special context exists solely to let an interrupt handler quickly respond to an interrupt, and then exit.

These contexts represent the breadth of the kernel's activities. In fact, in Linux, we can generalize that the processor is doing one of three things at any given moment:

- In kernel-space, in process context, executing on behalf of a specific process
- In kernel-space, in interrupt context, not associated with a process, handling an interrupt
- In user-space, executing user code in a process

Linux Versus Classic Unix Kernels

Owing to their common ancestry and same API, modern Unix kernels share various design traits. With few exceptions, Unix kernels are typically monolithic static binaries. That is, they exist as a large single-executable image that runs in a single address space. Unix systems typically require a system with a paged memory-management unit; this hardware enables the system to enforce memory protection and provide a unique virtual address space to each process. See the bibliography for my favorite books on the design of the classic Unix kernels.

As Linus and other kernel developers contribute to the Linux kernel, they decide how best to advance Linux without neglecting its Unix roots (and more importantly, the Unix API). Consequently, because Linux is not based on any specific Unix, Linus and company are able to pick and choose the best solution to any given problem—or at times, invent new solutions! Here is an analysis of characteristics that differ between the Linux kernel and other Unix variants:

- Linux supports the dynamic loading of kernel modules. Although the Linux kernel is monolithic, it is capable of dynamically loading and unloading kernel code on demand.
- Linux has symmetrical multiprocessor (SMP) support. Although many commercial variants of Unix now support SMP, most traditional Unix implementations did not.
- The Linux kernel is preemptive. Unlike traditional Unix variants, the Linux kernel is capable of preempting a task if it is running in the kernel. Of the other commercial Unix implementations, Solaris and IRIX have preemptive kernels.
- Linux takes an interesting approach to thread support: It does not differentiate between threads and normal processes. To the kernel, all processes are the same—some just happen to share resources.
- Linux ignores some common Unix features that are thought to be poorly implemented, such as STREAMS, or standards that are brain dead.
- Linux is free in every sense of the word. The feature set Linux implements is the result of the freedom of Linux's open development model. If a feature is without merit or poorly thought out, the Linux developers are under no obligation to

implement it. To the contrary, Linux has adopted an elitist attitude toward changes: Modifications must solve a specific real-world problem, have a sane design, and have a clean implementation. Consequently, features of some other modern Unix variants, such as pageable kernel memory, have received no consideration. Despite any differences, Linux remains an operating system with a strong Unix heritage.

Linux Kernel Versions

Linux kernels come in two flavors: stable or development. Stable kernels are production-level releases suitable for widespread deployment. New stable kernels are released typically only to provide bug fixes or new drivers. Development kernels, on the other hand, undergo rapid change where (almost) anything goes. As developers experiment with new solutions, often-drastic changes to the kernel are made.

Linux kernels distinguish between stable and development kernels with a simple naming scheme (see Figure 1.2). Three numbers, each separated by a dot, represent Linux kernels. The first value is the major release, the second is the minor release, and the third is the revision. The minor release also determines whether the kernel is a stable or development kernel; an even number is stable, whereas an odd number is development. Thus, for example, the kernel version 2.6.0 designates a stable kernel. This kernel has a major version of two, a minor version of six, and is revision zero. The first two values also describe the "kernel series"—in this case, the 2.6 kernel series.

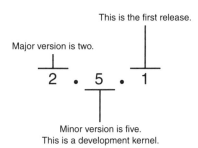

Figure 1.2   Kernel version naming convention.

Development kernels have a series of phases. Initially, the kernel developers work on new features and chaos ensues. Over time, the kernel matures and eventually a feature freeze is declared. At that point, no new features can be submitted. Work on existing features, however, can continue. After the kernel is considered nearly stabilized, a code freeze is put into effect. When that occurs, only bug fixes are accepted. Shortly thereafter (hopefully), the kernel is released as the first version of a new stable series. For example, 2.5 stabilized into 2.6.

The current Linux source code is always available in both a complete tarball and an incremental patch at `http://www.kernel.org`.

> **Where to install and hack on the source**
>
> The kernel source is typically installed in `/usr/src/linux`. Note that you should not use this source tree for development. The kernel version your *C library* is compiled against is often linked to this tree. Besides, you do not want to have to be root to make changes to the kernel—instead, work out of your home directory and use root only to install new kernels.

This book is based on the 2.6 stable kernel series.

The Linux Kernel Development Community

When you begin developing code for the Linux kernel, you become a part of the global kernel development community. The main forum for this community is the *linux-kernel mailing list*. Subscription information is available at `http://vger.kernel.org`. Note that this is a high-traffic list with upwards of 300 messages a day and that the other readers—which include all the core kernel developers, including Linus—are not open to dealing with nonsense. The list is, however, a priceless aide during development as it is the place where you will find testers, receive peer review, and ask questions.

Chapter 17 provides an overview of the kernel development process and a more complete description of participating successfully in the kernel-development community.

A Beast of a Different Nature

The kernel has several differences compared to normal user-space applications that, while not making it necessarily harder to program than user-space, certainly provide unique challenges to kernel development.

These differences make the kernel *a beast of a different nature*. Some of the usual rules are bent; other rules are entirely new. Although some of the differences are obvious (we all know the kernel can do anything it wants), others are not so obvious. The most important of these differences are

- The kernel does not have access to the C library.
- The kernel is coded in GNU C.
- The kernel lacks memory protection like user-space.
- The kernel cannot easily use floating point.
- The kernel has a small fixed-size stack.
- Because the kernel has asynchronous interrupts, is preemptive, and supports SMP, synchronization and concurrency are concerns within the kernel.
- Portability is important.

Let's briefly look at each of these issues because all kernel development must keep them in mind.

No libc

Unlike a user-space application, the kernel is not linked against the standard C library (or any other library, for that matter). There are multiple reasons for this, including some chicken and the egg situations, but the primary reason is speed and size. The full C library—or even a decent subset of it—is too large and too inefficient for the kernel.

Do not fret, because many of the usual libc functions have been implemented inside the kernel. For example, the common string manipulation functions are in `lib/string.c`. Just include `<linux/string.h>` and have at them. Note that when I talk about header files here—or elsewhere in this book—I am referring to the kernel headers files that are part of the kernel source tree. Kernel source files cannot include outside headers, just as they cannot use outside libraries.

Of the missing functions, the most familiar is `printf()`. The kernel does not have access to `printf()`, but it does have access to `printk()`. The `printk()` function copies the formatted string into the kernel log buffer, which is normally read by the syslog program. Usage is similar to `printf()`:

```
printk("Hello world! A string: %s and an integer: %d\n", a_string, an_integer);
```

One notable difference between `printf()` and `printk()` is that `printk()` allows you to specify a priority flag. This flag is used by syslog to decide where to display kernel messages. An example of these priorities:

```
printk(KERN_ERR "this is an error!\n");
```

We will use `printk()` throughout this book. Chapter 15, "Debugging," has more information on `printk()`.

GNU C

Like any self-respecting Unix kernel, the Linux kernel is programmed in C. Perhaps surprising, the kernel is not programmed in strict ANSI C. Instead, where applicable, the kernel developers make use of various language extensions available in *gcc* (gcc is the GNU Compiler Collection, which contains the C compiler used to compile the kernel).

The kernel developers use both ISO C99[5] and GNU C extensions to the C language. These changes wed the Linux kernel to gcc, although recently compilers, such as the Intel C compiler, have sufficiently supported enough gcc features that they too can compile the Linux kernel. The ISO C99 extensions that the kernel uses are nothing special and, because C99 is an official revision of the C language, are slowly cropping up in

---

[5]ISO C99 is the latest major revision to the ISO C standard. C99 adds numerous enhancements to the previous major revision, ISO C90, including named structure initializers and a `complex` type.

a lot of other code. The more interesting, and perhaps unfamiliar, deviations from standard ANSI C are those provided by GNU C. Let's look at some of the more interesting extensions that may show up in kernel code.

Inline Functions

GNU C supports *inline functions*. An inline function is, as its name suggests, inserted inline into each call site. This eliminates the overhead of function invocation and return (register saving and restore), and allows for potentially more optimization, as the compiler can optimize the caller and the called function together. As a downside (nothing in life is free), code size increases, which increases memory consumption and instruction cache footprint. Kernel developers use inline functions for small time-critical functions. Making large functions inline, especially those that are used more than once or are not time critical, is frowned against.

An inline function is declared using the keywords `static` and `inline` as part of the function definition. For example:

```
static inline void dog(unsigned long tail_size)
```

The function declaration must precede any usage, or else it cannot be inlined. Common practice is to place inline functions in header files. Because they are marked `static`, a non-inlined compilation unit is not created. If an inline function is only used by one file, it can also be placed toward the top of just that file.

In the kernel, using inline functions is preferred over complicated macros.

Inline Assembly

The gcc C compiler enables the embedding of assembly instructions in otherwise normal C functions. This feature, of course, is only used in parts of the kernel that are unique to a given system architecture.

The Linux kernel is programmed in a mixture of C and assembly, with assembly relegated to low-level architecture and fast path code. The vast majority of kernel code is programmed in straight C.

Branch Annotation

The gcc C compiler has a built-in directive that optimizes conditional branches as either very likely taken or very unlikely taken. The compiler uses the directive to appropriately optimize the branch. The kernel wraps the directive in very easy to use macros, `likely()` and `unlikely()`.

For example, consider an if statement such as:

```
if (foo) {
    /* .. */
}
```

To mark this branch as very unlikely taken (that is, likely not taken):

```
/* we predict foo is zero .. */
if (unlikely(foo)) {
    /* .. */
}
```

Conversely, to mark a branch as very likely taken:

```
/* we predict foo is nonzero .. */
if (likely(foo)) {
    /* .. */
}
```

You should only use these directives when the branch direction is overwhelmingly known a priori or when you want to optimize a specific case at the cost of the other case. This is an important point: These directives result in a performance boost when the branch is correctly predicted, but a performance loss when the branch is mispredicted. A very common usage for `unlikely()` and `likely()` is error conditions.

No Memory Protection

When a user-space application attempts an illegal memory access, the kernel can trap the error and kill the process. If the kernel attempts an illegal memory access, the results are less controlled. Memory violations in the kernel result in an *oops*, which is a major kernel error. It should go without saying that you must not access illegal memory, dereference a `NULL` pointer, and so on—but within the kernel, the stakes are much higher!

Additionally, kernel memory is not pageable. Therefore, every byte of memory you consume is one less byte of available physical memory. Keep that in mind next time you have to add *one more feature* to the kernel!

No (Easy) Use of Floating Point

When a user-space process uses floating point instructions, the kernel manages the transition from integer to floating point mode. What the kernel has to do when using floating point instructions varies by architecture.

Unlike user-space, the kernel does not have the luxury of seamless support for floating point. Using floating point inside the kernel requires manually saving and restoring the floating point registers, among possible other chores. The short answer is: D*on't do it*; no floating point in the kernel.

Small, Fixed Size Stack

User-space can get away with statically allocating tons of variables on the stack, including huge structures and many-element arrays. This behavior is legal because user-space has a large stack that can dynamically grow in size.

The kernel stack is neither large nor dynamic; it is small and fixed in size. The kernel stack is fixed at 4 KB on 32-bit architectures and 8 KB on 64-bit architectures.

For more discussion on the kernel stack, see the section *Statically Allocating on the Stack* in Chapter 10, "Memory Management."

Synchronization and Concurrency

The kernel is prone to race conditions. Unlike a single-threaded user-space application, a number of properties of the kernel allow for concurrent access of shared resources and thus require synchronization to prevent races. Specifically,

- The Linux kernel supports multiprocessing. Therefore, without proper protection, kernel code executing on two or more processors can access the same resource.
- Interrupts occur asynchronously with respect to the currently executing code. Therefore, without proper protection, an interrupt can occur in the midst of accessing a shared resource and the interrupt handler can access the same resource.
- The Linux kernel is preemptive. Therefore, without protection, kernel code can be preempted in favor of different code that then accesses the same resource.

Typical solutions to race conditions include spinlocks and semaphores.

For a thorough discussion of synchronization and concurrency, see Chapter 7, "Kernel Synchronization Introduction," and Chapter 8, "Kernel Synchronization Methods."

Portability Is Important

While user-space applications do not *have* to aim for portability, Linux is a portable operating system and should remain one. This means that architecture-independent C code must correctly compile and run on a wide range of systems.

A handful of rules—such as remain endian neutral, 64-bit clean, do not assume the word or page size, and so on—go a long way. Chapter 16, "Portability," is dedicated to the topic of portability.

Building the Kernel

Building the kernel is fairly easy. In fact, it is surprisingly easier than compiling and installing other system-level components, such as glibc. The 2.6 kernel series introduces a new configuration and build system, which makes the job even easier and is a welcome improvement over 2.4.

Before you can build the kernel, you must configure it. Because the kernel offers a myriad of features and supports tons of varied hardware, there is a *lot* to configure. Configuration options are represented by symbols prefixed by *CONFIG*, such as CON-FIG_PREEMPT, which represents whether or not kernel preemption is enabled. Configuration options are either *Booleans* or *tristates*. A Boolean option is either *yes* or *no*. Kernel features, such as CONFIG_PREEMPT, are usually Booleans. A tristate option is one of *yes*, *no*, or *module*. The *module* setting represents a configuration option which is set, but is to be compiled as a module (that is, a separate dynamically loadable object). Drivers are usually represented by tristates.

The kernel provides multiple tools to facilitate configuration. The simplest tool is a text-based command-line utility:

```
make config
```

This utility goes through each option, one by one, and asks the user to interactively select *yes*, *no*, or (for tristates) *module*. Because this takes a *long* time, unless you are paid by the hour, you should use an ncurses-based graphical utility:

```
make menuconfig
```

Or, an X11-based graphical utility:

```
make xconfig
```

These two utilities divide the various configuration options into categories, such as "Processor Features" and "Network Devices." You can move through the categories, view the kernel options, and of course change their values.

The configuration options are stored in the root of the kernel source tree, in a file named .config. You may find it easier—as most of the kernel developers do—to just edit this file directly. It is quite easy to search for, and it changes the value of the configuration options. After making changes to your configuration file, or when using an existing configuration file on a new kernel tree, you can validate and update the configuration:

```
make oldconfig
```

You should always run this before building a kernel, in fact. Once the kernel configuration is set, you can build it:

```
make
```

Unlike kernels before 2.6, you no longer need to run make dep before building the kernel—the dependency tree is maintained automatically. You also do not need to specify a specific build type, such as *bzImage*, as you did in old versions. The default Makefile rule will handle everything!

A trick to minimize build noise, but still see warnings and errors, is to redirect the output from make(1):

```
make > some_other_file
```

If you ever do need to see the build output, you can read the file. But since the warnings and errors *are* displayed, you normally do not need to.

Once the kernel is built, you need to install it. How it is installed is very architecture and boot loader dependent—consult the directions for your boot loader on where to copy the kernel image and how to add it to set it up to boot. Always keep a known-safe kernel or two around in case your new kernel has problems!

As an example, on x86 using grub, you might copy `arch/i386/boot/bzImage` to `/boot` and edit `/etc/grub/grub.conf` with a new entry for the new kernel.

The build process also creates the file `System.map` in the root of the kernel source tree. It contains a symbol lookup table, mapping kernel symbols to their start addresses. This is used during debugging to translate memory addresses to function and variable names.

Before We Begin

This book is about the Linux kernel: how it works, why it works, and why you should care. It covers the design and implementation of the core kernel subsystems as well as its interfaces and programming semantics. The book is practical, and takes a middle road toward explaining how all of this stuff works. This interesting approach—coupled with some personal anecdotes and tips on kernel hacking—should ensure this book gets you off the ground running.

I hope you have access to a Linux system and have the kernel source. Ideally, by this point, you are a Linux user and have been poking and prodding at the source, but require some help making it all come together. Conversely, you might never have used Linux but just want to learn the design of the kernel out of curiosity. However, if your desire is to write some code of your own, there is no substitute for the source. The source code is *freely* available; use it!

Oh, and above all else, *have fun!*

2

Process Management

THE *PROCESS* IS ONE OF THE FUNDAMENTAL abstractions in Unix operating systems[1]. A process is a program (object code stored on some media) in execution. It is, however, more than just the executing program code (often called the *text section* in Unix). Processes also include a *data section* containing global variables, a set of resources such as open files and pending signals, an address space, and one or more *threads of execution*.

Threads of execution, often shortened to *threads*, are the objects of activity within the process. Each thread includes a unique program counter, process stack, and set of processor registers. The kernel schedules individual threads, not processes. In traditional Unix systems, each process consists of one thread. In modern systems, however, multithreaded programs are common. As you will see later, Linux has a unique implementation of threads—it does not differentiate between threads and processes.

Processes provide two virtualizations: a virtualized processor and virtual memory. The virtual processor gives the process the illusion that it alone monopolizes the system, despite possibly sharing the processor amongst dozens of other processes. Chapter 3, "Scheduling," discusses this virtualization. Virtual memory lets the process allocate and manage memory as if it alone owned all the memory in the system. Virtual memory is covered in Chapter 10, "Memory Management and Addressing." Threads *share* the virtual memory abstraction while each receives their own virtualized processor.

Note that a program itself is not a process; a process is an *active* program and related resources. Indeed, two or more processes can exist that are executing the *same* program. In fact, two or more processes can exist that share various resources, such as open files or an address space. A process begins its life when, not surprisingly, it is created. In Linux, this occurs by means of the `fork()`[2] system call, which creates a new process by duplicating an existing one. The process that calls `fork()` is the *parent*, whereas the new process is the *child*. The parent resumes execution, and the child starts execution, at the same place, where the call returns. Often, following a fork it is desirable to execute a new, different, program. The `exec()`- family of function calls is used to create a new address space and load a new program into it.

[1] The other fundamental abstraction is files.

[2] In modern Linux kernels, `fork()` is actually implemented via the `clone()` system call, which is discussed in a following section.

Finally, a program exits via the `exit()` system call. This function terminates the process and frees all its resources. A parent process can inquire about the status of a terminated child, via the `wait4()`[3] system call that enables a process to wait for the termination of a specific process. When a process exits, it is placed into a special zombie state that is used to represent terminated processes until the parent calls `wait()` or `waitpid()`.

Another name for a process is a *task*. The Linux kernel often refers to processes as tasks. In this book, I will use the terms interchangeably, although I will try to denote the kernel representation of a running program as a *task* and the user-space representation as a *process*.

The Process Descriptor and Task Structure

The kernel stores the processes in a circular doubly linked list called the *task list*[4]. Each element in the task list is a *process descriptor* of the type `struct task_struct`, which is defined in `include/linux/sched.h`. The process descriptor contains all the information about a specific process.

The `task_struct` is a relatively large data structure at around 1.7 kilobytes on a 32-bit machine. This size, however, is quite small considering that the structure contains all the information the kernel needs about a process. The process descriptor contains the data that describe the executing program—open files, the process's address space, pending signals, the process's state, and much more (see Figure 2.1).

Allocating the Process Descriptor

The `task_struct` is allocated via the *slab allocator* to provide object reuse and cache coloring (see Chapter 10, "Memory Management"). Prior to the 2.6 kernel series, the `task_struct` was stored at the end of the kernel stack of each process. This allowed architectures with few registers, such as x86, to calculate the location of the process descriptor via the *stack pointer* without using an extra register to store the location. With the process descriptor now dynamically created via the slab allocator, a new structure, `struct thread_info`, was created that again lives at the bottom of the stack (for stacks that grow down) or at the top of the stack (for stacks that grow up)[5]. See Figure 2.2.

---

[3] The kernel implements the `wait4()` system call. Linux systems, via the C library, typically provide the `wait()`, `waitpid()`, `wait3()`, and `wait4()` functions. All these functions return status about a terminated process, albeit with slightly different semantics.

[4] Some texts on operating system design call this list the *task array*. Because the Linux implementation is a linked list and not a static array, it is called the *task list*.

[5] Register-impaired architectures were not the only reason for creating `struct thread_info`. The new structure also makes it rather easy to calculate offsets of its values for use in assembly code.

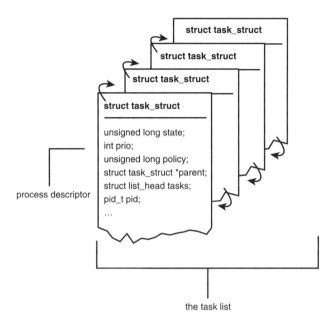

Figure 2.1   The process descriptor and task list.

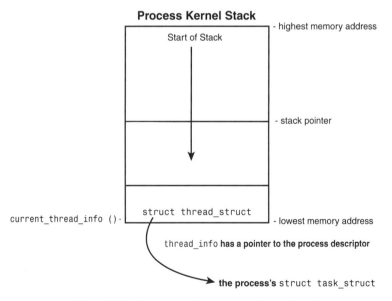

Figure 2.2   The process descriptor and kernel stack.

struct thread_info is defined on x86 in <asm/thread_info.h> as

```
struct thread_info {
        struct task_struct *task;
        struct exec_domain *exec_domain;
        unsigned long flags;
        __u32 cpu;
        __s32 preempt_count;
        mm_segment_t addr_limit;
        u8 supervisor_stack[0];
};
```

Each task's thread_info structure is allocated at the end of its stack. The task element of the structure is a pointer to the task's actual task_struct.

Storing the Process Descriptor

The system identifies processes by a unique *process identification* value or *PID*. The PID is a numerical value that is represented by the opaque type[6] pid_t, which is typically an int. Because of backward compatibility with earlier Unix and Linux versions, however, the default maximum value is only 32,767 (that of a short int). The kernel stores this value as pid inside each process descriptor.

This maximum value is important, as it is essentially the maximum number of processes that may exist concurrently on the system. Although 32,767 might be sufficient for a desktop system, large servers may require many more processes. If the system is willing to break compatibility with old applications, the administrator may increase the maximum value via /proc/sys/kernel/pid_max.

Inside the kernel, tasks are typically referenced directly by a pointer to their task_struct. In fact, most kernel code that deals with processes works directly with the task_struct. Consequently, it is very useful to be able to quickly lookup the process descriptor of the currently executing task, which is done via the current macro. This macro must be separately implemented by each supported architecture. Some architectures save a pointer to the task_struct of the currently running process in a register, allowing for efficient access. Other architectures, such as x86 with few registers to waste, make use of the fact that thread_info is stored on the kernel stack to calculate thread_info and subsequently the task_struct.

On x86, current is calculated by masking out the 13 least significant bits of the stack pointer to obtain the thread_info structure. This is done by the current_thread_info() function. The assembly is shown here:

```
movl $-8192, %eax
andl %esp, %eax
```

---

[6] An opaque type is a data type whose physical representation is unknown or irrelevant.

Finally, `current` dereferences the `task` member of `thread_info` to return the `task_struct`:

```
current_thread_info()->task;
```

Contrast this approach with that taken by PowerPC (IBM's modern RISC-based microprocessor), which stores the current `task_struct` in a register. Thus, `current` on PPC merely returns the value stored in the register `r2`. PPC can take this approach because, unlike x86, it has plenty of registers. Because accessing the process descriptor is a common and important job, the PPC kernel developers deem using a register worthy for the task.

Process State

The `state` field of the process descriptor describes the current condition of the process (see Figure 2.3). Each process on the system is in exactly one of five different states. This value is represented by one of five flags:

- **TASK_RUNNING**—The process is runnable; it is either currently running or on a runqueue waiting to run (runqueues are discussed in Chapter 3, "Scheduling").

- **TASK_INTERRUPTIBLE**—The process is sleeping (that is, it is blocked) waiting for some condition to occur. When this condition occurs, the kernel sets the process's state to `TASK_RUNNING`. The process also awakes prematurely and becomes runnable if it receives a signal.

- **TASK_UNINTERRUPTIBLE**—This state is identical to `TASK_INTERRUPTIBLE` except that it will *not* wake up and become runnable if it receives a signal. This is used in situations where the process must wait without interruption or when the event is expected to occur quite quickly. Because the task will not respond to signals in this state, `TASK_UNINTERRUPTIBLE` is less often used than `TASK_INTERRUPTIBLE`[7].

- **TASK_ZOMBIE**—The task has terminated, but its parent has not yet issued a `wait4()` system call. The task's process descriptor must remain in case the parent wants to access it. If the parent calls `wait4()`, the process descriptor is deallocated.

- **TASK_STOPPED**—Process execution has stopped; the task is not running nor is it eligible to run. This occurs if the task receives the `SIGSTOP`, `SIGTSTP`, `SIGTTIN`, or `SIGTTOU` signal or if it receives *any* signal while it is being debugged.

---

[7] This is why you have those dreaded unkillable processes with state D in ps(1). Because the task will not respond to signals, you cannot send it a SIGTERM signal. Further, even if you could terminate the task, it would not be wise as the task is supposedly in the middle of an important operation and may hold a semaphore.

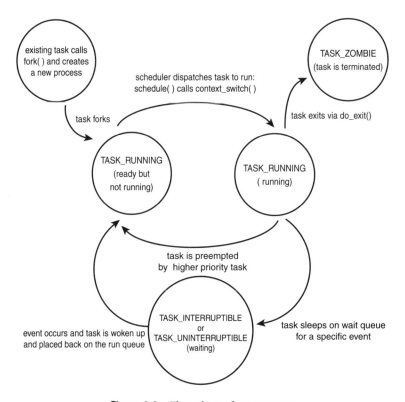

Figure 2.3   Flow chart of process states.

Manipulating the Current Process State

Kernel code often needs to change a process's state. The preferred mechanism is using the `set_task_state(task, state)` function, which sets the given task to the given state. If applicable, it also provides a memory barrier to force ordering on other processors (this is only needed on SMP systems). Otherwise, it is equivalent to

```
task->state = state;
```

The method `set_current_state(state)` is synonymous to `set_task_state(current, state)`.

Process Context

One of the most important parts of a process is the executing program code. This code is read in from an *executable file* and executed within the programs address space. Normal program execution occurs in *user-space*. When a program executes a system call (see Chapter 4, "System Calls") or triggers an exception, it enters *kernel-space*. At this point, the kernel is said to "be executing on behalf of the process" and is in *process context*. When in process context, the `current` macro is valid[8]. Upon exiting the kernel, the process resumes execution in user-space, unless a higher-priority process has become runnable in the interim, in which case the scheduler is invoked to select the higher priority process.

System calls and exception handlers are well-defined interfaces into the kernel. A process can begin executing in kernel-space only through one of these interfaces—all access to the kernel is through these interfaces.

A distinct hierarchy exists between processes in Linux. All processes are descendents of the `init` process whose PID is one. The kernel starts `init` in the last step of the boot process. The `init` process, in turn, reads the system *initscripts* and executes more programs, eventually completing the boot process.

Every process on the system has exactly one parent. Likewise, every process can have one or more children. Processes that are all direct children of the same parent are called *siblings*. The relationship between processes is stored in the process descriptor. Each `task_struct` has a pointer to the parent's `task_struct`, named `parent`, and a list of children, named `children`. Consequently, given the current process, it is possible to obtain the process descriptor of its parent with the following code:

```
struct task_struct *task = current->parent;
```

Similarly, it is possible to iterate over a process's children with

```
struct task_struct *task;
struct list_head *list;

list_for_each(list, &current->children) {
        task = list_entry(list, struct task_struct, sibling);
        /* task now points to one of current's children */
}
```

The init task's process descriptor is statically allocated as `init_task`. A good example of the relationship between all processes is that this code will always succeed:

```
struct task_struct *task;

for (task = current; task != &init_task; task = task->parent)
    ;
/* task now points to init */
```

In fact, you can follow the process hierarchy from any one process in the system to any other. Oftentimes, however, it is desirable simply to iterate over *all* processes in the

---

[8] Other than process context there is *interrupt context*, which we discuss in Chapter 5. In interrupt context, the system is not running on behalf of a process, but is executing an interrupt handler. There is no process tied to interrupt handlers and consequently no process context.

system. This is easy because the task list is a circular doubly linked list. To obtain the next task in the list, given any valid task:

```
list_entry(task->tasks.next, struct task_struct, tasks)
```

Obtaining the previous works the same way:

```
list_entry(task->tasks.prev, struct task_struct, tasks)
```

These two routines are provided by the macros `next_task(task)` and `prev_task(task)`. Finally, the macro `for_each_process(task)` is provided which iterates over the entire task list. On each iteration, `task` points to the next task in the list:

```
struct task_struct *task;

for_each_process(task) {
        /* this pointlessly prints the name and PID of each task */
        printk("%s[%d]\n", task->comm, task->pid);
}
```

Note, it can be expensive to iterate over every task in a system with many processes; code should have good reason (and no alternative) before doing so.

Process Creation

Process creation in Unix is unique. Most operating systems implement a *spawn* mechanism to create a new process in a new address space, read in an executable, and begin executing it. Unix takes the unusual approach of separating these steps into two distinct functions: fork() and exec()[9]. The first, fork(), creates a child process that is a copy of the current task. It differs from the parent only in its PID (which is unique), its PPID (parent's PID, which is set to the original process), and certain resources and statistics, such as pending signals, which are not inherited. The second function, exec(), loads a new executable into the address space and begins executing it. The combination of fork() followed by exec() is similar to the single function most operating systems provide.

Copy-on-Write

Traditionally, upon fork() all resources owned by the parent are duplicated and the copy is given to the child. This approach is significantly naïve and inefficient. With Linux, fork() is implemented using *copy-on-write* pages. Copy-on-write (or *COW*) is a technique to delay or altogether prevent copying of the data. Instead of duplicating the

---

[9] By exec() I mean any member of the exec() family of functions. The kernel implements the execve() system call on top of which execlp(), execle(), execv(), and execvp() are implemented.

process address space, the parent and the child can share a single copy. The data, however, is marked in such a way that if it is written to, a duplicate is made and each process receives a unique copy. Consequently, the duplication of resources occurs only when they are written; until then, they are shared read-only. This technique delays the copying of each page in the address space until it is actually written to. In the case that the pages are never written—for example, if exec() is called immediately after fork()—they never need to be copied. The only overhead incurred by fork() is the duplication of the parent's page tables and the creation of a unique process descriptor for the child. This optimization prevents the wasted copying of large amounts of data (the address space, easily tens of megabytes); in the common case a process executes a new executable image immediately after forking. This is an important optimization because the Unix philosophy encourages quick process execution. Chapter 10, "Memory Management," discusses how copy-on-write is implemented.

fork()

Linux implements fork() via the clone() system call. This call takes a series of flags that specify which resources, if any, the parent and child process should share (see the section on "The Linux Implementation of Threads" later in this chapter for more about the flags). The fork(), vfork(), and __clone() library calls call clone() with the requisite flags. The clone() system call, in turn, calls do_fork().

The bulk of the work in forking is handled by do_fork(), which is defined in kernel/fork.c. This function calls copy_process(), and then starts the process running. The interesting work is done by copy_process():

- Calls dup_task_struct() which creates a new kernel stack, thread_info structure, and task_struct for the new process whose values are identical to those of the current task. At this point, the child and parent process descriptors are identical.

- Check that the new child will not exceed the resource limits on the number of processes for the current user.

- Now the child needs to differentiate itself from its parent. Various members of the process descriptor are cleared or set to initial values.

- Next, the child's state is set to TASK_UNINTERRUPTIBLE, to insure it does not yet run.

- Calls copy_flags() to update the flags member of the task_struct. The PF_SUPERPRIV flag, which denotes whether a task used super-user privileges, is cleared. The PF_FORKNOEXEC flag, which denotes a process that has not called exec(), is set.

- Calls get_pid() to assign an available PID to the new task.

- Depending on the flags passed to clone(), either copy or share open files, filesystem information, signal handlers, process address space, and namespace. These resources are typically shared between threads in a given process; otherwise they are unique and thus copied here.

- Share the remaining timeslice between the parent and its child (this is discussed in Chapter 3, "Scheduling").
- Finally, cleanup and return a pointer to the new child.

Back in do_fork(), if copy_process() returns successfully, the new child is woken up and run. Deliberately, the kernel runs the child process first[10]. In the common case of the child simply calling exec() immediately, this eliminates any copy-on-write overhead that would occur if the parent ran first and began writing to the address space.

vfork()

The vfork() system call has the same effect as fork(), except that the page table entries of the parent process are not copied. Instead, the child executes as the sole thread in the parent's address space, and the parent is blocked until the child either calls exec() or exits. The child is *not* allowed to write to the address space. This was a welcome optimization in the old days of BSD 3.0 when the call was introduced because at the time fork() was not implemented using copy-on-write pages. Today, with copy-on-write and child-runs-first semantics, the only benefit to vfork() is not copying the parent page tables entries. If Linux one day gains copy-on-write page table entries there will no longer be any benefit[11]. Because the semantics of vfork() are tricky (what, for example, happens if the exec() fails?) it would be nice if vfork() died a slow painful death. It is entirely possible to implement vfork() as a normal fork()—in fact, this is what Linux did until 2.2.

The vfork() system call is implemented via a special flag to the clone() system call:

- In copy_process(), the task_struct member vfork_done is set to NULL.
- In do_fork(), if the special flag was given, vfork_done is pointed at a specific address.
- After the child is first run, instead of returning the parent waits for the child to signal it through the vfork_done pointer.
- In mm_release(), the function that is used when a task exits a memory address space, if vfork_done is not NULL the parent is signaled.
- Back in do_fork(), the parent wakes up and returns.

If this all goes as planned, the child is now executing in a new address space and the parent is again executing in its original address space. The overhead is lower, but the design is not pretty.

---

[10] Actually, this does not currently function correctly, although the intention is to run the child first.

[11] In fact, there are currently patches to add this functionality to Linux. Although we most likely will not see shared page tables in 2.6, such a feature may appear in 2.7.

The Linux Implementation of Threads

Threads are a popular modern programming abstraction. They provide multiple threads of execution within the same program in a shared memory address space. They can also share open files and other resources. Threads allow for *concurrent programming* and, on multiple processor systems, true *parallelism*.

Linux has a unique implementation of threads. To the Linux kernel, there is *no concept* of a thread. Linux implements all threads as standard processes. The Linux kernel does not provide any special scheduling semantics or data structures to represent threads. Instead, a thread is merely a process which shares certain resources. Each thread has a unique `task_struct` and appears to the kernel as a normal process (which shares resources, such as an address space, with other processes).

This approach to threads contrasts greatly with operating systems such as Microsoft Windows or Sun Solaris, which have *explicit* kernel support for threads (and sometimes call threads *lightweight processes*). The name "lightweight process" sums up the difference in philosophies between Linux and other systems. To these other operating systems, threads are an abstraction to provide a lighter, quicker execution unit than the heavy process. To Linux, threads are simply a manner of sharing resources between processes (which are already quite lightweight)[12]. For example, assume we have a process that consists of four threads. On systems with explicit thread support, there might exist one process descriptor that in turn points to the four different threads. The process descriptor describes the shared resources, such as an address space or open files. The threads than describe the resources they alone possess. Conversely, in Linux, there are simply four processes and thus four normal `task_struct` structures. The four processes are setup to share certain resources.

Threads are created like normal tasks with the exception that the `clone()` system call is passed flags corresponding to specific resources to be shared:

```
clone(CLONE_VM | CLONE_FS | CLONE_FILES | CLONE_SIGHAND, 0);
```

The previous code results in behavior identical to a normal `fork()`, except the address space, filesystem resources, file descriptors, and installed signal handlers are shared. In other words, the new task and its parent are threads.

In contrast, a normal `fork()` can be implemented as

```
clone(SIGCHLD, 0);
```

and `vfork()` as

```
clone(CLONE_VFORK | CLONE_VM | SIGCHLD, 0);
```

The flags provided to `clone()` help specify the behavior of the new process and detail what resources the parent and child will share. Table 2.1 lists the clone flags and their effect.

---

[12] As an example, benchmark process creation time in Linux versus process (or even thread!) creation time in these other operating systems. The results are quite nice.

Table 2.1 `clone()` **Flags**

Flag	Meaning
CLONE_CLEARTID	clear the TID
CLONE_DETACHED	the parent does not want a SIGCHLD signal sent on exit
CLONE_FILES	parent and child share open files
CLONE_FS	parent and child share filesystem information
CLONE_IDLETASK	set PID to zero (only used by the idle tasks)
CLONE_NEWNS	create a new namespace for the child
CLONE_PARENT	child is to have same parent as its parent
CLONE_PTRACE	continue tracing child
CLONE_SETTID	write the TID back to user-space
CLONE_SETTLS	create a new TLS for the child
CLONE_SIGHAND	parent and child share signal handlers
CLONE_SYSVSEM	parent and child share System V SEM_UNDO semantics
CLONE_THREAD	parent and child are in the same thread group
CLONE_VFORK	vfork() was used and the parent will sleep until the child wakes it
CLONE_VM	parent and child share address space

Kernel Threads

It is often useful for the kernel to perform some operations in the background. The kernel accomplishes this via *kernel threads*—standard processes that exist solely in kernel-space. The significant difference between kernel threads and normal processes is that kernel threads do not have an address space (in fact, their mm pointer is NULL). They operate only in kernel-space and do not context switch into user-space. Kernel threads are, however, schedulable and preemptable as normal processes.

Linux delegates several tasks to kernel threads, most notably the *pdflush* task and the *ksoftirqd* task. These threads are created on system boot by other kernel threads. Indeed, a kernel thread can only be created by another kernel thread. The interface for spawning a new kernel thread from an existing one is

```
int kernel_thread(int (*fn)(void *), void * arg, unsigned long flags)
```

The new task is created via the usual `clone()` system call with the specified `flags` argument. On return, the parent kernel thread exits with a pointer to the child's `task_struct`. The child executes the function specified by `fn` with the given argument `arg`. A special clone flag, CLONE_KERNEL, specifies the usual flags for kernel threads: CLONE_FS, CLONE_FILES, and CLONE_SIGHAND. Most kernel threads pass this for their `flags` parameter.

Typically, a kernel thread continues executing its initial function forever (or at least until the system reboots, but with Linux you never know). The initial function usually implements a loop in which the kernel thread wakes up as needed, performs its duties, and then returns to sleep.

We will discuss specific kernel threads in more detail in later chapters.

Process Termination

It is sad, but eventually processes must terminate. When a process terminates, the kernel must release the resources owned by the process and notify the child's parent of its unfortunate demise.

Typically, process destruction occurs when the process calls the exit() system call, either explicitly when it is ready to terminate or implicitly on return from the main subroutine of any program (that is, the C compiler will place a call to exit() after main() returns). A process can also terminate involuntarily. This occurs when the process receives a signal or exception it cannot handle or ignore. Regardless of how a process terminates, the bulk of the work is handled by do_exit(), which completes a number of chores:

- Set the PF_EXITING flag in the flags member of the task_struct.
- If BSD process accounting is enabled, call acct_process() to write out accounting information.
- Call __exit_mm() to release the mm_struct held by this process. If no other process is using it (in other words, if it is not shared) then deallocate it.
- Call sem_exit(). If the process is queued waiting for an IPC semaphore, it is dequeued here.
- Call __exit_files(), __exit_fs(), exit_namespace(), and exit_sighand() to decrement the usage count of objects related to file descriptors, filesystem data, the process namespace, and signal handlers, respectively. If any usage counts reach zero, then the object is no longer in use by any process and it is removed.
- Set the task's exit code, stored in the exit_code member of the task_struct, to the code provided by exit() or whatever kernel mechanism forced the termination.
- Call exit_notify() to send signals to the task's parent, reparent any of the task's children to another thread in their thread group or the init process, and set the task's state to TASK_ZOMBIE.
- Finally, call schedule() to switch to a new process (see Chapter 3). Because TASK_ZOMBIE tasks are never scheduled, this is the last code the task will ever execute.

The code for do_exit() is defined in kernel/exit.c.

At this point, all objects associated with the task (assuming the task was the sole user) are freed. The task is not runnable (and in fact no longer has an address space to run in) and is of the TASK_ZOMBIE state. The only memory it occupies is its kernel stack and slab object, which contain its thread_info and task_struct structures, respectively. The task exists solely to provide information to its parent.

Removal of the Process Descriptor

After do_exit() completes, the process descriptor for the terminated process still exists but the process is a zombie and is unable to run. As discussed, this allows the system to obtain information about a child process after it has terminated. Consequently, the acts of cleaning up after a process and removing its process descriptor are separate. After the parent has obtained information on its terminated child, the child's task_struct is deallocated.

The wait() family of functions are implemented via a single (and complicated) system call, wait4(). The standard behavior is to suspend execution of the calling task until one of its children exit at which time the function returns with the PID of the exited child. Additionally, a pointer is provided to the function that on return holds the exit code of the terminated child.

When it is time to finally deallocate the process descriptor, release_task() is invoked. It does the following:

- Call free_uid() to decrement the usage count of the process's user. Linux keeps a per-user cache of information related to how many processes and files a user has opened. If the usage count reaches zero, the user has no more open processes or files, and the cache is destroyed.

- Call unhash_process() to remove the process from the *pidhash* and remove the process from the task list.

- If the task was *ptraced*, reparent it to its original parent and remove it from the *ptrace* list.

- Finally, call put_task_struct() to free the pages containing the process's kernel stack and thread_info structure and deallocate the slab cache containing the task_struct.

At this point, the process descriptor and all resources belonging solely to the process have been freed.

The Dilemma of the Parentless Task

If a parent exits before its children, some mechanism must exist to *reparent* the child tasks to a new process or else parentless terminated processes would forever remain zombies, wasting system memory. The solution, hinted upon previously, is to reparent a task's children on exit to either another process in the current thread group or, if that fails, the init process. In do_exit(), notify_parent() is invoked, which calls forget_original_parent() to perform the reparenting:

```
struct task_struct *p, *reaper = father;
struct list_head *list;

if (father->exit_signal != -1)
        reaper = prev_thread(reaper);
else
        reaper = child_reaper;

if (reaper == father)
        reaper = child_reaper;
```

This code sets `reaper` to another task in the process's thread group. If there is not another task in the thread group, it sets `reaper` to `child_reaper`, which is the `init` process. Now that a suitable new parent for the children is found, each child needs to be located and reparented to `reaper`:

```
list_for_each(list, &father->children) {
        p = list_entry(list, struct task_struct, sibling);
        reparent_thread(p, reaper, child_reaper);
}

list_for_each(list, &father->ptrace_children) {
        p = list_entry(list, struct task_struct, ptrace_list);
        reparent_thread(p, reaper, child_reaper);
}
```

This code iterates over two lists: the *child list* and the *ptraced child list*, reparenting each child. The rationale behind having both lists is interesting; it is a new feature in the 2.6 kernel. When a task is *ptraced,* it is temporarily reparented to the debugging process. When the task's parent exits, however, it must be reparented along with its other siblings. In previous kernels, this resulted in a loop over *every process in the system* looking for children. The solution, as noted previously, is simply to keep a separate list of a process's children that are being ptraced—reducing the search for one's children from every process to just two relatively small lists.

With the process successfully reparented, there is no risk of stray zombie processes. The `init` process routinely calls `wait()` on its children, cleaning up any zombies assigned to it.

3

Scheduling

T HE *SCHEDULER* IS THE COMPONENT OF THE KERNEL that selects which process to run next. The scheduler (or *process scheduler*, as it is sometimes called) can be viewed as the code that divides the finite resource of processor time between the runnable processes on a system. The scheduler is the basis of a *multitasking* operating system such as Linux. By deciding what process can run, the scheduler is responsible for best utilizing the system and giving the impression that multiple processes are simultaneously executing.

The idea behind the scheduler is simple. To best utilize processor time, assuming there are runnable processes, a process should always be running. If there are more processes than processors in a system, some processes will not always be running. These processes are *waiting to run*. Deciding what process runs next, given a set of runnable processes, is a fundamental decision the scheduler must make.

Multitasking operating systems come in two flavors: *cooperative multitasking* and *preemptive multitasking*. Linux, like all Unix variants and most modern operating systems, provides preemptive multitasking. In preemptive multitasking, the scheduler decides when a process is to cease running and a new process is to resume running. The act of involuntarily suspending a running process is called *preemption*. The time a process runs before it is preempted is predetermined, and is called the *timeslice* of the process. The timeslice, in effect, gives each process a *slice* of the processor's time. Managing the timeslice enables the scheduler to make global scheduling decisions for the system. It also prevents any one process from monopolizing the system. As we will see, this timeslice is dynamically calculated in the Linux scheduler to provide some interesting benefits.

Conversely, in *cooperative multitasking,* a process does not stop running until it voluntary decides to do so. The act of a process voluntarily suspending itself is called *yielding*. The shortcomings of this approach are numerous: The scheduler cannot make global decisions regarding how long processes run, processes can monopolize the processor for longer than the user desires, and a hung process that never yields can potentially bring down the entire system. Thankfully, most operating systems designed in the last decade have provided preemptive multitasking, with Mac OS 9 and earlier being the most notable exceptions. Of course, Unix has been preemptively multitasked since the beginning.

During the 2.5 kernel series, the Linux kernel received a scheduler overhaul. A new scheduler, commonly called the *O(1) scheduler* because of its algorithmic behavior[1], solved the shortcomings of the previous Linux scheduler and introduced powerful new features and performance characteristics. In this section, we will discuss the fundamentals of scheduler design and how they apply to the new O(1) scheduler and its goals, design, implementation, algorithms, and related system calls.

Policy

Policy is the behavior of the scheduler that determines what runs when. A scheduler's policy often determines the overall feel of a system and is responsible for optimally utilizing processor time. Therefore, it is very important.

I/O-Bound Versus Processor-Bound Processes

Processes can be classified as either *I/O-bound* or *processor-bound*. The former is characterized as a process that spends much of its time submitting and waiting on I/O requests. Consequently, such a process is often runnable, but only for short periods, because it will eventually block waiting on more I/O (this is any type of I/O, such as keyboard activity, and not just disk I/O). Conversely, processor-bound processes spend much of their time executing code. They tend to run until they are preempted because they do not block on I/O requests very often. Because they are not I/O-driven, however, system response does not dictate that the scheduler run them often. The scheduler policy for processor-bound processes, therefore, tends to run such processes less frequently but for longer periods. Of course, these classifications are not mutually exclusive. The scheduler policy in Unix variants tends to explicitly favor I/O-bound processes.

The scheduling policy in a system must attempt to satisfy two conflicting goals: fast process response time (low latency) and high process throughput. To satisfy these requirements, schedulers often employ complex algorithms to determine the most worthwhile process to run, while not compromising fairness to other, lower priority, processes. Favoring I/O-bound processes provides improved process response time, because interactive processes are I/O-bound. Linux, to provide good interactive response, optimizes for process response (low latency), thus favoring I/O-bound processes over processor-bound processors. As you will see, this is done in a way that does not neglect processor-bound processes.

Process Priority

A common type of scheduling algorithm is *priority-based* scheduling. The idea is to rank processes based on their worth and need for processor time. Processes with a higher

---

[1] O(1) is an example of big-o notation. Basically, it means the scheduler can do its thing in constant time, regardless of the size of the input. A full explanation of big-o notation is in Appendix D, for the curious.

priority will run before those with a lower priority, while processes with the same priority are scheduled round-robin (one after the next, repeating). On some systems, Linux included, processes with a higher priority also receive a longer timeslice. The runnable process with timeslice remaining and the highest priority always runs. Both the user and the system may set a processes priority to influence the scheduling behavior of the system.

Linux builds on this idea and provides *dynamic priority-based* scheduling. This concept begins with the initial base priority, and then enables the scheduler to increase or decrease the priority dynamically to fulfill scheduling objectives. For example, a process that is spending more time waiting on I/O than running is clearly I/O bound. Under Linux, it receives an elevated dynamic priority. As a counterexample, a process that continually uses up its entire timeslice is processor bound—it would receive a lowered dynamic priority.

The Linux kernel implements two separate priority ranges. The first is the *nice* value, a number from −20 to 19 with a default of zero. Larger nice values correspond to a lower priority—you are being *nice* to the other processes on the system. Processes with a lower nice value (higher priority) run before processes with a higher nice value (lower priority). The nice value also helps determine how long a timeslice the process receives. A process with a nice value of −20 receives the maximum timeslice, whereas a process with a nice value of 19 receives the minimum timeslice. Nice values are the standard priority range used in all Unix systems.

The second range is the real-time priority, which will be discussed later. By default, it ranges from zero to 99. All real-time processes are at a higher priority than normal processes. Linux implements real-time priorities in accordance with POSIX. Most modern Unix systems implement a similar scheme.

Timeslice

The timeslice[2] is the numeric value that represents how long a task can run until it is preempted. The scheduler policy must dictate a default timeslice, which is not simple. A timeslice that is too long will cause the system to have poor interactive performance; the system will no longer feel as if applications are being concurrently executed. A timeslice that is too short will cause significant amounts of processor time to be wasted on the overhead of switching processes, as a significant percentage of the system's time will be spent switching from one process with a short timeslice to the next. Furthermore, the conflicting goals of I/O-bound versus processor-bound processes again arise; I/O-bound processes do not need longer timeslices, whereas processor-bound processes crave long timeslices (to keep their caches hot, for example).

With this argument, it would seem that *any* long timeslice would result in poor interactive performance. In many operating systems, this observation is taken to heart, and the default timeslice is rather low—for example, 20ms. Linux, however, takes advantage of the fact that the highest priority process always runs. The Linux scheduler bumps the

---

[2] Timeslice is sometimes called *quantum* or *processor slice* in other systems. Linux calls it timeslice.

priority of interactive tasks, enabling them to run more frequently. Consequently, the Linux scheduler offers a relatively high default timeslice (see Table 3.1). Furthermore, the Linux scheduler dynamically determines the timeslice of a process based on priority. This enables higher priority, allegedly more important, processes to run longer and more often. Implementing dynamic timeslices and priorities provides robust scheduling performance.

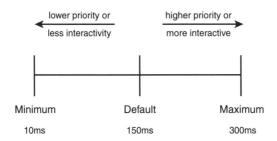

Figure 3.1   Process timeslice calculation.

Note that a process does not have to use all its timeslice at once. For example, a process with a 100 millisecond timeslice does not have to run for 100 milliseconds in one go or risk losing the remaining timeslice. Instead, the process can run on five different reschedules for 20 milliseconds each. Thus, a large timeslice also benefits interactive tasks—while they do not need such a large timeslice all at once, it ensures they remain runnable for as long as possible.

When a process's timeslice runs out, the process is considered expired. A process with no timeslice is not eligible to run until all other processes have exhausted their timeslice (that is, they all have zero timeslice remaining). At that point, the timeslices for all processes are recalculated. The Linux scheduler employs an interesting algorithm for handling timeslice exhaustion that is discussed in a later section.

Process Preemption

As mentioned, the Linux operating system is *preemptive*. When a process enters the `TASK_RUNNING` state, the kernel checks whether its priority is higher than the priority of the currently executing process. If it is, the scheduler is invoked to pick a new process to run (presumably the process that just became runnable). Additionally, when a process's timeslice reaches zero, it is preempted, and the scheduler is invoked to select a new process.

The Scheduling Policy in Action

Consider a system with two runnable tasks: a text editor and a video encoder. The text editor is I/O-bound because it spends nearly all its time waiting for user key presses (no matter how fast the user types, it is not *that* fast). Despite this, when it does receive a key press, the user expects the editor to respond *immediately*. Conversely, the video encoder is processor-bound. Aside from reading the raw data stream from the disk and later writing the resulting video, the encoder spends all its time applying the video codec to the raw data. It does not have any strong time constraints on when it runs—if it started running now or in half a second, the user could not tell. Of course, the sooner it finishes the better.

In this system, the scheduler gives the text editor a higher priority and larger timeslice than the video encoder, because the text editor is interactive. The text editor has plenty of timeslice available. Furthermore, because the text editor has a higher priority, it is capable of preempting the video encoder when needed. This ensure the text editor is capable of responding to user key presses immediately. This is to the detriment of the video encoder, but because the text editor runs only intermittently, the video encoder can monopolize the remaining time. This optimizes the performance of both applications.

The Scheduling Algorithm

The Linux scheduler is defined in `kernel/sched.c`. The scheduler algorithm and supporting code went through a large rewrite early in the 2.5 kernel development series. Consequently, the scheduler code is entirely new and unlike the scheduler in previous kernels. The new scheduler was designed to accomplish specific goals:

- Implement fully `O(1)` scheduling. Every algorithm in the new scheduler completes in constant-time, regardless of the number of running processes or any other input.

- Implement perfect SMP scalability. Each processor has its own locking and individual runqueue.

- Implement improved SMP affinity. Naturally attempt to group tasks to a specific CPU and continue to run them there. Only migrate tasks from one CPU to another to resolve imbalances in runqueue sizes.

- Provide good interactive performance. Even during considerable system load, the system should react and schedule interactive tasks immediately.

- Provide fairness. No process should find itself starved of timeslice for any reasonable amount of time. Likewise, no process should receive an unfairly high amount of timeslice.

- Optimize for the common case of only 1-2 runnable processes, yet scale well to multiple processors each with many processes.

The new scheduler accomplished these goals.

Runqueues

The basic data structure in the scheduler is the *runqueue*. The runqueue is defined in `kernel/sched.c` as `struct runqueue`. The runqueue is the list of runnable processes on a given processor; there is one runqueue per processor. Each runnable process is on exactly one runqueue. The runqueue additionally contains per-processor scheduling information. Consequently, the runqueue is the primary scheduling data structure for each processor. Why `kernel/sched.c` and not `include/linux/sched.h`? Because it is desired to abstract away the scheduler code and provide only certain interfaces to the rest of the kernel.

Let's look at the structure, with comments describing each field:

```
struct runqueue {
        spinlock_t          lock;                       /* spin lock which protects this
                                                           runqueue */
        unsigned long       nr_running;                 /* number of runnable tasks */
        unsigned long       nr_switches;                /* number of contextswitches */
        unsigned long       expired_timestamp;          /* time of last array swap */
        unsigned long       nr_uninterruptible;         /* number of tasks in
                                                           uinterruptible sleep */
        struct task_struct  *curr;                       /* this processor's currently
                                                           running task */
        struct task_struct  *idle;                       /* this processor's idle task */
        struct mm_struct    *prev_mm;                    /* mm_struct of last running task
                                                           */
        struct prio_array   *active;                     /* pointer to the active priority
                                                           array */
        struct prio_array   *expired;                    /* pointer to the expired
                                                           priority array */
        struct prio_array   arrays[2];                   /* the actual priority arrays */
        int                 prev_cpu_load[NR_CPUS];/* load on each processor */
        struct task_struct  *migration_thread;           /* the migration thread on this
                                                           processor */
        struct list_head    migration_queue;             /* the migration queue for this
                                                           processor */
        atomic_t            nr_iowait;                    /* number of tasks waiting on I/O
                                                           */
}
```

Because runqueues are the core data structure in the scheduler, a group of macros is used to obtain specific runqueues. The macro `cpu_rq(processor)` returns a pointer to the runqueue associated with the given processor. Similarly, the macro `this_rq()` returns the runqueue of the current processor. Finally, the macro `task_rq(task)` returns a pointer to the runqueue on which the given task is queued.

Before a runqueue can be manipulated, it must be locked (locking is discussed in-depth in Chapter 7, "Kernel Synchronization Introduction"). Because each runqueue is unique to the current processor, it is rare when a processor desires to lock a different processor's runqueue (it does happen, however, as we will see). The locking of the run-queue prohibits any changes to it while the lock-holder is reading or writing the run-queue's members. The most common way of locking a runqueue is when you want to lock the runqueue a specific task runs on. In that case, the `task_rq_lock()` and `task_rq_unlock()` functions are used:

```
struct runqueue *rq;
unsigned long flags;

rq = task_rq_lock(task, &flags);
/* manipulate the task's runqueue */
task_rq_unlock(rq, &flags);
```

Alternatively, the method `this_rq_lock()` locks the current runqueue and `rq_unlock(struct runqueue *rq)` unlocks the given runqueue.

To avoid deadlock, code that wants to lock multiple runqueues needs always to obtain the locks in the same order: by ascending runqueue address (again, Chapter 7 offers a full explanation). Example:

```
/* to lock ... */
if (rq1 < rq2) {
        spin_lock(&rq1->lock);
        spin_lock(&rq2->lock);
} else {
        spin_lock(&rq2->lock);
        spin_lock(&rq1->lock);
}

/* manipulate both runqueues ... */

/* to unlock ... */
spin_unlock(&rq1->lock);
spin_unlock(&rq2->lock);
```

These steps are made automatic by the `double_rq_lock()` and `double_rq_unlock()` functions. The above steps would then become:

```
double_rq_lock(rq1, rq2);

/* manipulate both runqueues ... */

double_rq_unlock(rq1, rq2);
```

Let's look at a quick example of why the order of obtaining the locks is important. The topic of deadlock is covered in Chapters 7 and 8, as this is not a problem unique to the runqueues; nested locks always need to be obtained in the same order. The spin locks are used to prevent multiple tasks from simultaneously manipulating the runqueues. They work like a key to a door. The first task to reach the door grabs the key and enters the door, locking the door behind it. If another task reaches the door and finds it locked (because another task is already inside), it must sit and wait for the first task to exit the door and return the key. This waiting is called *spinning* because the task actually sits in a tight loop, repeatedly checking for the return of the key. Now, consider if one task wants to lock the first runqueue and then the second, while another task wants to lock the second runqueue and then the first. Assume our first task succeeds in locking the first runqueue while simultaneously our second task succeeds in locking the second runqueue. Now, the first task tries to lock the second runqueue and the second task tries to lock the first runqueue. Neither task succeeds because the other task holds the lock. Both tasks wait forever for each other. Like an impasse creating a traffic deadlock, this out-of-order locking results in the tasks waiting for each other, forever, and thus, also deadlocking. If both tasks obtained the locks in the same order, this would not have happened. See Chapters 7 and 8 for the full scoop on locking.

The Priority Arrays

Each runqueue contains two *priority arrays*, the active and the expired array. Priority arrays are defined in `kernel/sched.c` as `struct prio_array`. Priority arrays are the data structure that provide O(1) scheduling. Each priority array contains one queue of runnable processors per priority level. These queues contain lists of the runnable processes at each priority level. The priority arrays also contain a *priority bitmap* used to efficiently discover the highest priority runnable task in the system.

```
struct prio_array {
        int               nr_active;          /* number of tasks */
        unsigned long     bitmap[BITMAP_SIZE]; /* priority bitmap */
        struct list_head  queue[MAX_PRIO];    /* priority queues */
};
```

`MAX_PRIO` is the number of priority levels on the system. By default, this is 140. Thus, there is one `struct list_head` for each priority. `BITMAP_SIZE` is the size that an array of `unsigned long` typed variables would have to be to provide one bit for each valid priority level. With 140 priorities and 32-bit words, this is five. Thus, `bitmap` is an array with five elements and a total of 160 bits.

Each priority array contains a `bitmap` field that has at least one bit for every priority on the system. Initially, all the bits are zero. When a task of a given priority becomes runnable (that is, its state becomes `TASK_RUNNING`), the corresponding bit in the bitmap is set to one. For example, if a task with priority seven is runnable, then bit seven is set. Finding the highest priority task on the system is therefore only a matter of finding the first set bit in the bitmap. Because the number of priorities is static, the time to complete this search is constant and unaffected by the number of running processes on the system. Furthermore, each supported architecture in Linux implements a fast *find first set* algorithm to quickly search the bitmap. This method is called `sched_find_first_bit()`.

Each priority array also contains an array called `queue` of `struct list_head` queues, one queue for each priority. Each list corresponds to a given priority and, in fact, contains all the runnable processes of that priority that are on this processor's runqueue. Finding the next task to run is as simple as selecting the next element in the list. Within a given priority, tasks are scheduled round robin.

The priority array also contains a counter, `nr_active`. This is the number of runnable tasks in this priority array.

Recalculating Timeslices

Many operating systems (older versions of Linux included) have an explicit method for recalculating each task's timeslice when they have all reached zero. Typically, this is implemented as a loop over each task, such as:

```
for (each task on the system) {
        recalculate priority
        recalculate timeslice
}
```

The priority and other attributes of the task are used to determine a new timeslice. This approach has some problems:

- It potentially can take a long time. Worse, it scales `O(n)` for n tasks on the system.
- The recalculation must occur under some sort of lock protecting the task list and the individual process descriptors. This results in high lock contention.
- The nondeterminism of a randomly occurring recalculation of the timeslices is a problem with deterministic real-time programs.
- It is just gross (which is a quite legitimate reason for improving something in the Linux kernel).

The new Linux scheduler alleviates the need for a recalculate loop. Instead, it maintains *two* priority arrays for each processor: both an *active* array and an *expired* array. The active array contains all the tasks in the associated runqueue that have timeslice left. The expired array contains all the tasks in the associated runqueue that have exhausted their timeslice. When each task's timeslice reaches zero, its timeslice is recalculated before it is moved to the expired array. Recalculating all the timeslices is then as simple as just switching the active and expired arrays. Because the arrays are accessed only via pointer, switching them is as fast as swapping two pointers. This is performed in `schedule()`:

```
struct prio_array array = rq->active;
if (!array->nr_active) {
        rq->active = rq->expired;
        rq->expired = array;
}
```

This swap is a key feature of the new O(1) scheduler. Instead of recalculating each process's priority and timeslice all the time, the O(1) scheduler performs a simple two-step array swap. This resolves the previously discussed problems.

schedule()

The act of picking the next task to run and switching to it is implemented via the schedule() function. This function is called explicitly by kernel code that wants to sleep and it is also invoked whenever a task is to be preempted.

The schedule() function is relatively simple for all it must accomplish. The following code determines the highest priority task:

```
struct task_struct *prev, *next;
struct list_head *queue;
struct prio_array array;
int idx;

prev = current;
array = rq->active;
idx = sched_find_first_bit(array->bitmap);
queue = array->queue + idx;
next = list_entry(queue->next, struct task_struct, run_list);
```

First, the active priority array is searched to find the first set bit. This bit corresponds to the highest priority task that is runnable. Next, the scheduler selects the first task in the list at that priority. This is the highest priority runnable task on the system and is the task the scheduler will run. See Figure 3.2.

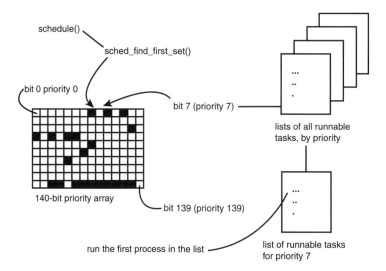

Figure 3.2   The Linux O(1) scheduler algorithm.

If prev does not equal next, then a new task has been selected to run. The architecture-specific function context_switch() is called to switch from prev to next. We will discuss context switching in a subsequent section.

Two important points should be noted from the previous code. First, it is very simple and consequently quite fast. Second, the number of processes on the system has no effect on how long this code takes to execute. There is no loop over any list to find the most suitable process. In fact, nothing affects how long the `schedule()` code takes to find a new task. It is constant in execution time.

Calculating Priority and Timeslice

At the beginning of this chapter, we looked at how priority and timeslice are used to influence the decisions the scheduler makes. Additionally, we looked at I/O-bound and processor-bound tasks and why it is beneficial to boost the priority of interactive tasks. Now, let's look at the actual code that implements this design.

Processes have an initial priority that is called the *nice* value. This value ranges from −20 to 19 with a default of zero. Nineteen is the lowest and −20 is the highest priority. This value is stored in the `static_prio` member of the process's `task_struct`. The value is called the static priority because it does not change from what the user specifies. The scheduler, in turn, bases its decisions on the dynamic priority that is stored in `prio`. The dynamic priority is calculated as a function of the static priority and the task's inter-activity.

The method `effective_prio()` returns the dynamic priority of a task. The method begins with the task's nice value and computes a bonus or penalty in the range −5 to +5 based on the interactivity of the task. For example, a highly interactive task with a nice value of ten can have a dynamic priority of five. Conversely, a mild processor hog with a nice value of ten can have a dynamic priority of 12. Tasks that are only mildly interactive receive no bonus or penalty and their dynamic priority is equal to their nice value.

Of course, the scheduler does not magically know whether a process is interactive. It requires some heuristic that is capable of accurately reflecting whether a task is I/O-bound or processor-bound. The most indicative metric is how long the task sleeps. If a task spends most of its time asleep it is I/O-bound. If a task spends more time runnable than sleeping, it is not interactive. This extends to the extreme; a task that spends nearly all the time sleeping is completely I/O-bound, whereas a task that spends nearly all its time runnable is completely processor-bound.

To implement this heuristic, Linux keeps a running tab on how much time a process is spent sleeping versus how much time the process spends in a runnable state. This value is stored in the `sleep_avg` member of the `task_struct`. It ranges from zero to `MAX_SLEEP_AVG`, which defaults to 10 milliseconds. When a task becomes runnable after sleeping, `sleep_avg` is incremented by how long it slept, until the value reaches `MAX_SLEEP_AVG`. For every timer tick the task runs, `sleep_avg` is decremented until it reaches zero.

This metric is surprisingly accurate. It is computed based not only on how long the task sleeps but also on how little it runs. Therefore, a task that spends a great deal of time sleeping, but also continually exhausts its timeslice will not be awarded a huge bonus—the metric works not just to award interactive tasks but also to punish processor-bound tasks. It is also not vulnerable to abuse. A task that receives a boosted priority and timeslice quickly loses the bonus if it turns around and hogs the processor. Finally, the metric provides quick response. A newly created interactive process quickly receives a large `sleep_avg`. Despite this, because the bonus or penalty is applied against the initial nice value, the user can still influence the system's scheduling decisions by changing the process's nice value.

Timeslice, on the other hand, is a much simpler calculation because dynamic priority is already based on nice value and interactivity (the metrics the scheduler assumes are most important). Therefore, timeslice can simply be based on the dynamic priority. When a process is first created, the new child and the parent split the parent's remaining timeslice. This provides fairness and prevents users from forking new children to get unlimited timeslice. After a task's timeslice is exhausted, however, it is recalculated based on the task's dynamic priority. The function `task_timeslice()` returns a new timeslice for the given task. The calculation is a simple scaling of the priority into a range of timeslices. The higher a task's priority the more timeslice it receives per round of execution. The maximum timeslice, given to the highest priority tasks, is `MAX_TIMESLICE`, which by default is 200 milliseconds. Even the lowest priority tasks receive at least the minimum timeslice, `MIN_TIMESLICE`, which is 10 milliseconds. Tasks with the default priority (nice value of zero and no interactivity bonus or penalty) receive a timeslice of 100 milliseconds. See Table 3.1.

Table 3.1 **Scheduler Timeslices**

Timeslice	Duration	Interactivity	Nice Value
Initial	half of parent's	N/A	parent's
Minimum	10ms	low	high
Default	100ms	average	zero
Maximum	3200ms	high	low

The scheduler provides one additional aide to interactive tasks: If a task is sufficiently interactive, when it exhausts its timeslice, it will not be inserted into the expired array, but instead reinserted back into the active array. Recall that timeslice recalculation is provided via the switching of the active and the expired arrays. Normally, as processes exhaust their timeslice, they are moved from the active array to the expired array. When there are no more processes in the active array, the two arrays are switched; the active becomes the expired, and the expired becomes the active. This provides `O(1)` timeslice recalculation. It also provides the possibility that an interactive task can become runnable, but fail to run again until the array switch occurs, because the task is stuck in the expired array. Reinserting interactive tasks back into the active array alleviates this problem. Note that the task will not run immediately, but will be scheduled round robin with the other tasks at its priority. The logic to provide this feature is implemented in `scheduler_tick()`, which is called via the timer interrupt (discussed in Chapter 9, "Timers and Time Management"):

```
struct task_struct *task = current;
struct runqueue *rq = this_rq();

if (!--task->time_slice) {
        if (!TASK_INTERACTIVE(task) || EXPIRED_STARVING(rq))
                enqueue_task(task, rq->expired);
        else
                enqueue_task(task, rq->active);
}
```

First, the code decrements the process's timeslice and checks if it is now zero. If it is, the task is expired and it needs to be inserted into an array, so the code first checks if the task is interactive via the `TASK_INTERACTIVE()` macro. This macro computes whether a task is "interactive enough" based on its nice value. The lower the nice value (the higher the priority), the less interactive a task needs to be. A nice 19 task can never be interactive enough to be reinserted. Conversely, a nice −20 task would need to be a heavy processor hog not to be reinserted. A task at the default nice value, zero, needs to be relatively interactive to be reinserted, but it is not too difficult. Next, the `EXPIRED_STARVING()` macro checks whether there are processes on the expired array that are *starving*—that is, if the arrays have not been switched in a relatively long time. If they have not been switched recently, reinserting the current task into the active array will further delay the switch; additionally starving the tasks on the expired array. If this is not the case, the process can be inserted into the active array. Otherwise, it is inserted into the expired array, which is the normal practice.

Sleeping and Waking Up

Tasks that are sleeping (blocked) are in a special non-runnable state. This is important because otherwise the scheduler would select tasks that did not want to run or, worse, sleeping would have to be implemented as busy looping. A task sleeps for a number of reasons, but always by waiting for some event. The event can be a specified amount of time, more data from a file I/O, or another hardware event. A task can also involuntarily go to sleep when it tries to obtain a contended semaphore in the kernel (this is covered in Chapter 8, "Kernel Synchronization Methods"). A common reason to sleep is file I/O—for example, the task issued a `read()` request on a file which needs to be read in from disk. As another example, the task could be waiting for keyboard input. Whatever the case, the kernel behavior is the same: The task marks itself as sleeping, puts itself on a wait queue, removes itself from the runqueue, and calls `schedule()` to select a new process to execute. Waking back up is the inverse; the task is set runnable, removed from the wait queue, and added back to the runqueue.

As discussed in the previous chapter, two states are associated with sleeping, `TASK_INTERRUPTIBLE` and `TASK_UNINTERRUPTIBLE`. They differ only in that tasks in the `TASK_UNINTERRUPTIBLE` state ignore signals, whereas tasks in the `TASK_INTERRUPTIBLE` state will wake up prematurely and respond to a signal if one is issued. Both types of sleeping tasks sit on a wait queue, waiting for an event to occur, and are not runnable.

Sleeping is handled via wait queues. A wait queue is a simple list of processes waiting for an event to occur. Wait queues are represented in the kernel by `wake_queue_head_t`. Wait queues are created statically via `DECLARE_WAIT_QUEUE_HEAD()` or dynamically via `init_waitqueue_head()`. Processes put themselves on a wait queue and mark themselves not runnable. When the event associated with the wait queue occurs, the processes on the queue are awakened. It is important to implement sleeping and waking correctly, to avoid race conditions.

Some simple interfaces for sleeping used to be in wide use. These interfaces, however, have races; it is possible to go to sleep *after* the condition becomes true. In that case, the task might sleep indefinitely. Therefore, the recommended method for sleeping in the kernel is a bit more complicated:

```
/* 'q' is the wait queue we wish to sleep on */
DECLARE_WAITQUEUE(wait, current);

add_wait_queue(q, &wait);
set_current_state(TASK_INTERRUPTIBLE); /* or TASK_UNINTERRUPTIBLE */
while (!condition) /* 'condition' is the event we are waiting for */
        schedule();
set_current_state(TASK_RUNNING);
remove_wait_queue(q, &wait);
```

The steps performed by the task to add itself to a wait queue are

- Create a wait queue entry via `DECLARE_WAITQUEUE()`.

- Add itself to a wait queue via `add_wait_queue()`. This wait queue will awaken the process when the condition it is waiting for occurs. Of course, there needs to be code elsewhere that calls `wake_up()` on the queue when the event actually does occur.

- Change the process state to `TASK_INTERRUPTIBLE` or `TASK_UNINTERRUPTIBLE`.

- Test if the condition is true; if it is, there is no need to sleep. If it is not true, call `schedule()`.

- When the task awakes, it will again check if the condition is true. If it is, it will exit the loop. Otherwise, it will again call `schedule()` and repeat.

- Now that the condition is true, the task can set itself to `TASK_RUNNING` and remove itself from the wait queue via `remove_wait_queue()`.

If the condition occurs before the task goes to sleep, the loop will terminate, and the task will not erroneously go to sleep. Note that kernel code often has to perform various other tasks in the body of the loop. For example, it might need to release locks before calling `schedule()` and reacquire them after, check if a signal was delivered and return `-ERESTARTSYS`, or react to other events.

Waking is handled via `wake_up()`, which wakes up all the tasks waiting on the given wait queue. It calls `try_to_wake_up()`, which sets the task's state to `TASK_RUNNING`, calls `activate_task()` to add the task to a runqueue, and sets `need_resched` if the woken task's priority is higher than the priority of the current task. The code that causes the event to occur typically calls `wake_up()` afterward. For example, when data arrives from the hard disk, the VFS calls `wake_up()` on the wait queue that holds the processes waiting for the data.

An important note about sleeping is that there are spurious wake ups. Just because a task is woken up does not mean the event it is waiting for has occurred; sleeping should always be handled in a loop that ensures the condition the task is waiting for has indeed occurred.

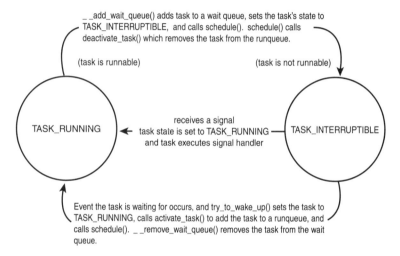

Figure 3.3   Sleeping and waking up.

The Load Balancer

As discussed, the Linux scheduler implements separate runqueues and locking for each processor on a symmetrical multiprocessing system. That is, each processor maintains its own list of processes and operates the scheduler only on those tasks. The entire scheduling system is, in effect, unique to each processor. How, then, does the scheduler enforce any sort of global scheduling policy on multiprocessing systems? What if the runqueues become unbalanced, say with five processes on one processor's runqueue, but only one on another? The solution is the load balancer, which works to ensure that the runqueues are balanced. The load balancer compares the current processor's runqueue to the other runqueues in the system. If it finds an imbalance, it *pulls* processes from the busier runqueue to the current runqueue. Ideally, every runqueue will have the same number of processes. That is a lofty goal, but the load balancer comes close.

The load balancer is implemented in `kernel/sched.c` as `load_balance()`. It has two methods of invocation. It is called by `schedule()` whenever the current runqueue is empty. It is also called via timer: every 1 millisecond when the system is idle and every 200 milliseconds otherwise. On uniprocessor systems, `load_balance()` is never called and, in fact, is not even compiled into the kernel image because there is only a single runqueue and thus, no balancing is needed.

The load balancer is called with the current processor's runqueue locked and with interrupts disabled to protect the runqueues from concurrent access. In the case where `schedule()` calls `load_balance()`, its job is pretty clear, because the current runqueue is empty and finding any process and pulling it onto this runqueue is advantageous. When the load balancer is called via timer, however, its job might be a less apparent; it needs to resolve any imbalance between the runqueues to keep them about even. See Figure 3.4.

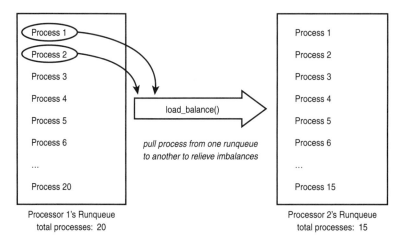

Figure 3.4   The load balancer.

The `load_balance()` function and related methods are fairly large and complicated although the steps they perform are comprehensible:

- First, `load_balance()` calls `find_busiest_queue()` to determine the busiest runqueue. In other words, this is the runqueue with the greatest number of processes in it. If there is no runqueue that has 25% or more processes than the current, `find_busiest_queue()` returns `NULL` and `load_balance()` returns. Otherwise, the busiest runqueue is returned.

- Second, `load_balance()` decides which priority array on the busiest runqueue it wants to pull from. The expired array is preferred because those tasks have not run in a relatively long time, thus are most likely not in the processor's cache (that is, they are not cache hot). If the expired priority array is empty, the active one is the only choice.

- Next, `load_balance()` finds the highest priority (smallest value) list that has tasks, because it is more important to fairly distribute high priority tasks than lower priority ones.

- Each task of the given priority is analyzed, to find a task that is not running, not prevented to migrate via processor affinity, and not cache hot. If the task meets this criteria, `pull_task()` is called to pull the task from the busiest runqueue to the current runqueue.

- As long as the runqueues remain imbalanced, the previous two steps are repeated and more tasks are pulled from the busiest runqueue to the current. Finally, when the imbalance is resolved, the current runqueue is unlocked and `load_balance()` returns.

Preemption and Context Switching

Context switching, the switching from one runnable task to another, is handled by the `context_switch()` function defined in `kernel/sched.c`. It is called by `schedule()` when a new process has been selected to run. It does two basic jobs:

- Calls `switch_mm()`, which is defined in `include/asm/mmu_context.h`, to switch the virtual memory mapping from the previous process's to that of the new process.

- Calls `switch_to()`, defined in `include/asm/system.h`, to switch the processor state from the previous process's to the current's. This involves saving and restoring stack information and the processor registers.

The kernel, however, must know when to call `schedule()`. If it only called `schedule()` when code explicitly did so, user-space programs could run indefinitely. Instead, the kernel provides the `need_resched` flag to signify whether a reschedule should be performed (See Table 3.2). This flag is set by `scheduler_tick()` when a process runs out of timeslice and by `try_to_wake_up()` when a process that has a higher priority than the currently running process is awakened. The kernel will check the flag, see that it is set, and call `schedule()` to switch to a new process. The flag is a message to the kernel that the scheduler should be invoked as soon as possible because another process deserves to run.

Table 3.2 **Functions for Accessing and Manipulating** `need_resched`

Function	Purpose
`set_tsk_need_resched(task)`	Set the `need_resched` flag in the given process
`clear_tsk_need_resched(task)`	Clear the `need_resched` flag in the given process
`need_resched()`	Test the value of the `need_resched` flag; return true if set and false otherwise

Upon returning to user-space or returning from an interrupt, the `need_resched` flag is checked. If it is set, the kernel invokes the scheduler before continuing.

The flag is per-process, and not simply global, because it is faster to access a value in the process descriptor (because of the speed of `current` and because it might be in a cache line) than a global variable. Historically, the flag was global before the 2.2 kernel. In 2.2 and 2.4, the flag was an `int` inside the `task_struct`. In 2.6, it was moved into a single bit of a special flag variable inside the `thread_info` structure. As you can see, the kernel developers are never satisfied.

User Preemption

User preemption occurs when the kernel is about to return to user-space, `need_resched` is set, and therefore, the scheduler is invoked. If the kernel is returning to user-space, it knows it is in a safe quiescent state. In other words, if it is safe to continue executing the current task, it is also safe to pick a new task to execute. Consequently, whenever the kernel is preparing to return to user-space, either on return from an interrupt or after a system call, the value of `need_resched` is checked. If it is set, the scheduler is invoked to select a new (more fit) process to execute. Both the return paths for return from interrupt and return from system call are architecture-dependent and typically implemented in assembly in `entry.S` (which, aside from kernel entry code, also contains kernel exit code).

In short, user preemption can occur

- When returning to user-space from a system call
- When returning to user-space from an interrupt handler

Kernel Preemption

The Linux kernel, unlike most other Unix variants and many other operating systems, is a fully preemptive kernel. In non-preemptive kernels, kernel code runs until completion. That is, the scheduler is not capable of rescheduling a task while it is in the kernel—kernel code is scheduled cooperatively, not preemptively. Kernel code runs until it finishes (returns to user-space) or explicitly blocks. In the 2.6 kernel, however, the Linux kernel became preemptive; it is now possible to preempt a task at any point, so long as the kernel is in a state in which it is safe to reschedule.

So when is it safe to reschedule? The kernel is capable of preempting a task running in the kernel so long as it does not hold a lock. That is, locks are used as markers of regions of non-preemptibility. Because the kernel is SMP-safe, if a lock is not held, the current code is reentrant and capable of being preempted.

The first change in supporting kernel preemption was the addition of a preemption counter, `preempt_count`, to each process's `task_struct`. This counter begins at zero and increments for each lock that is acquired and decrements for each lock that is released. When the counter is zero, the kernel is preemptible. Upon return from interrupt, if returning to kernel-space, the kernel checks the values of `need_resched` and `preempt_count`. If `need_resched` is set and `preempt_count` is zero, then a more important task is runnable and it is safe to preempt. Thus, the scheduler is invoked. If `preempt_count` is nonzero, a lock is held and it is unsafe to reschedule. In that case, the interrupt returns as usual to the currently executing task. When all the locks that the current task is holding are released, `preempt_count` returns to zero. At that time, the unlock code checks if `need_resched` is set. If so, the scheduler will be invoked. Enabling and disabling kernel preemption is sometimes required in kernel code and will be discussed in Chapter 8.

Kernel preemption can also occur explicitly, when a task in the kernel blocks or explicitly calls `schedule()`. This form of kernel preemption has always been supported because no additional logic is required to ensure the kernel is in a state that is safe to preempt. It is assumed that the code that explicitly calls `schedule()` knows it is safe to reschedule.

Kernel preemption can occur

- When returning to kernel-space from an interrupt handler
- When kernel code becomes preemptible again
- If a task in the kernel explicitly calls `schedule()`
- If a task in the kernel blocks (which results in a call to `schedule()`)

Real-Time

Linux provides two real-time scheduling policies, `SCHED_FF` and `SCHED_RR`. The normal, not real-time scheduling policy is `SCHED_OTHER`. `SCHED_FIFO` implements a simple first-in, first-out scheduling algorithm without timeslices. A runnable `SCHED_FIFO` task will always be scheduled over any `SCHED_OTHER` tasks. When a `SCHED_FIFO` task becomes runnable, it will continue to run until it blocks or explicitly yields the processor; it has no timeslice and can run indefinitely. Two or more `SCHED_FIFO` tasks at the same priority run round robin. If a `SCHED_FIFO` task is runnable, all tasks at a lower priority cannot run until it finishes.

`SCHED_RR` is identical to `SCHED_FIFO` except that each process can only run until it exhausts a predetermined timeslice. That is, `SCHED_RR` is `SCHED_FIFO` with timeslices—it is a real-time round-robin scheduling algorithm.

Both real-time scheduling policies implement static priorities. The kernel does not calculate dynamic priority values for real-time tasks. This ensures that a real-time process at a given priority will *always* preempt a process at a lower priority.

The real-time scheduling policies in Linux provide soft real-time behavior. Soft real-time refers to the notion that the kernel tries to schedule applications within timing deadlines, but the kernel does not promise to always be able to fulfill them. Conversely, hard real-time systems are guaranteed to meet any scheduling requirements within certain limits. Linux makes no guarantees on the ability to schedule real-time tasks. The

Linux scheduling policy, however, does ensure real-time tasks are running whenever they are runnable. Despite not having a design that guarantees hard real-time behavior, the real-time scheduling performance in Linux is quite good. The 2.6 kernel is capable of meeting very stringent timing requirements.

Real-time priorities range inclusively from one to MAX_RT_PRIO minus one. By default, MAX_RT_PRIO is 100—therefore, the default real-time priority range is one to 99. This priority space is shared with the nice values of SCHED_OTHER tasks; they use the space from MAX_RT_PRIO to (MAX_RT_PRIO + 40). By default, this means the −20 to +19 nice range maps directly onto the 100 to 140 priority range.

Scheduler-Related System Calls

Linux provides a family of system calls for the management of scheduler parameters. These system calls allow manipulation of process priority, scheduling policy, and processor affinity, as well as provide an explicit mechanism to *yield* the processor to other tasks.

Various books—and your friendly system man pages—provide reference to these system calls (which are all implemented in the C library without much wrapper—they just invoke the system call). Table 3.3 lists the system calls and provides a brief description. How system calls are implemented in the kernel is discussed in Chapter 4, "System Calls."

Table 3.3   **Scheduler-Related System Calls**

System Call	Description
nice()	Set a process's nice value
sched_setscheduler()	Set a process's scheduling policy
sched_getscheduler()	Get a process's scheduling policy
sched_setparam()	Set a process's real-time priority
sched_getparam()	Get a process's real-time priority
sched_get_priority_max()	Get the maximum real-time priority
sched_get_priority_min()	Get the minimum real-time priority
sched_rr_get_interval()	Get a process's timeslice value
sched_setaffinity()	Get a process's processor affinity
sched_getaffinity()	Set a process's processor affinity
sched_yield()	Temporarily yield the processor

Scheduling Policy and Priority-Related System Calls

The sched_setscheduler() and sched_getscheduler() system calls set and get a given process's scheduling policy and real-time priority, respectively. Their implementation, like most system calls, involves a lot of argument checking, setup, and cleanup. The important work, however, is merely to read or write the policy and rt_priority values in the process's task_struct.

The `sched_setparam()` and `sched_getparam()` system calls set and get a process's real-time priority. This call merely returns `rt_priority` encoded in a special `sched_param` structure. The calls `sched_get_priority_max()` and `sched_get_priority_min()` return the maximum and minimum priorities, respectively, for a given scheduling policy. The maximum priority for the real-time policies is `MAX_USER_RT_PRIO` minus one; the minimum is one.

For normal tasks, the `nice()` function increments the given process's static priority by the given amount. Only root can provide a negative value, thereby lowering the nice value and increasing the priority. The `nice()` function calls the kernel's `set_user_nice()` function, which sets the `static_prio` and `prio` values in the task's `task_struct`, as appropriate.

Processor Affinity System Calls

The Linux scheduler enforces hard processor affinity. That is, although it tries to provide soft or natural affinity by attempting to keep processes on the same processor, the scheduler also enables a user to say "this task must remain on this subset of the available processors no matter what." This hard affinity is stored as a bitmask in the task's `task_struct` as `cpus_allowed`. The bitmask contains one bit per possible processor on the system. By default, all bits are set and, therefore, a process is potentially runnable on any processor. The user, however, via `sched_setaffinity()`, can provide a different bitmask of any combination of one or more bits. Likewise, the call `sched_getaffinity()` will return the current `cpus_allowed` bitmask.

The kernel enforces hard affinity in a very simple manner. First, when a process is first created, it inherits its parent's affinity mask. Because the parent is running on an allowed processor, the child thus runs on an allowed processor. Second, when the affinity of a processor is changed, the kernel uses the *migration threads* to push the task onto a legal processor. Finally, the load balancer only pulls tasks to an allowed processor. Therefore, a process only ever runs on a processor whose bit is set in the `cpus_allowed` field of its process descriptor.

Yielding Processor Time

Linux provides the `sched_yield()` system call as a mechanism for a process to explicitly yield the processor to other waiting processes. It works by removing the process from the active array (where it currently is, because it is running) and inserting it into the expired array. This has the effect of not only preempting the process and putting it at the end of its priority list, but putting it on the expired list—guaranteeing it will not run for a while. Because real-time tasks never expire, they are a special case. Therefore, they are merely moved to the end of their priority list (and not inserted into the expired array). In earlier versions of Linux, the semantics of the `sched_yield()` call were quite different; at best, the task was only moved to the end of their priority list. The yielding was often not for a very long time. Nowadays, applications and even kernel code should be certain they truly want to give up the processor before calling `sched_yield()`.

Kernel code, as a convenience, can call `yield()`, which ensures the task's state is `TASK_RUNNING`, and then calls `sched_yield()`. User-space applications use the `sched_yield()` system call.

4

System Calls

THE KERNEL PROVIDES A SET OF INTERFACES for interacting with the system for process-es running in user-space. These interfaces give applications access to hardware and other operating system resources. The interfaces act as the messenger between applications and the kernel, with the applications issuing various requests, and the kernel fulfilling them (or telling the application to go away). The fact that these interfaces exist, and that appli-cations are not free to do directly whatever they please, is key to providing a stable sys-tem and avoiding a big mess.

System calls provide a layer between the hardware and user-space processes. This layer serves three primary purposes. First, it provides an abstracted hardware interface for user-space. When reading or writing from a file, for example, applications need not concern themselves with the type of disk, media, or even the filesystem on which the file resides. Second, system calls ensure system security and stability. With the kernel acting as a mid-dleman between system resources and user-space, the kernel can arbitrate access based on permissions and other criterion. For example, this prevents applications from incorrectly using hardware, stealing other process's resources, or doing harm to the system. Finally, a single common layer between user-space and the rest of the system allows for the virtual system afforded processes as discussed in Chapter 2, "Process Management." If applica-tions were free to access system resources without the kernel's knowledge, it would be nearly impossible to implement multitasking and virtual memory. In Linux, system calls are the only means user-space has of interfacing with the kernel; they are the only legal entry point into the kernel. Indeed, other interfaces, such as device files or /proc, are ultimately accessed via system calls. Interestingly, Linux implements far fewer system calls than most systems[1].

This chapter addresses the role and implementation of system calls in Linux.

---

[1] About 250 system calls are on x86 (each architecture is allowed to define unique system calls). Although not all operating systems publish their exact system calls, some operating systems are estimated to have over one thousand.

APIs, POSIX, and the C Library

Typically, applications are programmed against an Application Programming Interface (API), not directly to system calls. This is important, because no direct correlation is needed between the interface that applications make use of and the actual interface provided by the kernel. An API defines a set of programming interfaces used by applications. Those interfaces can be implemented as a system call, implemented using multiple system calls, or implemented without using system calls at all. In fact, the same API can exist on multiple systems and provide the same interface to applications while the implementation of the API itself can differ greatly from system to system.

One of the more popular application programming interfaces in the Unix world is based on the POSIX standard. Technically, POSIX is comprised of a series of standards from the IEEE[2] that aim to provide a portable operating system standard roughly based on Unix. Linux is POSIX compliant.

POSIX is an excellent example of the relationship between APIs and system calls. On most Unix systems, the POSIX-defined API calls have a strong correlation to the system calls. Indeed, the POSIX standard was created to resemble the interfaces provided by earlier Unix systems. On the other hand, some systems that are far from Unix, such as Windows NT, offer POSIX-compatible libraries.

The system call interface in Linux, as with most Unix systems, is provided in part by the C library. The C library implements the main API on Unix systems, including the standard C library and the system call interface. The C library is used by all C programs and, because of C's nature, is easily wrapped by other programming languages for use in their programs. The C library additionally provides the majority of the POSIX API.

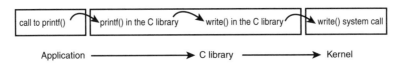

Figure 4.1   The relationship between applications, the C library, and the kernel with a call to `printf()`.

From the programmer's point of view, system calls are irrelevant; all the programmer is concerned with is the API. Conversely, the kernel is only concerned with the system calls; what library calls and applications make use of the system calls is not of the kernel's concern. Nonetheless, it is important for the kernel to keep in mind the potential uses of a system call and keep the system call as general and flexible as possible.

A common motto related to interfaces in Unix is "provide mechanism, not policy." In other words, Unix system calls exist to provide a specific function in a very abstract sense. The manner in which the function is used is not any of the kernel's business.

---

[2] IEEE (eye-triple-E) is the Institute of Electrical and Electronics Engineers. It is a nonprofit professional association involved in numerous technical areas and responsible for many important standards, such as POSIX. For more information, visit `http://www.ieee.org`.

Syscalls

System calls (often called *syscalls* in Linux) are typically accessed via function call. They can define one or more arguments (inputs) and might result in one or more side effects[3], for example writing to a file or copying some data into a provided pointer. System calls also provide a return value of type long[4] that signifies success or error. Usually, although not always, a negative return value denotes error. A return value of zero is usually (but again not always) a sign of success. Unix system calls, on error, will write a special error code into the global `errno` variable. This variable can be translated into human-readable errors via library functions such as `perror()`.

Finally, system calls, of course, have a defined behavior. For example, the system call `getpid()` is defined to return an integer that is the current process's PID. The implementation of this syscall in the kernel is very simple:

```
asmlinkage long sys_getpid(void)
{
        return current->tgid;
}
```

Note that the definition says nothing of the implementation. The kernel must provide the intended behavior of the system call, but is free to do so with whatever implementation it desires as long as the result is correct. Of course, this system call is as simple as they come and there are not too many other ways to implement it (certainly no simpler method exists)[5].

We can make a couple of observations about system calls even from this simple example. First, note the `asmlinkage` modifier on the function declaration. This is a bit of magic to tell the compiler to look only on the stack for this function's arguments. This is a required modifier for all system calls. Second, note that the `getpid()` system call is defined as `sys_getpid()` in the kernel. This is the naming convention taken with all system calls in Linux: system call `bar()` is implemented in the kernel as function `sys_bar()`.

System Call Numbers

In Linux, each system call is assigned a *syscall number*. This is a unique number that is used to reference a specific system call. When a user-space process executes a system call, the syscall number delineates which syscall was executed; the process does not refer to the syscall by name.

---

[3] Note the *might* here. Although nearly all system calls have a side effect (that is, they result in some change of the system's state), a few syscalls, such as `getpid()`, merely return some data from the kernel.

[4] The use of type `long` is for compatibility with 64-bit architectures.

[5] You might be wondering *why does `getpid()` return `tgid`, the thread group ID?* This is because, in normal processes, the TGID is equal to the PID. With threads, the TGID is the same for all threads in a thread group. This enables the threads to call `getpid()` and get the same PID.

The syscall number is important; when assigned, it cannot change, or else compiled applications will break. Likewise, if a system call is removed, its system call number cannot be recycled. Linux provides a "not implemented" system call, sys_ni_syscall(), which does nothing except return -ENOSYS, the error corresponding to an invalid system call. This function is used to "plug the hole" in the rare event a syscall is removed.

The kernel keeps a list of all registered system calls in the system call table, stored in sys_call_table. It is architecture-dependent and typically defined in entry.S. This table assigns each valid syscall to a unique syscall number.

System Call Performance

System calls in Linux are faster than in many other operating systems. This is partly because of Linux's incredibly fast context switch times; entering and exiting the kernel is a streamlined and simple affair. The other factor is the simplicity of the system call handler and the individual system calls themselves.

System Call Handler

It is not possible for user-space applications to execute kernel code directly. They cannot simply make a function call to a method existing in kernel-space because the kernel exists in a protected memory space. If applications could directly read and write to the kernel's address space, system security would go out the window.

Instead, user-space applications must somehow signal the kernel that they want to execute a system call and have the system switch to kernel mode, where the system call can be executed in kernel-space by the kernel on behalf of the application.

The mechanism to signal the kernel is a software interrupt: Incur an exception and then the system will switch to kernel mode and execute the exception handler. The exception handler, in this case, is actually the system call handler. The defined software interrupt on x86 is the int $0x80 instruction. It triggers a switch to kernel mode and the execution of exception vector 128, which is the system call handler. The system call handler is the aptly-named function system_call(). It is architecture-dependent and typically implemented in assembly in entry.S[6].

Denoting the Correct System Call

Simply entering kernel-space alone is not sufficient because there are multiple system calls, all of which enter the kernel in the same manner. Thus, the system call number must be passed into the kernel. On x86, storing the system call number in the eax register before issuing the software interrupt does this. The system call handler then reads the value from eax. Other architectures do something similar.

---

[6] Much of the following description of the system call handler is based on the x86 version. Do not fret, they are all very similar.

The `system_call()` function checks the validity of the given system call number by comparing it to `NR_syscalls`. If it is larger than or equal to `NR_syscalls`, the function returns `-ENOSYS`. Otherwise, the specified system call is invoked:

```
call *sys_call_table(,%eax,4)
```

Because each element in the system call table is 32-bits (four bytes), the kernel multiplies the given system call number by four to arrive at its location in the system call table. See Figure 4.2.

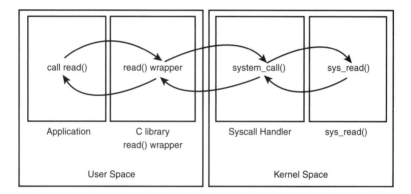

Figure 4.2   Invoking the system call handler and executing a system call.

Parameter Passing

In addition to the system call number, most syscalls require that one or more parameters be passed to them. Somehow, user-space must relay the parameters to the kernel during the exception trap. The easiest way to do this is via the same means the syscall number is passed: The parameters are stored in registers. On x86, the registers `ebx`, `ecx`, `edx`, `esi`, and `edi` contain, in order, the first five arguments. In the unlikely case of six or more arguments, a single register is used to hold a pointer to user-space where all the parameters exist.

The return value is sent to user-space also via register. On x86, it is written into the `eax` register.

System Call Implementation

The actual implementation of a system call in Linux does not need to concern itself with the behavior of the system call handler. Adding a new system call to Linux is relatively easy. The hard work lies in designing and implementing the system call; registering it with the kernel is simple. Let's look at the steps involved in writing a new system call for Linux.

The first step in implementing a system call is defining its purpose. What will it do? The syscall should have exactly one purpose. Multiplexing syscalls (a single system call that does wildly different things depending on a flag argument) is discouraged in Linux. Look at `ioctl()` as an example of what *not* to do.

What are the new system call's arguments, return value, and error codes? The system call should have a clean and simple interface with the smallest number of arguments possible. The semantics and behavior of a system call are important; they must not change, because existing applications will come to rely on them.

Designing the interface with an eye toward the future is important. Are you needlessly limiting the function? Design the system call to be as general as possible. Do not assume its use today will be the same as its use tomorrow. The *purpose* of the system call will remain constant but its *uses* may change. Is the system call portable? Do not make assumptions about an architecture's wordsize or endianness. Chapter 16, "Portability," discusses these issues. Make sure you are not making poor assumptions that will break the system call in the future. Remember the Unix motto: "provide mechanism, not policy."

When you write a system call, it is important to realize the need for portability and robustness, not just today but in the future. The basic Unix system calls have survived this test of time; most of them are just as useful and applicable as they were nearly thirty years ago!

Verifying the Parameters

System calls must carefully verify all their parameters to ensure they are valid and legal. The system call runs in kernel-space, and if the user is able to pass invalid input into the kernel without restraint, the system's security and stability can suffer.

For example, file I/O syscalls must check whether the file descriptor is valid. Process-related functions must check whether the provided PID is valid. Every parameter must be checked to ensure it is not just valid and legal, but correct.

One of the most important checks is the validity of the pointers that the user provides. Imagine if a process could pass any pointer into the kernel unchecked, even one for which it did not have read access! Processes could then trick the kernel into copying data for which they did not have permission to access, such as data belonging to another process. Before following a pointer into user-space, the system must ensure

- The pointer points to a region of memory in user-space.
- The pointer points to a region of memory in the process's address space.
- If reading, the memory is marked readable. If writing, the memory is marked writable.

The kernel provides two methods for performing the requisite checks and the desired copy to and from user-space. Note kernel code must never blindly follow a pointer into user-space! One of these two methods must always be used.

For writing into user-space, the method `copy_to_user()` is provided. It takes three parameters. The first is the destination memory address in the process's address space. The second is the source pointer in kernel-space. Finally, the third argument is the size in bytes of the data to copy.

For reading from user-space, the method `copy_from_user()` is analogous to `copy_to_user()`. The function reads from the second parameter into the first parameter the amount of bytes specified in the third parameter.

Both of these functions return the number of bytes they failed to copy on error. On success, they return zero. It is standard for the syscall to return `-EFAULT` in the case of such an error.

Let's consider an example system call that uses both `copy_from_user()` and `copy_to_user()`. This syscall, `silly_copy()`, is utterly worthless; it copies data from its first parameter into its second. This is highly suboptimal as it involves the intermediate extraneous copy into kernel-space for absolutely no reason. But it helps illustrate the point.

```
asmlinkage long sys_silly_copy(unsigned long *src, unsigned long *dst, unsigned
long len)
{
    unsigned long buf;

    /* fail if the kernel wordsize and user wordsize do not match */
    if (len != sizeof(buf))
        return -EINVAL;

    /* copy src, which is in the user's address space, into buf */
    if (copy_from_user(&buf, src, len))
        return -EFAULT;

    /* copy buf into dst, which is in the user's address space */
    if (copy_to_user(dst, &buf, len))
        return -EFAULT;

    /* return amount of data copied */
    return len;
}
```

Note that both `copy_to_user()` and `copy_from_user()` may block. This occurs, for example, if the page containing the user data is not in physical memory but swapped to disk. In that case, the process sleeps until the page fault handler can bring the page from the swap file on disk into physical memory.

A final check is for valid permission. In older versions of Linux, it was standard for syscalls that require *root* privilege to use `suser()`. This function merely checked whether a user was root or not; this is now removed and the finer-grained "capabilities" system is in place. The new system allows specific access checks on specific resources. A call to `capable()` with a valid capabilities flag returns nonzero if the caller holds the specified capability and zero otherwise. For example, `capable(CAP_SYS_NICE)` checks whether the caller has the ability to modify nice values of other processes. By default, the superuser possesses all capabilities and non-root possess none. See `<linux/capability.h>` for a list of all capabilities and what rights they entail.

System Call Context

As discussed in Chapter 2, "Process Management," the kernel is in process context during the execution of a system call. The `current` pointer points to the current task, which is the process that issued the syscall.

In process context, the kernel is capable of sleeping (for example, if the system call blocks on a call or explicitly calls `schedule()`) and is fully preemptible. These two points are important. First, the ability to sleep means system calls can make use of the majority of the kernel's functionality. As we will see in Chapter 5, "Interrupts and Interrupt Handlers," the ability to sleep greatly simplifies kernel programming[7]. The fact that process context is preemptible implies that, like user-space, the current task may be preempted by another task. Because the new task may then execute the same system call, care must be exercised to ensure that system calls are reentrant. Of course, this is the same concerns that symmetrical multiprocessing introduces. Protecting against reentrancy is covered in Chapter 7, "Kernel Synchronization Introduction," and Chapter 8, "Kernel Synchronization Methods."

When the system call returns, control continues in `system_call()`, which ultimately switches to user-space and continues the execution of the user process.

Final Steps in Binding a System Call

After the system call is written, it is trivial to register it as an official system call:

- Add an entry to the end of the system call table. This needs to be done for each architecture that supports the system call (which, for most calls, is all the architectures). The position of the syscall in the table, starting at zero, is its system call number. For example, the tenth entry in the list is assigned syscall number nine.

- For each architecture supported, the syscall number needs to be defined in `include/asm/unistd.h`.

- The syscall needs to be compiled into the kernel image (as opposed to compiled as a module). This can be as simple as putting the system call in a relevant file in `kernel/`.

Let us look at these steps in more detail with a fictional system call, `foo()`. First, we want to add `sys_foo()` to the system call table. For most architectures, the table is located in `entry.S` and it looks like

---

[7] Interrupt handlers cannot sleep, and thus are much more limited in what they can do than system calls running in process context.

```
ENTRY(sys_call_table)
    .long sys_restart_syscall    /* 0 */
    .long sys_exit
    .long sys_fork
    .long sys_read
    .long sys_write
    .long sys_open            /* 5 */

    ...

    .long sys_timer_delete
    .long sys_clock_settime
    .long sys_clock_gettime      /* 265 */
    .long sys_clock_getres
    .long sys_clock_nanosleep
```

We then append our new system call to the tail of this list:

```
    .long sys_foo
```

Although we did not explicitly specify it, our system call is then given the next subsequent syscall number, 268. For each architecture we wish to support, our system call must be added to the architecture's system call table (it need not receive the same syscall number under each architecture). Usually, you would want to make the system call available to each architecture. Note the convention of placing the number in a comment every five entries; this makes it easy to find out which syscall is assigned which number.

Next, we add our system call number to `include/asm/unistd.h`, which currently looks somewhat like

```
/*
 * This file contains the system call numbers.
 */

#define __NR_restart_syscall  0
#define __NR_exit         1
#define __NR_fork         2
#define __NR_read         3
#define __NR_write        4
#define __NR_open         5

...

#define __NR_timer_delete     263
#define __NR_clock_settime    264
#define __NR_clock_gettime    265
#define __NR_clock_getres     266
#define __NR_clock_nanosleep  267
```

We then add the following to the end of the list:

```
#define __NR_foo        268
```

Finally, we implement the actual `foo()` system call. Because the system call must be compiled into the core kernel image in all configurations, we will put it in `kernel/sys.c`. You should put it wherever the function is most relevant; for example, if the function is related to scheduling, you could put it in `sched.c`.

```
/*
 * sys_foo - everyone's favorite system call.
 *
 * An utterly worthless function that just returns
 * "out of memory" on each invocation.
 */
asmlinkage long sys_foo(void)
{
        return -ENOMEM;
}
```

User-space can now invoke the `foo()` system call.

Accessing the System Call from User-Space

Generally, the C library supports system calls. User applications can pull in function prototypes from the standard headers and link with the C library to use your system call (or the library routine that in turn uses your syscall call). If you just wrote the system call, however, it is doubtful that glibc already supports it!

Thankfully, Linux provides a set of macros for wrapping access to system calls. It sets up the register contents and issues the `int $0x80` instruction. These macros are named `_syscalln()`, where *n* is between zero and six. The number corresponds to the number of parameters passed into the syscall because the macro needs to know how many parameters to expect and, consequently, push into registers. For example, consider the system call `open()`, defined as

```
long open(const char *filename, int flags, int mode)
```

The syscall macro to use this system call without explicit library support would be

```
#define NR_open    5
_syscall3(long, open, const char *, filename, int, flags, int, mode)
```

Then, the application can simply call `open()`.

For each macro, there are *2+2*n* parameters. The first parameter corresponds to the return type of the syscall. The second is the name of the system call. Next follows the type and name for each parameter in order of the system call. The `NR_open` define is in `<asm/unistd.h>`, it is the system call number. This expands into a C function with inline assembly; the assembly performs the steps discussed in the previous section to push the system call number and parameters into the correct registers and issue the software interrupt to trap into the kernel. Placing this macro in an application is all that is required to use the `open()` system call.

Why Not to Implement a System Call

It is easy to implement a new system call, but that in no way should encourage you to do so. Often, much more viable alternatives to providing a new system call are available. Let's look at the pros, the cons, and the alternatives.

The pros of implementing a new interface as a syscall:

- System calls are simple to implement and easy to use.
- System call performance on Linux is blindingly fast.

The cons:

- You need a syscall number, which needs to be officially assigned to you during a developmental kernel series.
- After the system call is in a stable series kernel, it is written in stone. The interface cannot change without breaking user-space applications.
- Each architecture needs to separately register the system call and support it.
- For simple exchanges of information, a system call is overkill.

The alternatives:

- Implement a device node and `read()` and `write()` to it. Use `ioctl()` to manipulate specific settings or retrieve specific information.
- Certain interfaces, such as semaphores, can be represented as file descriptors and manipulated as such.
- The current trend is to implement a simple RAM-based filesystem where files represent the specific interfaces. Applications perform normal file I/O on the files to access the interface. Chapter 13, "Virtual Filesystems," provides more details.

For many interfaces, system calls *are* the correct answer. Linux, however, has tried to avoid simply adding a system call to support each new abstraction that comes along. The result has been an incredibly clean system call layer with very few regrets or deprecations (interfaces no longer used or supported).

The slow rate of addition of new system calls is a sign that Linux is a relatively stable and feature-complete operating system. Only a handful of system calls were added in total during the 2.3 and 2.5 kernel development series. The vast majority of these new calls were to provide performance enhancements.

5

Interrupts and Interrupt Handlers

O NE OF THE MAJOR RESPONSIBILITIES OF THE kernel is managing the hardware connected to the machine. As part of this work, the kernel needs to communicate with the machine's individual devices. Given that processors are typically magnitudes faster than the hardware they talk to, it is not ideal for the kernel to issue a request and wait for a response from the potentially slow hardware. Instead, because the hardware is comparatively slow to respond, the kernel must be free to go off and handle other work and deal with the hardware only after it has actually completed its work. One solution to this problem is *polling*. Periodically, the kernel can check the status of the hardware in the system and respond accordingly. This incurs overhead, however, regardless of whether the hardware is even active or ready because the polling occurs repeatedly at regular intervals. A better solution is to provide a mechanism for the hardware to signal the kernel when attention is needed. This solution is called interrupts.

Interrupts

Interrupts allow hardware to communicate with the processor. For example, when you type, the keyboard controller (the hardware device which controls the keyboard) issues an interrupt to alert the operating system to available key presses. Interrupts are special electrical signals sent from hardware devices to the processor. The processor receives the interrupt and signals the operating system so that the OS can process the new data. Hardware devices generate interrupts asynchronously with respect to the processor clock—they can occur at any time. In turn, the kernel can be interrupted at anytime to process interrupts.

An interrupt is physically produced by electronic signals originating from the devices and directed into input pins on an interrupt controller. The interrupt controller, in turn, sends a signal to the processor. The processor detects this signal and interrupts its current execution to handle the interrupt. The processor can then notify the operating system that an interrupt has occurred, and the operating system can handle the interrupt appropriately.

Different devices are associated with unique interrupts by means of a unique value associated with each interrupt. This way, interrupts from the keyboard are distinct from interrupts from the hard drive. This enables the operating system to differentiate between interrupts and to know which hardware device caused which interrupt. In turn, the operating system can service each interrupt with a unique handler.

These interrupt values are often called interrupt request (IRQ) lines. Typically, they are given a numeric value—for example, on a PC, IRQ zero is the timer interrupt and IRQ one is the keyboard interrupt. Not all interrupt numbers are so rigidly defined, however. Interrupts associated with devices on the PCI bus, for example, are dynamically assigned. Other non–PC architectures have similar dynamic assignments for interrupt values. The important notion is that a specific interrupt is associated with a specific device, and the kernel knows this.

Exceptions

Exceptions are often discussed at the same time as interrupts. Unlike interrupts, they occur synchronously with respect to the processor clock. In fact, they are often called synchronous interrupts. Exceptions are produced by the processor while executing instructions either in response to programming error (for example, divide by zero) or abnormal conditions that must be handled by the kernel (for example, a page fault). Because many processor architectures handle exceptions in a similar manner to interrupts, the kernel infrastructure for handling the two is similar. Much of the discussion of interrupts (asynchronous interrupts generated by hardware) in this chapter also pertains to exceptions (synchronous interrupts generated by the processor itself).

Interrupt Handlers

The function the kernel runs in response to a specific interrupt is called an *interrupt handler* or *interrupt service routine* (ISR). Each device that generates interrupts has an associated interrupt handler. For example, one function handles interrupts from the system timer, while another function handles interrupts generated by the keyboard. The interrupt handler for a device is part of the device's *driver*—the kernel code that manages the device.

In Linux, interrupt handlers are normal C functions. They match a specific prototype, which enables the kernel to pass the handler information in a standard way, but otherwise they are ordinary functions. What differentiates interrupt handlers from other kernel functions is that the kernel invokes them in response to interrupts and that they run in a special context, which we will discuss, called interrupt context.

Because an interrupt can occur at any time, an interrupt handler can in turn be executed at any time. It is imperative that the handler run quickly, to resume execution of the interrupted code as soon as possible. Therefore, although it is important to the hardware that the interrupt is serviced immediately, it is important to the rest of the system that the interrupt handler execute in as short a period as possible.

In the very least, an interrupt handler's job is to acknowledge the interrupt's receipt to the hardware. Usually, however, interrupt handlers often have a large amount of work to perform. For example, consider the interrupt handler for a network device. On top of responding to the hardware, the interrupt handler needs to copy networking packets from the hardware into memory, process it, and push it down to the appropriate protocol stack or application. Obviously, this can be a lot of work.

Top Halves Versus Bottom Halves

These two goals—that an interrupt handler execute quickly, but additionally perform a large amount of work—are plainly in contrast. Because of these conflicting goals, the processing of interrupts is split into two parts, or halves. The interrupt handler is the *top half*—it is run immediately upon receiving the interrupt and performs only the work that is time critical, such as acknowledging receipt of the interrupt or resetting the hardware. Work that can be performed later is delayed until the *bottom half*. The bottom half runs later, at a more convenient time, with all interrupts disabled—quite often, the bottom half runs as soon as the interrupt handler returns. Linux provides various mechanisms for implementing bottom halves, and they are all discussed in Chapter 6, "Bottom Halves and Deferring Work."

Registering an Interrupt Handler

Drivers can register an interrupt handler and enable a given interrupt line for handling via the function

```
int request_irq(unsigned int irq,
    irqreturn_t (*handler)(int, void *, struct pt_regs *),
    unsigned long irqflags,
    const char * devname,
    void *dev_id)
```

The first parameter, `irq`, specifies the interrupt number to allocate. For some devices, for example legacy PC devices such as the system timer or keyboard, this value is typically hard-coded. For most other devices, it is probed or otherwise determined dynamically.

The second parameter, `handler`, is a pointer to the actual interrupt handler that services this interrupt. This function is invoked whenever the interrupt is received by the operating system. Note the specific prototype of the handler function—it takes three parameters and has a return value of `irqreturn_t`. We will discuss this function later in this chapter.

The third parameter, `irqflags`, may be either zero or a bit mask of one or more of the following flags:

- `SA_INTERRUPT`: This flag specifies that the given interrupt handler is a *fast interrupt handler*. Historically, Linux differentiated between interrupt handlers that were fast versus slow. Fast handlers were assumed to execute quickly, but potentially very often, so the behavior of the interrupt handling was modified to enable them to execute as quickly as possible. Today, there is only one difference: fast interrupt handlers run with *all* interrupts disabled on the local processor. This enables a fast handler to complete quickly, without possible interruption from other interrupts. By default (without this flag), all interrupts are enabled except the interrupt lines of any running handlers, which are masked out on all processors. Sans the timer interrupt, most interrupts do not want to enable this flag.

- `SA_SAMPLE_RANDOM`: This flag specifies that interrupts generated by this device should contribute to the kernel entropy pool. The kernel entropy pool provides truly random numbers derived from various random events. If this flag is specified, the timing of interrupts from this device will be fed to the pool as entropy. Do *not* set this if your device issues interrupts at a predictable rate (for example, the system timer) or can be influenced by external attackers (for example, a networking device). On the other hand, most other hardware generates interrupts at nondeterministic times and is, therefore, a good source of entropy. For more information on the kernel entropy pool, see Appendix C, "Kernel Random Number Generator."

- `SA_SHIRQ`: This flag specifies that the interrupt line can be shared among multiple interrupt handlers. Each handler registered on a given line must specify this flag; otherwise, only one handler can exist per line. More information on shared handlers is provided in a following section.

The fourth parameter, `devname`, is an ASCII text representation of the device associated with the interrupt. For example, this value for the keyboard interrupt on a PC is `"keyboard"`. These text names are used by /proc/irq and /proc/interrupts for communication with the user, which we will discuss shortly.

The fifth parameter, `dev_id`, is used primarily for shared interrupt lines. When an interrupt handler is freed (discussed later) `dev_id` provides a unique cookie to allow the removal of only the desired interrupt handler from the interrupt line. Without this parameter, it would be impossible for the kernel to know *which* handler to remove on a given interrupt line. You can pass `NULL` here if the line is not shared, but you must pass a unique cookie if your interrupt line is shared (and unless your device lives on the ISA bus, there is good chance it must support sharing). This pointer is also passed into the interrupt handler on each invocation. A common practice is to pass the driver's device structure: This pointer is unique and might be useful to have within the handler.

On success, `request_irq()` returns zero. A nonzero value indicates error, in which case the specified interrupt handler was not registered. A common error is `-EBUSY`, which denotes that the given interrupt line is already in use (and either the current user or you did not specify `SA_SHIRQ`).

Note `request_irq()` might sleep and, therefore, cannot be called from interrupt context or other situations where code cannot block. It is a common mistake to assume `request_irq()` can be safely called from a context where it is not safe to sleep. This is partly due to *why* `request_irq()` can sleep—it is indeed unclear. On registration, an entry corresponding to the interrupt is created in /proc/irq. The function `proc_mkdir()` is used to create new procfs entries. This function calls `proc_create()` to set up the new procfs entries, which in turn calls `kmalloc()` to allocate memory. As we will discuss in Chapter 10, "Memory Management and Addressing," `kmalloc()` can sleep. So there you go!

To request an interrupt line and install a handler in a driver:

```
if (request_irq(irqn, my_interrupt, SA_SHIRQ, "my_device", dev)) {
    printk(KERN_ERR "my_device: cannot register IRQ %d\n", irqn);
    return -EIO;
}
```

In this example, `irqn` is the requested interrupt line, `my_interrupt` is the handler, the line can be shared, the device is named "`my_device`," and we passed `dev` for `dev_id`. On failure, the code prints an error and returns. If the call returned zero, the handler was successfully installed. From that point forward, the handler is invoked in response to an interrupt. It is important to initialize hardware and register an interrupt handler in the proper order to prevent the interrupt handler from running before the device is fully initialized.

Freeing an Interrupt Handler

To free an interrupt line, call

```
void free_irq(unsigned int irq, void *dev_id)
```

If the specified interrupt line is not shared, this function removes the handler and disables the line. If the interrupt line is shared, the handler identified via `dev_id` is removed. The line itself is only disabled when the last handler is removed. Now we can see why a unique `dev_id` is important. With shared interrupt lines, a unique cookie is required to differentiate between the multiple handlers on the single line and allow `free_irq()` to remove the correct handler. In either case (shared or unshared), if `dev_id` is non-`NULL`, it must match the desired handler.

A call to `free_irq()` must be made from process context.

Writing an Interrupt Handler

The following is a typical declaration of an interrupt handler:

```
static irqreturn_t intr_handler(int irq, void *dev_id, struct pt_regs *regs)
```

Note this matches the argument given to `request_irq()`. The first parameter, `irq`, is the numeric value of the interrupt line the handler is servicing. This is not entirely useful today, except perhaps in printing log messages. Prior to the 2.0 kernel, there was no `dev_id` parameter and, thus, `irq` was used to differentiate between multiple devices using the same driver and, therefore, the same interrupt handler (as an example, consider a computer with multiple hard drive controllers).

The second parameter, `dev_id`, is a generic pointer to the same `dev_id` that was given to `request_irq()` when the interrupt handler was registered. If this value is unique (which is recommended to support sharing), it can act as a cookie to differentiate between multiple devices potentially using the same interrupt handler. `dev_id` might also point to a structure of use to the interrupt handler. Because the device structure is both unique to each device and potentially useful to have within the handler, it is typically passed for `dev_id`.

The final parameter, `regs`, holds a pointer to a structure containing the processor registers and state prior to servicing the interrupt. They are rarely used, except for debugging.

The return value of an interrupt handler is the special type `irqreturn_t`. An interrupt handler can return two special values, `IRQ_NONE` or `IRQ_HANDLED`. The former is returned when the interrupt handler detects an interrupt for which its device was not the originator. The later is returned if the interrupt handler was correctly invoked, and its device did cause the interrupt. Alternatively, `IRQ_RETVAL(x)` may be used. If `x` is non-zero, this macro returns `IRQ_HANDLED`. Otherwise, the macro returns `IRQ_NONE`. These special values are used to let the kernel know if devices are issuing spurious (unrequested) interrupts. If all the interrupt handlers on a given interrupt line return `IRQ_NONE`, then the kernel can detect the problem. Note the curious return type, `irqreturn_t`, which is simply an `int`. This value is used to provide backward compatibility with earlier kernels, which did not have this feature—before 2.6, interrupt handlers returned `void`. Drivers may simply `typedef irqreturn_t` to `void` and then work in 2.4 without further modification.

The interrupt handler is normally marked `static`, since it is never called directly from another file.

The role of the interrupt handler depends entirely on the device and its reasons for issuing the interrupt. At a minimum, most interrupt handlers need to provide acknowledgment to the device that they received the interrupt. Devices that are more complex need to additionally send and receive data and perform extended work in the interrupt handler. As mentioned, the extended work is pushed as much as possible into the bottom half handler, which is discussed in the next chapter.

Reentrancy and Interrupt Handlers

Interrupt handlers in Linux need not be reentrant. When a given interrupt handler is executing, the corresponding interrupt line is masked out on all processors, preventing another interrupt on the same line from being received. Normally all other interrupts are enabled, so other interrupts are serviced, but the current line is always disabled. Consequently, the same interrupt handler is never invoked concurrently to service a nested interrupt.

Shared Handlers

A shared handler is registered and executed much like a non-shared handler. Three main differences are

- The `SA_SHIRQ` flag must be set in the `flags` argument to `request_irq()`.
- The `dev_id` argument must be unique to each registered handler. A pointer to any per-device structure is sufficient; a common choice is the device structure as it is

both unique and potentially useful to the handler. You *cannot* pass NULL for a shared handler!

- The interrupt handler must be capable of distinguishing whether its device actually generated an interrupt. This requires both hardware support and associated logic in the handler. If the hardware does not offer this capability, there would be no way for the interrupt handler to know whether its associated device or some other device sharing the line caused the interrupt.

All drivers sharing the interrupt line must meet the previous requirements. If any one device does not share fairly, none can share the line. When request_irq() is called with SA_SHIRQ specified, the call will succeed only if the interrupt line is currently not registered, or if all registered handlers on the line also specified SA_SHIRQ. Note that in 2.6, unlike the behavior in older kernels, shared handlers can mix usage of SA_INTERRUPT.

When the kernel receives an interrupt, it invokes sequentially each registered handler on the line. Therefore, it is important that the handler be capable of distinguishing whether it generated a given interrupt. The handler must quickly exit if its associated device did not generate the interrupt. This requires the hardware device to have a status register (or similar mechanism) that the handler can check. Most hardware does indeed have such a feature.

A Real Life Interrupt Handler

Let's look at a real interrupt handler, from the RTC (real-time clock) driver, found in drivers/char/rtc.c. An RTC is found in many machines, including PCs. It is a device, separate from the system timer, which is used to set the system clock, provide an alarm, or supply a periodic timer. Setting the system clock is typically done by writing into a specific register or I/O range. An alarm or periodic timer, however, is normally implemented via interrupt. The interrupt is equivalent to a real-world clock alarm: When the interrupt is sent, the alarm or timer is going off.

When the RTC driver loads, the function rtc_init() is invoked to initialize the driver. One of its duties is to register the interrupt handler:

```
if (request_irq(RTC_IRQ, rtc_interrupt, SA_INTERRUPT, "rtc", NULL) {
        printk(KERN_ERR "rtc: cannot register IRQ %d\n", rtc_irq);
        return -EIO;
}
```

From this, we see the interrupt line is stored in RTC_IRQ. This is a preprocessor define that specifies the RTC interrupt for a given architecture. On the PC, for example, the RTC is always located at IRQ 8. The second parameter is our interrupt handler, rtc_interrupt, which runs with all interrupts disabled, thanks to the SA_INTERRUPT flag. From the fourth parameter, we see that the driver name is "rtc". Because this device cannot share the interrupt line and the handler has no use for any special value, NULL is passed for dev_id.

Finally, the handler itself:

```
static irqreturn_t rtc_interrupt(int irq, void *dev_id, struct pt_regs *regs)
{
    /*
     * Can be an alarm interrupt, update complete interrupt,
     * or a periodic interrupt. We store the status in the
     * low byte and the number of interrupts received since
     * the last read in the remainder of rtc_irq_data.
     */

    spin_lock (&rtc_lock);

    rtc_irq_data += 0x100;
    rtc_irq_data &= ~0xff;
    rtc_irq_data |= (CMOS_READ(RTC_INTR_FLAGS) & 0xF0);

    if (rtc_status & RTC_TIMER_ON)
        mod_timer(&rtc_irq_timer, jiffies + HZ/rtc_freq + 2*HZ/100);

    spin_unlock (&rtc_lock);

    /*
     * Now do the rest of the actions
     */
    spin_lock(&rtc_task_lock);
    if (rtc_callback)
    rtc_callback->func(rtc_callback->private_data);
    spin_unlock(&rtc_task_lock);
    wake_up_interruptible(&rtc_wait);

    kill_fasync (&rtc_async_queue, SIGIO, POLL_IN);

    return IRQ_HANDLED;
}
```

This function is invoked whenever the machine receives the RTC interrupt. First, note the spin lock calls—the first set ensures that rtc_irq_data is not accessed concurrently by another processor on an SMP machine, and the second set protects rtc_callback from the same. Locks are discussed in Chapter 8, "Kernel Synchronization Methods."

rtc_irq_data stores information about the RTC and is updated on each interrupt to reflect the status of the interrupt.

Next, if an RTC periodic timer is set, it is updated via mod_timer(). Timers are discussed in Chapter 9, "Timers and Time Management."

The final bunch of code, wrapped with the second set of spin locks, executes a possible preset callback function. The RTC driver enables a callback function to be registered and executed on each RTC interrupt.

Finally, this function returns `IRQ_HANDLED` to signify that it properly handled this device. Because the interrupt handler does not support sharing, and there is no mechanism by which the RTC can detect a spurious interrupt, this handler always returns `IRQ_HANDLED`.

Interrupt Context

When executing an interrupt handler or bottom half, the kernel is in *interrupt context*. Recall that process context is the mode of operation the kernel is in while it is executing on behalf of a process—for example, executing a system call or running a kernel thread. In process context, the `current` macro points to the associated task. Furthermore, because a process is coupled to the kernel in process context, process context can sleep or otherwise invoke the scheduler.

Interrupt context, on the other hand, is not associated with a process. The `current` macro is not relevant (although it points to the interrupted process). Without a backing process, interrupt context cannot sleep—how would it ever reschedule? Therefore, you cannot call certain functions from interrupt context. If a function sleeps, you cannot use it from your interrupt handler—this limits the functions which one can call from an interrupt handler.

Interrupt context is time critical because the interrupt handler interrupted other code. Code should be quick and simple. Busy looping is discouraged. This is a very important point; always keep in mind that your interrupt handler interrupted other code (possibly even another interrupt handler on a different line!). Because of this asynchronous nature, it is imperative that all interrupt handlers are as quick and as simple as possible. As much as possible, work should be pushed out from the interrupt handler and performed in a bottom half, which runs at a more convenient time.

Finally, the interrupt handler does not receive its own stack. Instead, it shares the kernel stack of the process it interrupted. If no process is running, it uses the idle task's stack. Because interrupt handlers share the stack, they must be exceptionally frugal with what they allocate there. Of course, the kernel stack is limited to begin with[1], so all kernel code should be cautious.

Implementation of Interrupt Handling

Perhaps not surprising, the implementation of the interrupt handling system in Linux is very architecture-dependent. The implementation depends on the processor, the type of interrupt controller used, and the design of the architecture and machine itself.

Figure 5.1 is a diagram of the path an interrupt takes through hardware and the kernel.

---

[1] The kernel stack is 8KB on 32-bit architectures and 16KB on 64-bit architectures. This is shared by the executing process context code and *all* interrupts that occur.

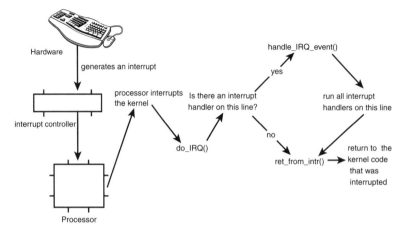

Figure 5.1 The path an interrupt takes from hardware and on through the kernel.

A device issues an interrupt by sending an electric signal over its bus to the interrupt controller. If the interrupt line is enabled (they can be masked out), the interrupt controller sends the interrupt to the processor. In most architectures, sending a signal to the processor over a special pin accomplishes this. Unless interrupts are disabled in the processor (which can also happen), the processor immediately stops what it is doing, disables the interrupt system, and jumps to a predefined location in memory and executes the code located there. This predefined point is setup by the kernel and is the entry point for interrupt handlers.

The interrupt's journey in the kernel begins at a predefined entry point, just like system calls. For each interrupt line, the processor jumps to a unique location. This way, the kernel knows the IRQ number of the incoming interrupt. The initial entry point simply saves this value and stores the current register values (which belong to the interrupted task) on the stack; then, the kernel calls do_IRQ(). From here onward, most of the interrupt handling code is written in C—however, it is still architecture-dependent.

do_IRQ() is declared as

```
unsigned int do_IRQ(struct pt_regs regs)
```

Because the C calling convention places function arguments at the top of the stack, the pt_regs structure contains the initial register values that were previously saved in the assembly entry routine. Because the interrupt value was also saved, do_IRQ() can extract it. The x86 code is

```
int irq = regs.orig_eax & 0xff;
```

After the interrupt line is calculated, do_IRQ() acknowledges the receipt of the interrupt and disables interrupt delivery on the line. On normal PC machines, these operations are handled by mask_and_ack_8259A(), which do_IRQ() calls.

Next, `do_IRQ()` ensures that a valid handler is registered on the line, and that it is enabled and not currently executing. If so, it calls `hardware_IRQ_event()` to run the installed interrupt handlers for the line. On x86, `handle_IRQ_event()` is

```
int handle_IRQ_event(unsigned int irq, struct pt_regs *regs, struct irqaction
*action)
{
    int status = 1;

    if (!(action->flags & SA_INTERRUPT))
        local_irq_enable();

    do {
        status |= action->flags;
        action->handler(irq, action->dev_id, regs);
        action = action->next;
    } while (action);

    if (status & SA_SAMPLE_RANDOM)
        add_interrupt_randomness(irq);
    local_irq_disable();

    return status;
}
```

First, because the processor disabled interrupts, they are turned back on unless `SA_INTERRUPT` was specified during the handler's registration. Recall that `SA_INTERRUPT` specifies that the handler must be run with interrupts disabled. Next, each potential handler is executed in a loop. If this line is not shared, the loop terminates after the first iteration. Otherwise, all handlers are executed. After that, `add_interrupt_randomness()` is called if `SA_SAMPLE_RANDOM` was specified during registration. This function uses the timing of the interrupt to generate entropy for the random number generator. Appendix C, "Kernel Random Number Generator," has more information on the kernel's random number generator. Finally, interrupts are again disabled (`do_IRQ()` expects them to still be off) and the function returns. Back in `do_IRQ()`, the function cleans up and returns to the initial entry point, which then jumps to `ret_from_intr()`.

The routine `ret_from_intr()` is, like the initial entry code, written in assembly. This routine checks whether a reschedule is pending (recall from Chapter 3, "Scheduling," that this implies `need_resched` is set). If a reschedule is pending, and the kernel is returning to user-space (that is, the interrupt interrupted a user process), `schedule()` is called. If the kernel is returning to kernel-space (that is, the interrupt interrupted the kernel itself), `schedule()` is called only if the `preempt_count` is zero (otherwise it is not safe to preempt the kernel). After `schedule()` returns, or if there is no work pending, the initial registers are restored and the kernel resumes whatever was interrupted.

On x86, the initial assembly routines are located in `arch/i386/kernel/entry.S`, and the C methods are located in `arch/i386/kernel/irq.c`. Other supported architectures are similar.

/proc/interrupts

Procfs is a virtual filesystem that exists only in kernel memory and is typically mounted as /proc. Reading or writing files in procfs invokes kernel functions that simulate reading or writing from a real file. A relevant example is the /proc/interrupts file, which is populated with statistics related to interrupts on the system. Here is sample output from a uniprocessor PC:

```
       CPU0
  0:  3602371   XT-PIC  timer
  1:  3048      XT-PIC  i8042
  2:  0         XT-PIC  cascade
  4:  2689466   XT-PIC  uhci-hcd, eth0
  5:  0         XT-PIC  EMU10K1
 12:  85077     XT-PIC  uhci-hcd
 15:  24571     XT-PIC  aic7xxx
NMI:  0
LOC:  3602236
ERR:  0
```

The first column is the interrupt line. On this system, interrupts numbered 0-2, 4, 5, 12, and 15 are present. Handlers are not installed on lines not displayed. The second column is a counter of the number of interrupts received. In fact, a column is present for each processor on the system, but this machine only has one processor. As we can see, the timer interrupt has received 3,602,371 interrupts[2], whereas the sound card (EMU10K1) has received none (which is an indication that it has not been used since the machine booted). The third column is the interrupt controller handling this interrupt. XT-PIC corresponds to the standard PC programmable interrupt controller. On systems with an I/O APIC, most interrupts would list IO-APIC-level or IO-APIC-edge as their interrupt controller. Finally, the last column is the device associated with this interrupt. This name is supplied by the `devname` parameter to `request_irq()`, as discussed previously. If the interrupt is shared, as is the case with interrupt four in this example, all the devices registered on the interrupt line are listed.

For the curious, procfs code is located primarily in `fs/proc`. The function that provides /proc/interrupts is, not surprisingly, architecture-dependent and named `show_interrupts()`.

---

[2] After reading Chapter 9, "Timers and Time Management," can you tell how long the system has been up (in terms of HZ) knowing the number of timer interrupts which have occurred?

Interrupt Control

The Linux kernel implements a family of interfaces for manipulating the state of interrupts on a machine. These interfaces enable you to disable the interrupt system for the current processor or mask out an interrupt line for the entire machine. These routines are all very architecture-dependent and can be found in <asm/system.h> and <asm/irq.h>. See Table 5.1 for a complete listing of the interfaces.

Reasons to control the interrupt system generally boil down to needing to provide synchronization. By disabling interrupts, you can guarantee that an interrupt handler won't preempt your current code. Moreover, disabling interrupts also disables kernel preemption. Neither disabling interrupt deliver nor disabling kernel preemption provides any protection from concurrent access from another processor, however. Because Linux supports multiple processors, kernel code more generally needs to obtain some sort of lock to prevent access to shared data simultaneously from another processor. These locks are often obtained in conjunction with disabling local interrupts. The lock provides protection against concurrent access from another processor, whereas disabling interrupts provides protection against concurrent access from a possible interrupt handler. Chapters 7 and 8 discuss the various problems of synchronization and their solutions. Nevertheless, understanding the kernel interrupt control interfaces is important.

Disabling and Enabling Interrupts

To disable interrupts locally for the current processor (and *only* the current processor) and later enable them:

```
local_irq_disable();
/* interrupts are disabled .. */
local_irq_enable();
```

These functions are usually implemented as a single assembly operation (of course, this depends on the architecture). Indeed, on x86, local_irq_disable() is a simple cli and local_irq_enable() is a simple sti instruction. For non-x86 hackers, cli and sti are the assembly calls to *clear* and *set* the *allow interrupts* flag, respectively. In other words, they disable and enable interrupt delivery on the issuing processor.

The local_irq_disable() routine is dangerous if interrupts were already disabled *prior* to its invocation. The corresponding call to local_irq_enable() unconditionally enables interrupts, despite the fact that they were off to begin with. Instead, a mechanism is needed to restore interrupts to a previous state. This is a common concern because a given code path in the kernel can be reached both with and without interrupts enabled, depending on the call chain. For example, imagine the previous code snippet is part of a larger function. This function is called by two other functions: one of which disables interrupts and one of which does not. Because it is becoming harder as the kernel grows to know all the code paths leading up to a function, it is much safer to save the state of the interrupt system before disabling it. Instead, when you are ready to enable them, you simply restore them to their original state:

```
unsigned long flags;


local_irq_save(flags);

/* interrupts are disabled .. */

local_irq_restore(flags); /* interrupts are restored to their previous state .. */
```

Note these methods are implemented at least in part as macros, so the `flags` parameter is seemingly passed by value. The parameter contains architecture-specific data containing the state of the interrupt systems. Because at least one supported architecture incorporates stack information into the value (SPARC), `flags` *cannot* be passed to another function (in other words, it must remain on the same stack frame). For this reason, the call to save and the call to restore must occur in the same function.

All of the previous functions can be called from both interrupt and process context.

> **No more global** `cli()`
>
> The kernel formerly provided a method to disable interrupts on *all* processors in the system. Furthermore, if another processor called this method, it would have to wait until interrupts were enabled before continuing. This function was named `cli()` and the corresponding enable call was named `sti()`—very x86 centric. These interfaces were removed during 2.5, and consequently all interrupt synchronization must now use a combination of local interrupt control and spin locks (discussed in Chapter 8, "Kernel Synchronization Methods"). This means that code that previously only had to disable interrupts globally to ensure mutual exclusive access to shared data now needs to do a bit more work.
>
> Previously, driver writers could assume a `cli()` used in their interrupt handler *and* anywhere else the shared data was accessed would provide mutual exclusion. The `cli()` call would ensure that no other interrupt handlers (and thus their specific handler) would run. Furthermore, if another processor entered a `cli()` protected region, it would not continue until the original processor exited their `cli()` protected region and called `sti()`.
>
> Removing the global `cli()` has a handful of advantages. First, it forces driver writers to implement real locking. A fine-grained lock with a specific purpose is faster than a global lock, which is effectively what `cli()` is. Second, it streamlined a lot of code and removed a bunch more. The resulting interrupt system is simpler and easier to comprehend.

Disabling a Specific Interrupt Line

In the previous section, we looked at functions that disable all interrupt deliver for an entire processor. In some cases, it is useful to disable only a *specific* interrupt line for the *entire* system. This is called *masking out* an interrupt line. As an example, you might want to disable delivery of a device's interrupts before manipulating its state. Linux provides four interfaces for this task:

```
void disable_irq(unsigned int irq);
void disable_irq_nosync(unsigned int irq);
```

```
void enable_irq(unsigned int irq);
void synchronize_irq(unsigned int irq);
```

The first two functions disable a given interrupt line in the interrupt controller. This disables delivery of the given interrupt to *all* processors in the system. Additionally, the `disable_irq()` function will not return until any currently executing handler completes. Thus, callers are assured not only that new interrupts will not be delivered on the given line, but also that any already executing handlers have exited. The function `disable_irq_nosync()` does not have this property.

The function `synchronize_irq()` will wait for a specific interrupt handler to exit, if it is executing, before returning.

Calls to these functions nest. For each call to `disable_irq()` or `disable_irq_nosync()` on a given interrupt line, a corresponding call to `enable_irq()` is required. Only on the last call to `enable_irq()` is the interrupt line actually enabled. For example, if `disable_irq()` is called twice, the interrupt line will not actually be enabled again until the second call to `enable_irq()`.

All three of these functions can be called from interrupt or process context and do not sleep. If calling from interrupt context, be careful! You do not want, for example, to enable an interrupt line while you are handling it (recall that the interrupt line of a handler is masked out while it is being serviced).

It would be rather rude to disable an interrupt line that is shared among multiple interrupt handlers. Disabling the line disables interrupt deliver for *all* devices on the line. Therefore, drivers for newer devices tend not to use these interfaces[3]. Because PCI devices have to support interrupt line sharing by specification, they should not use these interfaces at all. Thus, `disable_irq()` and friends are found more often in older legacy devices, such as the PC parallel port.

Status of the Interrupt System

It is often useful to know the state of the interrupt system (for example, whether interrupts are enabled or disabled) or whether you are currently executing in interrupt context.

The macro `irqs_disabled()`, defined in `<asm/system.h>`, returns nonzero if the interrupt system on the local processor is disabled. Otherwise, it returns zero.

Two macros, defined in `<asm/hardirq.h>`, provide an interface to check the kernel's current context. They are

```
in_interrupt()
in_irq()
```

---

[3] Many older devices, particularly ISA devices, do not provide a method of obtaining whether or not they generated an interrupt. Because of this, oftentimes interrupt lines for ISA devices cannot be shared. Because the PCI specification mandates the sharing of interrupts, modern PCI-based devices support interrupt sharing. In contemporary computers, nearly all interrupt lines can be shared.

The most useful is the first: It returns nonzero if the kernel is in interrupt context. This includes either executing an interrupt handler or a bottom half handler. The macro in_irq() returns nonzero only if the kernel is specifically executing an interrupt handler.

More often, you want to check if you are in process context. That is, you want to ensure you are *not* in interrupt context. This is often the case because code wants to do something that can only be done from process context, like sleep. If in_interrupt() returns zero, the kernel is in process context.

Table 5.1   **Listing of Interrupt Control Methods**

Function	Description
local_irq_disable()	Disable local interrupt deliver
local_irq_enable()	Enable local interrupt deliver
local_irq_save(unsigned long flags)	Save the current state of local interrupt deliver and then disable it
local_irq_restore(unsigned long flags)	Restore the local interrupt deliver to the given state
disable_irq(unsigned int irq)	Disable the given interrupt line and ensure no handler on the line is executing before returning
disable_irq_nosync(unsigned int irq)	Disable the given interrupt line
enable_irq(unsigned int irq)	Enable the given interrupt line
irqs_disabled()	Returns nonzero if local interrupt deliver is disabled; otherwise returns zero
in_interrupt()	Returns nonzero if in interrupt context and zero if in process context
in_irq()	Returns nonzero if currently executing an interrupt handler and zero otherwise

6

Bottom Halves and Deferring Work

I N THE PREVIOUS CHAPTER, WE LOOKED at interrupt handlers as the kernel mechanism for dealing with interrupts. Interrupt handlers are a useful—indeed, required—part of the kernel. Because of certain limitations, however, they form only the first half of the interrupt processing solution. The limitations include

- Interrupt handlers run asynchronously and thus interrupt other potentially important code (even other interrupt handlers). Therefore, they need to run as quickly as possible.
- Interrupt handlers run with the current interrupt level disabled at best, and at worst (if SA_INTERRUPT is set) with all interrupts disabled. Again, they need to run as quickly as possible.
- Interrupt handlers are often very timing-critical because they deal with hardware.
- Interrupt handlers do not run in process context, therefore, they cannot block.

It should now be obvious that interrupt handlers are only a piece of the whole solution to managing hardware interrupts. We certainly need a quick, asynchronous, simple handler for immediately responding to hardware and performing any time-critical actions. Interrupt handlers serve this function well, but other, less critical work, should be deferred to a later point when interrupts are enabled.

Consequently, managing interrupts is divided into two parts, or *halves*. The first part, interrupt handlers (*top halves*), are executed by the kernel asynchronously in immediate response to a hardware interrupt, as we discussed in the previous chapter. In this chapter, we look at the second part of managing interrupts, *bottom halves*.

Bottom Halves

The job of bottom halves is to perform any interrupt-related work not performed by the interrupt handler itself. In an ideal world, this is nearly all the work because we want the interrupt handler to perform as little work (and in turn be as fast) as possible. We want interrupt handlers to return as quickly as possible.

Nonetheless, the interrupt handler must perform some of the work. For example, the interrupt handler almost assuredly needs to acknowledge the receipt of the interrupt with the hardware. It might also need to copy data to or from the hardware. This work is timing-sensitive, so it makes sense to perform it in the interrupt handler itself.

Almost anything else is fair game for performing in the bottom half. For example, if you copy data from the hardware into memory in the top half, it certainly makes sense to process it in the bottom half. Unfortunately, no hard and fast rules exist about what work to perform where—the decision is left entirely up to the device driver author. Although no arrangement is *wrong*, an arrangement can easily be *suboptimal*. Remember, the interrupt handlers run asynchronously, with at least the current interrupt line disabled. Minimizing their duration is important. No strict rules about how to divide the work between the top and bottom half exist, but a couple useful tips might help:

- If the work is time-sensitive, perform it in the interrupt handler.
- If the work is related to the hardware itself, perform it in the interrupt handler.
- If the work needs to ensure that another interrupt (particularly the same interrupt) does not interrupt it, perform it in the interrupt handler.
- For everything else, consider performing the work in the bottom half.

When attempting to write your own device driver, looking at other interrupt handlers and their corresponding bottom halves will help. When deciding how to divide your interrupt processing work between the top and bottom half, ask yourself what *has* to be in the top half and what *can* be in the bottom half. Generally, the quicker the interrupt handler executes, the better.

Why Bottom Halves?

It is crucial to understand why to defer work, and when exactly to defer it. You want to limit the amount of work you perform in an interrupt handler because interrupt handlers run with the current interrupt line disabled. Worse, handlers that register with SA_INTERRUPT run with *all* local interrupts disabled (plus the local interrupt line globally disabled). Minimizing the time spent with interrupts disabled is important to system response and performance. Add to this the fact that interrupt handlers run asynchronously with respect to other code—even other interrupt handlers—and then it is clear that we should work to minimize how long interrupt handlers run. The solution is to defer some of the work until later.

But when is later? The important thing to realize is that *later* is often simply *not now*. The point of a bottom half is *not* to do work at some specified point in the future, but simply to defer work until *any* point in the future when the system is less busy and interrupts are again enabled. Often, bottom halves run immediately after the interrupt returns. The key is that they run with all interrupts enabled.

Not just Linux, but many operating systems separate the processing of hardware inter-rupts into two parts. The top half is quick and simple and runs with some or all inter-rupts disabled. The bottom half (however it is implemented) runs later with all interrupts enabled. This design keeps system response time low by running with interrupts disabled for as little time as necessary.

A World of Bottom Halves

Unlike the top half, which we implement entirely via the interrupt handler, multiple mechanisms are available for implementing a bottom half. These mechanisms are differ-ent interfaces and subsystems that allow you to implement bottom halves. Whereas in the previous chapter we looked at just a single way of implementing interrupt handlers, in this chapter we will look at multiple methods of implementing bottom halves. In fact, over the course of Linux's history there have been many bottom half mechanisms. Confusingly, some of these mechanisms have similar or even really dumb names.

In this chapter, we will discuss both the design and implementation of the bottom half mechanisms that exist in 2.6. We will also discuss how to use them in the kernel code you write. The old, but long since removed, bottom half mechanisms are historical-ly significant, so they'll be mentioned when relevant.

In the beginning, Linux provided only the "bottom half" for implementing bottom halves. The name was sane because that was the only means available for deferring work at the time. The infrastructure was also known as "BH," which is what we will call it to avoid confusion with the generic term "bottom half." The BH interface was very simple, like most things in those good old days. It provided a statically created list of 32 bottom halves. The top half could mark whether the bottom half would run by sitting a bit in a 32-bit integer. Each BH was globally synchronized. No two could run at the same time, even on different processors. This was easy-to-use, yet inflexible; simple, yet a bottleneck.

Later on, the kernel developers introduced *task queues* both as a method of deferring work and as a replacement for the BH mechanism. The kernel defined a family of queues. Each queue contained a linked list of functions to call. The queued functions were run at certain times, depending on which queue they were in. Drivers could regis-ter their bottom halves in the appropriate queue. This worked fairly well, but it was still too inflexible to replace entirely the BH interface. It also was not lightweight enough for performance critical subsystems, such as networking.

During the 2.3 development series, the kernel developers introduced *softirqs* and *tasklets*. With the exception of compatibility with existing drivers, softirqs and tasklets were capable of completely replacing the BH interface[1]. Softirqs are a set of 32 statically defined bottom halves that can run simultaneously on any processor—even two of the same type can run concurrently. Tasklets, which have an awful and confusing name[2], are

---

[1] Due to the global synchronization of any running BH with any other, it is nontrivial to convert them to softirqs or tasklets. It did eventually happen, however, in 2.5.

[2] They have nothing to do with tasks. Think of a tasklet as a simple and easy-to-use softirq.

flexible, dynamically created bottom halves that are built on top of softirqs. Two different tasklets can run concurrently on different processors, but two of the same type of tasklet cannot run simultaneously. Thus, tasklets are a good tradeoff between performance and ease-of-use. For most bottom half processing, the tasklet is sufficient. Softirqs are useful when performance is critical, such as with networking. Using softirqs requires more care, however, because two of the same softirq can run at the same time. In addition, softirqs must be registered statically at compile-time. Conversely, code can dynamically register tasklets.

To further confound the issue, some people refer to all bottom halves as software interrupts or softirqs. In other words, they call both the softirq mechanism and bottom halves in general softirqs. Ignore those people.

While developing the 2.5 kernel, the BH interface was finally tossed to the curb as all BH users were converted to the other bottom half interfaces. Additionally, the task queue interface was replaced by the work queue interface. Work queues are a very simple yet useful method of queueing work to later be performed in process context.

Consequently, today in 2.6 we have three bottom half mechanisms in the kernel: softirqs, tasklets, and work queues. The kernel used to have the BH and task queue interfaces, but today they are mere memories.

Kernel Timers

Another mechanism for deferring work is kernel timers. Unlike the mechanisms discussed in the chapter thus far, timers defer work for a specified amount of time. That is, although the tools discussed in this chapter are useful to defer work to *any time but now*, you use timers to defer work until at least a specific time has elapsed.

Therefore, timers have different uses than the general mechanisms discussed in this chapter. A full discussion of timers is given in Chapter 9, "Timers and Time Management."

Bottom Half Confusion

This is some real confusing stuff, but really it is just naming issues. Let's go over it again.

"Bottom half" is a generic operating system term referring to the deferred portion of interrupt processing. In Linux, it currently has this meaning, too. All the kernel's mechanisms for deferring work are "bottom halves." Some people also confusingly call all bottom halves "softirqs," but they are just being annoying.

"Bottom half" also refers to the original deferred work mechanism in Linux. This mechanism is also known as a "BH," so we call it by that name now and leave the former as a generic description. The BH mechanism was deprecated awhile back and fully removed in 2.5.

Currently, there are three methods for deferring work: softirqs, tasklets, and work queues. Tasklets are built on softirqs and work queues are entirely different. *Table 6.1* presents a history of bottom halves.

Table 6.1 **Bottom Half Status**

Bottom Half	Status
BH	Removed in 2.5
Task queues	Removed in 2.5
Softirq	Available since 2.3
Tasklet	Available since 2.3
Work queues	Available since 2.5

With this naming confusion settled, let's look at the individual mechanisms.

Softirqs

We begin our discussion of the actual bottom half methods with softirqs. Softirqs are rarely used; tasklets are a much more common form of bottom half. Nonetheless, because tasklets are built on softirqs we'll cover them first. The softirq code lives in `kernel/softirq.c`.

Implementation of Softirqs

Softirqs are statically allocated at compile-time. Unlike tasklets, you cannot dynamically register and destroy softirqs. Softirqs are represented by the `softirq_action` structure, which is defined in `<linux/interrupt.h>`:

```
/*
 * structure representing a single softirq entry
 */
struct softirq_action
{
    void (*action)(struct softirq_action *);    /* function to run */
    void *data;                    /* data to pass to function */
};
```

A 32-entry array of this structure is declared in `kernel/softirq.c`:

```
static struct softirq_action softirq_vec[32];
```

Each registered softirq consumes one entry in the array. Consequently, there can be a possible 32 softirqs. Note, this is fixed—the maximum number of registered softirqs cannot be dynamically changed. In the current kernel, however, only six of the 32 entries are used[3].

---

[3]Most drivers use tasklets for their bottom half. Tasklets are built off softirqs, as we shall see in the next section.

The Softirq Handler

The prototype of a softirq handler, `action`, looks like:

```
void softirq_handler(struct softirq_action *)
```

When the kernel runs a softirq handler, it executes this `action` function with a pointer
to the corresponding `softirq_action` structure as its lone argument. For example, if
`my_softirq` pointed to an entry in the `softirq_vec` array, the kernel would invoke the
softirq handler function as

```
my_softirq->action(my_softirq)
```

It might be a bit surprising that the kernel passes the entire structure, and not just the
`data` value, to the softirq handler. This trick allows future additions to the structure without requiring a change in every softirq handler. Softirq handlers can retrieve the data
value, if they need to, simply by dereferencing their argument and reading the `data`
member.

A softirq never preempts another softirq. In fact, the only event that can preempt a
softirq is an interrupt handler. Another softirq—even the same one—can run on another
processor, however.

Executing Softirqs

A registered softirq must be marked before it will execute. This is called *raising the softirq*.
Usually, an interrupt handler marks its softirq for execution before returning. Then, at a
suitable time, the softirq runs. Pending softirqs are checked for and executed in the following situations:

- After processing a hardware interrupt
- By the `ksoftirqd` kernel thread
- By code that explicitly checks and executes pending softirqs, such as the network-
  ing subsystem

Regardless of the method of invocation, softirq execution occurs in `do_softirq()`. The
function is really quite simple. If there are pending softirqs, `do_softirq()` loops over
each one, invoking its handler. Let's look at a simplified variant of the important part of
`do_softirq()`:

```
u32 pending = softirq_pending(cpu);

if (pending) {
    struct softirq_action *h = softirq_vec;

    softirq_pending(cpu) = 0;

    do {
        if (pending & 1)
```

```
        h->action(h);
    h++;
    pending >>= 1;
} while (pending);
}
```

This snippet is the heart of softirq processing. It checks for, and executes, any pending softirqs. Specifically,

- Set the `pending` local variable to the value returned by the `softirq_pending()` macro. This is a 32-bit mask of pending softirqs—if bit n is set, the softirq of that value is pending.

- Now that the pending bitmask of softirqs is saved, clear the actual bitmask[4].

- The pointer h is set to the first entry in the `softirq_vec`.

- If the first bit in `pending` is set, `h->action(h)` is called.

- The pointer h is incremented by one so that it now points to the second entry in the `softirq_vec` array.

- The bitmask `pending` is right-shifted by one. This tosses the first bit away, and moves all other bits one place to the right. Consequently, the second bit is now the first (and so on).

- The pointer h now points to the second entry in the array and the `pending` bitmask now has the second bit as the first. Repeat the previous steps.

- Continue repeating until `pending` is zero, at which point there are no more pending softirqs and our work is done. Note, this check is sufficient to ensure h always points to a valid entry in `softirq_vec` because `pending` has at most 32 set bits and thus this loop executes at most 32 times.

Using Softirqs

Softirqs are reserved for the most timing critical and important bottom half processing on the system. Currently, only two subsystems—networking and SCSI—directly use softirqs. Additionally, kernel timers and tasklets are built on top of softirqs. If you are adding a new softirq, you normally want to ask yourself why using a tasklet is insufficient. Tasklets are dynamically created and are simpler to use because of their weaker locking requirements, and they still perform quite well. Nonetheless, for timing-critical

---

[4]This actually occurs with local interrupts disabled, but that is omitted in this simplified version. If interrupts were not disabled, a softirq could have been raised (and thus be pending) in the intervening time between saving the mask and clearing it. This would result in incorrectly clearing a pending bit.

applications that are able to do their own locking in an efficient way, softirqs might be the correct solution.

Assigning an Index

You declare softirqs statically at compile-time via an enum in `<linux/interrupt.h>`. The kernel uses this index, which starts at zero, as a relative priority. Softirqs with the lowest numerical priority execute before those with a higher numerical priority.

Table 6.2   **Listing of Bottom Half Control Methods**

Tasklet	Priority	Softirq Description
HI_SOFTIRQ	0	High priority tasklets
TIMER_SOFTIRQ	1	Timer bottom half
NET_TX_SOFTIRQ	2	Send network packets
NET_RX_SOFTIRQ	3	Receive network packets
SCSI_SOFTIRQ	4	SCSI bottom half
TASKLET_SOFTIRQ	5	Tasklets

Creating a new softirq includes adding a new entry to this enum. When adding a new softirq you might not want to simply add your entry to the end of the list, as you would elsewhere. Instead, you need to insert the new entry depending on the priority you want to give it. Historically, HI_SOFTIRQ is always the first and TASKLET_SOFTIRQ is always the last entry. A new entry probably belongs somewhere after the network entries, but prior to TASKLET_SOFTIRQ.

Registering Your Handler

Next, the softirq handler is registered at run-time via `open_softirq()`, which takes three parameters: the softirq's index, its handler function, and a value for the `data` field. The networking subsystem, for example, registers its softirqs like this:

```
open_softirq(NET_TX_SOFTIRQ, net_tx_action, NULL);
open_softirq(NET_RX_SOFTIRQ, net_rx_action, NULL);
```

The softirq handlers run with interrupts enabled and cannot sleep. While a handler runs, softirqs on the current processor are disabled. Another processor, however, can execute other softirqs. In fact, if a softirq is raised again while it is executing, another processor can run it simultaneously. This means that any shared data—even global data used only within the softirq handler itself—needs proper locking (as discussed in the next two chapters). This is an important point, and it is the reason tasklets are usually preferred. Simply preventing your softirqs from running concurrently is not ideal. If a softirq obtained a lock to prevent itself from running simultaneously, there would be little reason to use a softirq. Consequently, most softirqs handlers resort to per-processor data (data unique to each processor and thus not requiring locking) or some other tricks to avoid explicit locking and provide excellent scalability.

Raising Your Softirq

After a handler is added to the `enum` list and registered via `open_softirq()`, it is ready to run. To mark it pending, so it is run at the next invocation of `do_softirq()`, call `raise_softirq()`. For example, the networking subsystem would call

```
raise_softirq(NET_TX_SOFTIRQ);
```

This raises the `NET_TX_SOFTIRQ` softirq. Its handler, `net_tx_action()`, runs the next time the kernel executes softirqs. This function disables interrupts prior to actually raising the softirq, and then restores them to their previous state. If interrupts are already off, the function `raise_softirq_irqoff()` can be used as a minor optimization. For example:

```
/*
 * interrupts must already be off!
 */
raise_softirq_irqoff(NET_TX_SOFTIRQ);
```

Softirqs are most often raised from within interrupt handlers. In the case of interrupt handlers, the interrupt handler performs the basic hardware-related work, raises the softirq, and then exits. When done processing interrupts, the kernel invokes `do_softirq()`. The softirq then runs and picks up where the interrupt handler left off. In this example, the "top half" and "bottom half" naming should make sense.

Tasklets

Tasklets are a bottom half mechanism built on top of softirqs. As already mentioned, they have nothing to do with tasks. Tasklets are similar in nature and work in a similar manner to softirqs; however, they have a simpler interface and relaxed locking rules.

The decision of whether to use softirqs versus tasklets is simple: You usually want to use tasklets. As we saw in the previous section, you can count on one hand the users of softirqs. Softirqs are required only for very high frequency and highly threaded uses. Tasklets, on the other hand, see much greater use. Tasklets work just fine for most cases and they are very easy to use.

Implementation of Tasklets

Because tasklets are implemented on top of softirqs, they *are* softirqs. As discussed, tasklets are represented by two softirqs: `HI_SOFTIRQ` and `TASKLET_SOFTIRQ`. The only real difference in these types is that the `HI_SOFTIRQ`-based tasklets run prior to the `TASKLET_SOFTIRQ` tasklets.

The Tasklet Structure

Tasklets are represented by the `tasklist_struct` structure. Each structure represents a unique tasklet. The structure is declared in `<linux/interrupt.h>`:

```
struct tasklet_struct {
```

```
    struct tasklet_struct *next;  /* pointer to the next tasklet in the list */
    unsigned long state;        /* state of the tasklet */
    atomic_t count;           /* reference counter */
    void (*func)(unsigned long);  /* tasklet handler function */
    unsigned long data;        /* argument to the tasklet function */
};
```

The func member is the tasklet handler (the equivalent of action to a softirq) and it receives data as its sole argument.

The state member is one of zero, TASKLET_STATE_SCHED, or TASKLET_STATE_RUN. TASKLET_STATE_SCHED denotes a tasklet that is scheduled to run and TASKLET_STATE_RUN denotes a tasklet that is running. As an optimization, TASKLET_STATE_RUN is only used on multiprocessor machines because a uniprocessor machine always knows whether the tasklet is running (it is either the currently executing code, or not).

The count field is used as a reference count for the tasklet. If it is nonzero, the tasklet is disabled and cannot run; if it is zero, the tasklet is enabled and can run if marked pending.

Scheduling Tasklets

Scheduled tasklets (the equivalent of raised softirqs)[5] are stored in two per-processor structures: tasklist_vec (for regular tasklets) and tasklet_hi_vec (for high-priority tasklets). Both of these structures are linked lists of tasklet_struct structures. Each tasklet_struct structure in the list represents a different tasklet.

Tasklets are scheduled via the tasklet_schedule() and tasklet_hi_schedule() functions, which receive a pointer to the tasklet's tasklet_struct as their lone argument. The two functions are very similar (the difference being one uses TASKLET_SOFTIRQ and one uses HI_SOFTIRQ). We will go over writing and using tasklets in the next section. For now, let's look at the details of tasklet_schedule():

- Check if the tasklet's state is TASKLET_STATE_SCHED. If it is, the tasklet is already scheduled to run and the function can return.

- Save the state of the interrupt system, and then disable local interrupts. This ensures nothing on this processor will mess with the tasklet code while we are.

- Add the tasklet to-be-scheduled to the head of the tasklet_vec or tasklist_hi_vec linked list, which is unique to each processor in the system.

- Raise the TASKLET_SOFTIRQ or HI_SOFTIRQ softirq, so this tasklet will execute in the near future by do_softirq().

- Restore interrupts to their previous state and return.

---

[5]Yet another example of the evil naming schemes at work here. Why are softirqs raised but tasklets scheduled? Who knows? Both terms mean to mark that bottom half pending so that it is executed soon.

At the next earliest convenience, `do_softirq()` is run as discussed in the previous section. Because most tasklets and softirqs are marked pending in interrupt handlers, `do_softirq()` most likely runs when the last interrupt returns. Because `TASKLET_SOFTIRQ` or `HI_SOFTIRQ` is now raised, `do_softirq()` executes the associated handlers. These handlers, `tasklet_action()` and `tasklet_hi_action()`, are the heart of tasklet processing. Let's look at what they do:

- Disable interrupts and retrieves the `tasklet_vec` or `tasklist_hi_vec` list for this processor.

- Clear the list for this processor by setting it equal to `NULL`.

- Enable interrupts (there is no need to restore them to their previous state because the code here is always called as a softirq handler, and thus, interrupts are always enabled).

- Loop over each pending tasklet in the retrieved list.

- If this is a multiprocessing machine, check if the tasklet is running on another processor by checking the `TASKLET_STATE_RUN` flag. If it is currently running, do not execute it now and skip to the next pending tasklet (recall, only one tasklet of a given type may run concurrently).

- If the tasklet is not currently running, set the `TASKLET_STATE_RUN` flag, so another processor will not run it.

- Check for a zero `count` value, to ensure that the tasklet is not disabled. If the tasklet is disabled, skip it and go to the next pending tasklet.

- We now know that the tasklet is not running elsewhere, is marked as running by us so it will not start running elsewhere, and has a zero `count` value. Run the tasklet handler.

- After the tasklet runs, clear the `TASKLET_STATE_RUN` flag in the tasklet's `state` field.

- Repeat for the next pending tasklet, until there are no more scheduled tasklets waiting to run.

The implementation of tasklets is simple, but rather clever. As we saw, all tasklets are multiplexed on top of two softirqs, `HI_SOFTIRQ` and `TASKLET_SOFTIRQ`. When a tasklet is scheduled, the kernel raises one of these softirqs. These softirqs, in turn, are handled by special functions that then run any scheduled tasklets. The special functions ensure that only one tasklet of a given type is running at the same time (but other tasklets can run simultaneously). All this complexity is then hidden behind a clean and simple interface.

Using Tasklets

In most cases, tasklets are the preferred mechanism with which to implement your bottom half for a normal hardware device. Tasklets are dynamically created, easy to use, and relatively quick.

Declaring Your Tasklet

You can create tasklets statically or dynamically. What option you choose depends on whether you have (or want) a direct or indirect reference to the tasklet. If you are going to statically create the tasklet (and thus have a direct reference to it), use one of two macros in `<linux/interrupt.h>`:

```
DECLARE_TASKLET(name, func, data)
DECLARE_TASKLET_DISABLED(name, func, data);
```

Both of these macros statically create a `struct tasklist_struct` with the given name. When the tasklet is scheduled, the given function `func` is executed and passed the argument `data`. The difference between the two macros is the initial reference count. The first macro creates the tasklet with a `count` of zero, and the tasklet is enabled. The second macro sets `count` to one, and the tasklet is disabled. Here is an example:

```
DECLARE_TASKLET(my_tasklet, my_tasklet_handler, dev);
```

This line is equivalent to

```
struct tasklet_struct my_tasklet = { NULL, 0, ATOMIC_INIT(0),
                                     tasklet_handler, dev };
```

This creates a tasklet named `my_tasklet` that is enabled with `tasklet_handler` as its handler. The value of `dev` is passed to the handler when it is executed.

To initialize a tasklet given an indirect reference (a pointer) to a dynamically created `struct tasklet_struct`, t:

```
tasklist_init(t, tasklet_handler, dev);  /* dynamically not statically */
```

Writing Your Tasklet Hander

The tasklet handler must match the correct prototype:

```
void tasklet_handler(unsigned long data)
```

As with softirqs, tasklets cannot sleep. This means you cannot use semaphores or other blocking functions in a tasklet. Tasklets also run with all interrupts enabled, so you must take precautions (for example, disable interrupts and obtain a lock) if your tasklet shares data with an interrupt handler. Unlike softirqs, however, two of the same tasklets never run concurrently—although two different tasklets can run at the same time on two different processors. If your tasklet shares data with another tasklet or softirq, you need to use proper locking (see Chapter 7, "Kernel Synchronization Introduction," and Chapter 8, "Kernel Synchronization Methods").

Scheduling Your Tasklet

To schedule a tasklet for execution, `tasklet_schedule()` is called and passed a pointer to the relevant `tasklet_struct`:

```
tasklet_schedule(&my_tasklet);   /* mark my_tasklet as pending */
```

After a tasklet is scheduled, it runs once at some time in the near future. If the same tasklet is scheduled again, before it has had a chance to run, it still runs only once. If it is already running, for example on another processor, the tasklet is rescheduled and runs again. As an optimization, a tasklet always runs on the processor that scheduled it—hopefully, making better use of the processor's cache.

You can disable a tasklet via a call to `tasklet_disable()`, which disables the given tasklet. If the tasklet is currently running, the function will not return until it finishes executing. Alternatively, you can use `tasklet_disable_nosync()`, which disables the given tasklet but does not wait for the tasklet to complete prior to returning. This is usually not safe, as you cannot assume the tasklet is not still running. A call to `tasklet_enable()` enables the tasklet. This function also must be called before a tasklet created with `DECLARE_TASKLET_DISABLED()` is usable. For example:

```
tasklet_disable(&my_tasklet);    /* tasklet is now disabled */

/* we can now do stuff knowing the tasklet cannot run .. */

tasklet_enable(&my_tasklet);     /* tasklet is now enabled */
```

You can remove a tasklet from the pending queue via `tasklet_kill()`. It receives a pointer as a lone argument to the tasklet's `tasklet_struct`. Removing a scheduled tasklet from the queue is useful when dealing with a tasklet that often reschedules itself. This function first waits for the tasklet to finish executing and then it removes it from queue. Nothing stops some other code from rescheduling the tasklet, of course. This function must not be used from interrupt context, as it sleeps.

ksoftirqd

Softirq (and thus tasklet) processing is aided by a set of per-processor kernel threads. These kernel threads help in the processing of softirqs when the system is overwhelmed with softirqs.

As we discussed, the kernel processes softirqs in a number of places, most commonly on return from handling an interrupt. Softirqs might be raised at very high rates (such as during intense network traffic). Worse, softirq functions can reactivate themselves. That is, while running, a softirq can raise itself so that it runs again (indeed, the networking subsystem does this). The possibility of a high frequency of softirqs in conjunction with their capability to remark themselves active can result in starving user-space programs of processor time. Not processing the reactivated softirqs in a timely manner, however, is unacceptable. This caused a dilemma that needed fixing, and neither obvious solution was a good one. First, let's look at each of the two obvious solutions.

The first solution is simply to keep processing softirqs as they come in and to recheck and reprocess any pending softirqs before returning. This ensures that the kernel processes softirqs in a timely manner and, most importantly, that any reactivated softirqs are also immediately processed. The problem lies in high load environments, in which many

softirqs occur, that continually reactivate themselves. The kernel might continually service softirqs without accomplishing much else. User-space is neglected—indeed, nothing
but softirqs and interrupt handlers run and, in turn, the system's users get mad. This
approach might work fine if the system is never under intense load; if the system, however, experiences even moderate interrupt levels this solution is not acceptable. User-
space cannot be starved for significant periods.

The second solution is *not* to handle reactivated softirqs. On return from interrupt,
the kernel merely looks at all pending softirqs and executes them as normal. If any
softirqs reactivate themselves, however, they will not run until the *next* time the kernel
handles pending softirqs. This is most likely not until the next interrupt occurs, which
can equate to a lengthy amount of time before any new (or reactivated) softirqs are executed. Worse, on an otherwise idle system it is beneficial to process the softirqs right
away. Unfortunately, this approach is oblivious to which processes may or may not be
runnable. Therefore, although this method prevents starving user-space, it does starve the
softirqs, and it does not take good advantage of an idle system.

Some sort of compromise was needed. The solution implemented in the kernel is to
not immediately process reactivated softirqs. Instead, if the number of softirqs grows
excessive, the kernel wakes up a family of kernel threads to handle the load. The kernel
threads run with the lowest possible priority (nice value of 19), which ensures they do
not run in lieu of anything important. They do run eventually, however, and this conces-
sion prevents heavy softirq activity from completely starving user-space of processor
time. Conversely, it also ensures that "excess" softirqs do run eventually. Finally, this solution has the nice property that on an idle system, the softirqs are handled rather quickly
(because the kernel threads will schedule immediately).

There is one thread per processor. The threads are each named `ksoftirqd/n` where n
is the processor number. On a two-processor system, you would have `ksoftirqd/0` and
`ksoftirqd/1`. Having a thread on each processor ensures an idle processor, if available, is
always able to service softirqs. After the threads are initialized, they run a tight loop similar to this:

```
for (;;) {
    if (!softirq_pending(cpu))
        schedule();

    set_current_state(TASK_RUNNING);

    while (softirq_pending(cpu)) {
        do_softirq();
        if (need_resched())
            schedule();
    }

    set_current_state(TASK_INTERRUPTIBLE);
}
```

If any softirqs are pending (as reported by `softirq_pending()`), `ksoftirqd` calls `do_softirq()` to handle them. Note that it does this repeatedly, to handle any reactivated softirqs, too. After each iteration, `schedule()` is called if needed, to allow more important processes to run. After all processing is complete the kernel thread sets itself `TASK_INTERRUPTIBLE` and invokes the scheduler to select a new runnable process.

The softirq kernel threads are awakened whenever `do_softirq()` detects an executed kernel thread reactivate itself.

The Old BH Mechanism

Although the old BH interface, thankfully, is no longer present in 2.6, it was around for a *long* time—since the earliest versions of the kernel. Seeing as it had immense staying power, it certainly carries some historical significance that requires more than a passing look. Nothing in this brief section actually pertains to 2.6, but the history is important.

The BH interface is ancient, and it shows. Each BH must be statically defined, and there are a maximum of 32. Because the handlers must all be defined at compile-time, modules could not directly use the BH interface. They could piggyback off an existing BH, however. Over time, this static requirement and the maximum of 32 bottom halves became an annoyance.

All BH handlers are strictly serialized—no two BH handlers, even of different types, can run concurrently. This made synchronization easy, but it wasn't a good thing for multiprocessing performance. A driver using the BH interface did not scale well to multiple processors. The networking layer, in particular, suffered.

Other than these attributes, the BH mechanism is similar to tasklets. In fact, the BH interface was implemented on top of tasklets in 2.4. The 32 possible bottom halves were represented by constants defined in `<linux/interrupt.h>`. To mark a BH as pending, the function `mark_bh()` was called and passed the number of the BH. In 2.4, this in turn scheduled the BH tasklet, `bh_action()`, to run. Prior to 2.4, the BH mechanism existed on its own; much like softirqs do today.

Because of the shortcomings of this form of bottom half, kernel developers introduced task queues to replace bottom halves. Task queues never accomplished this goal, although they did win many new users. In 2.3, the softirq and tasklet mechanisms were introduced to put an end to the BH. The BH mechanism was implemented on top of tasklets. Unfortunately, it was complicated to port bottom halves from the BH interface to tasklets or softirqs, because of the weaker inherent serialization of the new interfaces[6]. During 2.5, however, the conversion did occur when timers and SCSI—the remaining BH users—finally moved over to softirqs. The kernel developers summarily removed the BH interface. Good riddance, BH!

---

[6]That is, the weaker serialization was beneficial to performance but also harder to program. Converting a BH to a tasklet, for example, required careful thinking: *Is this code safe running at the same time as any other tasklet?* When finally converted, however, the performance was worth it.

Work Queues

Work queues are a different form of deferring work from what we have looked at so far. Work queues defer work into a kernel thread—the work always runs in process context. Thus, code deferred to a work queue has all the usual benefits of process context. Most importantly, work queues are schedulable and can therefore sleep.

Normally, there is little decision between work queues or softirqs/tasklets. If the deferred work needs to sleep, work queues are used. If the deferred work need not sleep, softirqs or tasklets are used. Indeed, the usual alternative to work queues is kernel threads. Because the kernel developers frown upon creating a new kernel thread (and, in some locales, it is a punishable offense), work queues are strongly preferred. They are *really* easy to use, too.

If you need a schedulable entity to perform your bottom half processing, you need work queues. They are the only bottom half mechanism that runs in process context, and thus, the only that can sleep. This means they are useful for situations where you need to allocate a lot of memory, obtain a semaphore, or perform block I/O. If you do not need a kernel thread to handle your deferred work, consider a tasklet instead.

Implementation of Work Queues

In its most basic form, the work queue subsystem is an interface for creating kernel threads to handle work that is queued from elsewhere. These kernel threads are called *worker threads*. Work queues let your driver create a special worker thread to handle deferred work. The work queue subsystem, however, implements and provides a default worker thread for handling work. Therefore, in its most common form, work queues are a simple interface for deferring work to a generic kernel thread.

The default worker threads are called events/n where n is the processor number; there is one per processor. For example, on a uniprocessor system there is one thread, events/0. A dual processor system would additionally have an events/1 thread. The default worker thread handles deferred work from multiple locations. Many drivers in the kernel defer their bottom half work to the default thread. Unless a driver or subsystem has a strong requirement for creating its own thread, the default thread is preferred.

Nothing stops code from creating its own worker thread, however. This might be advantageous if you are performing large amounts of processing in the worker thread. Processor-intense and performance-critical work might benefit from its own thread. This also lightens the load on the default threads, which prevents starving the rest of the queued work.

Data Structures Representing the Threads

The worker threads are represented by the workqueue_struct structure:

```
/*
 * The externally visible workqueue abstraction is an array of
 * per-CPU workqueues:
```

```
 */
struct workqueue_struct {
    struct cpu_workqueue_struct cpu_wq[NR_CPUS];
};
```

This structure contains an array of `struct cpu_workqueue_struct`, one per possible
processor on the system. Because the worker threads exist on each processor in the system, there is one of these structures per worker thread, per processor, on a given
machine. The `cpu_workqueue_struct` is the core data structure and is defined in
`kernel/workqueue.c`:

```
/*
 * The per-CPU workqueue:
 */
struct cpu_workqueue_struct {

    spinlock_t lock;

    atomic_t nr_queued;
    struct list_head worklist;
    wait_queue_head_t more_work;
    wait_queue_head_t work_done;

    struct workqueue_struct *wq;
    task_t *thread;
    struct completion exit;
};
```

Note that each *type* of worker thread has one `workqueue_struct` associated to it. Inside,
there is one `cpu_workqueue_struct` for every thread, and thus, every processor, because
there is one worker thread on each processor.

Data Structures Representing the Work

All worker threads are implemented as normal kernel threads running the
`worker_thread()` function. After initial setup, this function enters an infinite loop and
goes to sleep. When work is queued, the thread is awakened and processes the work.
When there is no work left to process, it goes back to sleep.

The work is represented by the `work_struct` structure, defined in
`<linux/workqueue.h>`:

```
struct work_struct {
    unsigned long pending;    /* is this work pending? */
    struct list_head entry;   /* link list of all work */
    void (*func)(void *);     /* handler function */
    void *data;               /* argument to handler */
    void *wq_data;            /* used internally */
    struct timer_list timer;  /* timer used by delayed work queues */
};
```

These structures are strung into a linked list, one for each type of queue on each processor. For example, there is one list of deferred work for the generic thread, per processor. When a worker thread wakes up, it runs any work in its list. As it completes work, it removes the corresponding `work_struct` entries from the linked list. When the list is empty, it goes back to sleep.

Let's look at the heart of `worker_thread()`, simplified:

```
for (;;) {
    set_task_state(current, TASK_INTERRUPTIBLE);
    add_wait_queue(&cwq->more_work, &wait);

    if (list_empty(&cwq->worklist))
        schedule();
    else
        set_task_state(current, TASK_RUNNING);
    remove_wait_queue(&cwq->more_work, &wait);

    if (!list_empty(&cwq->worklist))
        run_workqueue(cwq);
}
```

This function performs the following functions, in an infinite loop:

- The thread marks itself sleeping (state is set to `TASK_INTERRUPTIBLE`) and adds itself to a wait queue.
- If the linked list of work is empty, the thread calls `schedule()` and goes to sleep.
- If the list is not empty, the thread does not go to sleep. Instead, it marks itself `TASK_RUNNING` and removes itself from the wait queue.
- If the list is nonempty, call `run_workqueue()` to perform the deferred work.

run_workqueue()

The function `run_workqueue()`, in turn, actually performs the deferred work:

```
while (!list_empty(&cwq->worklist)) {
    struct work_struct *work = list_entry(cwq->worklist.next,
                    struct work_struct, entry);
    void (*f) (void *) = work->func;
    void *data = work->data;

    list_del_init(cwq->worklist.next);

    clear_bit(0, &work->pending);
    f(data);
}
```

This function loops over each entry in the linked list of pending work and executes the `func` member of the `workqueue_struct` for each entry in the linked list:

- While the list is not empty, grab the next entry in the list.
- Retrieve the function we want to call, `func`, and its argument, `data`.
- Remove this entry from the list and clear the pending bit in the structure itself.
- Invoke the function.
- Repeat.

Excuse Me?

The relationship between the different data structures is admittedly a bit convoluted. Figure 6.1 provides a graphical example, which should bring it all together.

At the highest level, there are worker threads. There can be multiple types of worker threads. There is one worker thread per processor of a given type. Parts of the kernel can create worker threads as needed. By default, there is the *events* worker thread. Each worker thread is represented by the `cpu_workqueue_struct` structure. The `workqueue_struct` structure represents all the worker threads of a given type.

For example, let's assume that in addition to the generic *events* worker type, I also create a *falcon* worker type. Also, I have a four-processor computer. Then, there are four *events* threads (and thus four `cpu_workqueue_struct` structures) and four *falcon* threads (and thus another four `cpu_workqueue_struct` structures). There is one `workqueue_struct` for the *events* type and one for the *falcon* type.

At the lowest level, there is work. Your driver creates work, which it wants to defer to later. The `work_struct` structure represents this work. Among other things, this structure contains a pointer to the function that will handle the deferred work. The work is submitted to a *specific* worker thread. The worker thread then wakes up and performs the queued work.

Most drivers use the existing default worker threads, named *events*. They are easy and simple. Some more serious situations, however, demand their own worker threads. The XFS file system, for example, creates two new types of worker threads.

Using Work Queues

Using work queues is easy. We will cover the default *events* queue first, and then we will look at creating new worker threads.

Creating Work

The first step is actually creating some work to defer. To create the structure statically at run-time:

```
DECLARE_WORK(name, void (*func)(void *), void *data);
```

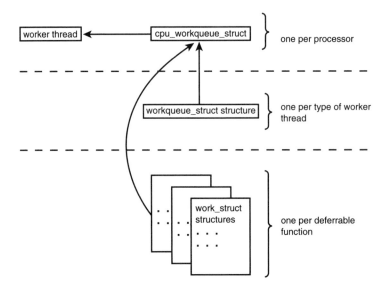

Figure 6.1   The relationship between work, work queues, and the worker threads.

This statically creates a `work_struct` structure named `name` with handler function `func` and argument `data`.

Alternatively, you can create work at run-time via a pointer:

```
INIT_WORK(struct work_struct *work, void (*func)(void *), void *data);
```

This dynamically initializes the work queue pointed to by `work` with handler function `func` and argument `data`.

Your Work Queue Handler

The prototype for the work queue handler is

```
void work_handler(void *data)
```

A worker thread executes this function, and thus, the function runs in process context. By default, interrupts are enabled and no locks are held. If needed, the function can sleep. Note that, despite running in process context, the work handlers cannot access user-space because there is no associated user-space memory map for kernel threads. The kernel only accesses user-space when running on behalf of a user-space process, when user memory is mapped in, such as when executing a system call.

Locking between work queues or other parts of the kernel is handled just as with any other process context code. This makes writing work handlers much easier. The next two chapters cover locking.

Scheduling Work

Now that the work is created, we can schedule it. To queue a given work's handler function with the default *events*, simply call

```
schedule_work(&work);
```

The work is scheduled immediately and is run as soon as the *events* worker thread on this processor wakes up.

Sometimes, you do not want the work to execute immediately, but instead after some delay. In those cases, you can schedule work to execute at a given time in the future:

```
schedule_delayed_work(&work, delay);
```

In this case, the `work_struct` pointed to by &work will not execute for at least `delay` timer ticks into the future. Using ticks as a unit of time is covered in Chapter 9.

Flushing Work

Queued work is executed when the worker thread next wakes up. Sometimes, you need to ensure that a given batch of work has completed before continuing. This is especially important for modules, which probably want to call this function before unloading. Other places in the kernel also might need to make certain no work is pending, to prevent race conditions.

For these needs, there is a function to flush a given work queue:

```
void flush_scheduled_work(void);
```

This function waits until all entries in the queue are executed before returning. While waiting for any pending work to execute, the function sleeps. Therefore, you can only call it from process context.

Note that this function does not cancel any delayed work. That is, any work that was scheduled via `schedule_delayed_work()`, and whose delay is not yet up, is not flushed via `flush_scheduled_work()`. To cancel delayed work, call

```
int cancel_delayed_work(struct work_struct *work);
```

This function cancels the pending work, if any, associated with the given `work_struct`.

Creating New Work Queues

If the default queue is insufficient for your needs, you can create a new work queue and corresponding worker threads. Because this creates one worker thread per processor, you should only create unique work queues if your code really needs the performance of a unique set of threads.

You create a new work queue and the associated worker threads via a simple function:

```
struct workqueue_struct *create_workqueue(const char *name);
```

The parameter name is used to name the kernel threads. For example, the default *events* queue is created via

```
struct workqueue_struct *keventd_wq = create_workqueue("events");
```

This creates *all* the worker threads (one for each processor in the system) and prepares them to handle work.

Creating work is handled the same regardless of the queue type. After the work is created, the following functions are analogous to `schedule_work()` and `schedule_delayed_work()`, except that they work on the given work queue and not the default *events* queue.

```
int queue_work(struct workqueue_struct *wq, struct work_struct *work);
```

```
int queue_delayed_work(struct workqueue_struct *wq,
          struct work_struct *work, unsigned long delay);
```

Finally, you can flush a wait queue via a call to the function

```
flush_workqueue(struct workqueue_struct *wq);
```

This function works identically to `flush_scheduled_work()` as previously discussed, except that it waits for the given queue to empty before returning.

The Old Task Queue Mechanism

Like the BH interface, which gave way to softirqs and tasklets, the work queue interface grew out of shortcomings in the task queue interface. The task queue interface (often called just *tq* in the kernel), like tasklets, also has nothing to do with tasks in the process sense[7]. The users of the task queue interface were ripped in half during the 2.5 development kernel. Half of the users were converted to tasklets. The other half continued using the task queue interface. What was left of the task queue interface then became the work queue interface. Briefly looking at task queues, which were around for some time, is a useful historical exercise.

Task queues work by defining a bunch of queues. The queues have names, such as the scheduler queue, the immediate queue, or the timer queue. Each queue is run at a specific point in the kernel. A kernel thread, *keventd*, ran the work associated with the scheduler queue. This was the precursor to the full work queue interface. The timer queue was run at each tick of the system timer and the immediate queue was run in a couple of places to ensure it was run "immediately." There were other queues, too. Additionally, you could dynamically create new queues.

All this might sound useful, but the reality is the task queue interface was a mess. All the queues were essentially arbitrary abstractions. The only meaningful queue was the scheduler queue, which provided the only way to defer work to process context.

The other good thing about task queues was the simple interface. Despite the myriad of queues and the arbitrary rules about when they ran, the interface was as simple as possible. But that's about it—the rest of task queues needed to go.

---

[7]Bottom half names are apparently a conspiracy to confuse new kernel developers.

The various task queue users were converted to other bottom half mechanisms. Most of them switched to tasklets. The scheduler queue users stuck around. Finally, the `keventd` code was generalized into the excellent work queue mechanism we have today and task queues were finally ripped out of the kernel.

Which Bottom Half Should I Use?

The decision over which bottom half to use is important. In the current 2.6 kernel, there are three choices: softirqs, tasklets, and work queues. Tasklets are built on softirqs and, therefore, both are similar. The work queue mechanism is entirely different and is built on kernel threads.

Softirqs, by design, provide the least serialization. This requires softirq handlers to go through extra steps to ensure shared data is safe, as two or more softirqs of the same type may run concurrently on different processors. If the code in question is already highly threaded, such as the networking subsystem that is entirely using per-processor variables, softirqs make a good choice. They are certainly the fastest alternative for timing-critical and high-frequency uses. Tasklets make more sense if the code is not finely threaded. They have a simpler interface and, because two tasklets of the same type might not run concurrently, they are easier to implement.

If your deferred work needs to run in process context, your only choice of the three is work queues. If process context is not a requirement—specifically, if you have no need to sleep—softirqs or tasklets are perhaps better suited. Work queues involve the highest overhead because they involve kernel threads and, therefore, context switching. This is not to say they are inefficient, but in light of thousands of interrupts hitting per second, as the networking subsystem might experience, other methods make more sense. For most situations, however, work queues are sufficient.

In terms of ease of use, work queues take the crown. Using the default *events* queue is child's play. Next, come tasklets, which also have a simple interface. Coming in last are softirqs, which need to be statically created.

Table 6.3 is a comparison between the three bottom half interfaces.

Table 6.3 **Bottom Half Comparison**

Bottom Half	Context	Serialization
Softirq	Interrupt	None
Tasklet	Interrupt	Against the same tasklet
Work queues	Process	None (scheduled as process context)

In short, normal driver writers have two choices. First, do you need a schedulable entity to perform your deferred work—do you need to sleep for any reason? Then work queues are your only option. Otherwise, tasklets are preferred. Only if scalability becomes a concern, then investigate softirqs.

Locking Between the Bottom Halves

We have not discussed locking yet, which is such a fun topic I devote the next two chapters to it. Nonetheless, it is important to understand that it is crucial to protect shared data from concurrent access while using bottom halves, even on a single processor machine. Remember, a bottom half can run at virtually any moment. You might want to come back to this section after reading the next two if the concept of locking is foreign to you.

One of the benefits of tasklets is that they are serialized with respect to themselves: The same tasklet will not run concurrently, even on two different processors. This means you do not have to worry about intratasklet concurrency issues. Intertasklet concurrency (that is, when two different tasklets share the same data) requires proper locking.

Because softirqs provide no serialization, (even two instances of the same softirq might run simultaneously) all shared data needs an appropriate lock.

If process context code and a bottom half share data, you need to disable bottom half processing and obtain a lock before accessing the data. Doing both ensures local and SMP protection and prevents a deadlock.

If interrupt context code and a bottom half share data, you need to disable interrupts and obtain a lock before accessing the data. This also ensures both local and SMP protection and prevents a deadlock.

Any shared data in a work queue requires locking, too. The locking issues are no different from normal kernel code because work queues run in process context.

In Chapter 7 we cover the magic behind locking. In Chapter 8 we cover the kernel locking primitives. These chapters will cover how to protect data that bottom halves use.

Disabling Bottom Halves

Normally, it is not sufficient only to disable bottom halves. More often, to safely protect shared data, you need to obtain a lock *and* disable bottom halves. Such methods, which you might use in a driver, are covered in Chapter 8. If you are writing core kernel code, however, you might need to disable just the bottom halves.

To disable all bottom half processing (specifically, all softirqs and thus all tasklets), call `local_bh_disable()`. To enable bottom half processing, call `local_bh_enable()`. Yes, the function is misnamed; no one bothered to change it when the BH interface gave way to softirqs. *Table 6.4* is a summary of these functions.

Table 6.4 **Listing of Bottom Half Control Methods**

Method	Description
`void local_bh_disable()`	Disable softirq and tasklet processing on the local processor
`void local_bh_enable()`	Enable softirq and tasklet processing on the local processor

The calls might be nested—only the final call to `local_bh_enable()` actually enables bottom halves. The functions accomplish this by maintaining a per-task counter via the `preempt_count` (interestingly, the same counter used by kernel preemption)[8]. When the counter reaches zero, bottom half processing is possible. Because bottom halves were disabled, `local_bh_enable()` also checks for any pending bottom halves and executes them.

The functions are unique to each supported architecture and are usually written as complicated macros in `<asm/softirq.h>`. The following are close C representations for the curious:

```
/*
 * disable local bottom halves by incrementing the preempt_count
 */
void local_bh_disable(void)
{
    struct thread_info *t = current_thread_info();

    t->preempt_count += SOFTIRQ_OFFSET;
}

/*
 * decrement the preempt_count - this will 'automatically' enable
 * bottom halves if the count returns to zero
 *
 * optionally run any bottom halves that are pending
 */
void local_bh_enable(void)
{
    struct thread_info *t = current_thread_info();

    t->preempt_count -= SOFTIRQ_OFFSET;

    /*
     * is preempt_count zero and are any bottom halves pending?
     * if so, run them
     */
    if (unlikely(!t->preempt_count && softirq_pending(smp_processor_id())))
        do_softirq();
}
```

[8]In fact, this counter is used both by the interrupt and bottom half subsystems. Thus, in Linux, a single per-task counter represents the atomicity of a task. This has proven very useful for work such as debugging sleeping-while-atomic bugs.

These calls do not disable the execution of work queues. Because work queues run in process context, there are no issues with asynchronous execution, and thus, there is no need to disable them. Because softirqs and tasklets can occur asynchronously (say, on return from handling an interrupt), however, kernel code may need to disable them. With work queues, on the other hand, protecting shared data is the same as in any process context. Chapters 7 and 8 give the details.

7

Kernel Synchronization Introduction

I N A SHARED MEMORY APPLICATION, care must be taken to ensure that shared resources are protected from concurrent access. The kernel is no exception. Shared resources require protection from concurrent access because if multiple threads of execution[1] access and manipulate the data at the same time, the threads may overwrite each other's changes or access data while it is in an inconsistent state. Concurrent access of shared data is a recipe for instability that often proves very hard to track down and debug—getting it right off the bat is important.

Properly protecting shared resources can be tough. Years ago, before Linux supported symmetrical multiprocessing, preventing concurrent access of data was simple. Because only a single processor was supported, the only way data could have been accessed concurrently was if an interrupt occurred or if kernel code explicitly rescheduled and allowed another task to run. Back then, life was simple.

Those days are over. Symmetrical multiprocessing support was introduced in the 2.0 kernel and has been continually enhanced ever since. Multiprocessing support implies that kernel code can simultaneously run on two or more processors. Consequently, without protection, code in the kernel, running on two different processors, can simultaneously access shared data at exactly the same time. With the introduction of the 2.6 kernel, the Linux kernel is preemptive. This implies that (again, in the absence of protection) the scheduler can preempt kernel code at virtually any point, and reschedule another task. Today, a number of scenarios allow for concurrency inside the kernel and they all require protection.

---

[1] The term *threads of execution* implies any instance of executing code. This includes, for example, a task in the kernel, an interrupt handler, or a kernel thread. This chapter may shorten *threads of execution* to simply *threads*. Keep in mind that this term describes *any* executing code.

This chapter discusses the issues of concurrency and synchronization, as they exist in an operating system kernel. The next chapter details the mechanisms and interfaces that the Linux kernel provides to solve these synchronization issues and prevent race conditions.

Critical Regions and Race Conditions

Code paths that access and manipulate shared data are called *critical regions*. It is usually unsafe for multiple threads of execution to access the same resource simultaneously. To prevent concurrent access during critical regions, the programmer (that's you) must ensure that the code executes *atomically*—that is, the code completes without interruption as if the entire critical region were one indivisible instruction. It is a bug if it is possible for two threads of execution to be simultaneously in the same critical region. When this actually occurs, we call it a *race condition* (named because the threads *raced* to get there). Note how rare this could be—debugging race conditions is often very hard because they are not easily reproducible. Ensuring concurrency is prevented and that race conditions do not occur is called *synchronization*.

Why Do We Need Protection?

To best identify race conditions, let's look at just how ubiquitous critical regions are. For a first example, consider a very simple shared resource, a single global integer, and a very simple critical region, the operation of merely incrementing it:

```
i++;
```

This might translate into instructions to the computer's processor that resemble:

```
get the current value of i and copy it into a register
add one to the value stored in the register
write back to memory the new value of i
```

Now, assume that there are two threads of execution, both enter this critical region, and the initial value of i is seven. The desired outcome is then similar to (each row represents a unit of time):

Thread 1	Thread 2
get i (7)	-
increment i (7 -> 8)	-
write back i (8)	-
-	get i (8)
-	increment i (8 -> 9)
-	write back i (9)

As expected, seven incremented twice is nine. A possible outcome, however, is

Thread 1	Thread 2
get i (7)	-
-	get i (7)
increment i (7 -> 8)	-
-	increment i (7 -> 8)
write back i (8)	-
-	write back i (8)

If both threads of execution read the initial value of i before it is incremented, both threads will increment and save the same value. As a result, the variable i contains the value eight when, in fact, it should now contain nine. This is one of the simplest examples of a critical region. Thankfully, the solution is equally as simple—we merely need a way to perform these operations in one indivisible step. Most processors provide an instruction to atomically read, increment, and write back a single variable. Using such an instruction would alleviate the problem. The kernel provides a set of interfaces that implement these atomic instructions; we will discuss them in the next chapter.

Locking

Now, let's consider a more complicated race condition that requires a more complicated solution. Assume we have a queue of requests that need to be serviced. How we implement the queue is irrelevant, but we can assume it is a linked list, where each node represents a request. Two functions manipulate the queue. One function adds a new request to the tail of the queue. Another function removes a request from the head of the queue and does something useful with the request. Various parts of the kernel invoke these two functions; thus, requests are continually being added, removed, and serviced.

Manipulating the request queues certainly requires multiple instructions. If one thread attempts to read from the queue while another is in the middle of manipulating it, the reading thread will find the queue in an inconsistent state. It should be apparent the sort of damage that can occur if access to the queue could occur concurrently. Often, when the shared resource is a complex data structure, the result of a race condition is corruption of the data structure.

The previous scenario, at first, might not have a clear solution. How can we prevent one processor from reading from the queue while another processor is updating it? Although it is feasible for a particular architecture to implement simple instructions, such as arithmetic and comparison atomically, it is ludicrous for architectures to provide instructions to support the indefinitely sized critical regions like the previous example. What is needed is a method of marking where a critical region begins and ends and preventing—or, *locking*—access to it while another thread of execution is in the region.

A lock provides such a mechanism; it works much like a lock on a door. Imagine the room beyond the door as the critical region. Inside the room, only one thread of execution can be present at a given time. When a thread enters the room, it locks the door behind it. When the thread is finished manipulating the shared data, it leaves the room and unlocks the door. If another thread reaches the door while it is locked, it must wait for the thread inside to exit the room and unlock the door before it can enter.

In the previous request queue example, a single lock could have been used to protect the queue. Whenever there was a new request to add to the queue, the thread would first obtain the lock. Then, it could safely add the request to the queue and ultimately release the lock. When a thread wanted to remove a request from the queue, it too would obtain the lock. Then, it could read the request and remove it from the queue. Finally, it would release the lock. Any other access to the queue would similarly need to obtain the lock. Because the lock can only be held by one thread at a time, only a single thread can manipulate the queue at a time. The lock prevents concurrency and protects the queue from race conditions.

Any code that accessed the queue would first need to obtain the relevant lock. If another thread of execution comes along, the lock will prevent concurrency:

Thread 1	Thread 2
try to lock the queue	try to lock the queue
succeeded: acquired lock	failed: waiting...
access queue...	waiting...
unlock the queue	waiting...
...	succeeded: acquired lock
	access queue...
	unlock the queue

Notice that locks are *advisory* and *voluntary*. Locks are entirely a programming construct that the programmer must take advantage of. Nothing prevents you from writing code that manipulates our fictional queue without the appropriate lock. Such a practice, of course, would eventually result in a race condition and corruption.

Locks come in various shapes and sizes—Linux alone implements a handful of different locking mechanisms. The most significant difference between the various mechanisms is the behavior when the lock is *contended* (already in use)—some locks simply busy wait[2], whereas other locks put the current task to sleep until the lock becomes available. The next chapter discusses the behavior of the different locks in Linux and their interfaces.

---

[2] That is, spin in a tight loop, waiting for the lock to become available.

What Causes Concurrency Anyway?

In user-space, the need for sychronization stems from the fact that programs are scheduled preemptively by the will of the scheduler. Because a process can be preempted at any time and another process can be scheduled onto the processor, it is possible for a process to be involuntarily preempted in the middle of accessing a critical region. If the newly scheduled process then enters the same critical region (say, if the two processes are threads and they access the same shared memory), a race can occur. The same problem can occur within a single program with signals, because signals can occur asynchronously. This type of concurrency—where two things do not actually happen at the same time, but interleave each other so that they might as well—is called *pseudo-concurrency*.

If you have a symmetrical multiprocessing machine, two processes can actually be executing in a critical region at the exact same time. That is called *true concurrency*. Although the causes and semantics of true versus pseudo concurrency are different, they both result in the same race conditions and require the same sort of protection. The kernel has similar causes of concurrency. They are

- Interrupts—An interrupt can occur asynchronously at almost any time, interrupting the currently executing code.

- Kernel preemption—Because the kernel is preemptive, one task in the kernel can preempt another.

- Sleeping and synchronization with user-space—A task in the kernel can sleep and thus invoke the scheduler, resulting in the running of a new process.

- Symmetrical multiprocessing—Two or more processors can be executing code at the exact same time.

It is important that kernel developers understand and prepare for these causes of concurrency. It is a bug if an interrupt occurs in the middle of code that is manipulating a resource and the interrupt handler can access the *same* resource. Similarly, it is a bug if kernel code can be preempted while it is accessing a shared resource. Likewise, it is an open invitation to race conditions if code in the kernel sleeps while in the middle of a critical section. Finally, two processors should never be able to simultaneously access the same shared data. With a clear picture of what data needs protection, it is not hard to provide the locking to keep the world safe. Rather, the hard part is identifying these conditions and realizing that to prevent concurrency, you need some form of protection. Let us reiterate this point, because it is quite important. Implementing the actual locking in your code to protect shared data is not hard, especially when done early on while designing the code. The tricky part is identifying the actual shared data and the corresponding critical sections. This is why designing locking into your code from the get go, and not as an afterthought, is of paramount importance. It can be very hard to go in, after the fact, and identify what needs locking and retrofit locking into the existing code. The result is usually not pretty, either. The moral of this is to *always* design proper locking into your code from the beginning.

Code that is safe from concurrent access from an interrupt handler is said to be *interrupt-safe*. Code that is safe from concurrency on symmetrical multiprocessing machines is *SMP-safe*. Code that is safe from concurrency with kernel preemption is *preempt-safe*[3]. The actual mechanisms used to provide synchronization and protect against race conditions in all of these cases will be covered in the next chapter.

What Needs Protecting?

Identifying what data specifically needs protection is vital. Since any code that can be accessed concurrently may need protection, it is probably easier to identify what data does *not* need protection and work from there. Obviously, any data that is local to one particular thread of execution does not need protection, because only that thread can access the data. For example, local automatic variables do not need any sort of locking, because they exist solely on the stack of the executing thread. Likewise, data that is only accessed by a specific task does not require locking.

What *does* need locking? Most global kernel data structures do. A good rule of thumb is if another thread of execution can access the data, it needs some sort of locking; if anyone else can see it, lock it.

CONFIG options: SMP versus UP

Because the Linux kernel is configurable at compile-time, it makes sense that you can tailor the kernel specifically for a given machine. Most importantly, whether the kernel supports SMP is provided via the CONFIG_SMP configure option. Many locking issues disappear on uniprocessor machines; consequently, when CONFIG_SMP is unset, unnecessary code is not compiled into the kernel image. For example, this enables uniprocessor machines to forgo the overhead of spin locks. The same trick applies to CONFIG_PREEMPT (the configure option enabling kernel preemption). This was an excellent design decision—the kernel maintains one clean source base, and the various locking mechanisms are used as needed. Different combinations of CONFIG_SMP and CONFIG_PREEMPT on different architectures compile in varying lock support.

In your code, provide appropriate protection for all issues and all scenarios will be covered.

Whenever you write kernel code, you should ask yourself these questions:

- Is the data global? Can a thread of execution other than the current access it?
- Is the data shared between process context and interrupt context? Is it shared between two different interrupt handlers?
- If a process is preempted while accessing this data, can the newly scheduled process access the same data?
- Can the current process sleep (block) on anything? If it does, what state does that leave any shared data in?
- What prevents the data from being freed out from under me?

---

[3] We will also see that, barring a few exceptions, being SMP-safe implies being preempt-safe.

- What happens if this function is called again on another processor?
- What are you going to do about it?

In short, nearly all global and shared data in the kernel requires some form of the synchronization methods discussed in the next chapter.

Deadlocks

A *deadlock* is a condition involving one or more threads of execution and one or more resources, such that each thread is waiting for one of the resources, but all the resources are already held. The threads are all waiting for each other, but they will never make any progress toward releasing the resources they already hold. Therefore, none of the threads can continue, which means we have a deadlock.

A good analogy is a four-way traffic stop. If each car at the stop decides to wait for the other cars before going, no car will ever go and we have a traffic deadlock.

The simplest example of a deadlock is the self-deadlock[4]: If a thread of execution attempts to acquire a lock it already holds, it will have to wait for the lock to be released. But it will never release the lock, because it is busy waiting for the lock, and the result is deadlock:

```
acquire lock
acquire lock, again
wait for lock to become available
...
```

Similarly, consider *n* threads and *n* locks. If each thread holds a lock the other thread wants, all threads will block waiting for their respective lock to become available. The most common example is with two threads and two locks, which is often called the *ABBA deadlock*:

Thread 1	Thread 2
`acquire lock A`	`acquire lock B`
`try to acquire lock B`	`try to acquire lock A`
`wait for lock B`	`wait for lock A`

Each thread is waiting for the other and neither thread will ever release their original lock; therefore, neither lock will ever become available. This type of deadlock is also known as the *deadly embrace*.

---

[4] Some kernels prevent this type of deadlock by having *recursive* locks that are locks that a single thread of execution may acquire multiple times. Linux, thankfully, does not provide recursive locks. This is usually considered a good thing. Although recursive locks might alleviate the self-deadlock problem, they very readily lead to sloppy locking semantics.

Prevention of deadlock scenarios is important. Although it is difficult to prove that code is free of deadlocks, it *is* possible to write deadlock free code. A few simple rules go a long way:

- Lock ordering is vital. Nested locks must *always* be obtained in the same order. This prevents the deadly embrace deadlock. Document the lock ordering so others will follow it.
- Prevent starvation. Ask, *does this code always finish? If* foo *does not occur, will* bar *wait forever?*
- Do not double acquire the same lock.
- Complexity in your locking scheme invites deadlocks—design for simplicity.

The first point is important, and worth stressing. If two or more locks are ever acquired at the same time, they must *always* be acquired in the same order. Let's assume we have the *cat*, *dog*, and *fox* locks that protect data structures of the same name. Now assume we have a function that needs to work on all three of these data structures simultaneously—perhaps to copy data between them. Whatever the case, the data structures require locking to ensure safe access. If one function acquires the locks in the order *cat*, *dog*, and then *fox*, then *every* other function must obtain these locks (or a subset of them) in this same order. For example, it is a potential deadlock (and hence a bug) to first obtain the *fox* lock, and then obtain the *dog* lock (because the *dog* lock must always be acquired prior to the *fox* lock). Once more, here is an example where this would cause a deadlock:

Thread 1	Thread 2
acquire lock cat	acquire lock fox
acquire lock dog	try to acquire lock dog
try to acquire lock fox	wait for lock dog
wait for lock fox	-

Thread one is waiting for the fox lock, which thread two holds, while thread two is waiting for the dog lock, which thread one holds. Neither ever releases their locks and hence both wait forever—bam, deadlock. If the locks were always obtained in the same order, a deadlock in this manner would not be possible.

Whenever locks are nested with other locks, a specific ordering must be obeyed. It is good practice to place the ordering in a comment above the lock. Something like the following is a good idea:

```
/*
 * cat_lock - always obtain before the dog lock
 * (and always obtain the dog lock before the fox lock)
 */
```

Note the order of *unlock* does not matter with respect to deadlock, although it is good practice to release the locks in the inverse order they were acquired.

Preventing deadlocks is very important. The Linux kernel has some basic debugging facilities for detecting deadlock scenarios in a running kernel. These features are discussed in the next chapter.

Contention and Scalability

The term *lock contention*, or simply *contention*, is used to describe a lock that is currently in use, but that another thread is trying to acquire. A lock that is *highly contended* often has threads waiting to acquire it. Because a lock's job is to serialize access to a resource, it comes as no surprise that locks can slow down the performance of a system. A highly contended lock can become a bottleneck in the system, quickly limiting its performance. Of course, the locks are also required to prevent the system from tearing itself to shreds, so a solution to high contention must continue to provide the necessary concurrency protection.

Scalability is a measurement of how well a system can be expanded. In operating systems, we talk of the scalability with large number of processes, large number of processors, or large amounts of memory. We can discuss scalability in relation to virtually any component of a computer to which we can attach a quantity. Ideally, doubling the number of processors should result in a doubling of the system's processor performance. This, of course, is never the case.

The scalability of Linux on a large number of processors has increased dramatically in the time since multiprocessing support was introduced in the 2.0 kernel. In the early days of Linux multiprocessing support, only one task could execute in the kernel at a time. During 2.2, this limitation was removed as the locking mechanisms grew more fine-grained. Through 2.4 and onward, kernel locking became even finer grained.

The granularity of locking is a description of the size or amount of data that a lock protects. A very coarse lock protects a large amount of data—for example, an entire subsystem's set of data structures. On the other hand, a very fine grained lock protects a very small amount of data—say, only a single element in a larger structure. In reality, most locks fall somewhere in between these two extremes, protecting neither an entire subsystem nor an individual element, but perhaps a single structure. Most locks start off fairly coarse, and are made more fine-grained as lock contention proves to be a problem.

One example of evolving to finer-grained locking is the scheduler runqueues, discussed in Chapter 3, "Scheduling." In 2.4 and prior kernels, the scheduler had a single runqueue (recall, a runqueue is the list of runnable processes). In 2.6, the O(1) scheduler introduced per-processor runqueues each with a unique lock. The locking evolved from a single global lock to separate locks for each processor.

Generally, this scalability improvement is a very good thing, as it improves the performance of Linux on larger and more powerful systems. Rampant scalability "improvements" can lead to a decrease in performance on smaller SMP and UP machines, however, because smaller machines may need not such fine grained locking, but will nonetheless have to put up with the increased complexity and overhead. Consider a linked list. An initial locking scheme would provide a single lock for the list. In time, this single lock might prove to be a scalability bottleneck on very large multiprocessor machines that frequently access this linked list. In response, the single lock could be broken up into one lock per node in the linked list. For each node you wanted to read or write, you obtained the node's unique lock. Now there is only lock contention when multiple processors are accessing the same exact node. What if there is still lock contention, however? Do we provide a lock for each element in each node? (Answer: No.) Seriously, even though this very fine-grained locking might perform excellent on very large SMP machines, how does it perform on dual processor machines? The overhead of all those extra locks is wasted if a dual processor machine does not see significant lock contention to begin with.

Nonetheless, scalability is an important consideration. Designing your locking from the beginning to scale well is important. Coarse locking of major resources can easily become a bottleneck on even small machines. There is a thin line between too coarse locking and too fine locking. Too coarse of locking results in poor scalability if there is high lock contention, whereas too fine of locking results in wasteful overhead if there is little lock contention. Both scenarios equate to poor performance. *Start simple and grow in complexity only as needed. Simplicity is key.*

Locking and Your Code

Making your code SMP-safe is not something that can be added as an afterthought. Proper synchronization—locking that is free of deadlocks, scalable, and clean—requires design decisions from start through finish. Whenever you write kernel code, whether it is a new system call or a rewritten driver, protecting data from concurrent access needs to be a primary concern.

Provide sufficient protection for every scenario—SMP, kernel preemption, and so on—and rest assured the data will be safe on any given machine and configuration. The next chapter will discuss just how to do this.

8

Kernel Synchronization Methods

THE PREVIOUS CHAPTER DISCUSSED THE SOURCES of and solutions to race conditions. Thankfully, the Linux kernel implements a large family of synchronization methods. This chapter discusses these methods and their interface, behavior, and use.

Atomics Operations

Atomic operations provide instructions that execute *atomically*—without interruption. Just as the atom was originally thought to be an indivisible particle, atomic operators are indivisible instructions. For example, as discussed in the previous chapter, an atomic increment can read and increment a variable by one in a single indivisible and uninterruptible step. Instead of the race discussed in the previous chapter, the outcome is always similar to (assume i is initially seven):

Thread 1	Thread 2
increment i (7 -> 8)	-
-	increment i (8 -> 9)

The resulting value, nine, is correct. It is never possible for the two atomic operations to occur on the same variable concurrently. Therefore, it is not possible for the increments to race.

The kernel provides two sets of interfaces for atomic operations—one that operates on integers and another that operates on individual bits. These interfaces are implemented on every architecture that Linux supports. Most architectures either directly support simple atomic operations or provide an operation to lock the memory bus for a single operation (and thus ensure another operation cannot occur simultaneously). Architectures that cannot easily support primitive atomic operations, such as SPARC, somehow cope.

Atomic Integer Operations

The atomic integer methods operate on a special data type, `atomic_t`. This special type is used, as opposed to having the functions work directly on the C `int` type, for a couple of reasons. First, having the atomic functions accept only the `atomic_t` type ensures that the atomic operations are only used with these special types. Likewise, it also ensures that the data types are not passed to any other nonatomic functions. Indeed, what good would atomic operations be if sometimes they were used and other times they were not? Next, the use of `atomic_t` ensures the compiler does not (erroneously but cleverly) optimize access to the value—it is important the atomic operations receive the correct memory address and not an alias. Finally, use of `atomic_t` can hide any architecture-specific differences in its implementation.

Despite being an integer, and thus 32-bits on all the machines that Linux supports, code must assume an `atomic_t` is no larger than 24-bits in size. This is because of the SPARC architecture, which has an odd implementation of atomic operations: A lock is embedded in the lower 8-bits of the 32-bit `int` (it looks like Figure 8.1). The lock is used to protect concurrent access to the atomic type, because the SPARC architecture lacks appropriate support at the instruction-level. Consequently, only 24-bits are usable on SPARC machines. Although code that assumes the full 32-bit range exists will work on other machines, it can fail in strange and subtle ways on SPARC machines—and that is just rude.

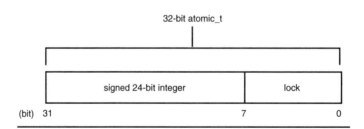

Figure 8.1   Layout of the 32-bit atomic_t on SPARC.

The declarations needed to use the atomic integer operations are in `<asm/atomic.h>`. Some architectures provide additional methods which are unique to that architecture, but all architectures provide at least a minimum set of operations which are used throughout the kernel. When you write kernel code, you can ensure these operations are correctly implemented on all architectures.

Defining an `atomic_t` is done in the usual manner. Optionally, you can set it to an initial value:

```
atomic_t u;                    /* define u */
atomic_t v = ATOMIC_INIT(0);     /* define v and initialize it to zero */
```

Operations are all simple:

```
atomic_set(&v, 4);      /* v = 4 (atomically) */
atomic_add(2, &v);      /* v = v + 2 = 6 (atomically) */
atomic_inc(&v);         /* v = v + 1 = 7 (atomically) */
```

If you ever need to convert an `atomic_t` to an `int`, use `atomic_read()`:

```
printk("%d\n", atomic_read(&v)); /* will print "7" */
```

A common use of the atomic integer operations is to implement counters. Protecting a sole counter with a complex locking scheme is silly, so instead developers use `atomic_inc()` and `atomic_dec()`, which are much lighter in weight. Another use of the atomic integer operators is atomically performing an operation and testing the result. A common example is the atomic decrement and test:

```
int atomic_dec_and_test(atomic_t *v)
```

This function decrements by one the given atomic value. If the result is zero, it returns true; otherwise, it returns false. A full listing of the standard atomic integer operations (those found on all architectures) is in *Table 8.1*. All the operations implemented on a specific architecture can be found in `<asm/atomic.h>`.

Table 8.1   **Full Listing of Atomic Integer Operations**

Atomic Integer Operation	Description
`ATOMIC_INIT(int i)`	At declaration, initialize an atomic_t to i
`int atomic_read(atomic_t *v)`	Atomically read the integer value of v
`void atomic_set(atomic_t *v, int i)`	Atomically set v equal to i
`void atomic_add(int i, atomic_t *v)`	Atomically add i to v
`void atomic_sub(int i, atomic_t *v)`	Atomically subtract i from v
`void atomic_inc(atomic_t *v)`	Atomically add one to v
`void atomic_dec(atomic_t *v)`	Atomically subtract one from v
`int atomic_sub_and_test(int i, atomic_t *v)`	Atomically subtract i from v and return true if the result is zero; otherwise false
`int atomic_add_negative(int i, atomic_t *v)`	Atomically add i to v and return true if the result is negative; otherwise false
`int atomic_dec_and_test(atomic_t *v)`	Atomically decrement v by one and returns true if zero; false otherwise
`int atomic_inc_and_test(atomic_t *v)`	Atomically increment v by one and return true if the result is zero; otherwise false

The atomic operations are typically implemented as inline functions with inline assembly (kernel developers like inlines). In the case where a specific function is inherently atomic, the given function is usually just a macro. For example, on most sane architectures, a word-sized read is atomic. That is, a read of a single word cannot complete in the middle of a write to that word. Consequently, `atomic_read()` is usually just a macro returning the integer value of the `atomic_t`.

In your code, preferring atomic operations to more complicated locking mechanisms when applicable is usually preferred. On most architectures, one or two atomic operations incur less overhead and less cache-line thrashing than a more complicated synchronization method. As with any performance-sensitive code, however, testing multiple approaches is always smart.

Atomic Bitwise Operations

In addition to atomic integer operations, the kernel also provides a family of functions that operate at the bit-level. Not surprisingly, they are architecture-specific and defined in `<asm/bitops.h>`.

What may be surprising is that the bitwise functions operate on generic memory addresses. The arguments are a pointer and a bit number. Bit zero is the least significant bit of the given address. On 32-bit machines, bit 31 is the most significant bit and bit 32 is the least significant bit of the following word. There are no limitations on the bit number supplied, although most uses of the functions provide a word and, consequently, a bit number between 0 and 31 (or 63, on 64-bit machines).

Because the functions operate on a generic pointer, there is no equivalent of the atomic integer's `atomic_t` type. Instead, you can work with a pointer to whatever data you desire. Let us consider an example:

```
unsigned long word = 0;

set_bit(0, &word);      /* bit zero is now set (atomically) */
set_bit(1, &word);      /* bit one is now set (atomically) */
printk("%ul\n", word);  /* will print "3" */
clear_bit(1, &word);    /* bit one is now unset (atomically) */
change_bit(0, &word);   /* bit zero is flipped; now it is unset (atomically) */

/* atomically sets bit zero and returns the previous value (zero) */
if (test_and_set_bit(0, &word)) {
        /* never true ... */

}
```

A listing of the standard atomic bit operations is in *Table 8.2*.

Table 8.2 **Listing of Atomic Bitwise Operations**

Atomic Bitwise Operation	Description
`void set_bit(int nr, void *addr)`	Atomically set the nr-*th* bit starting from `addr`
`void clear_bit(int nr, void *addr)`	Atomically clear the nr-*th* bit starting from `addr`
`void change_bit(int nr, void *addr)`	Atomically flip the value of the nr-*th* bit starting from `addr`
`int test_and_set_bit(int nr, void *addr)`	Atomically set the nr-*th* bit starting from `addr` and return the previous value
`int test_and_clear_bit(int nr, void *addr)`	Atomically clear the nr-*th* bit starting from `addr` and return the previous value
`int test_and_change_bit(int nr, void *addr)`	Atomically flip the nr-*th* bit starting from `addr` and return the previous value
`int test_bit(int nr, void *addr)`	Atomically return the value of the nr-*th* bit starting from `addr`

Conveniently, nonatomic versions of all the bitwise functions are also provided. They behave identical to their atomic siblings, except they do not guarantee atomicity and their names are prefixed with double underscores. For example, the nonatomic form of `test_bit()` is `__test_bit()`. If you do not require atomicity (say, for example, because a lock already protects your data), these variants of the bitwise functions might be faster.

The kernel also provides routines to find the first set (or unset) bit starting at a given address:

```
int find_first_bit(unsigned long *addr, unsigned int size)
int find_first_zero_bit(unsigned long *addr, unsigned int size)
```

Both functions take a pointer as their first argument and the number of bits in total to search as their second. They return the bit number of the first set or first unset bit, respectively. If your code is only searching a word, the routines `__ffs()` and `ffz()`, which take a single parameter of the word in which to search, are optimal.

Unlike the atomic integer operations, code typically has no choice whether to use the bitwise operations—they are the only portable way to set a specific bit. The only question is whether to use the atomic or nonatomic variants. If your code is inherently safe from race conditions, you can use the nonatomic versions, which might be faster depending on the architecture.

Spin Locks

Although it would be nice if every critical region were as simple as incrementing a variable, reality is much crueler. In real life, critical regions can span multiple functions. For example, it is often the case that data must be removed from one structure, formatted and parsed, and added to another structure. This entire operation must occur atomically; it must not be possible for other code to read either structure before we are done updating it. Because simple atomic operations are clearly incapable of providing the needed protection, a more complex method of synchronization is needed—locks.

The most common lock in the Linux kernel is the *spin lock*. A spin lock is a lock that can be held at most by one thread of execution. If a thread of execution attempts to acquire a spin lock while it is *contended* (already held), the thread will busy loop—*spin*—waiting for the lock to become available. If the lock is not contended, the thread can immediately acquire the lock and continue. The spinning prevents more than one thread of execution from entering the critical region at any one time. Note the same lock can be used in multiple locations—so all access to a given data structure, for example, can be protected and synchronized.

The fact that a contended spin lock causes threads to spin (essentially wasting processor time) while waiting for the lock to become available is important. It is *not* wise to hold a spin lock for a long time. In fact, this is the nature of the spin lock: a lightweight single-holder lock that should be held for short durations. An alternative behavior when the lock is contended is to put the current thread to sleep and wake it up when it becomes available. Then, the processor can go off and execute other code. This incurs a bit of overhead—most notably the two context switches to switch out of and back into the blocking thread. Therefore, it is wise to hold spin locks for less than the duration of two context switches. Because most of us have better things to do than measure context switches, just try to hold the lock as short as possible[1]. The next section will cover *semaphores*, which provide a lock that makes the waiting thread sleep, instead of spin, when contended.

Spin locks are architecture-dependent and implemented in assembly. The architecture-dependent code is defined in `<asm/spinlock.h>`. The actual usable interfaces are defined in `<linux/spinlock.h>`. The basic use of a spin lock is

```
spinlock_t mr_lock = SPIN_LOCK_UNLOCKED;

spin_lock(&mr_lock);
/* critical region ... */
spin_unlock(&mr_lock);
```

---

[1]This is especially important now that the kernel is preemptive. The duration of locks held is equivalent to the scheduling latency of the system.

The lock can only be held simultaneously by at most one thread of execution. Consequently, only one thread is allowed in the critical region at a time. This provides the needed protection from concurrency on multiprocessing machines. Note on UP machines, the locks compile away and do not exist. They simply act as markers to disable and enable kernel preemption. If kernel preempt is turned off, the locks compile away entirely.

Warning: Spin Locks Are Not Recursive!

Unlike spin lock implementations in other operating systems, the Linux kernel's spin locks are not recursive. This means that if you attempt to acquire a lock you already hold, you will spin, waiting for yourself to release the lock. But because you are busy spinning, you will never release the lock and you will deadlock. Be careful!

Spin locks can be used in interrupt handlers (semaphores, however, cannot because they sleep). If a lock is used in an interrupt handler, you must also disable local interrupts (interrupt requests on the current processor) before obtaining the lock. Otherwise, it is possible for an interrupt handler to interrupt kernel code while the lock is held and attempt to reacquire the lock. The interrupt handler spins, waiting for the lock to become available. The lock holder, however, will not run until the interrupt handler completes. This is an example of the double-acquire deadlock discussed in the previous chapter. Note, you only need to disable interrupts on the *current* processor. If an interrupt occurs on a different processor, and it spins on the same lock, it will not prevent the lock holder (which is on a different processor) from eventually releasing the lock.

The kernel provides an interface that conveniently disables interrupts and acquires the lock. Usage is

```
spinlock_t mr_lock = SPIN_LOCK_UNLOCKED;
unsigned long flags;

spin_lock_irqsave(&mr_lock, flags);
/* critical region ... */
spin_unlock_irqrestore(&mr_lock, flags);
```

The routine `spin_lock_irqsave()` saves the current state of interrupts, disables them locally, and then obtains the given lock. Conversely, `spin_unlock_irqrestore()` unlocks the given lock and returns interrupts to their previous state. This way, if they are initially disabled, your code will not erroneously enable them. Note that the `flags` variable is seemingly passed by value. This is because the lock routines are implemented partially as macros.

On uniprocessor systems, the previous example must still disable interrupts to prevent an interrupt handler from accessing the shared data, but the lock mechanism is compiled away. The lock and unlock also disable and enable kernel preemption, respectively.

What Do I Lock?

It is important that each lock is clearly associated with what it is locking. More importantly, it is important that you protect *data* and not *code*. Despite the examples in this chapter explaining the importance of protecting the critical sections, it is the actual data inside that needs protection and not the code. Locks that simply lock code regions are hard to understand and prone to race conditions. Instead, associate data with a specific lock. For example, *"the* struct foo *is locked by* foo_lock." Always associate each piece of global data with a given lock. Whenever you access the data, make sure it is safe. Most likely, this means obtaining the appropriate lock before manipulating the data and releasing the lock when finished.

If you know that interrupts are initially enabled, there is no need to restore their previous state. You can unconditionally enable them on unlock. In those cases, spin_lock_irq() and spin_unlock_irq() are optimal:

```
spinlock_t mr_lock = SPIN_LOCK_UNLOCKED;

spin_lock_irq(&mr_lock);
/* critical section … */
spin_unlock_irq(&mr_lock);
```

It is increasingly hard to ensure that interrupts are always enabled in any given code path in the kernel. Because of this, use of spin_lock_irq() is not recommended. If you do use it, you had better be positive that interrupts were originally off or someone will be upset when they find them on!

Debugging Spin Locks

The configure option CONFIG_DEBUG_SPINLOCK enables a handful of debugging checks in the spin lock code. For example, with this option the spin lock code will check for the use of uninitialized spin locks and unlocking a lock that is not yet locked. When testing your code, you should always run with spin lock debugging enabled.

Other Spin Lock Methods

The method spin_lock_init() can be used to initialize a dynamically created spin lock (a spinlock_t that you do not have a direct reference to, just a pointer).

The method spin_try_lock() attempts to obtain the given spin lock. If the lock is contended, instead of spinning and waiting for the lock to be released, the function immediately returns nonzero. If it succeeds in obtaining the lock, it returns zero. Similarly, spin_is_locked() returns nonzero if the given lock is currently acquired. Otherwise, it returns zero. In neither case does this function actually obtain the lock[2].

See *Table 8.3* for a complete list of the standard spin lock methods.

[2]Use of these two functions can lead to gross code. You should not frequently have to check the values of spin locks—your code should either always acquire the lock itself or always be called while the lock is already held. Some legitimate uses do exist, however, so these interfaces are provided.

Table 8.3 **Listing of Spin Lock Methods**

Method	Description
`spin_lock()`	Acquires given lock
`spin_lock_irq()`	Disables local interrupts and acquire given lock
`spin_lock_irqsave()`	Saves current state of local interrupts, disable local interrupts, and acquires given lock
`spin_unlock()`	Releases given lock
`spin_unlock_irq()`	Releases given lock and enables local interrupts
`spin_unlock_irqrestore()`	Releases given lock and restores local interrupts to given previous state
`spin_lock_init()`	Initializes given `spinlock_t`
`spin_trylock()`	Tries to acquire given lock; if unavailable, returns nonzero
`spin_is_locked()`	Returns nonzero if the given lock is currently acquired, else it returns zero

Spin Locks and Bottom Halves

As mentioned in Chapter 6, "Bottom Halves and Deferring Work," certain locking precautions must be taken when working with bottom halves. The function `spin_lock_bh()` obtains the given lock and disables all bottom halves. The function `spin_unlock_bh()` performs the inverse.

Because a bottom half may preempt process context code, if data is shared between a bottom half process context, you must protect the data in process context with both a lock and the disabling of bottom halves. Likewise, because an interrupt handler may preempt a bottom half, if data is shared between an interrupt handler and a bottom half, you must both obtain the appropriate lock and disable interrupts.

Recall that two tasklets of the same type do not ever run simultaneously. Thus, there is no need to protect data used only within a single type of tasklet. If the data is shared between two different tasklets, however, you must obtain a normal spin lock before accessing the data in the bottom half. You do not need to disable bottom halves because a tasklet will never preempt another running tasklet on the same processor.

With softirqs, regardless of whether it is the same softirq type or not, if data is shared by softirqs it must be protected with a lock. Recall that softirqs, even two of the same type, may run simultaneously on multiple processors in the system. A softirq will never preempt another softirq running on the same processor, however, so disabling bottom halves is not needed.

Reader–Writer Spin Locks

Sometimes, lock usage can be clearly divided into readers and writers. For example, consider a list that is both updated and searched. When the list is updated (written to), it is important no other code is concurrently writing to *or* reading from the list. Writing demands mutual exclusion. On the other hand, when the list is searched (read from), it is only important that nothing else is writing to the list. Multiple concurrent readers are safe so long as there are no writers. The task list (discussed in Chapter 2, "Process Management") is very similar to this description. Not surprisingly, the task list is protected by a reader-writer spin lock.

When a data structure is neatly split into reader/writer paths like this, it makes sense to use a locking mechanism that provides similar semantics. In this case, Linux provides reader-writer spin locks. Reader-writer spin locks provide separate reader and writer variants of the lock. One or more readers can concurrently hold the reader lock. The writer lock, conversely, can be held by at most one writer with no concurrent readers. Usage is similar to spin locks. The reader-writer spin lock is initialized via

```
rwlock_t mr_rwlock = RW_LOCK_UNLOCKED;
```

Then, in the reader code path:

```
read_lock(&mr_rwlock);
/* critical section (read only) ... */
read_unlock(&mr_rwlock);
```

Finally, in the writer code path:

```
write_lock(&mr_rwlock);
/* critical section (read and write) ... */
write_unlock(&mr_rwlock);
```

Normally, the readers and writers are in entirely separate code paths, such as in this example.

Note that you cannot "upgrade" a read lock to a write lock. This code

```
read_lock(&mr_rwlock);
write_lock(&mr_rwlock);
```

will deadlock as the writer lock will spin, waiting for all readers to release the lock, including yourself. If you ever need to write, obtain the write lock from the very start. If the line between your readers and writers is muddled, it might be an indication that you do not need to use reader-writer locks. In that case, a normal spin lock is optimal.

It is safe for multiple readers to obtain the same lock. In fact, it is safe for the same thread to recursively obtain the same read lock. This lends itself to a useful and common optimization. If you only have readers in interrupt handlers but no writers, you can mix use of the "interrupt disabling" locks. You can use `read_lock()` instead of `read_lock_irqsave()` for reader protection. You still need to disable interrupts for write access, ala `write_lock_irqsave()`, otherwise a reader in an interrupt could deadlock on the held write lock. See *Table 8.4* for a full listing of the reader-writer spin lock methods.

Table 8.4 **Listing of Reader-Writer Spin Lock Methods**

Method	Description
read_lock()	Acquires given read-lock
read_lock_irq()	Disables local interrupts and acquires given read-lock
read_lock_irqsave()	Saves the current state of local interrupts, disables local interrupts, and acquires the given read-lock
read_unlock()	Releases given read-lock
read_unlock_irq()	Releases given read-lock and enables local interrupts
read_unlock_irqrestore()	Releases given read-lock and restores local interrupts to the given previous state
write_lock()	Acquires given write-lock
write_lock_irq()	Disables local interrupts and acquires the given write-lock
write_lock_irqsave()	Saves current state of local interrupts, disables local interrupts, and acquires the given write-lock
write_unlock()	Releases given write-lock
write_unlock_irq()	Releases given write-lock and enables local interrupts
write_unlock_irqrestore()	Releases given write-lock and restores local interrupts to given previous state
write_trylock()	Tries to acquire given write-lock; if unavailable, returns nonzero
rw_lock_init()	Initializes given rwlock_t
rw_is_locked()	Returns nonzero if the given lock is currently acquired, else it returns zero

A final important consideration in using the Linux reader-writer spin locks is that they favor readers over writers. If the read lock is held and a writer is waiting for exclusive access, readers that attempt to acquire the lock will continue to succeed. The spinning writer will not acquire the lock until all readers release the lock. Therefore, a sufficient number of readers can starve pending writers. This is important to keep in mind when designing your locking.

Spin locks provide a very quick and simple lock. The spinning behavior is optimal for short hold times and code that cannot sleep (interrupt handlers, for example). In cases where the sleep time might be long or you potentially need to sleep *while* holding the lock, the semaphore is a solution.

Semaphores

Semaphores in Linux are sleeping locks. When a task attempts to acquire a semaphore that is already held, the semaphore places the task onto a wait queue and puts the task to sleep. The processor is then free to execute other code. When the processes[3] holding the

---

[3]As we will see, multiple processes can simultaneously hold a semaphore, if desired.

semaphore release the lock, one of the tasks on the wait queue will be awakened up so that it can acquire the semaphore.

We can draw some interesting conclusions from the sleeping behavior of semaphores:

- Because the contending tasks sleep while waiting for the lock to become available, semaphores are well suited to locks that can be held a long time.

- Conversely, semaphores are not optimal for locks that are held for very short periods because the overhead of sleeping can outweigh the total lock hold time.

- Because a thread of execution sleeps on lock contention, semaphores can only be obtained in process context, as interrupt context is not schedulable.

- You can (although you may not want to) sleep while holding a semaphore because you will not deadlock when another process acquires the same semaphore (as it will just go to sleep and eventually let you continue).

- You cannot hold a spin lock while you acquire a semaphore, because you might have to sleep while waiting for the semaphore, and you cannot sleep while holding a spin lock.

These facts highlight the uses of semaphores versus spin locks. In most uses of semaphores, there is little choice as to what lock to use. If your code needs to sleep, which is often the case when synchronizing with user-space, semaphores are the sole solution. It is often easier, if not necessary, to use semaphores because they allow you the flexibility of sleeping. When you do have a choice, the decision between semaphore and spin lock should be based on lock hold time. Ideally, all your locks should be held as short as possible. With semaphores, however, longer lock hold times are more acceptable. Additionally, unlike spin locks, semaphores do not disable kernel preemption and, consequently, code holding a spin lock can be preempted. This means semaphores do not adversely affect scheduling latency.

A final useful feature of semaphores is that they can allow for an arbitrary number of simultaneous lock holders. Whereas spin locks permit at most one task to hold the lock at a time, the number of permissible simultaneous holders of semaphores can be set at declaration time. This value is called the *usage count* or simply *count*. The most common value is to allow, like spin locks, only one lock holder at a time. In this case, the count is equal to one and the semaphore is called a *binary semaphore* (because it is either held by one task or not held at all) or a *mutex* (because it enforces mutual exclusion). Alternatively, the count can be initialized to a nonzero value greater than one. In this case, the semaphore is called a *counting semaphore,* and it allows at most *count* holders of the lock at a time. Counting semaphores are not used to enforce mutual exclusion, because they allow multiple threads of execution in the critical region at once. Instead, they are used to enforce limits in certain code. They are not used much in the kernel. If you use a semaphore, you almost assuredly want to use a mutex (a semaphore with a count of one).

Semaphores were formalized by Edsger Wybe Dijkstra[4] in 1968 as a generalized locking mechanism. A semaphore supports two atomic operations, `P()` and `V()`, named after the Dutch word *Proberen*, to test (literally, to probe), and the Dutch word *Verhogen*, to increment. Later systems called these methods `down()` and `up()`, respectively, and so does Linux. The `down()` method is used to acquire a semaphore by decrementing the count by one. If it is zero or greater, the lock is acquired and the task can enter the critical region. If the count is negative, the task is placed on a wait queue and the processor moves on to something else. The function is used as a verb; you *down* a semaphore to acquire it. The `up()` method is used to release a semaphore upon completion of a critical region. This is called *upping* the semaphore. The method increments the count value; if the semaphore's wait queue is not empty, one of the waiting tasks is awakened and allowed to acquire the semaphore.

Creating and Initializing Semaphores

The semaphore implementation is architecture-dependent and defined in `<asm/semaphore.h>`. The `struct semaphore` type represents semaphores. Statically declared semaphores are created via

```
static DECLARE_SEMAPHORE_GENERIC(name, count);
```

where `name` is the variable's name and `count` is the usage count of the semaphore. As a shortcut to create the more common mutex, use

```
static DECLARE_MUTEX(name);
```

where, again, `name` is the variable name of the semaphore. More frequently, semaphores are created dynamically, often as part of a larger structure. In this case, to initialize a dynamically created semaphore to which you have only an indirect pointer reference, use

```
sema_init(sem, count);
```

where `sem` is a pointer and `count` is the usage count of the semaphore. Similarly, to initialize a dynamically created mutex, you can use

```
init_MUTEX(sem);
```

Using Semaphores

The function `down_interruptible()` attempts to acquire the given semaphore. If it fails, it sleeps in the `TASK_INTERRUPTIBLE` state. Recall from Chapter 2 that this process state implies a task can be woken up with a signal, which is generally a good thing. If a

[4]Dr. Dijkstra (1930-2002) is one of the most accomplished computer scientists in the (admittedly brief) history of computer scientists. His numerous contributions include work in OS design, algorithm theory, and the concept of semaphores. He was born in Rotterdam, The Netherlands and taught at the University of Texas for 15 years. He is probably *not* happy with the large number of GOTO statements in the Linux kernel, however.

signal is received while waiting for the semaphore, the task is woken up and
`down_interruptible()` returns `-EINTR`. Alternatively, the function `down()` places the
task in the `TASK_UNINTERRUPTIBLE` state if it sleeps. You most likely do not want this
because the process waiting for the semaphore will not respond to signals. Therefore, use
of `down_interruptible()` is much more common than `down()`. Yes, the naming is not
ideal.

You can use `down_trylock()` to nonblockingly try to acquire the given semaphore. If
the semaphore is already held, the function immediately returns nonzero. Otherwise, it
returns zero and you successfully hold the lock.

To release a given semaphore, call `up()`. Let's look at an example:

```
static DECLARE_MUTEX(mr_sem);

...

if (down_interruptible(&mr_sem))
        /* signal received, semaphore not acquired */

/* critical region ... */

up(&mr_sem);
```

A complete listing of the semaphore methods is in *Table 8.5*.

Table 8.5   **Listing of Semaphore Methods**

Method	Description
`sema_init(struct semaphore *, int)`	Initializes the dynamically created semaphore to the given count
`init_MUTEX(struct semaphore *)`	Initializes the dynamically created semaphore with a count of one
`init_MUTEX_LOCKED(struct semaphore *)`	Initializes the dynamically created semaphore with a count of zero (so it is initially locked)
`down_interruptible(struct semaphore *)`	Tries to acquire the given semaphore and enter interruptible sleep if it is contended
`down(struct semaphore *)`	Tries to acquire the given semaphore and enter uninterruptible sleep if it is contended
`down_trylock(struct semaphore *)`	Tries to acquire the given semaphore and immediately return nonzero if it is contended
`up(struct semaphore *)`	Releases the given semaphore and wake a waiting task, if any

Reader–Writer Semaphores

Semaphores, like spin locks, also come in a reader-writer flavor. The situations where reader-writer semaphores are preferred over standard semaphores are the same as with reader-writer spin locks versus standard spin locks.

Reader-writer semaphores are represented by the `struct rw_semaphore` type, which is defined in `<linux/rwsem.h>`. Statically declared reader-writer semaphores are created via

```
static DECLARE_RWSEM(name);
```

where `name` is the declared name of the new semaphore.

Reader-writer semaphores that are created dynamically can be initialized via

```
init_rwsem(struct rw_semaphore *sem)
```

All reader-writer semaphores are mutexes (that is, their usage count is one). Any number of readers can concurrently hold the read lock, so long as there are no writers. Conversely, only a sole writer (with no readers) can acquire the write variant of the lock. All reader-writer locks use uninterruptible sleep, so there is only one version of each `down()`. For example:

```
static DECLARE_RWSEM(mr_rwsem);

...

down_read(&mr_rwsem);

/* critical region (read only) ... */

up_read(&mr_rwsem);

...

down_write(&mr_rwsem);

/* critical region (read and write) ... */

up_write(&mr_rwsem);
```

As with semaphores, implementations of `down_read_trylock()` and `down_write_try-lock()` are provided. Each has one parameter: a pointer to a reader-writer semaphore. They both return nonzero if the lock is successfully acquired and zero if it is currently contended. Be careful—for admittedly no good reason—this is the opposite of normal semaphore behavior!

Reader-writer semaphores have a unique method that their reader-writer spin lock cousins do not have: `downgrade_writer()`. This function atomically converts an acquired write lock to a read lock.

Reader-writer semaphores, as spin locks of the same nature, should not be used unless there is a clear separation between write paths and read paths in your code. Supporting the reader-writer mechanisms has a cost, and it is only worthwhile if your code naturally splits along a reader/writer boundary.

Knowing when to use a spin lock versus a semaphore is important to writing optimal code. In many cases, however, there is little choice. Only a spin lock can be used in interrupt context, whereas only a semaphore can be held while a task sleeps. *Table 8.6* reviews the requirements that dictate which lock to use.

Table 8.6   **What to Use: Spin Locks Versus Semaphores**

Requirement	Recommended Lock
Low overhead locking	Spin lock is preferred
Short lock hold time	Spin lock is preferred
Long lock hold time	Semaphore is preferred
Need to lock from interrupt context	Spin lock is required
Need to sleep while holding lock	Semaphore is required

Completion Variables

Condition variables are an easy way to synchronize between two tasks in the kernel, when one task needs to signal to the other that an event has occurred. One task waits on the completion variable while another task performs some work. When the other task has completed the work, it uses the completion variable to wake up any waiting tasks. If this sounds like a semaphore, you are right—the idea is much the same. In fact, completion variables merely provide a simple solution to a problem whose answer is otherwise semaphores.

Completion variables are represented by the `struct completion` type, which is defined in `<linux/completion.h>`. A statically created completion variable is created and initialized via

```
DECLARE_COMPLETION(mr_comp);
```

A dynamically created completion variable is initialized via `init_completion()`.

On a given completion variable, the tasks that want to wait call `wait_for_completion()`. After the event has occurred, calling `complete()` signals all waiting tasks to wake up. *Table 8.7* has a listing of the completion variable methods.

Table 8.7   **Completion Variables Methods**

Method	Description
`init_completion(struct completion *)`	Initializes the given dynamically created completion variable

Table 8.7   **Continued**

Method	Description
`wait_for_completion(struct completion *)`	Waits for the given completion variable to be signaled
`complete(struct completion *)`	Signals any waiting tasks to wake up

For sample usages of completion variables, see `kernel/sched.c` and `kernel/fork.c`. A common usage is to have a completion variable dynamically created as a member of a data structure. Kernel code waiting for the initialization of the data structure calls `wait_for_completion()`. When the initialization is complete, the waiting tasks are awakened via a call to `completion()`.

BKL: The Big Kernel Lock

Welcome to the redheaded stepchild of the kernel. The Big Kernel Lock (BKL) is a global spin lock which was created to ease the transition from Linux's original SMP implementation to fine-grained locking. The BKL has some interesting properties:

- You can sleep while holding the BKL. The lock is automatically dropped when the task is unscheduled and reacquired when the task is rescheduled. Of course, this does not mean it is *safe* to sleep while holding the BKL, merely that you *can* and you will not deadlock.
- The BKL is a recursive lock. A single process can acquire the lock multiple times and not deadlock, as it would with a spin lock.
- You can only use the BKL in process context.
- It is evil.

These features helped ease the transition from kernel version 2.0 to 2.2. When SMP support was introduced in kernel version 2.0, only one task could be in the kernel at a time (of course, now the kernel is quite finely threaded—we have come a long way). A goal of 2.2 was to allow multiple processors to execute in the kernel concurrently. The BKL was introduced to help ease the transition to finer grained locking. It was a great aide then; now it is a scalability burden[5].

Use of the BKL is discouraged. In fact, new code should never introduce locking using the BKL. The lock is still fairly well used in parts of the kernel, however. Therefore, understanding the BKL and its interfaces is important. The BKL behaves like a spin lock, with the additions discussed previously. The function `lock_kernel()` acquires the lock and the function `unlock_kernel()` releases the lock. A single thread of execution may acquire the lock recursively, but must then call `unlock_kernel()` an

---

[5]Although, it may not be as terrible as some make it out to be - some people believe it to be the kernel incarnation of the devil.

equal number of times to release the lock. On the last unlock call the lock will be released. The function `kernel_locked()` returns nonzero if the lock is currently held; otherwise, it returns zero. These interfaces are declared in `<linux/smp_lock.h>`. Sample usage:

```
lock_kernel();

/*
 * Critical section, synchronized against all other BKL users...
 * Note, you can safely sleep here and the lock will be transparently
 * released. When you reschedule, the lock will be transparently
 * reacquired. This implies you will not deadlock, but you still do
 * not want to sleep if you need the lock to protect data here!
 */

unlock_kernel();
```

The BKL also disables kernel preemption while it is held. On UP kernels, the BKL code does not actually perform any physical locking. *Table 8.8* has a complete list of the BKL functions.

Table 8.8   **List of BKL functions**

Function	Description
`lock_kernel()`	Acquires the BKL
`unlock_kernel()`	Releases the BKL
`kernel_locked()`	Returns nonzero if the lock is held and zero otherwise (UP always returns nonzero)

One of the major issues concerning the BKL is determining what the lock is protecting. Too often, the BKL is seemingly associated with code (for example, "it synchronizes callers to `foo()`") instead of data ("it protects the `foo` structure"). This makes replacing BKL uses with a spin lock difficult because it is not easy to determine just what is being locked. The replacement is made even harder in that the relationship between all BKL users needs to be determined.

Seq Locks

Seq locks are a new type of lock introduced in the 2.6 kernel. They provide a very simple mechanism for reading and writing shared data. They work by maintaining a sequence counter. Whenever the data in question is written to, a lock is obtained and a sequence number is incremented. Prior to and after reading the data, the sequence number is read. If the values are the same, then a write did not begin in the middle of the read. Further, if the values are even then a write is not underway (grabbing the write lock makes the value odd while releasing it makes it even, since the lock starts at zero).

To define a seq lock, do

```
seqlock_t mr_seq_lock = SEQLOCK_UNLOCKED;
```

The write path is then

```
write_seqlock(&mr_seq_lock);
/* write lock is obtained... */
write_sequnlock(&mr_seq_lock);
```

This looks like normal spin lock code. The oddness comes in with the read path, which is quite a bit different:

```
unsigned long seq;

do {
        seq = read_seqbegin(&mr_seq_lock);
        /* read data here ... */
} while (read_seqretry(&mr_seq_lock, seq));
```

Seq locks are useful to provide a very lightweight and scalable look for use with many readers and a few writers. Seq locks, however, favor writers over readers. The write lock will always succeed in being obtained so long as there are no other writers. Readers will not effect the write lock, as is the case with reader-writer spin locks and semaphores. Furthermore, pending writers will continually cause the read loop (the previous example) to repeat, until there are no longer any writers holding the lock.

Preemption Disabling

Because the kernel is preemptive, a process in the kernel can stop running at any instant to allow a process of higher priority to run. This means a task can begin running in the same critical region as a task that was preempted. To prevent this, the kernel preemption code uses spin locks as markers of nonpreemptive regions. If a spin lock is held, the kernel is not preemptive. Because the concurrency issues with kernel preemption and SMP are the same, and the kernel is already SMP-safe, this simple change makes the kernel preempt-safe, too.

Or so we hope. In reality, some situations do not require a spin lock, but do need kernel preemption disabled. The most frequent of these situations is per-processor data. If the data is unique to each processor, there may be no need to protect it with a lock because only that one processor can access the data. If there are no spin locks held, the kernel is preemptive, and it would be possible for a newly scheduled task to access this same variable, as shown here

```
task A manipulates variable foo
task A is preempted
task B is scheduled
task B manipulates variable foo
task B completes
```

```
task A is scheduled
task A manipulates variable foo
```

Consequently, even if this were a uniprocessor computer, the variable could pseudo-concurrently be accessed by multiple processes. Normally, this variable would require a spin lock (to prevent true concurrency on multiprocessing machines). If this were a per-processor variable, however, it might not require a lock.

To solve this, kernel preemption can be disabled via `preempt_disable()`. The call is nestable; you may call it any number of times. For each call, a corresponding call to `preempt_enable()` is required. The final corresponding call to `preempt_enable()` will re-enable preemption. For example:

```
preempt_disable();

/* preemption is disabled ... */

preempt_enable();
```

The preemption count stores the number of held locks and `preempt_disable()` calls. If the number is zero the kernel is preemptive. If it is one or greater, the kernel is not preemptive. This count is incredibly useful—it is a great way to do atomicity and sleep debugging. The function `preempt_count()` returns this value. See *Table 8.9* for a listing of kernel preemption-related functions.

Table 8.9   **Kernel Preemption-Related Functions**

Function	Description
`preempt_disable()`	Disables kernel preemption
`preempt_enable()`	Enables kernel preemption and check and service any pending reschedules
`preempt_enable_no_resched()`	Enables kernel preemption but do not reschedule
`preempt_count()`	Returns the preemption count

As a cleaner solution to per-processor data issues, you can obtain the processor number (which presumably is used to index into the per-processor data) via `get_cpu()`. This function will disable kernel preemption prior to returning the current processor number:

```
int cpu = get_cpu();

/* manipulate per-processor data ... */

put_cpu(); /* all done, reenable kernel preemption */
```

Barriers

When dealing with synchronization between multiple processors or with hardware devices, it is sometimes a requirement that memory-reads (loads) and memory-writes (stores) issue in the order specified in your program code. When talking with hardware, you often need to ensure a given read occurs before another read or write. Additionally, on symmetrical multiprocessing systems, it may be important for writes to appear in the order your code issues them (usually to ensure subsequent reads see the data in the same order). Complicating these issues is the fact that both the compiler and the processor can reorder reads and writes[6] for performance reasons. Thankfully, all processors that do reorder reads or writes provide machine instructions to enforce ordering requirements. It is also possible to instruct the compiler not to reorder instructions around a given point. These instructions are called *barriers*.

Basically, on some processors the code

```
a = 1;
b = 2;
```

may store the new value in b *before* they store the new value in a. The processor and the compiler, however, will never reorder writes such as

```
a = 1;
b = a;
```

because there is clearly a data dependency between a and b. Neither the compiler nor the processor, however, know about code in other contexts. Occasionally, it is important that writes are seen by other code and the outside world in the specific order you intend. This is often the case with hardware devices, but is also a commonality on multiprocessing machines.

The rmb() method provides a read memory barrier. It ensures that no loads are reordered across the rmb() call. That is, no loads prior to the call will be reordered to after the call and no loads after the call will be reordered to before the call.

The wmb() method provides a write barrier. It functions in the same manner as rmb(), but with respect to stores instead of loads—it ensures no stores are reordered across the barrier.

The mb() call provides both a read barrier and a write barrier. No loads *or* stores will be reordered across a call to mb(). It is provided because a single instruction (often the same instruction used by rmb()) can provide both the load and store barrier.

A variant of rmb(), read_barrier_depends(), provides a read barrier, but *only for loads that subsequent loads depend on*. All reads prior to the barrier are guaranteed to complete before any reads after the barrier that depend on the reads prior to the barrier. Got

---

[6]Although, Intel x86 processors do *not* ever reorder writes. That is, they do not do out-of-order stores. But other processors do.

it? Basically, it enforces a read barrier, like `rmb()`, but only for certain reads—those that depend on each other. On some architectures, `read_barrier_depends()` is much quicker than `rmb()` because it is not needed and, thus, is a *noop*.

Let's consider an example using `mb()` and `rmb()`. The initial value of a is one and b is two.

Thread 1	Thread 2
a = 3;	–
mb();	–
b = 4;	c = b;
–	rmb();
–	d = a;

Without using the memory barriers, on some processors it is possible that c receives the *new* value of b, while d receives the *old* value of a. For example, c could equal four (what we expect), yet d could equal one (not what we expect). Using the `mb()` ensured a and b were written in the intended order, while the `rmb()` insured c and d were read in the intended order.

This sort of reordering occurs because modern processors dispatch and commit instructions out-of-order, to optimize use of their pipelines. What can end up happening in the above example is that the instructions associated with the loads of b and a occur out of order. The `rmb()` and `wmb()` functions corresponds to instructions which tell the processor to commit any pending load or store instructions, respectively, before continuing.

Let's look at a similar example, but one in which we can use `read_barrier_depends()` instead of `rmb()`. In this example, initially a is one, b is two, and p is &b.

Thread 1	Thread 2
a = 3;	–
mb();	–
p = &a;	pp = p;
–	read_barrier_depends();
–	b = *pp;

Again, without memory barriers, it would be possible for b to be set to pp before pp was set to p. The `read_barrier_depends()`, however, provides a sufficient barrier because the load of *pp depends on the load of p. It would also be sufficient to use `rmb()` here, but because the reads are data-dependent, we can use the potentially faster `read_barrier_depends()`. Note in either case, the `mb()` is required to enforce the intended load/store ordering in the left thread.

The macros `smp_rmb()`, `smp_wmb()`, `smp_mb()`, and `smp_read_barrier_depends()` provide a useful optimization. On SMP kernels they are defined as the usual memory barriers, while on UP kernels they are defined only as a compiler barrier. You can use these SMP variants when the ordering constraints are specific to SMP systems.

The `barrier()` method prevents the compiler from optimizing loads or stores across the call. The compiler knows not to rearrange stores and loads in ways that would change the effect of the C code and existing data dependencies. It does not have knowledge, however, of events that can occur outside of the current context. For example, the compiler cannot know about interrupts that might read the same data you are writing. For this reason, you might want to ensure a store is issued before a load, for example. The previous memory barriers also function as compiler barriers, but a compiler barrier is much lighter in weight (it is practically free) than a memory barrier.

Table 8.10 has a full listing of the memory and compiler barrier methods provided by all architectures in the Linux kernel.

Table 8.10 **Memory and Compiler Barrier Methods**

Barrier	Description
`rmb()`	Prevents loads being reordered across the barrier
`read_barrier_depends()`	Prevents data-dependent loads being reordered across the barrier
`wmb()`	Prevents stores being reordered across the barrier
`mb()`	Prevents load or stores being reordered across the barrier
`smp_rmb()`	On SMP, provides a `rmb()` and on UP provides a `barrier()`
`smp_read_barrier_depends()`	On SMP, provides a `read_barrier_depends()` and on UP provides a `barrier()`
`smp_wmb()`	On SMP, provides a `wmb()` and on UP provides a `barrier()`
`smp_mb()`	On SMP, provides a `mb()` and on UP provides a `barrier()`
`barrier()`	Prevents the compiler from optimizing stores or loads across the barrier

Note the actual effects of the barriers vary for each architecture. For example, if a machine does not perform out-of-order stores (for example, Intel x86 chips do not) then `wmb()` does nothing. You can use the appropriate memory barrier for the worst case (that is, the weakest ordering processor) and your code will compile optimally for your architecture.

9

Timers and Time Management

THE PASSING OF TIME IS VERY IMPORTANT to the kernel. A large number of kernel functions are time driven, as opposed to event driven[1]. Some of these functions are periodic, such as balancing the scheduler runqueues or refreshing the screen. They occur on a fixed schedule, such as 100 times per second. The kernel schedules other functions, such as delayed disk I/O, at a relative time in the future. For example, the kernel might schedule work for 500 milliseconds from now. Finally, the kernel must also manage the system uptime and the current date and time.

Note the differences between relative and absolute time. Scheduling an event for five seconds in the future requires no concept of the *absolute* time—only the *relative* time (for example, five seconds from now). Conversely, managing the current time of day requires the kernel to understand not just the passing of time, but also some absolute measurement of it. Both of these concepts are crucial to the management of time.

Also, note the differences between events that occur periodically and events the kernel schedules for a fixed point in the future. Events that occur periodically—say, every 10 milliseconds—are driven by the *system timer*. The system timer is a programmable piece of hardware that issues an interrupt at a fixed frequency. The interrupt handler for this timer—called the *timer interrupt*—updates the system time and performs periodic work. The system timer and its timer interrupt are central to Linux, and a large focus of this chapter.

The other focus is *dynamic timers*—the facility used to schedule events that run once after a specified time has elapsed. For example, the floppy device driver uses a timer to shut off the floppy drive motor after a specified period of inactivity. The kernel can create and destroy timers dynamically. This chapter covers the kernel implementation of dynamic timers, as well as the interface available for their use in your code.

---

[1] More accurately, time-driven events are also event driven—the event being the passing of time.

Kernel Notion of Time

Certainly, the concept of *time* to a computer is a bit obscure. Indeed, the kernel must work with the system's hardware to comprehend and manage time. The hardware provides a system timer that the kernel uses to gauge the passing of time. This system timer works off an electronic time source, such as a digital clock or the frequency of the processor. The system timer goes off (often called *hitting* or *popping*) at a preprogrammed frequency, called the *tick rate*. When the system timer goes off, it issues an interrupt that the kernel handles via a special interrupt handler.

Because the kernel knows the preprogrammed tick rate, it knows the time between any two successive timer interrupts. This period is called a *tick* and is equal to *one-over-the-tick-rate* seconds. As you'll see, this is how the kernel keeps track of both wall time and system uptime. Wall time—the actual time of day—is of most importance to user-space applications. The kernel keeps track of it simply because the kernel controls the timer interrupt. A family of system calls provide the date and time of day to user-space. The system uptime—the relative time since the system booted—is useful to both the kernel and user-space. This is because a lot of code must be aware of the *passing* of time. The difference between two uptime readings—now and then—is a simple measure of this relativity.

The timer interrupt is very important to the management of the operating system. A large number of kernel functions live and die by the passing of time. Some of the work executed periodically by the timer interrupt includes:

- Update the system uptime
- Update the time of day
- On an SMP system, ensure that the scheduler runqueues are balanced, and if not, balance them (as discussed in Chapter 3, "Scheduling")
- Check if the current process has exhausted its timeslice and, if so, cause a reschedule (also discussed in Chapter 3)
- Run any dynamic timers that have expired
- Update resource usage and processor time statistics

Some of this work occurs on *every* timer interrupt—that is, the work is carried out with the frequency of the tick rate. Other functions still execute periodically, but only every *n* timer interrupts. That is, these functions occur at some fraction of the tick rate. In the section "The Timer Interrupt Handler," we will look at the timer interrupt handler itself.

The Tick Rate: HZ

The frequency of the system timer (the tick rate) is programmed on system boot based on a static preprocessor define, HZ. The value of HZ differs for each supported architecture. In fact, on some supported architectures, it even differs between machine types.

The kernel defines the value in `<asm/param.h>`. The tick rate has a frequency of HZ hertz and a period of 1/HZ seconds. For example, in `include/asm-i386/param.h`, the i386 architecture defines:

```
#define HZ 1000        /* internal kernel time frequency */
```

Therefore, the timer interrupt on i386 has a frequency of 1000 Hz and occurs 1000 times per second (every one-thousandth of a second, which is every millisecond). Most other architectures have a tick rate of 100. *Table 9.1* is a complete listing of each supported architecture and their defined tick rate.

Table 9.1 **Frequency of the Timer Interrupt**

Architecture	Frequency (in Hertz)
alpha	1024
arm	100
cris	100
h8300	100
i386	1000
ia64	32 or 1024[2]
m68k	100
m68knommu	50, 100, or 1000
mips	100
mips64	100
parisc	100 or 1000
ppc	100
ppc64	1000
s390	100
sh	100
sparc	100
sparc64	100
um	100
v850	24, 100, or 122
x86-64	1000

When writing kernel code, do not assume HZ has any given value. This is not a common mistake these days because so many architectures have varying tick rates. In the past, however, Alpha was the only architecture with a tick rate not equal to 100 Hz, and it

---

[2] The IA-64 simulator has a tick rate of 32 Hz. Real IA-64 machines have a tick rate of 1024 Hz.

was common to see code incorrectly hard-code the value `100` when the `HZ` value should have been used. Examples of using `HZ` in kernel code will be shown later.

The frequency of the timer interrupt is rather important. As we saw, the timer interrupt performs a lot of work. Indeed, the kernel's entire notion of time derives from the periodicity of the system timer. Picking the right value, like a successful relationship, is all about compromise.

The Ideal `HZ` Value

The i386 architecture, ever since the initial version of Linux, has had a timer interrupt frequency of 100 Hz. During the 2.5 development series, however, the frequency was raised to 1000 Hz and was (as such things are) controversial. Because so much of the system is dependent on the timer interrupt, changing its frequency has a reasonable impact on the system. Of course, there are pros and cons to larger versus smaller `HZ` values.

Increasing the tick rate means the timer interrupt runs more frequently. Consequently, the work it performs occurs more often. This has the following benefits:

- The timer interrupt has a higher resolution and, consequently, all timed events have a higher resolution.
- The accuracy of timed events improve.

The resolution increases by the same factor that the tick rate increases. For example, the granularity of timers with `HZ=100` is 10 milliseconds. In other words, all periodic events occur on the timer interrupt's 10 millisecond boundary and no finer *precision*[3] is guaranteed. With `HZ=1000`, however, resolution is 1 millisecond—10x finer. Although kernel code can create timers with 1 millisecond resolution, there is no guarantee the precision afforded with `HZ=100` is sufficient to execute the timer on anything better than 10 millisecond intervals.

Likewise, accuracy improves in the same manner. Assuming the kernel starts timers at random times, the average timer is off by half the period of the timer interrupt because timers might expire at any time, but are only executed on occurrences of the timer interrupt. For example, with `HZ=100`, the average event occurs +/– 5 millisecond off from the desired time. Thus, error is 5 millisecond on average. With `HZ=1000`, the average error drops to 0.5 millisecond—a 10x improvement.

This higher resolution and greater accuracy provides multiple advantages:

- Kernel timers execute with finer resolution and increased accuracy (this provides a large number of improvements, one of which is the following).
- System calls, such as `poll()` and `select()`, which optionally employ a timeout value, execute with improved precision.

---

[3]Use *precision* here in the computer sense, not the scientific. Precision in science is a statistical measurement of repeatability. In computers, precision is the number of significant figures used to represent a value.

- Measurements, such as resource usage or the system uptime, are recorded with a finer resolution.

- Process preemption occurs more accurately.

Some of the most readily noticeable performance benefits come from the improved precision of `poll()` and `select()` timeouts. The improvement might be quite large; an application that makes heavy use of these system calls might waste a great deal of time waiting for the timer interrupt, when, in fact, the timeout has actually expired. Remember, the average error (that is, potentially wasted time) is half the period of the timer interrupt.

Another benefit of a higher tick rate is the greater accuracy in process preemption, which results in decreased scheduling latency. Recall from Chapter 3, that the timer interrupt is responsible for decrementing the running process's timeslice count. When the count reaches zero, `need_resched` is set and the kernel will run the scheduler as soon as possible. Now, assume a given process is running and has 2 milliseconds of its timeslice remaining. In 2 milliseconds, the scheduler *should* preempt the running process and begin executing a new process. Unfortunately, this event will not occur until the next timer interrupt, which might not be in 2 milliseconds. In fact, at worst the next timer interrupt might be $1/HZ$ of a second away! With HZ=100, a process might get nearly ten extra milliseconds to run. Of course, this all balances out and fairness is preserved, because all tasks receive the same imprecision in scheduling—but that is not the issue. The problems stems from the latency created by the delayed preemption. If the to-be-scheduled task had something time sensitive to do, such as refill an audio buffer, the delay might not be acceptable. Increasing the tick rate to 1000 Hz lowers the worst-case scheduling overrun to just 1 millisecond, and the average-case overrun to just 0.5 milliseconds.

Now, there must be *some* downside to increasing the tick rate or it would have been 1000 Hz to start (or even higher). Indeed, there is one large issue: A higher tick rate implies more frequent timer interrupts, which implies higher overhead, because the processor must spend more time executing the timer interrupt handler. The higher the tick rate the more time the processor spends executing the timer interrupt. This adds up to not just less processor time available for other work, but also a more frequent periodic thrashing of the processor's cache. The issue of the overhead's impact is debatable. A move from HZ=100 to HZ=1000 clearly brings with it a 10x greater overhead from the timer interrupt. However, how substantial is the overhead to begin with? Ten times nothing is still nothing! The final agreement is that, at least on modern systems, HZ=1000 does not create unacceptable overhead. Nevertheless, it is possible in 2.6 to compile the kernel with a different value for HZ[4].

---

[4] Due to architectural and NTP-related issues, however, not just any value is acceptable for HZ. On x86, 100, 500, and 1000 all work fine.

> **A tickless OS?**
>
> You might wonder if an operating system even needs a fixed timer interrupt. Is it possible to design an OS without ticks? Yes, *it is possible* but *it might not be pretty.*
>
> There is no absolute need for a fixed timer interrupt. Instead, the kernel can use a dynamically programmed timer for each pending event. This quickly adds a lot of timer overhead, so a better idea is to have just *one* timer, and program it to occur when the next earliest event is due. When that timer executes, create a timer for the next event and repeat. With this approach, there is no periodic timer interrupt and no HZ value.
>
> Two issues need to be overcome with this approach. The first is how to manage some concept of ticks, at least so the kernel can keep track of relative time. This is not too hard to solve. The second issue—how to overcome the overhead of managing all the dynamic timers, even with the optimized version—is a bit harder. The overhead and complexity is high enough that the Linux kernel does not take this approach. Nonetheless, people have tried and the results are interesting—search online archives if interested.

Jiffies

The global variable `jiffies` holds the number of ticks that have occurred since the system booted. On boot, the kernel initializes the variable to zero, and it is incremented by one during each timer interrupt. Thus, because there are HZ timer interrupts in a second, there are HZ jiffies in a second. The system uptime is thus `jiffies`/HZ seconds.

The `jiffies` variable is declared in `<linux/jiffies.h>` as:

```
extern unsigned long volatile jiffies;
```

In the next section, we will look at its actual definition, which is a bit peculiar. For now, let's look at some example kernel code. To convert from seconds to `jiffies`:

```
(seconds * HZ)
```

Likewise, to convert from `jiffies` to seconds:

```
(jiffies / HZ)
```

The former is more common. For example, code often needs to set a value for some time in the future:

```
unsigned long time_stamp = jiffies;          /* now */
unsigned long next_tick = jiffies + 1;       /* one tick from now */
unsigned long later = jiffies + 5*HZ;        /* five seconds from now */
```

The latter is typically reserved for communicating with user-space, as the kernel itself rarely cares about any sort of absolute time.

Note that `jiffies` is prototyped as `unsigned long` and storing it in anything else is incorrect.

Internal Representation of Jiffies

The actual internal representation of `jiffies` is rather strange. For 2.6, the variable type changed from an `unsigned long` to a `u64`. In other words, it is an unsigned 64-bit integer, even on 32-bit machines. The declaration for the full 64-bit tick count is in `<linux/jiffies.h>`:

```
extern u64 jiffies_64;
```

A 32-bit `jiffies` value, with a timer tick occurring 100 times per second, will overflow in about 497 days, which is pretty reasonable. Increasing HZ to 1000, however, will bring the overflow down to just 49.7 days. Conversely, a 64-bit value will not overflow in anyone's lifetime. In the next section, we will look at the potential problems with overflow (while undesirable, overflow in the tick count is a normal and expected occurrence).

The transition from a 32-bit to a 64-bit value would normally require care. The kernel developers applied some smart thinking, however. Because existing code references the `jiffies` variable and most code only cares about the lower 32-bits, the original `jiffies` variable is still used. Using some magic linker scripts, the `jiffies` variable is overlaid onto the new `jiffies_64` variable. *Figure 9.1* shows the layout of `jiffies` versus `jiffies_64`.

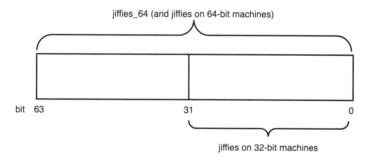

Figure 9.1   Layout of `jiffies` versus `jiffies_64`.

Code that accesses `jiffies` simply reads the lower 32-bits of `jiffies_64`. The function `get_jiffies_64()` can be used to read the full 64-bit value[5]. Such a need is rare, consequently, most code simply continues to read the lower 32-bits directly via the `jiffies` variable.

---

[5] A special function is needed because 32-bit architectures cannot atomically access both 32-bit words in a 64-bit value. The special function locks the jiffies count via the `xtime_lock` lock before reading.

On 64-bit architectures, however, `jiffies_64` and `jiffies` simply refer to the same thing. Code can read either `jiffies` or call `get_jiffies_64()` because both have the same effect.

Jiffies Wraparound

The `jiffies` variable, like any C integer, experiences *overflow* when its value is increased beyond its maximum storage limit. For a 32-bit unsigned integer, the maximum value is $2^{32} - 1$. Thus, a possible 4294967295 timer ticks can occur before the tick count overflows. When the tick count is equal to this maximum and it is incremented, it wraps around to zero.

Let's look at an example of a wraparound:

```
unsigned long timeout = jiffies + HZ/2;        /* timeout in 0.5s */

/* do some work, then see if we took too long ... */
if (timeout < jiffies) {
        /* we did not time out, good ... */
} else {
        /* we timed out, error ... */
}
```

The intention of this code snippet is to set a timeout for some time in the future—for one half second from now, to be precise. The code then proceeds to perform some work, presumably poking hardware and waiting for a response. When done, if the whole ordeal took longer than the timeout, the code handles the error as appropriate.

Multiple potential overflow issues are here, but let's study one of them: Consider what happens if `jiffies` wrapped back to zero after setting `timeout`. Then, the first conditional would fail as the `jiffies` value would be smaller than `timeout` despite logically being larger. Conceptually, the `jiffies` value should be a very large number—larger than `timeout`. Because it overflowed its maximum value, however, it is now a very small value—perhaps only a handful of ticks over zero. Because of the wraparound, the results of the `if` statement are switched. Whoops!

Thankfully, the kernel provides four macros for comparing tick counts that correctly handle wraparound in the tick count. They are in `<linux/jiffies.h>`:

```
#define time_after(unknown, known) ((long)(known) - (long)(unknown) < 0)
#define time_before(unknown, known) ((long)(unknown) - (long)(known) < 0)
#define time_after_eq(unknown, known) ((long)(unknown) - (long)(known) >= 0)
#define time_before_eq(unknown, known) ((long)(known) - (long)(unknown) >= 0)
```

The `unknown` parameter is typically `jiffies` and the `known` parameter is the value you want to compare against.

The `time_after(unknown, known)` macro returns true if time `unknown` is after time `known`; otherwise, it returns false. The `time_before(unknown, known)` macro returns true if time `unknown` is before time `known`; otherwise, it returns false. The final two macros perform identically to the first two, except they also return true if the parameters are equal.

The timer-wraparound-safe version of the previous example would look like:

```
unsigned long timeout = jiffies + HZ/2;        /* timeout in 0.5s */

/* ... */
if (time_after(jiffies, timeout)) {
        /* we did not time out, good ... */
} else {
        /* we timed out, error ... */
}
```

If you are curious as to why these macros prevent errors because of wraparound, try various values for the two parameters. Then assume one parameter wrapped to zero and see what happens.

User-Space and HZ

Previously, changing the value of HZ resulted in user-space anomalies. This was because of values that were exported to user-space in units of ticks-per-second. As these interfaces became permanent, applications grew to rely on a specific value of HZ. Consequently, changing HZ scales various exported values by some constant—without user-space knowing! Uptime would read 20 hours when it was in fact two!

To remedy this, the kernel must scale all exported jiffies values. It does this by defining USER_HZ, which is the HZ value that user-space *expects*. On x86, because HZ was historically 100, USER_HZ=100. The macro jiffies_to_clock_t() is then used to scale a tick count count in terms of HZ to a tick count in terms of USER_HZ. The macro used depends on whether USER_HZ and HZ are integer multiples of themselves. If so, the macro is rather simple:

```
#define jiffies_to_clock_t(x)                ((x) / (HZ / USER_HZ))
```

A more complicated algorithm is used if the values are not integer multiples.

Finally, the function jiffies_64_to_clock_t() is provided to convert a 64-bit jiffies value from HZ to USER_HZ units.

These functions are used anywhere a value in ticks-per-seconds needs to be exported to user-space. Example:

```
unsigned long start = jiffies;
unsigned long total_time;

/* do some work ... */
total_time = jiffies - start;
printk("That took %lu ticks\n", jiffies_to_clock_t(total_time));
```

User-space expects the previous value as if HZ=USER_HZ. If they are not equivalent, the macro scales as needed and everyone is happy. Of course, this example is silly: It would make more sense to print the message in seconds, not ticks, that is

```
printk("That took %lu seconds\n", total_time / HZ);
```

Hardware Clocks and Timers

Architectures provide two hardware devices to help with time keeping—the system timer, which we have been discussing, and the real-time clock. The actual behavior and implementation of these devices varies between different machines, but the general purpose and design is about the same for each.

Real-Time Clock

The real-time clock (RTC) provides a nonvolatile device for storing the system time. The RTC continues to keep track of time even when the system is off, by way of a small battery typically included on the system board. On the PC architecture, the RTC and the CMOS are integrated and a single battery keeps the RTC running and the BIOS settings preserved.

On boot, the kernel reads the RTC and uses it to initialize the wall time, which is stored in the xtime variable. The kernel does not typically read the value again; however, some supported architectures, such as x86, periodically save the current wall time back to the RTC. Nonetheless, the real time clock's primary importance is only during boot, when xtime is initialized.

System Timer

The system timer serves a much more important (and frequent) role in the kernel's timekeeping. The idea behind the system timer, regardless of architecture, is the same—to provide a mechanism for driving an interrupt at a periodic rate. Some architectures implement this via an electronic clock that oscillates at a programmable frequency. Other systems provide a decrementer—a counter is set to some initial value and decrements at a fixed rate until the counter reaches zero. When the counter reaches zero, an interrupt is triggered. In any case, the effect is the same.

On x86, the primary system timer is the programmable interrupt timer (PIT). The PIT exists on all PC machines and has been driving interrupts since the days of DOS. The kernel programs the PIT on boot to drive the system timer interrupt (interrupt zero) at HZ frequency. It is a simple device with limited functionality, but it gets the job done. Other x86 time sources include the local APIC timer and the time stamp counter (TSC).

The Timer Interrupt Handler

Now that we have an understanding of HZ, jiffies, and what the system timer's role is, let's look at the actual implementation of the timer interrupt handler. The timer interrupt is broken into two pieces: an architecture-dependent and an architecture-independent routine.

The architecture-dependent routine is registered as the interrupt handler for the system timer and, thus, runs when the timer interrupt hits. Its exact job depends on the given architecture, of course, but most handlers perform at least the following work:

- Obtain the `xtime_lock` lock, which protects access to `jiffies_64` and the wall time value, `xtime`.

- Acknowledge or reset the system timer as required.

- Periodically save the updated wall time to the real time clock.

- Call the architecture-independent timer routine, `do_timer()`.

The architecture-independent routine, `do_timer()`, performs much more work:

- Increment the `jiffies_64` count by one (this is safe, even on 32-bit architectures, as the `xtime_lock` lock was previously obtained).

- Update resource usages, such as consumed system and user time, for the currently running process.

- Run any dynamic timers that have expired (discussed in the following section).

- Execute `scheduler_tick()` as discussed in Chapter 3.

- Update the wall time, which is stored in `xtime`.

- Calculate the infamous load average.

The actual routine is very simple, as other functions handle most of the previously discussed work:

```
void do_timer(struct pt_regs *regs)
{
        jiffies_64++;

        update_process_times(user_mode(regs));
        update_times();
}
```

The `user_mode()` macro looks at the state of the processor registers, `regs`, and returns one if the timer interrupt occurred in user-space and zero if the interrupt occurred in kernel mode. This enables `update_process_times()` to attribute the previous tick to the proper mode, either user or system:

```
void update_process_times(int user_tick)
{
        struct task_struct *p = current;
        int cpu = smp_processor_id();
        int system = user_tick ^ 1;

        update_one_process(p, user_tick, system, cpu);
        run_local_timers();
        scheduler_tick(user_tick, system);
}
```

The `update_one_process()` function does the actual updating of the process's times. It is rather elaborate, but note how one of either the `user_tick` or the `system` value is equal to one and the other is zero, because of the XOR. Therefore, `updates_one_process()` can simply add each value to the corresponding counter without a branch:

```
/*
 * update by one jiffy the appropriate time counter
 */
p->utime += user;
p->stime += system;
```

The appropriate value is increased by one and the other value remains the same. You might realize that this implies that the kernel credits a process for running the *entire* previous tick in whatever mode the processor was in when the timer interrupt occurred. In reality, the process might have entered and exited kernel mode many times during the last tick. In fact, the process might not even have been the only process running in the last tick! Unfortunately, without much more complex accounting, this is the best the kernel can provide. It is also another reason for a higher frequency tick rate.

Next, the `run_local_timers()` function marks a softirq (see Chapter 6, "Bottom Halves and Deferring Work") to handle the execution of any expired timers. We will look at timers in a following section, "Timers."

Finally, the `scheduler_tick()` function decrements the currently running process's timeslice and sets `need_resched` if needed. On SMP machines, it also balances the per-processor runqueues as needed. This was all discussed in Chapter 3.

When `update_process_times()` returns, `do_timer()` calls `update_times()` to update the wall time:

```
void update_times(void)
{
        unsigned long ticks;

        ticks = jiffies - wall_jiffies;
        if (ticks) {
                wall_jiffies += ticks;
                update_wall_time(ticks);
        }
        last_time_offset = 0;
        calc_load(ticks);
}
```

The `ticks` value is calculated to be the change in ticks since the last update. In normal cases, this is, of course, one. In rare situations, timer interrupts can be missed and the ticks are said to be *lost*. This can occur if interrupts are off for a long time. It is not the norm and quite often a bug. The `wall_jiffies` value is increased by the `ticks` value—thus, it is equal to the `jiffies` value of the most recent wall time update—and update_wall_time() is called to update xtime, which stores the wall time. Finally, calc_load() is called to update the load average and update_times() returns.

The do_timer() function returns to the original architecture-dependent interrupt handler, which performs any needed clean up, releases the xtime_lock lock, and finally returns.

All this occurs every 1/HZ of a second. That is *1000* times per second on your PC.

The Time of Day

The current time of day (the wall time) is defined in kernel/timer.c:

```
struct timespec xtime;
```

The timespec data structure is defined in <linux/time.h> as:

```
struct timespec {
        time_t tv_sec;                  /* seconds */
        long tv_nsec;                   /* nanoseconds */
};
```

The xtime.tv_sec value stores the number of seconds that have elapsed since January 1, 1970 (UTC). This date is called the *epoch*. Most Unix systems base their notion of the current wall time as relative to this epoch. The xtime.v_nsec value stores the number of nanoseconds that have elapsed in the last second.

Reading or writing the xtime variable requires the xtime_lock lock, which is *not* a normal spinlock but a *seqlock*. Chapter 8, "Kernel Synchronization Methods," discusses seqlocks.

To update xtime, a write seqlock is required:

```
write_seqlock(&xtime_lock);

/* update xtime ... */

write_sequnlock(&xtime_lock);
```

Reading xtime requires use of the read_seqbegin() and read_seqretry() functions:

```
do {
        unsigned long lost;
        seq = read_seqbegin(&xtime_lock);

        usec = timer->get_offset();
        lost = jiffies - wall_jiffies;
        if (lost)
                usec += lost * (1000000 / HZ);
        sec = xtime.tv_sec;
        usec += (xtime.tv_nsec / 1000);
} while (read_seqretry(&xtime_lock, seq));
```

This loop repeats until the reader is assured it read the data without an intervening write. If the timer interrupt occurred and updated `xtime` during the loop, the returned sequence number is invalid and the loop repeats.

The primary user-space interface for retrieving the wall time is `gettimeofday()`, which is implemented as `sys_gettimeofday()`:

```
asmlinkage long sys_gettimeofday(struct timeval *tv, struct timezone *tz)
{
        if (likely(tv != NULL)) {
                struct timeval ktv;
                do_gettimeofday(&ktv);
                if (copy_to_user(tv, &ktv, sizeof(ktv)))
                        return -EFAULT;
        }
        if (unlikely(tz != NULL)) {
                if (copy_to_user(tz, &sys_tz, sizeof(sys_tz)))
                        return -EFAULT;
        }
        return 0;
}
```

If the user provided a non-`NULL` `tv` value, the architecture-dependent `do_gettimeofday()` is called. This function primarily performs the `xtime` read loop previously discussed. Likewise, if `tz` is non-`NULL`, the system time zone (stored in `sys_tz`) is returned to the user. If there were errors copying the wall time or time zone back to user-space, the function returns `-EFAULT`. Otherwise, it returns zero for success.

The kernel also implements the `time()`[6] system call, but `gettimeofday()` largely supersedes it. The C library also provides other wall time-related library calls, such as `ftime()` and `ctime()`.

The `settimeofday()` system call sets the wall time to the specified value. It requires the `CAP_SYS_TIME` capability.

Other than updating `xtime`, the kernel does not make nearly as frequent use of the current wall time as user-space. One notable exception is in the filesystem code, which stores access timestamps in inodes.

Timers

Timers—sometimes called *dynamic timers* or *kernel timers*—are essential for managing the flow of time in kernel code. Kernel code often needs to delay execution of some function until a later time. In previous chapters, we looked at using the bottom half mechanisms, which are great for deferring work until later. Unfortunately, the definition of *later* is intentionally quite vague. The purpose of bottom halves is not so much to *delay work*,

---

[6]Some architectures, however, do not implement `sys_time()` and instead specify that it is emulated in the C library using `gettimeofday()`.

but simply to *not do the work now.* What we need is a tool for delaying work a specified amount of time—certainly no less, and with hope, not much longer. The solution is kernel timers.

A timer is very easy to use. You perform some initial setup, specify an expiration time, specify a function to execute upon said expiration, and activate the timer. The given function will run after the timer expires. Timers are *not* cyclic. The timer is destroyed once it expires. This is one reason for the *dynamic* nomenclature[7]; timers are constantly created and destroyed, and there is no limit on the number of timers. Timers are very popular throughout the entire kernel.

Using Timers

Timers are represented by `struct timer_list`, which is defined in `<linux/timer.h>`:

```
struct timer_list {
        struct list_head entry;          /* timers are part of linked list */
        unsigned long expires;           /* expiration value, in jiffies */
        spinlock_t lock;                 /* lock protecting this timer */
        void (*function)(unsigned long); /* the timer handler function */
        unsigned long data;              /* lone argument to the handler */
        struct tvec_t_base_s *base;      /* internal timer field, don't touch */
};
```

Fortunately, the usage of timers requires little understanding of this data structure. In fact, toying with it is discouraged to keep code forward compatible with changes. The kernel provides a family of timer-related interfaces to make timer management easy. Everything is declared in `<linux/timer.h>`. Most of the actual implementation is in `kernel/timer.c`.

The first step in creating a timer is defining it:

```
struct timer_list my_timer;
```

Next, the timer's internal values must be initialized. This is done via a helper function and must be done prior to calling *any* timer management functions on the timer:

```
init_timer(&my_timer);
```

Now, you fill out the remaining values as required:

```
my_timer.expires = jiffies + delay;   /* timer expires in delay ticks */
my_timer.data = 0;                     /* zero is passed to the timer handler */
my_timer.function = my_function;       /* function to run when timer expires */
```

---

[7]Another reason is because of the existence of *static timers* in older (pre-2.3) kernels. They were created at compile-time, not runtime. They were lame, so no one shed tears over their demise.

The `my_timer.expires` value specifies the timeout value, in absolute ticks. When the current `jiffies` count is equal to or greater than `my_timer.expires`, the handler function `my_timer.function` is run with the lone argument of `my_timer.data`. As we see from the `timer_list` definition, the function must match this prototype:

```
void my_timer_function(unsigned long data);
```

The `data` parameter enables you to register multiple timers with the same handler, and differentiate between them via the argument. If you do not need the argument, you can simply pass zero (or any other value).

Finally, you activate the timer:

```
add_timer(&my_timer);
```

And, voila, the timer is off and running! Note the significance of the `expired` value. The kernel runs the timer handler when the current tick count is *equal to or greater* than the specified expiration. Although the kernel guarantees to run no timer handler *prior* to the timer's expiration, there may be a delay in running the timer. Typically, timers are run fairly close to their expiration; however, they might be delayed until the next timer tick. Consequently, timers cannot be used to implement any sort of hard real-time processing.

Sometimes you might need to modify the expiration of an already active timer. The kernel implements a function, `mod_timer()`, which changes the expiration of a given timer:

```
mod_timer(&my_timer, jiffies + new_delay);
```

The `mod_timer()` function can operate on timers that are initialized but not active, too. If the timer is inactive, `mod_timer()` will activate it. The function returns zero if the timer was inactive and one if the timer was active. In either case, upon return from `mod_timer()`, the timer is activated and set to the new expiration.

If you need to deactivate a timer prior to its expiration, use the `del_timer()` function:

```
del_timer(&my_timer);
```

The function works both on active and inactive timers. If the timer is already inactive, the function returns zero; otherwise, the function returns one. Note you do *not* need to call this for timers that have expired because they are automatically deactivated.

A potential race condition that must be guarded against exists when deleting timers. When `del_timer()` returns, it guarantees only that the timer is no longer active (that is, that it will not be executed in the future). On a multiprocessing machine, however, the timer handler might be executing on another processor. To deactivate the timer and wait until a potentially executing handler for the timer exits, use `del_timer_sync()`:

```
del_timer_sync(&my_timer);
```

Unlike `del_timer()`, `del_timer_sync()` cannot be used from interrupt context.

Timer Race Conditions

Because timers run asynchronously with respect to the currently executing code, several potential race conditions exist. First, never do the following as a substitute for a mere `mod_timer()`, because this is unsafe on multiprocessing machines:

```
del_timer(my_timer)
my_timer->expires = jiffies + new_delay;
add_timer(my_timer);
```

Second, in almost all cases, you should use `del_timer_sync()` over `del_timer()`. Otherwise, you cannot assume the timer is not currently running, and that is why you made the call in the first place! Imagine if, after deleting the timer, the code goes on to free or otherwise manipulate resources used by the timer handler. Therefore, the synchronous version is preferred.

Finally, you must make sure to protect any shared data used in the timer handler function. The kernel runs the function asynchronously with respect to other code. Shared data should be protected as discussed in Chapter 8.

The Timer Implementation

The kernel executes timers in bottom half context, as a softirq, after the timer interrupt completes. The timer interrupt handler runs `update_process_times()` which calls `run_local_timers()`:

```
void run_local_timers(void)
{
        raise_softirq(TIMER_SOFTIRQ);
}
```

The `TIMER_SOFTIRQ` softirq is handled by `run_timer_softirq()`. This function runs all the expired timers (if any) on the current processor.

Timers are stored in a linked list. However, it would be unwieldy for the kernel to either constantly traverse the entire list looking for expired timers, or keep the list sorted by expiration value, as the insertion and deletion of timers would then become very expensive. Instead, the kernel partitions timers into five groups based on their expiration value. Timers move down through the groups as their expiration time draws closer. The partitioning ensures that, in most executions of the timer softirq, the kernel has to do little work to find the expired timers. Consequently, the timer management code is very efficient.

Delaying Execution

Often, kernel code (especially drivers) needs a way to delay execution for some time without using timers or a bottom half mechanism. This is usually to allow hardware time to complete a given task. The time is typically quite short. For example, the specifications for a network card might list the time to change Ethernet modes as two microseconds.

After setting the desired speed, the driver should wait at least the two microseconds before continuing.

The kernel provides a number of solutions, depending on the semantics of the delay. The solutions have different characteristics. Some hog the processor while delaying, effectively preventing the accomplishment of any real work. Other solutions do not hog the processor, but offer no guarantee that your code will resume in exactly the required time[8].

Busy Looping

The simplest solution to implement (although rarely the optimal solution) is *busy waiting* or *busy looping*. This technique only works when the time you want to delay is some integer multiple of the tick rate or precision is not very important.

The idea is simple: Spin in a loop until the desired number of clock ticks pass. For example,

```
unsigned long delay = jiffies + 10;                    /* ten ticks */

while (time_before(jiffies, delay))
        ;
```

The loop will continue until `jiffies` is larger than `delay`, which will occur only after 10 clock ticks have passed. On x86 with `HZ` equal to 1000, this is 10 milliseconds. Similarly,

```
unsigned long delay = jiffies + 2*HZ;                    /* two seconds */

while (time_before(jiffies, delay))
        ;
```

This will spin until `2*HZ` clock ticks has passed, which is always two seconds regardless of the clock rate.

This approach is not nice to the rest of the system. While your code waits, the processor is tied up spinning in a silly loop—no useful work is accomplished! In fact, you rarely want to take this brain-dead approach, and it is shown here because it is a clear and simple method for delaying execution. You might also encounter it in someone else's not-so-pretty code.

A better solution would reschedule the processor to accomplish other work while your code waits:

```
unsigned long delay = jiffies + 5*HZ;
```

---

[8]Actually, no approach guarantees that the delay will be *exactly* for the time requested. Some come extremely close, however - and they all promise to wait *at least* as long as needed. Some just wait longer.

```
while (time_before(jiffies, delay))
        cond_resched();
```

The call to `cond_resched()` schedules a new process, but only if `need_resched` is set. In other words, this solution conditionally invokes the scheduler only if there is some more important task to run. Note that because this approach invokes the scheduler, you cannot make use of it from an interrupt handler—only process context. In fact, all these approaches are best used from process context, because interrupt handlers should execute as quickly as possible (and busy looping does not help accomplish that goal!). Furthermore, delaying execution in any manner, if at all possible, should not occur while a lock is held or interrupts are disabled.

C aficionados might wonder what guarantee is given that the previous loops even work. The C compiler is usually free to perform a given load only once. Normally, no assurance is given that the `jiffies` variable in the loop conditional is even reloaded on each iteration. We require, however, that `jiffies` be reread on each iteration as the value is incremented behind our back, in the timer interrupt. Indeed, this is why the variable is marked `volatile` in `<linux/jiffies.h>`. The `volatile` keyword instructs the compiler to reload the variable on each access from main memory and never alias the variables value in a register, guaranteeing that the previous loop completes as expected.

Small Delays

Sometimes, kernel code (again, usually drivers) requires very short (smaller than a clock tick) and rather precise delays. This is often to synchronize with hardware, which again usually lists some minimum time for an activity to complete—often less than a millisecond. It would be impossible to use `jiffies`-based delays, like the previous examples, for such a short wait. With a timer interrupt of 100 Hz, the clock tick is a rather large 10 milliseconds! Even with a 1000 Hz timer interrupt, the clock tick is still one millisecond. We clearly need another solution for smaller, more precise delays.

Thankfully, the kernel provides two functions for microsecond and millisecond delays, both defined in `<linux/delay.h>`, which do not use `jiffies`:

```
void udelay(unsigned long usecs);
void mdelay(unsigned long msecs);
```

The former function delays execution by busy looping for the specified number of *microseconds*. The later function delays execution for the specified number of *milliseconds*. Recall one second equals 1000 milliseconds, which equals 1000000 microseconds. Usage is trivial,

```
udelay(150);        /* delay for 150 µs */
```

The `udelay()` function is implemented as a loop which knows how many iterations can be executed in a given period of time. The `mdelay()` function is then implemented in terms of `udelay()`. Because the kernel knows how many loops the processor can complete in a second (see the sidebar on BogoMIPS), the `udelay()` function simply scales that value to the correct number of loop iterations for the given delay.

> **My BogoMIPS are Bigger than Yours!**
>
> The BogoMIPS value has always been a source of confusion and humor. In reality, the BogoMIPS calculation has very little to do with the performance of your computer and is primarily used only for the `udelay()` and `mdelay()` functions. Its name is a contraction of *bogus* (that is, fake) and *MIPS* (million of instructions per second). Everyone is familiar with a boot message similar to the following (this is on a 1GHz Pentium 3):
>
> ```
> Detected 1004.932 MHz processor.
> Calibrating delay loop... 1990.65 BogoMIPS
> ```
>
> The BogoMIPS value is the number of busy loop iterations the processor can perform in a given period. In effect, BogoMIPS are a measurement of how fast a processor can do nothing! This value is stored in the `loops_per_jiffy` variable and is readable from `/proc/cpuinfo`. The delay loop functions use the `loops_per_jiffy` value to figure out (fairly precisely) how many busy loop iterations they need to execute to provide the requisite delay.
>
> The kernel computes `loops_per_jiffy` on boot via `calibrate_delay()` in init/main.c.

The `udelay()` function should only be called for small delays because larger delays on fast machines might result in overflow. As a general rule, try to not use `udelay()` for delays of over one millisecond in duration. For such longer durations, `mdelay()` works fine. Like the other busy waiting solutions to delaying execution, neither of these functions (especially `mdelay()`, because it is used for such long delays) should be used unless absolutely needed. Remember that it is rude to busy loop with locks held or interrupts disabled, because system response and performance will be adversely effected. If you require precise delays, however, these calls are your best bet. Typical uses of these busy waiting functions delay for a very small amount of time, usually in the microsecond range.

schedule_timeout()

A more optimal method of delaying execution is to use `schedule_timeout()`. This call will put your task to sleep until at least the specified time has elapsed. There is no guarantee that the sleep duration will be *exactly* the specified time—only that the duration is at least as long as specified. When the specified time has elapsed, the kernel wakes the task up and places it back on the runqueue. Usage is easy:

```
set_current_state(TASK_INTERRUPTIBLE);
schedule_timeout(s * HZ);
```

The lone parameter is the desired relative timeout, in jiffies. This example puts the task in interruptible sleep for s seconds. Because the task is marked `TASK_INTERRUPTIBLE`, it wakes up prematurely if it receives a signal. If the code does not want to process signals, you can use `TASK_UNINTERRUPTIBLE` instead. The task must be in one of these two states prior to calling `schedule_timeout()` or else the task will not go to sleep.

Note that because `schedule_timeout()` invokes the scheduler, code which calls it must be capable of sleeping. See Chapter 8 for a discussion of atomicity and sleeping. Briefly, you must be in process context and must not hold a lock.

The `schedule_timeout()` function is fairly straightforward. Indeed, it is a simple application of kernel timers, so let's take a look at it:

```
signed long schedule_timeout(signed long timeout)
{
        timer_t timer;
        unsigned long expire;

        switch (timeout)
        {
        case MAX_SCHEDULE_TIMEOUT:
                schedule();
                goto out;
        default:
                if (timeout < 0)
                {
                        printk(KERN_ERR "schedule_timeout: wrong timeout "
                            "value %lx from %p\n", timeout,
                            __builtin_return_address(0));
                        current->state = TASK_RUNNING;
                        goto out;
                }
        }

        expire = timeout + jiffies;

        init_timer(&timer);
        timer.expires = expire;
        timer.data = (unsigned long) current;
        timer.function = process_timeout;

        add_timer(&timer);
        schedule();
        del_timer_sync(&timer);

        timeout = expire - jiffies;

 out:
        return timeout < 0 ? 0 : timeout;
}
```

The function creates a timer, `timer`, and sets it to expire in `timeout` clock ticks in the future. It sets the timer to execute the `process_timeout()` function when the timer expires. It then enables the timer and calls `schedule()`. Because the task is supposedly marked TASK_INTERRUPTIBLE or TASK_UNINTERRUPTIBLE, the scheduler will *not* run the task, but pick a new one.

When the timer expires, it runs process_timeout():

```
void process_timeout(unsigned long data)
{
        wake_up_process((task_t *) data);
}
```

This function puts the task in the TASK_RUNNING state and places it back on the run-queue.

When the task reschedules, it returns to where it left off in schedule_timeout() (right after the call to schedule()). In case the task was woken up prematurely (if a signal was received), the timer is destroyed. The function then returns the time slept.

The code in the switch() statement is for special cases and not part of the general usage of the function. The MAX_SCHEDULE_TIMEOUT check enables a task to sleep indefinitely. In that case, no timer is set (because there is no bound on the sleep duration) and the scheduler is immediately invoked. If you do this, you had better have another method of waking your task up!

Sleeping on a Wait Queue, with a Timeout

In Chapter 3 we looked at how process context code in the kernel can place itself on a wait queue to wait for a specific event, and then invoke the scheduler to select a new task. Elsewhere, when the event finally occurs, wake_up() is called and the tasks sleeping on the wait queue are woken up and can continue running.

Sometimes, it is desirable to wait for a specific event *or* wait for a specified time to elapse—whichever comes first. In those cases, code might simply call schedule_timeout() instead of schedule() after placing itself on a wait queue. The task wakes up when the desired event occurs or the specified time elapses. The code needs to check *why* it woke up—it might be because of the event occurring, the time elapsing, or a received signal—and continue as appropriate.

10

Memory Management

MEMORY ALLOCATION *INSIDE* THE KERNEL is not as easy as memory allocation *outside* the kernel. A lot of factors contribute to this. Primarily, the kernel simply lacks the luxuries enjoyed by user-space. Unlike user-space, the kernel is not always afforded the capability to easily allocate memory. For example, often the kernel cannot sleep. Furthermore, the kernel cannot easily deal with memory errors. Because of these limitations, and the need for a lightweight memory allocation scheme, getting hold of memory in the kernel is more complicated than in user-space. This is not to say that kernel memory allocations are difficult, however, as we'll see.

This chapter discusses the methods used to obtain memory inside the kernel. Before we can delve into the actual allocation interfaces, we need to look at how the kernel handles memory.

Pages

The kernel treats physical pages as the basic unit of memory management. Although the processor's smallest addressable unit is usually a word, the memory management unit (MMU, the hardware that manages memory and performs virtual to physical address translations) typically deals in pages. Because of this, the MMU manages the system's page tables with page-sized granularity (hence their name). In terms of virtual memory, pages are the smallest unit that matters.

As we'll see in Chapter 16, "Portability," each architecture supports its own page size. Many architectures even support multiple page sizes. Most 32-bit architectures have 4KB pages, whereas most 64-bit architectures have 8KB pages. This implies that on a machine with 4KB pages and 1GB of physical memory, physical memory is divided up into 262,144 distinct pages.

The kernel represents *every* physical page on the system with a `struct page` structure. This structure is defined in `<linux/mm.h>`:

```
struct page {
        unsigned long        flags;
```

```
        atomic_t                count;
        struct list_head        list;
        struct address_space    *mapping;
        unsigned long           index;
        struct list_head        lru;
        union {
                struct pte_chain    *chain;
                pte_addr_t          direct;
        } pte;
        unsigned long           private;
        void                    *virtual;
};
```

Let's look at the important fields. The `flags` field stores the status of the page. Such flags include whether the page is dirty or whether it is locked in memory. Bit flags represent the various values, so at least 32 different flags are simultaneously available. The flag values are defined in `<linux/page-flags.h>`.

The `count` field stores the usage count of the page—that is, how many references there are to this page. When this count reaches zero, no one is using the page, and it becomes available for use in a new allocation.

The `mapping` field points to the `address_space` object that is associated with this page.

The `virtual` field is the page's virtual address. Normally, this is simply the address of the page in virtual memory. Some memory (called high memory) is not permanently mapped into the kernel's address space. In that case, this field is `NULL` and the page must be dynamically mapped when needed. We'll discuss high memory shortly.

The important point to understand is that the `page` structure is associated with physical pages, not virtual pages. Therefore, what the structure describes is transient at best. Even if the data contained in the page continues to exist, it might not always be associated with the same `page` structure because of swapping and so on. The kernel uses this data structure to describe whatever is stored in the associated physical page at that moment. The data structure's goal is to describe physical memory, not the data contained therein.

The kernel uses this structure to keep track of all the pages in the system, because the kernel needs to know whether a page is free (that is, if the page is not allocated). If a page is not free, the kernel needs to know who owns the page. Possible owners include user-space processes, dynamically allocated kernel data, static kernel code, the page cache, and so on.

Developers are often surprised that an instance of this structure is allocated for each physical page in the system. They think, "*What a lot of memory used!*" Let's look at just how bad (or good) the space consumption is from all these pages. Assume `struct page` consumes 40 bytes of memory, the system has 4KB physical pages, and the system has

128MB of physical memory. Then, all the `page` structures in the system consume slightly more than 1MB of memory—not too high a cost for managing all the physical pages.

Zones

Because of hardware limitations, the kernel cannot treat all pages as identical. Some pages, because of their physical address in memory, cannot be used for certain tasks. Because of this limitation, the kernel divides pages into different *zones*. The kernel uses the zones to group pages of similar properties. In particular, Linux has to deal with two shortcomings of hardware with respect to memory addressing:

- Some hardware devices are capable of performing DMA (direct memory access) only to certain memory addresses.

- Some architectures are capable of physically addressing larger amounts of memory than they can virtually address. Consequently, some memory is not permanently mapped into the kernel address space.

Because of these constraints, there are three memory zones in Linux:

- `ZONE_DMA`
  This zone contains pages that are capable of undergoing DMA.

- `ZONE_NORMAL`
  This zone contains normal, regularly mapped, pages.

- `ZONE_HIGHMEM`
  This zone contains "high memory," which are pages not permanently mapped into the kernel's address space.

The actual use and layout of the memory zones is architecture independent. For example, some architectures have no problem performing DMA into any memory address. In those architectures, `ZONE_DMA` is empty and `ZONE_NORMAL` is used for allocations regardless of their use. As a counterexample, on the x86 architecture, ISA devices[1] cannot perform DMA into the full 32-bit address space, because ISA devices can only access the first 16MB of physical memory. Consequently, `ZONE_DMA` on x86 consists of all memory in the range 0–16MB.

`ZONE_HIGHMEM` works in the same regard. What an architecture can and cannot directly map varies. On x86, `ZONE_HIGHMEM` is all memory above the physical 896MB mark. On other architectures, `ZONE_HIGHMEM` is empty as all memory is directly mapped. The memory contained in `ZONE_HIGHMEM` is called *high memory*[2]. The rest of the system's memory is called *low memory*.

---

[1] Some broken PCI devices can only perform DMA into a 24-bit address space. But they are broken.
[2] This has nothing to do with high memory in DOS.

ZONE_NORMAL tends to be whatever is left over after the previous two zones claim their requisite share. On x86, for example, ZONE_NORMAL is all physical memory from 16MB to 896MB. On other (more fortunate) architectures, ZONE_NORMAL is all available memory. *Table 10.1* is a listing of each zone and its consumed pages on x86.

Table 10.1   **Zones on x86**

Zone	Description	Physical Memory
ZONE_DMA	DMA-able pages	< 16MB
ZONE_NORMAL	Normally addressable pages	16–896MB
ZONE_HIGHMEM	Dynamically mapped pages	> 896MB

Linux partitions the system's pages into zones to have a pooling in place to satisfy allocations as needed. For example, having a ZONE_DMA pool gives the kernel the capability to satisfy memory allocations needed for DMA. If such memory is needed, the kernel can simply pull the required number of pages from ZONE_DMA. Note that the zones do not have any physical relevance; they are simply logical groupings used by the kernel to keep track of pages.

Although some allocations may require pages from a particular zone, the zones are not hard requirements in both directions. While an allocation for DMA-able memory must originate from ZONE_DMA, a normal allocation can come from ZONE_DMA or ZONE_NORMAL. The kernel will prefer to satisfy normal allocations from the normal zone, of course, to save the pages in ZONE_DMA for allocations that need it. But if push comes to shove (if memory should get low), the kernel can dip its fingers in whatever zone is available and suitable.

Each zone is represented by struct zone, which is defined in <linux/mmzone.h>:

```
struct zone {
        spinlock_t              lock;
        unsigned long           free_pages;
        unsigned long           pages_min;
        unsigned long           pages_low;
        unsigned long           pages_high;
        spinlock_t              lru_lock;
        struct list_head        active_list;
        struct list_head        inactive_list;
        atomic_t                refill_counter;
        unsigned long           nr_active;
        unsigned long           nr_inactive;
        int                     all_unreclaimable;
        unsigned long           pages_scanned;
        struct free_area        free_area[MAX_ORDER];
        wait_queue_head_t       *wait_table;
        unsigned long           wait_table_size;
```

```
        unsigned long           wait_table_bits;
        struct per_cpu_pageset  pageset[NR_CPUS];
        struct pglist_data      *zone_pgdat;
        struct page             *zone_mem_map;
        unsigned long           zone_start_pfn;
        char                    *name;
        unsigned long           spanned_pages;
        unsigned long           present_pages;
};
```

The structure is big, but there are only three zones in the system and, thus, only three of these structures. Let's look at the more important fields.

The `lock` field is a spin lock that protects the structure from concurrent access. Note that it protects just the structure, and not all the pages that reside in the zone. A specific lock does not protect individual pages, although parts of the kernel may lock the data that happens to reside in said pages.

The `free_pages` field is the number of free pages in this zone. The kernel tries to keep at least `pages_min` pages free (through swapping, if needed), if possible.

The `name` field is, unsurprisingly, a NULL-terminated string representing the name of this zone. The kernel initializes this value during boot in `mm/page_alloc.c` and the three zones are given the names "DMA," "Normal," and "HighMem."

Getting Pages

Now with an understanding of how the kernel manages memory—via pages, zones, and so on—let's look at the interfaces the kernel implements to allow you to allocate and free memory within the kernel.

The kernel provides one low-level mechanism for requesting memory, along with several interfaces to access it. All these interfaces allocate memory with page-sized granularity and are declared in `<linux/gfp.h>`. The core function is

```
struct page * alloc_pages(unsigned int gfp_mask, unsigned int order)
```

This allocates 2^{order} (that is, `1 << order`) contiguous physical pages and returns a pointer to the first page's `page` structure; on error it returns NULL. We will look at the `gfp_mask` parameter in a later section. You can convert a given page to its logical address with the function

```
void * page_address(struct page *page)
```

This returns a pointer to the logical address where the given physical page currently resides. If you have no need for the actual `struct page`, you can call

```
unsigned long __get_free_pages(unsigned int gfp_mask, unsigned int order)
```

This function works the same as `alloc_pages()`, except that it directly returns the logical address of the first requested page. Because the pages are contiguous, the other pages simply follow from the first.

If you only need one page, two functions are implemented as wrappers to save you a bit of typing:

```
struct page * alloc_page(unsigned int gfp_mask)

unsigned long __get_free_page(unsigned int gfp_mask)
```

These functions work the same as their brethren but pass zero for the order (2^0 = one page).

Getting Zeroed Pages

If you need the returned page filled with zeros, use the function

```
unsigned long get_zeroed_page(unsigned int gfp_mask)
```

This function works the same as __get_free_page(), except that the allocated page is then filled with zeros. This is useful for pages given to user-space, as the random garbage in an allocated page is not so random—it might "randomly" contain sensitive data. All data must be zeroed or otherwise cleaned before returning to user-space, to ensure system security is not compromised. *Table 10.2* is a listing of all the low-level page allocation methods.

Table 10.2   **Low-Level Page Allocations Methods**

Flag	Description
alloc_page(gfp_mask)	Allocate a single page and return a pointer to its page structure
alloc_pages(gfp_mask, order)	Allocate 2^{order} pages and return a pointer to the first page's page structure
get_free_page(gfp_mask)	Allocate a single page and return a pointer to its logical address
__get_free_pages(gfp_mask, order)	Allocate 2^{order} pages and return a pointer to the first page's logical address
get_zeroed_page(gfp_mask)	Allocate a single page, zero its contents, and return a pointer to its logical address

Freeing pages

To free allocated pages when you no longer need them:

```
void __free_pages(struct page *page, unsigned int order)
void free_pages(unsigned long addr, unsigned int order)
void free_page(unsigned long addr)
```

You must be careful to only free pages you allocate. Passing the wrong struct page or address, or the incorrect order, can result in corruption. Remember, the kernel trusts itself. Unlike user-space, the kernel happily hangs itself if you ask it.

Let's look at an example. Here, we want to allocate 8 pages:

```
unsigned long page;

page = __get_free_pages(GFP_KERNEL, 3);
if (!page)
        /* insufficient memory: you must handle this error! */

/* 'page' is now the address of the first of eight contiguous pages ... */

free_pages(page, 3);

/*
 * our pages are now freed and we should no
 * longer access the address stored in 'page'
 */
```

The GFP_KERNEL parameter is an example gfp_mask flag. We will look at it shortly.

Make note of the error checking after the call to __get_free_pages(). A kernel allocation *can* fail and your code *must* check for and handle such errors. This might mean unwinding everything you have done thus far. Because of this, it often makes sense to allocate your memory at the start of the routine, to make handling the error easier. Otherwise, by the time you attempt to allocate memory, it may be rather hard to bail out.

These low-level page functions are useful when you need page-sized chunks of physically contiguous pages, especially if you need exactly a single page or a large number of pages. For more general byte-sized allocations, the kernel provides kmalloc().

kmalloc()

The kmalloc() function works very similar to user-space's familiar malloc() routine, with the exception of the addition of a *flags* parameter. The kmalloc() function is a simple interface for obtaining kernel memory in byte-sized chunks. If you need whole pages—especially if you need an amount close to a power of two—the previously discussed interfaces might be a better choice. For most kernel allocations, however, kmalloc() is the preferred interface.

The function is declared in <linux/slab.h>:

```
void * kmalloc(size_t size, int flags)
```

The function returns a pointer to a region of memory that is at *least* size bytes in length[3]. The region of memory allocated is physically contiguous. On error, it returns

---

[3]It may allocate more than you asked, although you have no way of knowing how much more! Because at its heart the kernel allocator is page-based, some allocations may be rounded up to fit within the available memory. The kernel will never return *less* memory than requested. If the kernel is unable to find at least the requested amount, the allocation will fail and the function will return NULL.

NULL. Kernel allocations always succeed, unless there is an insufficient amount of memory available. Thus, you must check for NULL after all calls to kmalloc() and handle the error appropriately.

Let's look at an example. Assume we need to dynamically allocate enough room for a fictional dog structure:

```
struct dog *ptr;
```

```
ptr = kmalloc(sizeof(struct dog), GFP_KERNEL);
if (!ptr)
        /* handle error ... */
```

If the kmalloc() call succeeds, ptr now points to a block of memory that is at least the requested size. The GFP_KERNEL flag specifies the behavior of the memory allocator while trying to obtain the memory to return to the caller of kmalloc().

gfp_mask **Flags**

We have looked at various examples of allocator flags in both the low-level page allocation functions and kmalloc(). Now, let's discuss these flags in depth.

The flags are broken up into three categories: action modifiers, zone modifiers, and types. Action modifiers specify *how* the kernel is supposed to allocate the requested memory. In certain situations, only certain methods can be employed to allocate memory. For example, interrupt handlers must instruct the kernel not to sleep (because interrupt handlers cannot reschedule) in the course of allocating memory. Zone modifiers specify from *where* to allocate memory. As we saw, the kernel divides physical memory into multiple zones, each of which serves a different purpose. Zone modifiers specify which of these zones to allocate from. Type flags specify a combination of action and zone modifiers as needed by a certain *type* of memory allocation. Type flags simplify specifying numerous modifiers; instead, you generally specify just one type flag. The GFP_KERNEL is a type flag, which is used for code in process context inside the kernel. Let's look at the flags.

Action Modifiers

All the flags, the action modifiers included, are declared in <linux/gfp.h>. Including <linux/slab.h> includes this header, however, so you often need not include it directly. In reality, you will usually use only the type modifiers, which we will look at later. Nonetheless, it is good to have an understanding of these individual flags. *Table 10.3* is a list of the action modifiers.

Table 10.3   **Action Modifiers**

Flag	Description
__GFP_WAIT	The allocator can sleep.
__GFP_HIGH	The allocator can access emergency pools.

Table 10.3 **Continued**

Flag	Description
__GFP_IO	The allocator can start disk I/O.
__GFP_FS	The allocator can start filesystem I/O.
__GFP_COLD	The allocator should use cache cold pages.
__GFP_NOWARN	The allocator will not print failure warnings.
__GFP_REPEAT	The allocator will repeat the allocation if it fails.
__GFP_NOFAIL	The allocator will indefinitely repeat the allocation.
__GFP_NORETRY	The allocator will never retry if the allocation fails.
__GFP_NO_GROW	Used internally by the slab layer.

These allocations can be specified together. For example,

```
ptr = kmalloc(size, __GFP_WAIT | __GFP_IO | __GFP_FS);
```

instructs the page allocator (ultimately alloc_pages()) that the allocation can block, perform I/O, and perform filesystem operations, if needed. This allows the kernel great freedom in how it can find the free memory to satisfy the allocation.

Most allocations specify these modifiers, but do so indirectly, by way of the type flags we will discuss shortly. Do not worry, you will not have to figure out which of these weird flags to use every time you allocate memory!

Zone Modifiers

Zone modifiers specify from which memory zone the allocation should originate. Normally, allocations can be fulfilled from any zone. The kernel prefers ZONE_NORMAL, however, to ensure that the other zones have free pages when they are needed.

There are only two zone modifiers because there are only two zones other than ZONE_NORMAL (which is where, by default, allocations orginate). *Table 10.4* is a listing of the zone modifiers.

Table 10.4 **Zone Modifiers**

Flag	Description
__GFP_DMA	Allocate only from ZONE_DMA
__GFP_HIGHMEM	Allocate from ZONE_HIGHMEM or ZONE_NORMAL

Specifying one of these two flags modifies the zone from which the kernel attempts to satisfy the allocation. The __GFP_DMA flag forces the kernel to satisfy the request from ZONE_DMA. Conversely, with the __GFP_HIGHMEM flag, the allocation is satisfied from either ZOME_NORMAL or (preferentially) ZONE_HIGHMEM. If neither flag is specified, the kernel fulfills the allocation from either ZONE_DMA or ZONE_NORMAL, with a strong preference to satisfy the allocation from ZONE_NORMAL.

You cannot specify __GFP_HIGHMEM to either __get_free_pages() or kmalloc(). Because both of these return a logical address, and not a page structure, it is possible that these functions would allocate memory that is not currently mapped in the kernel's virtual address space and, thus, does not have a logical address. Only `alloc_pages()` can allocate high memory. The majority of your allocations, however, will not specify a zone modifier, as `ZONE_NORMAL` is sufficient.

Type Flags

The type flags specify the required action and zone modifiers to fulfill a particular type of transaction. Because of this, kernel code tends to use the correct type flag and not specify the myriad of other flags it might need. This is both simpler and less error prone. *Table 10.5* is a list of the type flags and *Table 10.6* shows which modifiers are associated with each type flag.

Table 10.5 **Type Flags**

Flag	Description
GFP_ATOMIC	The allocation is high-priority and must not sleep. This is the flag to use in interrupt handlers, bottom halves, and other situations where you cannot sleep.
GFP_NOIO	This allocation might block, but will not initiate disk I/O. This is the flag to use in block I/O code when you cannot cause more disk I/O.
GFP_NOFS	This allocation might block and might initiate disk I/O, but will not initiate a filesystem operation. This is the flag to use in filesystem code when you cannot start another filesystem operation.
GFP_KERNEL	This is a normal allocation and might block. This is the flag to use in process context code when it is safe to sleep.
GFP_USER	This is a normal allocation and might block. This flag is used to allocate memory for user-space processes.
GFP_HIGHUSER	This is an allocation from `ZOME_HIGHMEM` and might block. This flag is used to allocate memory for user-space processes.
GFP_DMA	This is an allocation from `ZONE_DMA`. Device drivers that need DMA-able memory use this flag, usually in combination with one of the above.

Table 10.6 **Listing of the Modifiers Behind Each Type Flag**

Flag	Modifier Flags
GFP_ATOMIC	__GFP_HIGH
GFP_NOIO	__GFP_WAIT
GFP_NOFS	(__GFP_WAIT | __GFP_IO)
GFP_KERNEL	(__GFP_WAIT | __GFP_IO | __GFP_FS)
GFP_USER	(__GFP_WAIT | __GFP_IO | __GFP_FS)
GFP_HIGHUSER	(__GFP_WAIT | __GFP_IO | __GFP_FS | __GFP_HIGHMEM)
GFP_DMA	__GFP_DMA

Let's look at the frequently used flags and when and why you might need them. The vast majority of allocations in the kernel use the GFP_KERNEL flag. The resulting allocation is a normal priority allocation that might sleep. Because the call can block, this flag can only be used from process context that can safely reschedule (that is, no locks are held and so on). As this flag does not make any stipulations to how the kernel may obtain the requested memory, the memory allocation has a high probability of succeeding.

On the far other end of the spectrum is the GFP_ATOMIC flag. Because this flag specifies a memory allocation that cannot sleep, the allocation is very restrictive in the memory it can obtain for the caller. If no sufficiently sized contiguous chunk of memory is available, the kernel will not be very likely to free memory because it cannot put the caller to sleep. Conversely, the GFP_KERNEL allocation can put the caller to sleep to swap pages to disk, flush dirty pages to disk, and so on. Because GFP_ATOMIC is unable to perform any of these actions, it has less of a chance of succeeding (at least when memory is low) compared to GFP_KERNEL allocations. Nonetheless, the GFP_ATOMIC flag is the only option when the current code is unable to sleep, such as with interrupt handlers and bottom halves.

In between these two flags are GFP_NOIO and GFP_NOFS. Allocations initiated with these flags might block, but they refrain from performing certain other operations. A GFP_NOIO allocation will not initiate any disk I/O whatsoever to fulfill the request. On the other hand, GFP_NOFS might initiate disk I/O, but will not initiate filesystem I/O. Why might you need these flags? They are needed for certain low-level block I/O or filesystem code, respectively. Imagine if a common path in the filesystem code allocated memory *without* the GFP_NOFS flag. If the allocation resulted in *more* filesystem operations, the allocations might cause more filesystem operations, which would then result in another allocation and, thus, more filesystem operations! This could continue indefinitely. Code such as this that invokes the allocator must ensure that the allocator also does not execute it, or else the allocation can create a deadlock. Not surprisingly, the kernel uses these two flags only in a handful of places.

The GFP_DMA flag is used to specify that the allocator must satisfy the request from ZONE_DMA. This flag is used by device drivers, which need DMA-able memory for their devices. Normally, you combine this flag with the GTP_ATOMIC or GFP_KERNEL flag.

In the vast majority of the code that you write you will use either GFP_KERNEL or GFP_ATOMIC. *Table 10.7* is a list of the common situations and the flags to use. Regardless of the allocation type, you must check for and handle failures.

Table 10.7 **Which Flag to Use When**

Situation	**Solution**
Process context, can sleep	Use GFP_KERNEL
Process context, cannot sleep	Use GFP_ATOMIC, or perform your allocations with GFP_KRENEL at an earlier or later point when you can sleep
Interrupt handler	Use GFP_ATOMIC

Table 10.7   **Continued**

Situation	Solution
Bottom Half	Use GFP_ATOMIC
Need DMA-able memory, can sleep	Use (GFP_DMA | GFP_KERNEL)
Need DMA-able memory, cannot sleep	Use (GFP_DMA | GFP_ATOMIC), or perform your allocation at an earlier point when you can sleep

kfree()

The other end of kmalloc() is kfree(), which is declared in <linux/slab.h>:

```
void kfree(const void *ptr)
```

The kfree() method will free a block of memory previously allocated with kmalloc().
Calling this function on memory not previously allocated with kmalloc(), or on memory which has already been freed, will result in very bad things, such as freeing memory
belonging to another part of the kernel. Just like in user-space, be careful to balance your
allocations with your deallocations to prevent memory leaks and other bugs. Note, calling kfree(NULL) is explicitly checked for and safe.

Let's look at an example of allocating memory in an interrupt handler. In this example, an interrupt handler wants to allocate a buffer to hold incoming data. The preprocessor define BUF_SIZE is the size in bytes of this desired buffer, which is presumably larger
than just a couple bytes.

```
char *buf;

buf = kmalloc(BUF_SIZE, GFP_ATOMIC);
if (!buf)
        /* error allocting memory ! */
```

Later, when we no longer need the memory, do not forget to free it:

```
kfree(buf);
```

vmalloc()

The vmalloc() function works similar to kmalloc(), except it allocates memory that is
only virtually contiguous and not necessarily physically contiguous. This is also how a
user-space allocation function works: The pages returned by malloc() are contiguous
within the virtual address space of the processor, but there is no guarantee that they are
actually contiguous in physical RAM. The kmalloc() function guarantees that the pages
are physically contiguous (and virtually contiguous). The vmalloc() function only
ensures that the pages are contiguous within the virtual address space. It does this by
allocating potentially noncontiguous chunks of physical memory and "fixing up" the
page tables to map the memory into a contiguous chunk of the logical address space.

For the most part, only hardware devices require physically contiguous memory allocations. Hardware devices live on the other side of the memory management unit and, thus, do not understand virtual addresses. Consequently, any regions of memory that hardware devices work with must exist as a physically contiguous block and not merely a virtually contiguous one. Blocks of memory used only by software—for example, process-related buffers—are fine using memory that is only virtually contiguous. In your programming, you will never know the difference. All memory appears to the kernel as logically contiguous.

Despite the fact that physically contiguous memory is only required in certain cases, most kernel code uses `kmalloc()` and not `vmalloc()` to obtain memory. Primarily, this is for performance. The `vmalloc()` function, to make nonphysically contiguous pages contiguous in the virtual address space, must specifically set up the page table entries. Worse, pages obtained via `vmalloc()` must be mapped by their individual pages (because they are not physically contiguous), which results in much greater TLB[4] thrashing than when using directly mapped memory. Because of these concerns, `vmalloc()` is only used when absolutely necessary—typically, to obtain very large regions of memory. For example, when modules are dynamically inserted into the kernel, they are loaded into memory created via `vmalloc()`.

The `vmalloc()` function is declared in `<linux/vmalloc.h>` and defined in `mm/vmalloc.c`. Usage is identical to user-space's `malloc()`:

```
void * vmalloc(unsigned long size)
```

The function returns a pointer to at least `size` bytes of virtually contiguous memory. On error, the function returns `NULL`. The function might sleep, and thus cannot be called from interrupt context or other situations where blocking is not permissible.

To free an allocation obtained via `vmalloc()`, use

```
void vfree(void *addr)
```

This function frees the block of memory beginning at `addr` that was previously allocated via `vmalloc()`. The function can also sleep and, thus, cannot be called from interrupt context. It has no return value.

Usage of these functions is simple:

```
char *buf;

buf = vmalloc(16 * PAGE_SIZE); /* get 16 pages */
if (!buf)
        /* error! failed to allocate memory */
```

---

[4]The TLB (translation lookaside buffer) is a hardware buffer used by most architectures to cache the mapping of virtual addresses to physical addresses. This greatly improves the performance of the system, because most memory access is done via virtual addressing.

```
/*
 * buf now points to at least a 16*PAGE_SIZE bytes
 * of virtually contiguous block of memory
 */
```

After you are done with the memory, make sure to free it using

```
vfree(buf);
```

Slab Layer

Allocating and freeing data structures is one of the most common operations inside any kernel. To facilitate frequent allocations and deallocations of data, programmers often introduce *free lists*. A free list contains a block of available, already allocated, data structures. When code requires a new instance of a data structure, it can grab one of the structures off the free list instead of allocating a sufficient amount of memory and setting it up for the data structure. Later on, when the data structure is no longer needed, it is returned to the free list instead of deallocated. In this sense, the free list acts as an object cache, caching a frequently used *type* of object.

One of the main problems with free lists in the kernel is that there exists no global control. When available memory is low, there is no way for the kernel to communicate to every free list that it should shrink the sizes of its cache to free up memory. In fact, the kernel has no understanding of the random free lists at all. To remedy this, and to consolidate code, the Linux kernel provides the slab layer (also called the slab allocator). The slab layer acts as a generic data structure-caching layer.

The concept of a slab allocator was first implemented in Sun Microsystem's SunOS 5.4 operating system[5]. The Linux data structure-caching layer shares the same name and basic design.

The slab layer attempts to leverage several basic tenets:

- Frequently used data structures tend to be allocated and freed often, so cache them.

- Frequent allocation and deallocation can result in memory fragmentation (the inability to find large contiguous chunks of available memory). To prevent this, the cached free lists are arranged contiguously. Because freed data structures return to the free list, there is no resulting fragmentation.

- The free list provides improved performance during frequent allocation and deallocation, as a freed object can be immediately returned to the next allocation.

- If part of the cache is made per-processor (separate and unique to each processor on the system), allocations and frees can be performed without an SMP lock.

- Stored objects can be *colored* to prevent multiple objects from mapping to the same cache lines.

The slab layer in Linux was designed and implemented with these premises in mind.

---

[5]And subsequently documented in Bonwick, J. "The Slab Allocator: An Object-Caching Kernel Memory Allocator," USENIX, 1994.

Design of the Slab Layer

The slab layer divides different objects into groups called *caches*, each of which stores a different type of object. There is one cache per object type. For example, one cache is for process descriptors (a free list of `task_struct` structures), whereas another cache is for inode objects (`struct inode`). Interestingly, the `kmalloc()` interface is built on top of the slab layer using a family of general purpose caches.

The caches are then divided into *slabs* (hence the name of this subsystem). The slabs are composed of one or more physically contiguous pages. Typically, slabs are composed of only a single page. Each cache may consist of multiple slabs.

Each slab contains some number of *objects*, which are the data structures being cached. Each slab is in one of three states: full, partial, or empty. A full slab has no free objects (all objects in the slab are allocated). An empty slab has no allocated objects (all objects in the slab are free). A partial slab has some allocated objects and some free objects. When some part of the kernel requests a new object, the request is satisfied from a partial slab, if one exists. Otherwise, the request is satisfied from an empty slab. If there exists no empty slab, one is created. Obviously, a full slab can never satisfy a request because it does not have any free objects. This strategy reduces fragmentation.

Let's look at the `inode` structure as an example, which is the in-memory representation of a disk inode (see Chapter 11). These structures are frequently created and destroyed, so it makes sense to manage them via the slab allocator. Thus, `struct inode` is allocated from the `inode_cachep` cache (such a naming convention is standard). This cache is made up of one or more slabs—probably a lot of slabs because there are a lot of objects. Each slab contains as many `struct inode` objects as possible. When the kernel requests a new `inode` structure, the kernel returns a pointer to an already allocated, but unused structure from a partial slab or, if there is no partial slab, an empty slab. When the kernel is done using the `inode` object, the slab allocator marks the object as free. Figure 10.1 diagrams the relationship between caches, slabs, and objects.

Each cache is represented by a `kmem_cache_s` structure. This structure contains three lists, `slabs_full`, `slabs_partial`, and `slabs_empty`, stored inside a `kmem_list3` structure. These lists contain all the slabs associated with the cache. A slab descriptor, `struct slab`, represents each slab:

```
struct slab {
        struct list_head  list;       /* full, partial, or empty list */
        unsigned long     colouroff;  /* offset for the slab coloring */
        void              *s_mem;     /* first object in the slab */
        unsigned int      inuse;      /* number of allocated objects */
        kmem_bufctl_t     free;       /* first free object, if any */
};
```

Slab descriptors are allocated either outside of the slab in a general cache or inside the slab itself, at the beginning. The descriptor is stored inside the slab if the total size of the slab is sufficiently small, or if internal slack space is sufficient to hold the descriptor.

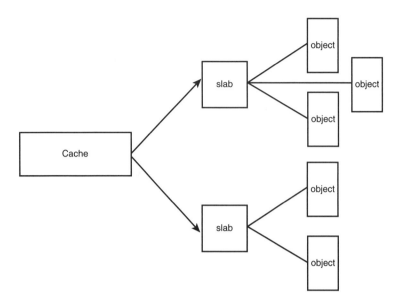

Figure 10.1   The relationship between caches, slabs, and objects.

The slab allocator creates new slabs by interfacing with the low-level kernel page allocator via __get_free_pages():

```
static inline void * kmem_getpages(kmem_cache_t *cachep, unsigned long flags)
{
        void *addr;

        flags |= cachep->gfpflags;
        addr = (void*) __get_free_pages(flags, cachep->gfporder);

        return addr;
}
```

The first parameter to this function points to the specific cache that needs more pages. The second parameter points to the flags given to __get_free_pages(). Note how this value is binary OR'ed against another value. This adds default flags that the cache requires to the flags parameter.

Memory is then freed using kmem_freepages(), which calls free_pages() on the given cache's pages. Of course, the point of the slab layer is to refrain from allocating and freeing pages. In turn, the slab layer only invokes the page allocation function when there does not exist any partial or empty slabs in a given cache. The freeing function is only called when available memory grows low and the system is attempting to free memory, or when a cache is explicitly destroyed.

The slab layer is managed on a per-cache basis through a simple interface, which is exported to the entire kernel. The interface allows the creation and destruction of new caches and the allocation and freeing of objects within the caches. The sophisticated management of caches and the slabs within is entirely handled by the internals of the slab layer. After you create a cache, the slab layer works just like a specialized allocator for the specific type of object.

Slab Allocator Interface

A new cache is created via

```
kmem_cache_t * kmem_cache_create(const char *name, size_t size,
                                size_t offset, unsigned long flags,
                                void (*ctor)(void*, kmem_cache_t *,
                                    unsigned long),
                                void (*dtor)(void*, kmem_cache_t *,
                                    unsigned long))
```

The first parameter is a string storing the name of the cache. The second parameter is the size of each element in the cache. The third parameter is the offset of the first object within a slab. This is done to ensure a particular alignment within the page. Normally, zero is sufficient, which results in the standard alignment. The `flags` parameter specifies optional settings controlling the behavior of the cache. It can be zero, specifying no special behavior, or one or more of the following flags OR'ed together:

`SLAB_NO_REAP`   This flag instructs the slab layer not to automatically reap objects (that is, free the memory backing unused objects) when memory is low. Normally, you do *not* want to set this flag as your cache could then prevent the system from recovering enough memory to continue operation when memory is low.

`SLAB_HWCACHE_ALIGN`   This flag instructs the slab layer to align each object within a slab to a cache line. This prevents "false sharing" (two or more objects mapping to the same cache line despite existing at different addresses in memory). This improves performance, but comes at a cost of increased memory footprint because the stricter alignment results in more wasted slack space. How large the increase in memory consumption is depends on the size of the objects and how they naturally align with respect to the system's cache lines. For frequently used caches in performance critical code, setting this option is a good idea; otherwise, think twice.

`SLAB_MUST_HWCACHE_ALIGN`   If debugging is enabled, it might be infeasible to both perform debugging and cache align the objects. This flag forces the slab layer to cache align the objects. Normally, this flag is not needed and the previous is sufficient. Specifying this flag while slab debugging is enabled (it is disabled by default) might result in a large increase in memory consumption. Only objects where cache alignment is critical, such as the process descriptor, should set this flag.

`SLAB_CACHE_DMA`   This flag instructs the slab layer to allocate each slab in DMA-able memory. This is needed if the allocated object is used for DMA and must reside in `ZONE_DMA`. Otherwise, you do not need this and you should not set it.

The final two parameters, `ctor` and `dtor` are a constructor and destructor for the cache, respectively. The constructor is called whenever new pages are added to the cache. The destructor is called whenever pages are removed from the cache. Having a destructor requires a constructor. In practice, caches in the Linux kernel do not utilize a constructor or destructor. You can pass `NULL` for both of these parameters.

On success, `kmem_cache_create()` returns a pointer to the created cache. Otherwise, it returns `NULL`. This function must not be called from interrupt context as it can sleep.

To destroy a cache, call

```
int kmem_cache_destroy(kmem_cache_t *cachep)
```

This destroys the given cache. This function is generally invoked from module shutdown code in modules that create their own caches. It must not be called from interrupt context as it may sleep. The caller of this function must ensure two conditions are true prior to invoking this function:

- All slabs in the cache are empty. Indeed, if an object in one of the slabs were still allocated and in use, how could the cache be destroyed?

- No one accesses the cache during (and obviously after) a call to `kmem_cache_destroy()`. The caller must ensure this synchronization.

On success, the function returns zero; it returns nonzero otherwise.

After a cache is created, an object is obtained from the cache via

```
void * kmem_cache_alloc(kmem_cache_t *cachep, int flags)
```

This function returns a pointer to an object from the given cache `cachep`. If no free objects are in any slabs in the cache, and the slab layer must obtain new pages via `kmem_getpages()`, the value of `flags` is passed to `__get_free_pages()`. These are the same flags we looked at earlier. You probably want `GFP_KERNEL` or `GFP_ATOMIC`.

To later free an object and return it to its originating slab, use the function

```
void kmem_cache_free(kmem_cache_t *cachep, void *objp)
```

This marks the object `objp` in `cachep` as free.

Example of Using the Slab Allocator

Let's look at a real-life example using the `task_struct` structure (the process descriptor). This code, in slightly more complicated form, is in `kernel/fork.c`.

First, the kernel has a global variable that stores a pointer to the `task_struct` cache:

```
kmem_cache_t *task_struct_cachep;
```

During kernel initialization, in `fork_init()`, the cache is created:

```
task_struct_cachep = kmem_cache_create("task_struct", sizeof(struct
task_struct),
                                0, SLAB_MUST_HWCACHE_ALIGN, NULL,
NULL);
if (!task_struct_cachep)
        panic("fork_init(): cannot create task_struct SLAB cache");
```

This creates a cache named `task_struct`, which stores objects of type `struct task_struct`. The objects are created with the default offset within the slab and are all cache aligned. There is no constructor or destructor. Note the return value is checked for `NULL`, which denotes failure—you must check the return! In this case, if the kernel was unable to create the `task_struct_cachep` cache, it panics (halts the machine), because this is a requisite cache for system operation (the machine is not much good without process descriptors).

Each time a process calls `fork()`, a new process descriptor must be created (recall Chapter 2, "Process Management"). This is done in `dup_task_struct()`, which is called from `do_fork()`:

```
struct task_struct *tsk;

tsk = kmem_cache_alloc(task_struct_cachep, GFP_KERNEL);
if (!tsk) {
        /* failed to allocate process descriptor, cleanup and return error */
        free_thread_info(ti);
        return NULL;
}
```

After a task dies, if it has no children waiting on it, its process descriptor is freed and returned to the `task_struct_cachep` slab cache. This is done in `free_task_struct()` (where `tsk` is the exiting task):

```
kmem_cache_free(task_struct_cachep, tsk);
```

Because process descriptors are part of the core kernel and always needed, the `task_struct_cachep` cache is never destroyed. If it were, however, we would destroy the cache via

```
int err;

err = kmem_cache_destroy(task_struct_cachep);
if (err)
        /* error destroying cache */
```

Easy enough? The slab layer handles all the low-level alignment, coloring, allocations, freeing, and reaping during low-memory conditions. If you are frequently creating many objects of the same type, consider using the slab cache. Definitely do not implement your own free list!

Statically Allocating on the Stack

In user-space, allocations, such as some of the examples discussed thus far, could have occurred on the stack because we knew the size of the allocation a priori. User-space is afforded the luxury of a very large and dynamically-growing stack, whereas the kernel has no such luxury—the kernel's stack is small and fixed. On most 32-bit architectures, the stack is 8KB. On most 64-bit architectures, the stack is 16KB. This is primarily done for efficiency reasons. By giving each process a small, fixed kernel stack, memory consumption is minimized and the kernel need not burden itself with stack management code.

Each process receives its own kernel stack. The entire call chain of a process executing inside the kernel must be capable of fitting on the stack. Interrupt handlers also use the stack of the process they interrupt. This means that, at worst, the 8KB kernel stack might need to be shared by a multiple function-deep call chain and a couple of interrupt handlers. Obviously, unbounded recursion is out!

In any given function, you must keep stack usage to a minimum. There is no hard and fast rule, but you should keep the sum of all local variables (also known as automatic variables or variables on the stack) in a particular function to a maximum of a couple hundred bytes. Performing a large static allocation on the stack, such as of a large array or structure, is dangerous. Otherwise, stack allocations are performed in the kernel just as in user-space. Stack overflows occur silently and will undoubtedly result in problems. Because the kernel does not make any effort to manage the stack, when the stack overflows, the excess data simply spills into whatever exists at the tail end of the stack. First, this is the `thread_info` structure (recall from Chapter 2 that this structure is allocated at the end of each process's kernel stack). Beyond the stack, any kernel data might lurk. At best, the machine will crash when the stack overflows. At worst, the overflow will silently corrupt the kernel.

Therefore, it is wise to use a dynamic allocation scheme, such as one of those discussed earlier in this chapter for any large memory allocations.

High Memory Mappings

By definition, pages in high memory might not be permanently mapped into the kernel's address space. Thus, pages obtained via `alloc_pages()` with the `__GFP_HIGHMEM` flag might not have a logical address.

On the x86 architecture, all physical memory beyond the 896MB mark is high memory and is not permanently or automatically mapped into the kernel's address space, despite x86 processors being capable of physically addressing up to 4GB (64GB with PAE[6]) of physical RAM. Once allocated, these pages must be mapped into the kernel's logical address space. On x86, pages in high memory are mapped somewhere between the 3 and 4GB mark.

Permanent Mappings

To map a given `page` structure into the kernel's address space, use

```
void *kmap(struct page *page)
```

---

[6]PAE stands for *Physical Address Extension*. It is a feature of x86 processors that allow them to physically address 36-bits (64GB) worth of memory, despite having only a 32-bit virtual address space.

This function works on either high or low memory. If the `page` structure belongs to a page in low memory, the page's virtual address is simply returned. If the page resides in high memory, a permanent mapping is created and the address is returned. The function may sleep, so `kmap()` only works in process context.

Because the number of permanent mappings are limited (if not, we would not be in this mess and could just permanently map all memory), high memory should be unmapped when no longer needed. This is done via

```
void kunmap(struct page *page)
```

which unmaps the given `page`.

Temporary Mappings

For times when a mapping must be created but the current context is unable to sleep, the kernel provides *temporary mappings* (which are also called *atomic mappings*). These are a set of reserved permanent mappings that can temporarily hold a mapping on-the-fly. The kernel can atomically map a high memory page into one of these reserved mappings. Consequently, a temporary mapping can be used in places that cannot sleep, such as interrupt handlers, because obtaining the mapping never blocks.

Setting up a temporary mapping is done via

```
void *kmap_atomic(struct page *page, enum km_type type)
```

The `type` parameter is one of the following enumerations, which describe the purpose of the temporary mapping. They are defined in `<asm/kmap_types.h>`:

```
enum km_type {
        KM_BOUNCE_READ,
        KM_SKB_SUNRPC_DATA,
        KM_SKB_DATA_SOFTIRQ,
        KM_USER0,
        KM_USER1,
        KM_BIO_SRC_IRQ,
        KM_BIO_DST_IRQ,
        KM_PTE0,
        KM_PTE1,
        KM_PTE2,
        KM_IRQ0,
        KM_IRQ1,
        KM_SOFTIRQ0,
        KM_SOFTIRQ1,
        KM_TYPE_NR
};
```

This function does not block and thus can be used in interrupt context and other places that cannot reschedule. It also disables kernel preemption, which is needed because the mappings are unique to each processor (and a reschedule might change which task is running on which processor).

The mapping is undone via

```
void kunmap_atomic(void *kvaddr, enum km_type type)
```

This function also does not block. In fact, in many architectures it does not do anything at all except enable kernel preemption, because a temporary mapping is only valid until the next temporary mapping. Thus, the kernel can just "forget about" the `kmap_atomic()` mapping and `kunmap_atomic()` does not need to do anything special. The next atomic mapping will then simply overwrite the previous one.

Which Allocation Method Should I Use?

If you need contiguous physical pages, use one of the low-level page allocators or `kmalloc()`. This is the standard manner of allocating memory from within the kernel, and most likely, how you will allocate most of your memory. Recall that the two most common flags given to these functions are GFP_ATOMIC and GFP_KERNEL. Specify the GFP_ATOMIC flag to perform a high priority allocation that will not sleep. This is a requirement of interrupt handlers and other pieces of code that cannot sleep. Code that can sleep, such as process context code that does not hold a spin lock, should use GFP_KERNEL. This flag specifies an allocation that can sleep, if needed, to obtain the requested memory.

If you want to allocate from high memory, use `alloc_pages()`. The `alloc_pages()` function returns a `struct page`, and not a pointer to a logical address. Because high memory might not be mapped, the only way to access it might be via the corresponding `struct page` structure. To obtain an actual pointer, use `kmap()` to map the high memory into the kernel's logical address space.

If you do not need physically contiguous pages—only virtually contiguous—use `vmalloc()` (although bear in mind the slight performance hit taken with `vmalloc()` over `kmalloc()`). The `vmalloc()` function allocates kernel memory that is virtually contiguous but not, per se, physically contiguous. It performs this feat much like user-space allocations, by mapping chunks of physical memory into a contiguous logical address space.

If you are creating and destroying many large data structures, consider setting up a slab cache. The slab layer will maintain a per-processor object cache (a free list), which might greatly enhance object allocation and deallocation performance. Instead of frequently allocating and freeing memory, the slab layer will store a cache of already allocated objects for you. When you need a new chunk of memory to hold your data structure, the slab layer often does not need to allocate more memory and can instead simply return an object from the cache.

11

The Virtual Filesystem

THE VIRTUAL FILESYSTEM (SOMETIMES CALLED the *Virtual File Switch* or simply the *VFS*) is the subsystem of the kernel that implements the filesystem interface provided to user-space programs. All filesystems rely on the VFS to allow them not only to coexist, but also to interoperate. This enables you to use standard Unix system calls to read and write to different filesystems on different media, as shown in Figure 11.1.

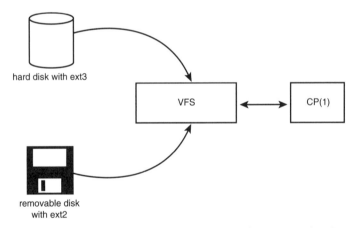

Figure 11.1   The VFS in action: Using the `cp(1)` utility to move data from a hard disk mounted as ext3 to a removable disk mounted as ext2.

Common Filesystem Interface

The VFS is the glue that enables system calls such as `open()`, `read()`, and `write()` to work regardless of the filesystem or underlying physical medium. It might not sound impressive these days—we have long been taking such a feature for granted—but it is a nontrivial feat for such generic system calls to work across all supported filesystems and media. More so, the system calls work *between* these different filesystems and media—we can copy or move from one filesystem to another using standard system calls. In older operating systems (think DOS), this would never have worked; any access to a nonnative filesystem would require special tools. It is only because modern operating systems, Linux included, abstract access to the filesystems via a virtual interface is such interoperation and generic access possible.

Filesystem Abstraction Layer

A generic interface for any type of filesystem is only feasible because the kernel itself implements an abstraction layer around its low-level filesystem interface. This abstraction layer enables Linux to support different filesystems, even if they differ greatly in supported features or behavior. This is possible because the VFS provides a common file model that is capable of representing any conceivable filesystem's general features and behavior. Of course, it is biased toward Unix-style filesystems (we will see what constitutes a Unix-style filesystem in the proceeding sections). Regardless, wildly different filesystems are still supportable in Linux.

The abstraction layer works by defining the basic abstract interfaces and data structures all filesystems support. The filesystems mold their view of concepts such as "*this is how I open files*" and "*this is what a directory is to me*" to match the expectations of the VFS. The actual filesystem code hides the implementation details. To the VFS layer and the rest of the kernel, however, each filesystem looks the same. They all support notions, such as files and directories, and they all support operations, such as create file and delete file.

The result is a general abstraction layer that enables the kernel to support many types of filesystems easily and cleanly. The filesystems are programmed to provide the abstracted interfaces and data structures the VFS expects; in turn, the kernel easily works with any filesystem and the exported user-space interface seamlessly works on any filesystem.

In fact, nothing in the kernel needs to understand the underlying details of the filesystems, except the filesystems themselves. For example, consider a simple user-space program that does

```
write(f, &buf, len);
```

This writes the `len` bytes pointed to by `&buf` into the current position in the file represented by the file descriptor `f`. This system call is first handled by a generic `sys_write()` system call that determines the actual file writing method for the filesystem on which `f` resides. The generic write system call then invokes this method, which is part of the filesystem implementation, to write the data to the media (or whatever this filesystem does on write). Figure 11.2 shows the flow from user-space's `write()` call through the data arriving on the physical media. We will look at how the VFS achieves this abstraction and provides its interfaces throughout the rest of this chapter.

Unix Filesystems

Historically, Unix provided four basic filesystem-related abstractions: files, directory entries, inodes, and mount points.

A filesystem is a hierarchical storage of data adhering to a specific structure. Filesystems contain files, directories, and associated control information. Typical operations performed on filesystems are creation, deletion, and mounting. In Unix, filesystems are mounted at a specific mount point in a global hierarchy[1] known as a *namespace*. This enables all mounted filesystems to appear as entries in a single tree[2].

A file is an ordered string of bytes. The first byte marks the beginning of the file and the last byte marks the end of the file. Each file is assigned a human-readable name for identification by both the system and the user. Typical file operations are read, write, create, and delete.

Files are laid out in directories. A directory is analogous to a folder and usually contains related files. Directories can also contain subdirectories; in this fashion, directories may be nested to form paths. Each component of a path is called a directory entry. An example path is "/home/wolfman/foo"—the root directory /, the directories home and wolfman, and the file foo are all directory entries, called *dentries*. In Unix, directories are actually normal files that simply list the files contained therein. Because a directory is a file to the VFS, the same operations performed on files can be performed on directories.

Unix systems separate the concept of a file from any associated information about it (such as access permissions, size, owner, creation time, and so on). This information is sometimes called *file metadata* (that is, data about data) and is stored in a separate data structure from the file, called the *inode*. This name is short for *index node*, although these days the term "inode" is much more ubiquitous.

All this information is tied together with the filesystem's control information, which is stored in the superblock. The superblock is a data structure containing information about the filesystem as a whole. Sometimes, the collective data is referred to as *filesystem metadata*. Filesystem metadata includes information about both the individual files and the filesystem as a whole.

Traditionally, Unix filesystems implement these notions as part of their physical on-disk layout. For example, file information is stored as an inode in a separate block on the disk, directories are files, control information is stored centrally in a superblock, and so on. The Linux VFS is designed to work with filesystems that understand and implement such concepts. Non-Unix filesystems, such as FAT or NTFS, still work in Linux, but their filesystem code must provide the appearance of these concepts. For example, even if a filesystem does not support distinct inodes, it must assemble the inode data structure in

---

[1] Recently, Linux has made this hierarchy per-process, to give a unique namespace to each process. Although, by default, each process inherits its parent's namespace and, thus, there is seemingly one global namespace.

[2] As opposed to at a given drive letter, like "C:".

memory as if it did. Or, if a filesystem treats directories as a special object, to the VFS they must represent directories as mere files. Oftentimes, this involves some special processing done on the fly by the non-Unix filesystems to cope with the Unix paradigm and the requirements of the VFS. Such filesystems still work, however, and usually suffer very little.

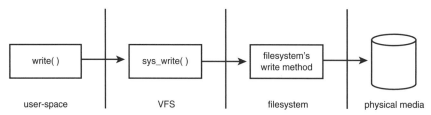

Figure 11.2   The flow of data from user-space issuing a `write()` call, through the VFS's generic system call, into the filesystem's specific write method, and finally arriving at the physical media.

VFS Objects and Their Data Structures

The VFS is object-oriented[3]. A family of data structures represents the common file model. These data structures are akin to objects. Because the kernel is programmed strictly in C, without the benefit of a language directly supporting object-oriented paradigms, the data structures are represented as C structures. The structures contain both data and pointers to filesystem-implemented functions that operate on the data.

The four primary object types of the VFS are

- The *superblock* object, which represents a specific mounted filesystem.
- The *inode* object, which represents a specific file.
- The *dentry* object, which represents a specific directory entry.
- The *file* object, which represents an open file as associated with a process.

Note that, because the VFS treats directories as normal files, there is not a specific directory object. Recall from earlier in this chapter that a dentry represents a component in a path, which might include a regular file. In other words, a dentry is not the same as a directory, but a directory is the same as a file. Got it?

---

[3] People often miss this, or even deny it, but there are many examples of object-oriented programming in the kernel. Although the kernel developers may shun C++ and other explicitly object-oriented languages, *thinking* in terms of objects is often useful. The VFS is a good example of how to do clean and efficient OOP in C, which is a language that lacks any OOP constructs.

An *operations* object is contained within each of these primary objects. These objects describe the methods that the kernel invokes against the primary objects. Specifically, we have

- The `super_operations` object, which contains the methods the kernel can invoke on a specific filesystem, such as `read_inode()` and `sync_fs()`.

- The `inode_operations` object, which contains the methods the kernel can invoke on a specific file, such as `create()` and `link()`.

- The `dentry_operations` object, which contains the methods the kernel can invoke on a specific directory entry, such as `d_compare()` and `d_delete()`.

- The *file* object, which contains the methods a process can invoke on an open file, such as `read()` and `write()`.

The operations objects are implemented as a structure of pointers to functions that operate on the parent object. For many methods, the objects can inherit a generic function if basic functionality is sufficient. Otherwise, the specific instance of the particular filesystem fills in the pointers with its own filesystem-specific methods.

Again, note that by *object* we mean structures—not explicit object data types, such as those in C++ or Java. These structures, however, represent specific instances of an object, their associated data, and methods to operate on themselves. They are very much objects.

Other VFS Objects

The VFS loves structures, and it is composed of a couple more than the primary objects previously discussed. Each registered filesystem is represented by a `file_system_type` structure. This object describes the filesystem and its capabilities. Furthermore, each mount point is represented by the `vfsmount` structure. This structure contains information about the mount point, such as its location and mount flags.

Finally, three per-process structures describe the filesystem and files associated with a process. They are the `file_struct`, `fs_struct`, and `namespace` structures.

The rest of this chapter concentrates on discussing these objects and the role they play in implementing the VFS layer.

The Superblock Object

The superblock object is implemented by each filesystem, and is used to store information describing that specific filesystem. This object usually corresponds to the *filesystem superblock* or the *filesystem control block*, which is stored in a special sector on disk (hence the object's name). Filesystems that are not disk-based (a virtual memory-based filesystem, such as *sysfs*, for example) generate the superblock on the fly and store it in memory.

The superblock object is represented by `struct super_block` and defined in `<linux/fs.h>`. Here is what it looks like, with comments describing each entry:

```
struct super_block {
    struct list_head        s_list;          /* list of all superblocks */
    dev_t                   s_dev;           /* identifier */
    unsigned long           s_blocksize;     /* block size in bytes */
    unsigned long           s_old_blocksize; /* old block size in bytes */
    unsigned char           s_blocksize_bits; /* block size in bits */
    unsigned char           s_dirt;          /* dirty flag */
    unsigned long long      s_maxbytes;      /* max file size */
    struct file_system_type s_type;          /* filesystem type */
    struct super_operations s_op;            /* superblock methods */
    struct dquot_operations *dq_op;          /* quota methods */
    struct quotactl_ops     *s_qcop;         /* quota control methods */
    struct export_operations *s_export_op;   /* export methods */
    unsigned long           s_flags;         /* mount flags */
    unsigned long           s_magic;         /* filesystem's magic number */
    struct dentry           *s_root;         /* directory mount point */
    struct rw_semaphore     s_umount;        /* unmount semaphore */
    struct semaphore        s_lock;          /* superblock semaphore */
    int                     s_count;         /* superblock reference count */
    int                     s_syncing;       /* filesystem syncing flag */
    int                     s_need_sync_fs;  /* not-yet-synced flag */
    atomic_t                s_active;        /* active reference count */
    void                    *s_security;     /* security module */
    struct list_head        s_dirty;         /* list of dirty inodes */
    struct list_head        s_io;            /* list of writebacks */
    struct hlist_head       s_anon;          /* anonymous dentries for export */
    struct list_head        s_files;         /* list of assigned files */
    struct block_device     *s_bdev;         /* associated block device driver */
    struct list_head        s_instances;     /* list of filesystems of this type */
    struct quota_info       s_dquot;         /* quota-specific options */
    char                    s_id[32];        /* text name */
    struct kobject          kobj;            /* sysfs object */
    void                    *s_fs_info;      /* filesystem-specific info */
    struct semaphore        s_vfs_rename_sem;/* directory rename semaphore */
};
```

The code for creating, managing, and destroying superblock objects lives in `fs/super.c`. A superblock object is created and initialized via the `alloc_super()` function. When mounted, a filesystem invokes this function, reads its superblock off the disk, and fills in its superblock object.

Superblock Operations

The most important item in the superblock object is `s_op`, which is the superblock operations table. The superblock operations table is represented by `struct super_operations` and is defined in `<linux/fs.h>`. It looks like

```
struct super_operations {
        struct inode *(*alloc_inode) (struct super_block *sb);
        void (*destroy_inode) (struct inode *);
        void (*read_inode) (struct inode *);
        void (*dirty_inode) (struct inode *);
        void (*write_inode) (struct inode *, int);
        void (*put_inode) (struct inode *);
        void (*drop_inode) (struct inode *);
        void (*delete_inode) (struct inode *);
        void (*put_super) (struct super_block *);
        void (*write_super) (struct super_block *);
        int (*sync_fs) (struct super_block *, int);
        void (*write_super_lockfs) (struct super_block *);
        void (*unlockfs) (struct super_block *);
        int (*statfs) (struct super_block *, struct statfs *);
        int (*remount_fs) (struct super_block *, int *, char *);
        void (*clear_inode) (struct inode *);
        void (*umount_begin) (struct super_block *);
        int (*show_options) (struct seq_file *, struct vfsmount *);
};
```

Each item in this structure is a pointer to a function that operates on a superblock object. The superblock operations perform low-level operations on the filesystem and its inodes.

When a filesystem needs to perform an operation on its superblock, it follows the pointers from its superblock object to the desired method. For example, if a filesystem wanted to write to its superblock, it would invoke

```
sb->s_op->write_super(sb);
```

where sb is a pointer to the filesystem's superblock. Following that pointer into s_op yields the superblock operations table and ultimately the desired write_super() function, which is then directly invoked. Note how the write_super() call must be passed a superblock, despite the method being associated with one. This is because of the lack of object-oriented support in C. In C++, a call such as

```
sb.write_super();
```

would suffice. In C, there is no way for the method to cleanly obtain its parent, so we have to pass it.

Let's look at the superblock operations, which are specified by super_operations:

- struct inode * alloc_inode(struct super_block *sb)
  This function creates and initializes a new inode object under the given superblock.

- void destroy_inode(struct inode *inode)
  This function deallocates the given inode.

- `void read_inode(struct inode *inode)`
  This function reads the inode specified by `inode->i_ino` from disk and fills in the rest of the inode structure.

- `void dirty_inode(struct inode *inode)`
  This function is invoked by the VFS when an inode is dirtied (modified). Journaling filesystems (such as ext3) use this function to perform journal updates.

- `void write_inode(struct inode inode*, int wait)`
  Writes the given inode to disk. The `wait` parameter specifies whether the operation should be synchronous.

- `void put_inode(struct inode *inode)`
  This function releases the given inode.

- `void drop_inode(struct inode *inode)`
  This function is called by the VFS when the last reference to an inode is dropped. Normal Unix filesystems do not define this function, in which case the VFS simply deletes the inode. The caller must hold the `inode_lock`.

- `void delete_inode(struct inode *inode)`
  This function deletes the given inode from the disk.

- `void put_super(struct super_block *sb)`
  This function is called by the VFS on unmount to release the given superblock object.

- `void write_super(struct super_block *sb)`
  This function updates the on-disk superblock with the specified superblock. The VFS uses this function to synchronize a modified in-memory superblock with the disk.

- `int sync_fs(struct super_block *sb, int wait)`
  This function synchronizes filesystem metadata with the on-disk filesystem. The `wait` parameter specifies whether the operation is synchronous.

- `void write_super_lockfs(struct super_block *sb)`
  This function prevents changes to the filesystem, and then updates the on-disk superblock with the specified superblock. It is currently used by LVM (the Logical Volume Manager).

- `void unlockfs(struct super_block *sb)`
  This function unlocks the filesystem against changes as done by `write_super_lockfs()`.

- `int statfs(struct super_block *sb, struct statfs *statfs)`
  This function is called by the VFS to obtain filesystem statistics. The statistics related to the given filesystem are placed in `statfs`.

- `int remount_fs(struct super_block *sb, int *flags, char *data)`
  This function is called by the VFS when the filesystem is remounted with new mount options.

- `void clear_inode(struct inode *)`
  This function is called by the VFS to release the inode and clear any pages containing related data.

- `void umount_begin(struct super_block *sb)`
  This function is called by the VFS to interrupt a mount operation. It is used by network filesystems, such as NFS.

All these functions are invoked by the VFS, in process context. They may all block if needed.

Some of these functions are optional; the filesystem can then set their value in the superblock operations structure to NULL. If the associated pointer is NULL, the VFS either calls a generic function or does nothing, depending on the operation.

The Inode Object

The inode object represents all the information needed by the kernel to manipulate a file or directory. For Unix-style filesystems, this information is simply read from the on-disk inode and used to populate the VFS's inode object. If a filesystem does not have inodes, however, the filesystem must obtain the information from wherever it is stored on the disk[4].

The inode object is represented by `struct inode` and is defined in `<linux/fs.h>`. Here is the structure, with comments describing each entry

```
struct inode {
        struct hlist_node    i_hash;        /* hash list */
        struct list_head     i_list;        /* linked list of inodes */
        struct list_head     i_dentry;      /* linked list of dentries */
        unsigned long        i_ino;         /* inode number */
        atomic_t             i_count;       /* reference counter */
        umode_t              i_mode;        /* access permissions */
        unsigned int         i_nlink;       /* number of hard links */
        uid_t                i_uid;         /* user id of owner */
        gid_t                i_gid;         /* group id of owner */
        kdev_t               i_rdev;        /* real device node */
        loff_t               i_size;        /* file size in bytes */
```

---

[4]Filesystems without inodes generally store the information as part of the file itself. Some modern filesystems also employ a database to store the file's data. Whatever the case, the inode object is constructed in whatever manner is applicable to the filesystem.

```
        struct timespec        i_atime;                /* last file access */
        struct timespec        i_mtime;                /* last file modify */
        struct timespec        i_ctime;                /* file creation timestamp */
        unsigned int           i_blkbits;              /* block size in bits */
        unsigned long          i_blksize;              /* block size in bytes */
        unsigned long          i_version;              /* version number */
        unsigned long          i_blocks;               /* file size in blocks */
        unsigned short         i_bytes;                /* bytes consumed */
        spinlock_t             i_lock;                 /* lock protecting fields */
        struct semaphore       i_sem;                  /* inode semaphore */
        struct inode_operations *i_op;                 /* inode operations table */
        struct file_operations *i_fop;                 /* file operations */
        struct super_block     *i_sb;                  /* associated superblock */
        struct file_lock       *i_flock;               /* file lock list */
        struct address_space   *i_mapping;             /* backing address space */
        struct address_space   i_data;                 /* device address space */
        struct dquot           *i_dquot[MAXQUOTAS];    /* disk quotas for inode */
        struct list_head       i_devices;              /* list of block devices */
        struct pipe_inode_info *i_pipe;                /* pipe information */
        struct block_device    *i_bdev;                /* block device driver */
        unsigned long          i_dnotify_mask;         /* Directory notify events */
        struct dnotify_struct  *i_dnotify;             /* dir notifications */
        unsigned long          i_state;                /* state flags */
        unsigned int           i_flags;                /* filesystem flags */
        unsigned char          i_sock;                 /* is this a socket? */
        atomic_t               i_writecount;           /* write usage counter */
        void                   *i_security;            /* security module */
        __u32                  i_generation;           /* inode version number */
        union {
                void           *generic_ip;            /* fs-specific info */
        } u;
};
```

An inode represents each file on a filesystem (although an inode object is only constructed in memory as the files are accessed). This includes special files, such as device files or pipes. Consequently, some of the entries in `struct inode` are related to these special files. For example, the `i_pipe` entry points to a named pipe data structure. If the inode does not refer to a named pipe, this field is simply NULL. Other special file-related fields are `i_devices`, `i_bdev`, and `i_cdev`.

It might occur that a given filesystem does not support a property represented in the inode object. For example, some filesystems might not record a creation timestamp. In that case, the filesystem is free to implement the feature however it sees fit; it can store zero for i_ctime, make i_ctime equal to i_mtime, or whatever floats its boat.

Inode Operations

As with the superblock operations, the inode_operations member is very important, as it describes the filesystem's implemented functions that the VFS can invoke on an inode. As with the superblock, inode operations are invoked via

```
i->i_op->truncate(i)
```

where i is a reference to a particular inode. In this case, the truncate() operation defined by the filesystem on which i exists is called on the given inode. The inode_operations structure is defined in <linux/fs.h>:

```
struct inode_operations {
        int create(struct inode *dir, struct dentry *dentry, int mode)
        struct dentry * (*lookup) (struct inode *, struct dentry *);
        int (*link) (struct dentry *, struct inode *, struct dentry *);
        int (*unlink) (struct inode *, struct dentry *);
        int (*symlink) (struct inode *, struct dentry *, const char *);
        int (*mkdir) (struct inode *, struct dentry *, int);
        int (*rmdir) (struct inode *, struct dentry *);
        int (*mknod) (struct inode *, struct dentry *, int, dev_t);
        int (*rename) (struct inode *, struct dentry *, struct inode *, struct
dentry *);
        int (*readlink) (struct dentry *, char *, int);
        int (*follow_link) (struct dentry *, struct nameidata *);
        void (*truncate) (struct inode *);
        int (*permission) (struct inode *, int);
        int (*setattr) (struct dentry *, struct iattr *);
        int (*getattr) (struct vfsmount *, struct dentry *, struct kstat *);
        int (*setxattr) (struct dentry *, const char *, const void *, size_t,
int);
        ssize_t (*getxattr) (struct dentry *, const char *, void *, size_t);
        ssize_t (*listxattr) (struct dentry *, char *, size_t);
        int (*removexattr) (struct dentry *, const char *);
};
```

Let's look at these operations:

- int create(struct inode *dir,
                    struct dentry *dentry, int mode)

  The VFS calls this function from the creat() and open() system calls to create a new inode associated with the given dentry object with the specified initial mode.

- `struct dentry * lookup(struct inode *dir, struct dentry *dentry)`
  This function searches a directory for an inode corresponding to a filename specified in the given dentry.

- `int link(struct dentry *old_dentry, struct inode *dir,`
  `                struct dentry *dentry)`
  The function is invoked by the `link()` system call to create a hard link of the file `old_dentry` in the directory `dir` with the new filename `dentry`.

- `int unlink(struct inode *dir,`
  `                struct dentry *dentry)`
  This function is called from the `unlink()` system call to remove the inode specified by the directory entry `dentry` from the directory `dir`.

- `int symlink(struct inode *dir,`
  `                struct dentry *dentry,`
  `                const char *symname)`
  This function is called from the `symlink()` system call to create a symbolic link named `symname` to the file represented by `dentry` in the directory `dir`.

- `int mkdir(struct inode *dir, struct dentry *dentry, int mode)`
  This function is called from the `mkdir()` system call to create a new directory with the given initial mode.

- `int rmdir(struct inode *dir, struct dentry *dentry)`
  This function is called by the `rmdir()` system call to remove the directory referenced by `dentry` from the directory `dir`.

- `int mknod(struct inode *dir,`
  `                struct dentry *dentry,`
  `                int mode, dev_t rdev)`
  This function is called by the `mknod()` system call to create a special file (device file, named pipe, or socket) as referenced by `rdev` with the directory entry `dentry` in the directory `dir` with the given initial mode.

- `int rename(struct inode *old_dir,`
  `                struct dentry *old_dentry,`
  `                struct inode *new_dir,`
  `                struct dentry *new_dentry)`
  This function is called by the VFS to move the file specified by `old_dentry` from the `old_dir` directory to the directory `new_dir` with the filename specified by `new_dentry`.

- `int readlink(struct dentry *dentry, char *buffer, int buflen)`
  This function is called by the `readlink()` system call to copy at most `buflen` bytes of the full path associated with the symbolic link specified by `dentry` into the specified buffer.

- `int follow_link(struct dentry *dentry, struct nameidata *nd)`
  This function is called by the VFS to translate a symbolic link to the inode it points to.

- `void truncate(struct inode *inode)`
  This function is called by the VFS to modify the size of the given file. Before invocation, the inode's `i_size` field must be set to the desired new size.

- `int permission(struct inode *inode, int mask)`
  This function checks whether the specified access mode is allowed for the file referenced by `inode`. This function returns zero if the access is allowed and a negative error code otherwise. Most filesystems set this field to NULL and use the generic VFS method, which simply compares the mode bits in the inode's objects to the given mask. More complicated filesystems, such as those supporting access control lists (ACL's), have a specific `permission()` method.

- `int setattr(struct dentry *dentry, struct iattr *attr)`
  This function is called from `notify_change()` to notify a "change event" after modifying an inode.

- `int getattr(struct vfsmount *mnt,`
  `            struct dentry *dentry,`
  `            struct kstat *stat)`
  This function is invoked by the VFS upon noticing that an inode needs to be refreshed from disk.

- `int setxattr(struct dentry *dentry,`
  `             const char *name,`
  `             const void *value, size_t size,`
  `             int flags)`
  This function is used by the VFS to set the extended attribute[5] name to the value value on the file referenced by `denty`.

---

[5]Extended attributes are a new feature introduced in the 2.6 kernel for pairing name/value tags to files, similar to a database. Although a few filesystems currently support them, they have not yet seen widespread use.

- `ssize_t getxattr(struct dentry *dentry,`
                              `const char *name,`
                              `void *value, size_t size)`

  This function is used by the VFS to copy into `value` the value of the extended attribute `name` for the specified file.

- `ssize_t listxattr(struct dentry *dentry, char *list, size_t size)`

  This function copies the list of all attributes for the specified file into the buffer `list`.

- `int removexattr(struct dentry *dentry, const char *name)`

  This function removes the given attribute from the given file.

The Dentry Object

As discussed, the VFS treats directories as files. In the path /bin/vi, both `bin` and `vi` are files—`bin` being the special directory file and `vi` being a regular file. An inode object represents both of these components. Despite this useful unification, the VFS often needs to perform directory-specific operations, such as path name lookup. Path name lookup involves translating each component of a path, ensuring it is valid, and following it to the next component.

To facilitate this, the VFS employs the concept of a directory entry (dentry). A dentry is a specific component in a path. Using the previous example, /, `bin`, and `vi` are all dentry objects. The first two are directories and the last is a regular file. This is an important point; dentry objects are *all* components in a path, including files.

They might also include mount points. In the path /mnt/cdrom/foo, the components /, `mnt`, `cdrom`, and `foo` are all dentry objects. The VFS constructs dentry objects on the fly, as needed, when performing directory operations.

Dentry objects are represented by `struct dentry` and defined in `<linux/dcache.h>`. Here is the structure, with comments describing each member:

```
struct dentry {
        atomic_t            d_count;        /* usage count */
        unsigned long       d_vfs_flags;    /* dentry cache flags */
        spinlock_t          d_lock;         /* per-dentry lock */
        struct inode        *d_inode;       /* associated inode */
        struct list_head    d_lru;          /* unused list */
        struct list_head    d_child;        /* list of dentries in parent */
        struct list_head    d_subdirs;      /* subdirectories */
        struct list_head    d_alias;        /* list of alias inodes */
        unsigned long       d_time;         /* revalidate time */
```

```
    struct dentry_operations *d_op;        /* dentry operations table */
    struct super_block       *d_sb;        /* superblock of file */
    unsigned int             d_flags;      /* dentry flags */
    int                      d_mounted;    /* is this dentry a mount point? */
    void                     *d_fsdata;    /* filesystem-specific data */
    struct rcu_head          d_rcu;        /* RCU locking */
    struct dcookie_struct    *d_cookie;    /* cookie */
    unsigned long            d_move_count; /* did we move during RCU? */
    struct qstr              *d_qstr;      /* dentry name used during RCU
                                              lookup */
    struct dentry            *d_parent;    /* dentry object of parent
                                              directory */
    struct qstr              d_name;       /* dentry name */
    struct hlist_node        d_hash;       /* list of hash table entries */
    struct hlist_head        *d_bucket;    /* hash bucket */
    unsigned char            d_iname
                             [DNAME_INLINE_LEN_MIN]; /* short filenames */
};
```

Unlike the previous two objects, the dentry object does not correspond to any sort of on-disk data structure. The VFS creates it on the fly from a string-representation of a path name. Because the dentry object is not physically stored on the disk, no flag in struct dentry specifies whether the object is modified (that is, whether it is dirty and needs to be written back to disk).

Dentry State

A valid dentry object can be in one of three states: used, unused, or negative.

A used dentry corresponds to a valid inode (that is, d_inode points to an associated inode) and there are one or more users of the object (that is, d_count is positive). A used dentry is in use by the VFS and points to valid data and, thus, cannot be discarded.

An unused dentry corresponds to a valid inode (d_inode points to an inode), but the VFS is not currently using the dentry object (d_count is zero). Because the dentry object still points to a valid object, the dentry is kept around in case it is needed again. By not destroying the dentry prematurely, the dentry need not be recreated if it is needed in the future and path name lookups can complete quicker. If it is necessary to reclaim memory, however, the dentry can be discarded because it is not in use.

A negative dentry[6] is not associated with a valid inode (d_inode is NULL) because either the inode was deleted or the path name was never correct to begin with. The dentry is kept around, however, so that future lookups are resolved quickly. Although the dentry is useful, it can be destroyed, if needed, because nothing can actually be using it.

---

[6]The name is misleading. There is nothing particularly negative about a negative dentry. A better name might be *invalid dentry*.

A dentry object can also be freed, sitting in the slab object cache, as discussed in the previous chapter. In that case, there is no valid reference to the dentry object in any VFS or any filesystem code.

The Dentry Cache

After the VFS layer goes through the trouble of resolving each element in a path name into a dentry object and arriving at the end of the path, it would be quite wasteful to throw away all that work. Instead, the kernel caches dentry objects in the dentry cache, or, simply, the *dcache*.

The dentry cache consists of three parts:

- Lists of "used" dentries that are linked off their associated inode via the i_dentry field of the inode object. Because a given inode can have multiple links, there might be multiple dentry objects; consequently, a list is used.

- A doubly linked "least recently used" list of unused and negative dentry objects. The list is insertion sorted by time, such that entries toward the head of the list are newest. When the kernel must remove entries to reclaim memory, the entries are removed from the tail because those are the oldest and have the least chance of being used in the near future.

- A hash table and hashing function used to quickly resolve a given path into the associated dentry object.

The hash table is represented by the dentry_hashtable array. Each element is a pointer to a list of dentries that hash to the same value. The size of this array depends on the amount of physical RAM in the system.

The actual hash value is determined by d_hash(). This enables filesystems to provide a unique hashing function.

Hash table lookup is performed via d_lookup(). If a matching dentry object is found in the dcache, it is returned. On failure, NULL is returned.

As an example, assume you are editing a source file in your home directory, /home/dracula/src/foo.c. Each time this file is accessed (for example, when you first open it, later save it, then compile it, and so on), the VFS must follow each directory entry to resolve the full path: /, home, dracula, src, and finally foo.c. To prevent this time-consuming operation each time this (or any) path name is accessed, the VFS can first try to lookup the path name in the dentry cache. If the lookup succeeds, the required final dentry object is obtained without much effort. Conversely, if the dentry is not in the dentry cache, the VFS must manually resolve the path. Once completed, it will add the dentry objects to the dcache to speed up any future lookups.

The dcache also provides the front end to an inode cache, the *icache*. Inode objects that are associated with dentry objects are not freed because the dentry maintains a positive usage counter over the inode. This enables dentry objects to pin inodes in memory. As long as the dentry is cached, the corresponding inodes are cached, too. Consequently, when a path name lookup succeeds from cache, as in the previous example, the associated inodes are already cached in memory.

Dentry Operations

The `dentry_operations` structure specifies the methods that the VFS invokes on directory entries on a given filesystem.

The `dentry_operations` structure is defined in `<linux/dcache.h>`:

```
struct dentry_operations {
        int (*d_revalidate) (struct dentry *, int);
        int (*d_hash) (struct dentry *, struct qstr *);
        int (*d_compare) (struct dentry *, struct qstr *, struct qstr *);
        int (*d_delete) (struct dentry *);
        void (*d_release) (struct dentry *);
        void (*d_iput) (struct dentry *, struct inode *);
};
```

The methods:

- `int d_revalidate(struct dentry *dentry, int flags)`
  This function determines whether the given dentry object is valid. The VFS calls this function whenever it is preparing to use a dentry from the dcache. Most filesystems set this method to NULL because their dentry objects in the dcache are always valid.

- `int d_hash(struct dentry *dentry, struct qstr *name)`
  This function creates a hash value from the given dentry. The VFS calls this function whenever it adds a dentry to the hash table.

- `int d_compare(struct dentry *dentry,`
  `                       struct qstr *name1,`
  `                       struct qstr *name2)`
  This function is called by the VFS to compare two filenames, `name1` and `name2`. Most filesystems leave this at the VFS default, which is a simple string compare. For some filesystems, such as FAT, a simple string compare is insufficient. The FAT filesystem is case insensitive and therefore needs to implement a comparison function that disregards case. This function requires the `dcache_lock`.

- `int d_delete (struct dentry *dentry)`
  This function is called by the VFS when the specified dentry object's `d_count` reaches zero. This function requires the `dcache_lock`.

- `void d_release(struct dentry *dentry)`
  This function is called by the VFS when the specified dentry is going to be freed. The default function does nothing.

- `void d_iput(struct dentry *dentry, struct inode *inode)`

This function is called by the VFS when a dentry object loses its associated inode (say, because the entry was deleted from the disk). By default, the VFS simply calls the `iput()` function to release the inode. If a filesystem overrides this function, it must also call `iput()` in addition to performing whatever filesystem-specific work it requires.

The File Object

The final primary VFS object we look at is the file object. The file object is used to represent a file opened by a process. When we think of the VFS from the perspective of user space, the file object is what readily comes to mind. Processes deal directly with files, not superblocks, inodes, or dentries. It is not surprising that the information in the file object is the most familiar (data such as access mode and current offset) or that the file operations are familiar system calls like `read()` and `write()`.

The file object is the in-memory representation of an open file. The object (but not the physical file) is created in response to the `open()` system call and destroyed in response to the `close()` system call. All these file-related calls are actually methods defined in the file operations table. Because multiple processes can open and manipulate a file at the same time, there can be multiple file objects in existence for the same file. The file object merely represents a process's view of an open file. The object points back to the dentry (which in turn points back to the inode) that actually represents the open file. The inode and dentry objects, of course, are unique.

The file object is represented by `struct file` and is defined in `<linux/fs.h>`. Let's look at the structure, again with comments added to describe each entry:

```
struct file {
        struct list_head        f_list;       /* list of file objects */
        struct dentry           *f_dentry;    /* associated dentry object */
        struct vfsmount         *f_vfsmnt;    /* associated mounted filesystem */
        struct file_operations  *f_op;        /* file operations table */
        atomic_t                f_count;      /* file object's usage count */
        unsigned int            f_flags;      /* flags specified on open */
        mode_t                  f_mode;       /* file access mode */
        loff_t                  f_pos;        /* file offset (file pointer) */
        struct fown_struct      f_owner;      /* owner data for signals */
        unsigned int            f_uid;        /* user's UID */
        unsigned int            f_gid;        /* user's GID */
        int                     f_error;      /* error code */
        struct file_ra_state    f_ra;         /* read-ahead state */
        unsigned long           f_version;    /* version number */
        void                    *f_security;  /* security module */
        void                    *private_data; /* tty driver hook */
        struct list_head        f_ep_links;   /* list of eventpoll links */
        spinlock_t              f_ep_lock;    /* eventpoll lock */
};
```

Similar to the dentry object, the file object docs not actually correspond to any on-disk data. Therefore, no flag is in the object to represent whether the object is dirty and requires writeback to disk. The file object does point to its associated dentry object via the f_dentry pointer. The dentry in turn points to the associated inode, which reflects whether the file is dirty.

File Operations

As with all the other VFS objects, the file operations table is quite important. The operations associated with struct file are the familiar system calls that form the basis of the standard Unix system calls.

The file object methods are specified in file_operations and defined in <linux/fs.h>:

```
struct file_operations {
        struct module *owner;
        loff_t (*llseek) (struct file *, loff_t, int);
        ssize_t (*read) (struct file *, char *, size_t, loff_t *);
        ssize_t (*aio_read) (struct kiocb *, char *, size_t, loff_t);
        ssize_t (*write) (struct file *, const char *, size_t, loff_t *);
        ssize_t (*aio_write) (struct kiocb *, const char *, size_t, loff_t);
        int (*readdir) (struct file *, void *, filldir_t);
        unsigned int (*poll) (struct file *, struct poll_table_struct *);
        int (*ioctl) (struct inode *, struct file *, unsigned int, unsigned long);
        int (*mmap) (struct file *, struct vm_area_struct *);
        int (*open) (struct inode *, struct file *);
        int (*flush) (struct file *);
        int (*release) (struct inode *, struct file *);
        int (*fsync) (struct file *, struct dentry *, int);
        int (*aio_fsync) (struct kiocb *, int);
        int (*fasync) (int, struct file *, int);
        int (*lock) (struct file *, int, struct file_lock *);
        ssize_t (*readv) (struct file *, const struct iovec *, unsigned long,
                loff_t *);
        ssize_t (*writev) (struct file *, const struct iovec *, unsigned long,
                loff_t *);
        ssize_t (*sendfile) (struct file *, loff_t *, size_t, read_actor_t, void
                *);
        ssize_t (*sendpage) (struct file *, struct page *, int, size_t, loff_t *,
                int);
        unsigned long (*get_unmapped_area) (struct file *, unsigned long, unsigned
                long,
                                          unsigned long, unsigned long);
};
```

Filesystems can implement unique functions for each of these operations or they can use a generic method if one exists. The generic methods tend to work fine on normal

Unix-based filesystems. A filesystem is under no obligation to implement all these methods—although not implementing the basics is silly—and can simply set the method to NULL if not interested.

Let's look at the individual operations:

- `loff_t llseek(struct file *file, loff_t offset, int origin)`
  This function updates the file pointer to the given offset. It is called via the `llseek()` system call.

- `ssize_t read(struct file *file,`
                `char *buf, size_t count,`
                `loff_t *offset)`
  This function reads count bytes from the given file at position offset into buf. The file pointer is then updated. This function is called by the `read()` system call.

- `ssize_t aio_read(struct kiocb *iocb,`
                `char *buf, size_t count,`
                `loff_t offset)`
  This function begins an asynchronous read of count bytes into buf of the file described in iocb. This function is called by the `aio_read()` system call.

- `ssize_t write(struct file *file,`
                `const char *buf, size_t count,`
                `loff_t *offset)`
  This function writes count bytes from buf into the given file at position offset. The file pointer is then updated. This function is called by the `write()` system call.

- `ssize_t aio_write(struct kiocb *iocb,`
                `const char *buf,`
                `size_t count, loff_t offset)`
  This function begins an asynchronous write of count bytes into buf of the file described in iocb. This function is called by the `aio_write()` system call.

- `int readdir(struct file *file, void *dirent, filldir_t filldir)`
  This function returns the next directory in a directory listing. This function is called by the `readdir()` system call.

- `unsigned int poll(struct file *file,`
                `struct poll_table_struct *poll_table)`
  This function sleeps, waiting for activity on the given file. It is called by the `poll()` system call.

- `int ioctl(struct inode *inode,`
                `struct file *file,`
                `unsigned int cmd,`
                `unsigned long arg)`

This function is used to send a command and argument pair to a device. It is used when the file is an open device node. This function is called from the `ioctl()` system call.

- `int mmap(struct file *file, struct vm_area_struct *vma)`
  This function memory maps the given file onto the given address space and is called by the `mmap()` system call.

- `int open(struct inode *inode, struct file *file)`
  This function creates a new file object and links it to the corresponding inode object. It is called by the `open()` system call.

- `int flush(struct file *file)`
  This function is called by the VFS whenever the reference count of an open file decreases. Its purpose is filesystem-dependent.

- `int release(struct inode *inode, struct file *file)`
  This function is called by the VFS when the last remaining reference to the file is destroyed — for example, when the last process sharing a file descriptor calls `close()` or exits. Its purpose is filesystem-dependent.

- `int fsync(struct file *file,`
  `                struct dentry *dentry,`
  `                int datasync)`
  This function is called by the `fsync()` system call to write all cached data for the file to disk.

- `int aio_fsync(struct kiocb *iocb, int datasync)`
  This function is called by the `aio_fsync()` system call to write all cached data for the file associated with `iocb` to disk.

- `int fasync(int fd, struct file *file, int on)`
  This function enables or disables signal notification of asynchronous I/O.

- `int lock(struct file *file, int cmd, struct file_lock *lock)`
  This function manipulates a file lock on the given file.

- `ssize_t readv(struct file *file,`
  `                const struct iovec *vector,`
  `                unsigned long count,`
  `                loff_t *offset)`
  This function is called by the `readv()` system call to read from the given file and put the results into the `count` buffers described by `vector`. The file offset is then incremented.

- ```
  ssize_t writev(struct file *file,
                           const struct iovec *vector,
                           unsigned long count,
                           loff_t *offset)
  ```
  This function is called by the `writev()` system call to write from the `count` buffers described by `vector` into the file specified by `file`. The file offset is then incremented.

- ```
  ssize_t sendfile(struct file *file,
                           loff_t *offset,
                           size_t size,
                           read_actor_t actor,
                           void *target)
  ```
  This function is called by the `sendfile()` system call to copy data from one file to another. It performs the copy entirely in the kernel and avoids an extraneous copy to user-space.

- ```
  ssize_t sendpage(struct file *file,
                           struct page *page,
                           int offset, size_t size,
                           loff_t *pos, int more)
  ```
  This function is used to send data from one file to another.

- ```
  unsigned long get_unmapped_area(struct file
                      *file,
                      unsigned long addr,
                      unsigned long len,
                      unsigned long offset,
                      unsigned long flags)
  ```
  This function gets unused address space to map the given file.

Data Structures Associated with Filesystems

In addition to the fundamental VFS objects, the kernel uses other standard data structures to manage data related to filesystems. The first object is used to describe a specific variant of filesystem, such as ext3 or XFS. The second data structure is used to describe a mounted instance of a filesystem.

Because Linux supports so many different filesystems, the kernel must have a special structure for describing the abilities and behavior of each filesystem.

```
struct file_system_type {
        const char              *name;     /* filesystem's name */
        struct subsystem        subsys;    /* sysfs subsystem object */
        int                     fs_flags;  /* filesystem type flags */
```

```
        /* the following is a function used to read the superblock off the disk */
        struct super_block     *(*get_sb) (struct file_system_type *, int, char
                *, void *);

        /* this is a function used to terminate access to the superblock */
        void                    (*kill_sb) (struct super_block *);

        struct module          *owner;     /* associated module (if any) */
        struct file_system_type *next;     /* next file_system_type in list */
        struct list_head        fs_supers; /* list of superblock objects */
};
```

The `get_sb()` function is used to read the superblock from the disk and populate the superblock object when the filesystem is loaded. The remaining functions describe the properties of the filesystem.

There is only one `file_system_type` per filesystem, regardless of how many instances of the filesystem are mounted on the system, or if the filesystem is even mounted at all.

Things get more interesting when the filesystem is actually mounted, at which point the `vfsmount` structure is created. This structure is used to represent a specific instance of a filesystem—in other words, a mount point.

The `vfsmount` structure is defined in `<linux/mount.h>`. Here it is

```
struct vfsmount {
        struct list_head    mnt_hash;       /* hash table list */
        struct vfsmount     *mnt_parent;    /* parent filesystem */
        struct dentry       *mnt_mountpoint; /* dentry of this mount point */
        struct dentry       *mnt_root;      /* dentry of root of this fs */
        struct super_block *mnt_sb;         /* superblock of this filesystem */
        struct list_head    mnt_mounts;     /* list of children */
        struct list_head    mnt_child;      /* parent-relative children */
        atomic_t            mnt_count;      /* usage count */
        int                 mnt_flags;      /* mount flags */
        char                *mnt_devname;   /* device file name */
        struct list_head    mnt_list;       /* list of descriptors*/
};
```

The complicated part of maintaining the list of all mount points is the relation between the filesystem and all the other mount points. The various linked lists in `vfsmount` keep track of this information.

The `vfsmount` structure also stores the flags, if any, specified on mount in the `mnt_flags` field. Table 11.1 is a list of the standard mount flags.

Table 11.1   **Listing of Standard Mount Flags**

Flag	Description
MNT_NOSUID	Forbids setuid and setgid flags on binaries on this filesystem
MNT_NODEV	Forbids access to device files on this filesystem
MNT_NOEXEC	Forbids execution of binaries on this filesystem

These flags are most useful on removable devices that the administrator does not trust.

Data Structures Associated with a Process

Each process on the system has its own list of open files, root filesystem, current working directory, mount points, and so on. Three data structures tie together the VFS layer and the processes on the system: the files_struct, fs_struct, and namespace structure.

The files_struct is defined in <linux/file.h>. The address of this table is pointed to by the files entry in the processor descriptor. All per-process information about open files and file descriptors is contained therein. Here it is, with comments:

```
struct files_struct {
        atomic_t    count;          /* structure's usage count */
        spinlock_t  file_lock;      /* lock protecting this structure */
        int         max_fds;        /* maximum number of file objects */
        int         max_fdset;      /* maximum number of file descriptors */
        int         next_fd;        /* next file descriptor number */
        struct file **fd;           /* array of all file objects */
        fd_set      *close_on_exec; /* file descriptors to close on exec() */
        fd_set      *open_fds;      /* pointer to open file descriptors */
        fd_set      close_on_exec_init; /* initial files to close on exec() */
        fd_set      open_fds_init;  /* initial set of file descriptors */
        struct file *fd_array[NR_OPEN_DEFAULT]; /* array of file objects */
};
```

The fd array points to the list of open file objects. By default, this is the fd_array array. Because NR_OPEN_DEFAULT is equal to 32, this includes room for 32 file objects. If a process opens more than 32 file objects, the kernel allocates a new array and points the fd pointer at it. In this fashion, access to a reasonable number of file objects is quick, taking place in a static array. In the case that a process opens an abnormal number of files, the kernel can create a new array. If the majority of processes on a system open more than 32 files, for optimum performance, the administrator can increase the NR_OPEN_DEFAULT preprocessor define to match.

The second process-related structure is `fs_struct`, which contains filesystem information related to a process and is pointed at by the `fs` field in the process descriptor. The structure is defined in `<linux/fs_struct.h>`. Here it is, with comments:

```
struct fs_struct {
        atomic_t        count;        /* structure usage count */
        rwlock_t        lock;         /* lock protecting structure */
        int             umask;        /* default file permissions*/
        struct dentry   *root;        /* dentry of the root directory */
        struct dentry   *pwd;         /* dentry of the current working directory */
        struct dentry   *altroot;     /* dentry of the alternative root */
        struct vfsmount *rootmnt;     /* mount object of the root directory */
        struct vfsmount *pwdmnt;      /* mount object of the cwd */
        struct vfsmount *altrootmnt;  /* mount object of the alt root dir */
};
```

This structure holds the current working directory and root directory of the current process.

The third and final structure is the `namespace` structure, which is defined in `<linux/namespace.h>` and pointed at by the `namespace` field in the process descriptor. Per-process namespaces were added to the 2.4 Linux kernel. They enable each process to have a unique view of the mounted filesystems on the system—not just a unique root directory, but an entirely unique filesystem hierarchy, if desired. Here is the structure, with the usual comments:

```
struct namespace {
        atomic_t            count;  /* structure usage count */
        struct vfsmount     *root;  /* mount object of root directory */
        struct list_head    list;   /* list of mount points */
        struct rw_semaphore sem;    /* semaphore protecting the namespace */
};
```

The `list` member specifies a doubly linked list of the mounted filesystems that make up the namespace.

These data structures are linked from each process descriptor. For most processes, their process descriptor points to unique `files_struct` and `fs_struct` structures. For processes created with the clone flag CLONE_FILES or CLONE_FS, however, these structures are shared[7]. Consequently, multiple process descriptors might point to the same `files_struct` or `fs_struct` structure. The `count` member of each structure provides a reference count to prevent destruction while a process is still using the structure.

---

[7]Threads usually specify CLONE_FILES and CLONE_FS and, thus, share a single `files_struct` and `fs_struct` amongst themselves. Normal processes, on the other hand, do not specify these flags and consequently have their own filesystem information and open files table.

The `namespace` structure works the other way around. By default, all processes share the same namespace (that is, they all see the same filesystem hierarchy). Only when the `CLONE_NEWNS` flag is specified during `clone()` is the process given a unique copy of the namespace structure.

Filesystems in Linux

Linux supports a wide range of filesystems, from native filesystems, such as ext2 and ext3, to networked filesystems, such as NFS and Coda, more than 50 filesystems alone in the official kernel. The VFS layer provides these disparate filesystems with both a framework for their implementation and an interface for working with the standard system calls. The VFS layer, thus, makes it both clean to implement new filesystems in Linux, and it allows those filesystems to automatically interoperate via the standard Unix system calls.

12

The Block I/O Layer

BLOCK DEVICES ARE HARDWARE DEVICES DISTINGUISHED by their random (that is, not necessarily sequential) access of fixed-size chunks of data, called blocks. The most common block device is a hard disk, but many other block devices exist, such as floppy drives, CD-ROM drives, and flash memory. Notice how these are all devices on which you mount a filesystem—this is how block devices are normally accessed.

The other basic type of device is a character device. Character devices, or char devices, are accessed as a stream of sequential data, one byte after another. Example character devices are serial ports and keyboards. If the hardware device is accessed as a stream of data, it is implemented as a character device. On the other hand, if the device is accessed randomly (nonsequentially), it is a block device.

Basically, the difference comes down to whether you access the device randomly—in other words, whether the device can *seek* to one position from another. As an example, consider the keyboard. As a driver, the keyboard provides a stream of data. You type "dog" and the keyboard driver returns a stream with those three letters in exactly that order. Reading the letters out of order, or reading any letter but the next one in the stream, makes little sense. The keyboard driver is thus a char device; it provides a stream of the characters typed by the user onto the keyboard. Reading from the keyboard returns a stream first with "*d*," then "*o*," and finally "*g*." When there are no keystrokes waiting, the stream is empty. A hard drive, conversely, is quite different. The hard drive's driver might ask to read the contents of one arbitrary block and then read the contents of a different block; the blocks need not be consecutive. Therefore, the hard disk is accessed randomly, and not as a stream, and thus is a block device.

Managing block devices in the kernel requires more care, preparation, and work than managing character devices. This is because character devices have only one position—the current one—while block devices must be able to navigate back and forth between any location on the media. Indeed, the kernel does not have to provide an entire subsystem dedicated to the management of character devices, but block devices receive exactly that. Partly, such a subsystem is a necessity because of the complexity of block devices. A large reason, however, for such extensive support is that block devices are quite performance sensitive; getting every last drop out of your hard disk is much more important than squeezing an extra percent of speed out of your keyboard. Furthermore, as we will see, the complexity of block devices provides a lot of room for such optimizations. The topic of this chapter is how the kernel manages block devices and their requests. This part of the kernel is known as the *block I/O layer*. Interestingly, revamping the block I/O layer was the primary goal for the 2.5 development kernel.

Anatomy of a Block Device

The smallest addressable unit on a block device is known as a *sector*. Sectors come in various powers of two, but 512 bytes is the most common size. The sector size is a physical property of the device and the sector is the fundamental unit of all block devices—the device cannot address or operate on a unit smaller than the sector, although many block devices can transfer multiple sectors at once. Although most block devices have 512 byte sectors, other sizes are common (for example, many CD-ROM discs have two kilobyte sectors).

Software has different goals, however, and therefore imposes its own smallest logically addressable unit, which is the block. The block is an abstraction of the filesystem—filesystems can only be accessed in multiples of a block. Although the physical device itself is addressable at the sector-level, the kernel performs all disk operations in terms of blocks. Because the device's smallest addressable unit is the sector, the block size can be no smaller than the sector and must be a multiple of a sector. Furthermore, the kernel (like hardware with the sector) needs the block to be a power-of-two. The kernel also requires that a block be no larger than the page size (see Chapter 10, "Memory Management," and Chapter 16, "Portability")[1]. Therefore, block sizes are a power-of-two multiple of the sector size and not greater than the page size. Common block sizes are 512 bytes, one kilobyte, and four kilobytes.

Somewhat confusingly, some people refer to sectors and blocks with different names. Sectors, the smallest addressable unit to the device, are sometimes called "hard sectors" or "device blocks." Meanwhile, blocks, the smallest addressable unit to the filesystem, are sometimes referred to as "filesystem blocks" or "I/O blocks." This chapter continues to call the two notions "sectors" and "blocks," but you should keep these other terms in mind. Figure 12.1 is a diagram of the relationship between sectors and buffers.

Other terminology, at least with respect to hard disks, is common—terms such as *clusters*, *cylinders*, and *heads*. Those notions are specific only to certain block devices and, for the most part, are invisible to user-space software—we will not cover them here. The reason the sector is important to the kernel is because all device I/O must be done in units of sectors. In turn, the higher-level concept used by the kernel, blocks, is built on top of sectors.

---

[1] This is an artificial constraint that could go away in the future. Forcing the block to remain equal to or smaller than the page size, however, simplifies the kernel.

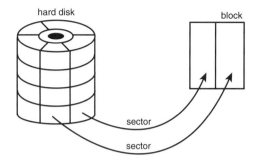

hard disk   block

sector

sector

mapping from sectors to blocks

Figure 12.1   Relationship between sectors and buffers.

Buffers and Buffer Heads

When a block is stored in memory (say, after a read or pending a write), it is stored in a
buffer. Each buffer is associated with exactly one block. The buffer serves as the object
that represents a disk block in memory. Recall a block is composed of one or more sectors, but is no more than a page in size. Therefore, a single page can hold one or more
blocks in memory. Because the kernel requires some associated control information to
accompany the data (such as which block device and which specific block is the buffer
from), each buffer is associated with a descriptor. The descriptor is called a *buffer head* and
is of type `struct buffer_head`. The `buffer_head` structure holds all the information
the kernel needs to manipulate buffers and is defined in `<linux/buffer_head.h>`.

Let's look at this structure, with comments describing each field:

```
struct buffer_head {
        unsigned long       b_state;        /* buffer state flags */
        atomic_t            b_count;        /* buffer usage counter */
        struct buffer_head  *b_this_page;   /* list of buffers on the page */
        struct page         *b_page;        /* associated page */
        sector_t            b_blocknr;      /* logical block number */
        u32                 b_size;         /* block size (in bytes) */
        char                *b_data;        /* pointer to buffer in the page */
        struct block_device *b_bdev;        /* associated block device */
        bh_end_io_t         *b_end_io;      /* I/O completion method */
        void                *b_private;     /* completion method data */
        struct list_head    b_assoc_buffers; /* list of associated mappings */
};
```

The b_state field specifies the state of this particular buffer. It can be one or more of the flags in *Table 12.1*. The legal flags are stored in the bh_state_bits enumeration, which is defined in <linux/buffer_head.h>.

Table 12.1 bh_state **Flags**

Status Flag	Meaning
BH_Uptodate	Buffer contains valid data
BH_Dirty	Buffer is dirty (the contents of the buffer are newer than the contents of the block on disk and therefore the buffer must be written back to disk)
BH_Lock	Buffer is undergoing disk I/O and is locked to prevent concurrent access
BH_Req	Buffer is involved in a request
BH_Mapped	Buffer is a valid buffer mapped to an on-disk block
BH_New	Buffer is newly allocated and not yet accessed
BH_Async_Read	Buffer is undergoing asynchronous read I/O
BH_Async_Write	Buffer is undergoing asynchronous write I/O
BH_Delay	Buffer does not yet have an associated on-disk block
BH_Boundary	Buffer forms the boundary of contiguous blocks —the next block is discontinuous

The bh_state_bits enumeration also contains as the last value in the list a BH_PrivateStart flag. This is not a valid state flag, but instead corresponds to the first usable bit that other code can make use of. All bit values equal to and greater than BH_PrivateStart are not used by the block I/O layer proper, so these bits are safe to use by individual drivers who want to store information in the b_state field. Drivers can base the bit values of their internal flags off this flag and rest assured that they are not encroaching on an official bit used by the block I/O layer.

The b_count field is the usage count of the buffer. The value is incremented and decrements by two inline functions, both of which are defined in <linux/buffer_head.h>:

```
static inline void get_bh(struct buffer_head *bh)
{
        atomic_inc(&bh->b_count);
}

static inline void put_bh(struct buffer_head *bh)
{
        atomic_dec(&bh->b_count);
}
```

Before manipulating a buffer head, you must increment its reference count via `get_bh()` to ensure that the buffer head is not deallocated out from under you. When finished with the buffer head, decrement the reference count via `put_bh()`.

The physical block on disk that a given buffer corresponds to is the `b_blocknr`-th logical block on the block device described by `b_bdev`.

The physical page in memory that a given buffer corresponds to is the page described by `b_page`. More specifically, `b_data` is a pointer directly to the block (that exists somewhere in `b_page`), which is `b_size` bytes in length. Therefore, the block is located in memory starting at address `b_data` and ending at address (`b_data + b_size`).

The purpose of a buffer head is to describe this mapping between the on-disk block and the physical in-memory buffer (which is a sequence of bytes on a specific page). Acting as a descriptor of this buffer-to-block mapping is the data structure's only role in the kernel.

Before the 2.6 kernel, the buffer head was a much more important data structure. In essence, it was *the* unit of I/O in the kernel. Not only did the buffer head describe the disk-block-to-physical-page mapping, but it also acted as the container used for all block I/O. This had two primary problems. First, the buffer head was a large and unwieldy data structure (it has shrunken a bit nowadays) and it was neither clean nor simple to manipulate data in terms of buffer heads. Instead, the kernel prefers to work in terms of pages, which are simple and allow for greater performance. A large buffer head describing each individual buffer (which might be smaller than a page) was inefficient. Consequently, in the 2.6 kernel, much work has gone into making the kernel work directly with pages and address spaces instead of buffers. Some of this work is discussed in Chapter 14, "The Page Cache and Page Writeback," where we discuss the `address_space` structure and the `pdflush` daemons.

The second issue with buffer heads is that they describe only a single buffer. When used as the container for all I/O operations, the buffer head forces the kernel to break up potentially large block I/O operations (say, a write) into many multiple `buffer_head` structures. This results in needless overhead and space consumption. As a result, the primary goal of the 2.5 development kernel was to introduce a new, flexible, and lightweight container for block I/O operations. The result is the `bio` structure, which we discuss in the next section.

The `bio` structure

The basic container for block I/O within the kernel is the `bio` structure, which is defined in `<linux/bio.h>`. This structure represents block I/O operations that are in-flight (active) as a list of *segments*. A segment is a chunk of a buffer that is contiguous in memory. Thus, individual buffers need not be contiguous in memory. By allowing the buffers to be described in chunks, the `bio` structure provides the capability to perform block I/O operations of even a single buffer from multiple locations in memory. Here is `struct bio`, with comments added for each field:

```
struct bio {
        sector_t              bi_sector;          /* associated sector on disk */
        struct bio            *bi_next;           /* list of requests */
        struct block_device   *bi_bdev;           /* associated block device */
        unsigned long         bi_flags;           /* status and command flags */
        unsigned long         bi_rw;              /* read or write? */
        unsigned short        bi_vcnt;            /* number of bio_vec's off
                                                    bi_io_vec */
        unsigned short        bi_idx;             /* current index in bi_io_vec */
        unsigned short        bi_phys_segments;   /* number of segments after
                                                    coalescing */
        unsigned short        bi_hw_segments;     /* number of segments after
                                                    remapping */
        unsigned int          bi_size;            /* I/O count */
        unsigned int          bi_max_vecs;        /* maximum bio_vecs possible */
        struct bio_vec        *bi_io_vec;         /* bio_vec list */
        bio_end_io_t          *bi_end_io;         /* I/O completion method */
        atomic_t              bi_cnt;             /* usage counter */
        void                  *bi_private;        /* owner-private method */
        bio_destructor_t      *bi_destructor;     /* destructor method */
};
```

The primary purpose of a bio structure is to represent an in-flight block I/O operation.
To this end, the majority of fields in the structure are housekeeping-related. The most
important fields are bi_io_vecs, bi_vcnt, and bi_idx.

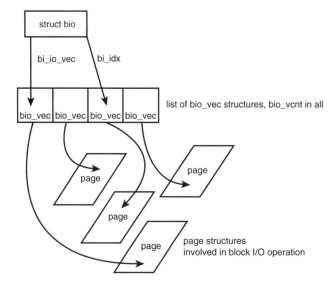

Figure 12.2 Relationship between struct bio,
struct bio_vec, and struct page.

The bi_io_vecs field points to an array of bio_vec structures. These structures are used as lists of individual segments in this specific block I/O operation. Each bio_vec is treated as a vector of the form <page, offset, len>, which describes a specific segment: the physical page it lies on, the location of the block as an offset into the page, and the length of the block. The full array of these vectors describes the entire buffer. The bio_vec structure is defined in <linux/bio.h>, which is shown here:

```
struct bio_vec {
        struct page   *bv_page    /* the physical page on which we reside */;
        unsigned int  bv_len      /* the length of the block */;
        unsigned int  bv_offset   /* the offset within the page */;
};
```

In each given block I/O operation, there are bi_vcnt vectors in the bio_vec array starting with bi_io_vecs. As the block I/O operation is carried out, the bi_idx field is used to point to the current index into the array.

In summary, each block I/O request is represented by a bio structure. Each request is composed of one or more blocks, which are stored in an array of bio_vec structures. These structures act as a vector and describe each segment's location in a physical page in memory. The first segment in the I/O operation is pointed to by b_io_vec. Each additional segment follows after the first, for a total of bi_vcnt segments in the list. As the block I/O layer submits segments in the request, the bi_idx field is updated to point to the current segment. Table 12.3 is a diagram of the relationship between the bio structure, the bio_vec structure, and the page structure.

The bi_idx field is used to point to the current bio_vec in the list, which helps the block I/O layer keep track of partially completed block I/O operations. A more important usage, however, is to allow the splitting of bio structures. With this feature, drivers such as for RAID (Redundant Array of Inexpensive Disks, a hard disk setup that allows single volumes to span multiple disks for performance and reliability purposes) can take a single bio structure, initially intended for a single device, and split it up among the multiple hard drives in the RAID array. All the RAID driver needs to do is copy the bio structure and update the bi_idx field to point to where the individual drive should start its operation.

The bio structure maintains a usage count in the bi_cnt field. When this field reaches zero, the structure is destroyed and the backing memory is freed. Two functions, which follow, manage the usage counters for you.

```
void bio_get(struct bio *bio)
void bio_put(struct bio *bio)
```

The former increments the usage count, whereas the latter decrements the usage count (and, if the count reaches zero, destroys the bio structure). Before manipulating an in-flight bio structure, be sure to increment its usage count to make sure it does not complete and deallocate out from under you. When done, decrement the usage count in turn.

Finally, the `bi_private` field is a private field for the owner (that is, creator) of the structure. As a rule, you can only read or write this field if you allocated the `bio` structure.

The Old Versus the New

The difference between buffers heads and the new `bio` structure is important. The `bio` structure represents an I/O operation, which may include one or more pages in memory. On the other hand, the `buffer_head` structure represents a single buffer, which describes a single block on the disk. Because buffer heads are tied to a single disk block in a single page, buffer heads result in the unnecessary dividing of requests into block-sized chunks, only to later reassemble them. Because the `bio` structure is lightweight, it can describe discontiguous blocks, and does not unnecessarily split I/O operations; it has none of these problems.

Switching from `struct buffer_head` to `struct bio` provided other benefits, as well:

- The `bio` structure can easily represent high memory (see Chapter 10), because `struct bio` only deals with physical pages and not direct pointers.

- The `bio` structure can represent both normal page I/O and direct I/O (I/O operations that do not go through the page cache—see Chapter 14 for a discussion on the page cache).

- The `bio` structure makes it easy to perform scatter-gather (vectored) block I/O operations, with the data involved in the operation originating from multiple physical pages.

- The `bio` structure is much more lightweight than a buffer head because it only contains the minimum information needed to represent a block I/O operation and not unnecessary information related to the buffer itself.

The concept of buffer heads is still required, however, to function as a descriptor mapping disk blocks to pages. The `bio` structure does not contain any information about the state of a buffer—it is simply an array of vectors describing one or more segments of data for a single block I/O operation, plus related information. The `buffer_head` structure is still needed to contain information about buffers. Keeping the two structures separate allows each to remain as small as possible.

Request Queues

Block devices maintain *request queues* to store their pending block I/O requests. The request queue is represented by the `request_queue` structure and is defined in `<linux/blkdev.h>`. The request queue contains a doubly linked list of requests and associated control information. Requests are added to the queue by higher level code in the kernel, such as filesystems. As long as the request queue is nonempty, the block device driver associated with the queue grabs the request from the head of the queue and submits it to its associated block device. Each item in the queue's request list is a single request, of type `struct request`.

Requests

Individual requests on the queue are represented by `struct request`, which is also defined in `<linux/blkdev.h>`. Each request can be composed of more than one `bio` structure because individual requests can operate on multiple consecutive disk blocks. Note that although the blocks on disk must be adjacent, the blocks in memory need not be—each `bio` structure can describe multiple segments (recall, segments are contiguous chunks of a block in memory) and the request can be composed of multiple `bio` structures.

I/O Schedulers

Simply sending out requests to the block devices in the order that the kernel issues them, as soon as it issues them, results in awful performance. One of the slowest operations in an *entire computer* is disk seeks. Each seek—positioning the hard disk's head at the location of a specific block—takes many milliseconds. Minimizing seeks is absolutely crucial to the performance of the system.

Therefore, the kernel does not issue block I/O requests to the disk in the order they are received or as soon as they are received. Instead, it performs operations called *merging* and *sorting* to greatly improve the performance of the system as a whole[2]. The subsystem of the kernel that performs these operations is called the *I/O scheduler*.

The I/O scheduler divides the resource of disk I/O among the pending block I/O requests in the system. It does this through the merging and sorting of pending requests in the request queue. The I/O scheduler is not to be confused with the process scheduler (see Chapter 3, "Scheduling"), which divides the resource of the processor among the processes on the system. The two subsystems are related but not the same. Both the process scheduler and the I/O scheduler virtualize a resource among multiple objects. In the case of the process scheduler, the processor is virtualized and shared among the processes on the system. This provides the illusions inherit in a multitasking and time-sharing operating system, such as any Unix. On the other hand, the I/O scheduler virtualizes block devices among multiple outstanding block requests. This is done to minimize disk seeks and ensure optimum disk performance.

The Job of an I/O Scheduler

An I/O scheduler works by managing a block device's request queue. It decides the order of requests in the queue and at what time each request is dispatched to the block

---

[2]This point must be stressed. A system without these features, or wherein these features are poorly implemented, would perform horribly with even a modest amount of block I/O operations.

device. It manages the request queue with the goal of reducing seeks, which will result in greater *global throughput*. The "global" modifier here is important. An I/O scheduler, very openly, is unfair to some requests at the expense of improving the *overall* performance of the system.

I/O schedulers perform two primary actions to minimize seeks: merging and sorting. Merging is the coalescing of two or more requests into one. Consider an example request that is submitted to the queue by a filesystem—say, to read a chunk of data from a file (at this point, of course, everything is occurring in terms of sectors and blocks and not files). If a request is already in the queue to read from an adjacent sector on the disk (for example, an earlier chunk of the same file), the two requests can be merged into a single request operating on one or more adjacent on-disk sectors. By merging requests, the I/O scheduler reduced the overhead of multiple requests down to a single request. More importantly, only a single command needs to be issued to the disk and servicing the multiple requests can be done without seeking. Consequently, merging requests reduces overhead and minimizes seeks.

Now, assume our fictional read request is submitted to the request queue, but there is no read request to an adjacent sector. We are therefore unable to merge this request with any other request. Now, we could simply stick this request onto the tail of the queue. But, what if there are other requests to a similar location on the disk? Would it not make sense to insert this new request into the queue at a spot near other requests operating on physically near sectors? In fact, I/O schedulers do exactly this. The entire request queue is kept sorted, sector-wise, so that all requests along the queue move (as much as possible) sequentially over the sectors of the hard disk. The goal is not just to minimize each individual seek, but to minimize all seeking by keeping the disk head moving in a straight line. This is similar to the algorithm employed in elevators—elevators do not jump all over, wildly, from floor to floor. Instead, they try to move gracefully in a single direction. When the final floor is reached in one direction, the elevator can reverse course and move in the other direction. Because of this similarity, I/O schedulers (or sometimes just their sorting algorithm) are called *elevators*.

The Linus Elevator

Now let's look at some real-life I/O schedulers. The first I/O scheduler we will look at is called the *Linus Elevator* (this is not a typo; Linus has an elevator named after him!). It was the default I/O scheduler in 2.4. In 2.6, it was replaced by the following two I/O schedulers we will look at—however, because this elevator is simpler than the subsequent ones, and performs many of the same functions, it still deserves discussion.

The Linus Elevator performs both merging and sorting. When a request is added to the queue, it is first checked against every other pending request to see if it is a possible candidate for merging. The Linus Elevator I/O scheduler performs both *front* and *back merging*. The type of merging describes where on the existing request exists the adjacency. If the new request immediately precedes an existing request, it is front merged.

Conversely, if the new request immediately precedes an existing request, it is back merged. Because of the way files are laid out (usually by increasing sector number) and the I/O operations performed in a typical workload (we normally read data start to finish and not in reverse), front merging is very rare compared to back merging. Nonetheless, the Linus Elevator checks for and performs either type of merge.

If the merge attempt fails, a possible insertion point in the queue (a location in the queue where the new request fits sector-wise between the existing requests) is then sought. If one is found, the new request is inserted there. If a suitable location is not found, the request is added to the tail of the queue. Additionally, if an existing request is found in the queue that is suitably old, the new request is also added to the tail of the queue. This prevents many requests to nearby on-disk locations from indefinitely starving requests to other locations on the disk. Unfortunately, this "age" check is not very efficient. It does not provide any real attempt to service requests in a given time frame—it merely stops insertion-sorting requests after a suitable delay. This leads to request starvation, which was the big must-fix of the 2.4 I/O scheduler.

In summary, when a request is added to the queue, four operations are possible. In order, they are

- First, if a request to an adjacent on-disk sector is in the queue, the existing request and the new request are merged into a single request.

- Second, if a request in the queue is sufficiently old, the new request is inserted at the tail of the queue to prevent starvation of the other, older, requests.

- Next, if there is a suitable location sector-wise in the queue, the new request is inserted there. This keeps the queue sorted by physical location on disk.

- Finally, if no such suitable insertion point exists, the request is inserted at the tail of the queue.

The Deadline I/O Scheduler

The Deadline I/O scheduler sought to prevent the starvation caused by the Linus Elevator. In the interest of minimizing seeks, heavy disk I/O operations to one area of the disk can indefinitely starve request operations to another part of the disk. Indeed, a stream of requests to the same area of the disk can result in other far-off requests never being serviced. This starvation is unfair.

Worse, the general issue of request starvation introduces a specific problem known as *writes-starving-reads*. Write operations can usually be committed to disk whenever the kernel gets around to them, entirely asynchronous with respect to the submitting application. Read operations are quite different. Normally, when an application submits a read request, the application blocks until the request is fulfilled. That is, read requests occur synchronously with respect to the submitting application. Although system response is largely unaffected by write latency (the time required to commit a write request), read latency (the time required to commit a read request) is very important. Write latency has little bearing on application performance[3], but an application must wait, twiddling its thumbs, for the completion of each read request. Consequently, read latency is very important to the performance of the system.

Compounding the problem, read requests tend to be dependent on each other. For example, consider the reading of a large number of files. Each read occurs in small buffered chunks. The application will not start reading the next chunk (or the next file, for that matter) until the previous chunk is read from disk and returned to the application. Consequently, if each read request is individually starved, the total delay to such applications compounds and can grow enormous. Recognizing that the asynchrony and interdependency of read requests results in a much stronger bearing of read latency on the performance of the system, the Deadline I/O scheduler implements several features to ensure that request starvation, in general, and read starvation, in specific, is minimized.

Note that reducing request starvation comes at a cost to global throughput. Even the Linus Elevator makes this compromise, albeit in a much milder manner—the Linus Elevator could provide better overall throughput (through a greater minimization of seeks) if it *always* inserted requests into the queue sector-wise and never checked for old requests and reverted to insertion at the tail. Although minimizing seeks is very important, indefinite starvation is not good either. The Deadline I/O scheduler, therefore, works harder to limit starvation. Make no mistake, it is a tough act to provide request fairness, yet maximize global throughput.

In the Deadline I/O scheduler, each request is associated with an expiration time. By default, the expiration time is 500 milliseconds in the future for read requests and five seconds in the future for write requests. The Deadline I/O scheduler operates similarly to the Linus Elevator in that it maintains a request queue sorted by physical location on disk. It calls this queue the sorted queue. When a new request is submitted to the sorted queue, the Deadline I/O scheduler performs merging and insertion like the Linus Elevator[4]. The Deadline I/O scheduler also, however, inserts the request into a second queue, depending on the type of request. Read requests are sorted into a special read FIFO queue and write requests are inserted into a special write FIFO queue. Although the normal queue is sorted by on-disk sector, these queues are kept FIFO (effectively, they are sorted by time). Consequently, new requests are always added to the tail of the queue. Under normal operation, the Deadline I/O scheduler pulls requests from the head of the sorted queue into the dispatch queue. The dispatch queue is then fed to the disk drive. This results in minimal seeks.

If the request at the head of either the write FIFO queue or the read FIFO queue expires (that is, if the current time becomes greater than the expiration time associated with the request), the Deadline I/O scheduler then begins servicing requests from the

---

[3]This is not an incentive to delay writes indefinitely, however. Write requests need to promptly go out to the disk too, just not as critically as reads requests.

[4]Performing front merging is optional in the Deadline I/O scheduler, however, as it is not always worth the trouble since many workloads have very few requests that can be front merged.

FIFO queue. In this manner, the Deadline I/O scheduler attempts to ensure that no request is outstanding longer than its expiration time. See Figure 12.3.

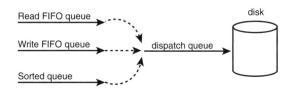

Figure 12.3   The three queues of the Deadline I/O scheduler.

Note that the Deadline I/O scheduler does not make any strict guarantees over request latency. It is capable, however, of generally committing requests on or before their expiration. This prevents request starvation. Because read requests are given a substantially smaller expiration value than write requests, the Deadline I/O scheduler also works to ensure that write requests do not starve read requests. This preference toward read requests provides minimized read latency.

The Deadline I/O scheduler lives in `drivers/block/deadline-iosched.c`.

The Anticipatory I/O Scheduler

Although the Deadline I/O scheduler does a great job minimizing read latency, it does so at the expense of global throughput. Consider a system undergoing heavy write activity. Every time a read request is submitted, the I/O scheduler quickly rushes to handle the read request. This results in the disk seeking over to where the read is, performing the read operation, and then seeking back to continue the ongoing write operation, repeating this little charade for each read request. The preference toward read requests is a good thing, but the resulting pair of seeks (one to the location of the read request and another back to the ongoing write) is detrimental to global disk throughput. The Anticipatory I/O scheduler aims to continue to provide excellent read latency, but also provide excellent global throughput.

First, the Anticipatory I/O scheduler starts with the Deadline I/O scheduler as its base. Therefore, it is not entirely different. The Anticipatory I/O scheduler implements three queues (plus the dispatch queue) and expirations for each request, just like the Deadline I/O scheduler. The major change is the addition of an *anticipation heuristic*.

The Anticipatory I/O scheduler attempts to minimize the seek storm that accompanies read requests issued during other disk I/O activity. When a read request is issued, it is handled within its usual expiration period, as usual. After the request is submitted, however, the Anticipatory I/O scheduler does not immediately seek back and return to handling any other requests. Instead, it does absolutely nothing for a few milliseconds (the actual value is configurable; by default it is six milliseconds). In those few milliseconds, there is a good chance that the application will submit another read request. Any requests issued to an adjacent area of the disk are immediately handled. After the waiting period elapses, the Anticipatory I/O scheduler seeks back to where it left off and continues handling the previous requests.

It is important to note that the few milliseconds that are spent waiting for more requests (basically, the time is spent in anticipation of more requests) are well worth it if they minimize even a modest percentage of the back-and-forth seeking that results from the servicing of read requests during other heavy requests. If an adjacent I/O request is issued within the waiting period, the I/O scheduler just saved a pair of seeks. As more and more reads are issued to the same area of disk, many more seeks are prevented.

Of course, if no activity occurs within the waiting period, the Anticipatory I/O scheduler loses and a few milliseconds are wasted. The key to reaping maximum benefit from the Anticipatory I/O scheduler is correctly anticipating the actions of applications and filesystems. This is done via a set of heuristics and statistics. The Anticipatory I/O scheduler keeps track of per-application statistics pertaining to block I/O habits in hopes of correctly anticipating the actions of applications. With a sufficiently high percentage of correct anticipations, the Anticipatory I/O scheduler can greatly reduce the penalty of seeking to service read requests, while still providing the attention to such requests that system response requires. This allows the Anticipatory I/O scheduler to minimize read latency, while also minimizing the number and duration of seeks. This results in low system latency and high system throughput.

The Anticipatory I/O scheduler lives in `drivers/block/as-iosched.c`. Both the Deadline I/O and the Anticipatory I/O scheduler are part of the standard 2.6 kernel. Which I/O scheduler a given block device uses is configurable. The default I/O scheduler—and of course the best choice for most users—is the Anticipatory I/O scheduler.

13

The Process Address Space

IN CHAPTER 10, "MEMORY MANAGEMENT," we looked at how the kernel manages physical memory. In addition to managing its own memory, the kernel also has to manage the process address space—the view of memory given to each user-space process on the system. Linux is a virtual memory operating system, and thus the resource of memory is virtualized among the processes on the system. To an individual process, the view is as if it alone has full access to the system's physical memory. More importantly, the address space of even a single process can be much larger than physical memory. This chapter discusses how the kernel manages the process address space.

The process address space consists of the linear address range presented to each process and, more importantly, the addresses within this space that the process is allowed to use. Each process is given a *flat* [1] 32 or 64-bit address space, with the size depending on the architecture. Normally, the address space is unique to each process. A memory address in one process's address space tells nothing of that memory address in another process's address space. Processes can elect to share their address space with other processes, however. We know these processes as threads.

A memory address is a given value within the address space, such as 4021f000. This particular value identifies a specific byte in a process's 32-bit address space. The interesting part of the address space is the intervals of memory addresses, such as `08048000-0804c000`, that the process has permission to access. These intervals of legal addresses are called *memory areas*. The process, through the kernel, can dynamically add and remove memory areas to its address space.

The process can only access a memory address in a valid area. Furthermore, the area can be marked read-only or nonexecutable. If a process accesses a memory address not in

---

[1] The term "flat" describes the fact that the address space exists in a single range (as an example, a 32-bit address space extends from the address zero to 429496729). Some operating systems provide a *segmented address space*, with the address space not existing in a single linear range, but instead in segments. Modern virtual memory operating systems generally have flat address spaces.

a valid memory area, or if it accesses a valid area in an invalid manner, the kernel kills the process with the dreaded "Segmentation Fault" message.

Memory areas can contain all sorts of goodies, such as

- A memory map of the executable file's code, called the *text section*
- A memory map of the executable file's initialized global variables, called the *data section*
- A memory map of the zero page (a page consisting of all zeros, used for purposes such as this) containing uninitialized global variables, called the *bss section*[2]
- A memory map of the zero page used for the process's user-space stack (do not confuse this with the process's kernel stack, which is separate and maintained by the kernel)
- An additional text, data, and bss section for each shared library, such as the C library and dynamic linker, loaded into the process's address space
- Any memory mapped files
- Any shared memory segments
- Any anonymous memory mappings, such as those associated with `malloc()`[3]

All valid addresses in the process address space exist in exactly one area (memory areas do not overlap). As we see, there is a separate memory area for each different chunk of memory in a running process: the stack, the object code, global variables, mapped file, and so on.

The Memory Descriptor

The kernel represents a process's address space with a data structure called the *memory descriptor*. This structure contains all of the information related to the process address space. The memory descriptor is represented by `struct mm_struct` and defined in `<linux/sched.h>`[4].

Let's look at the memory descriptor, with comments added describing each field:

---

[2]The term "BSS" is historic and quite old. It stands for `block started by symbol`. Uninitialized variables are not stored in the executable object, because they do not have any associated value. But the C standard decrees that uninitialized global variables are assigned certain default values (basically, all zeros), so the kernel loads the variables (without value) from the executable into memory and maps the zero page over the area, thereby giving the variables the value zero, without having to waste space in the object file with explicit initializations.

[3]Newer versions of glibc implement `malloc()` via `mmap()` and not `brk()`.

[4]There is a rather tangled interdependency between the process descriptor, the memory descriptor, and their related functions. Consequently, struct mm_struct ends up in sched.h.

```
struct mm_struct {
        struct vm_area_struct  *mmap;                /* list of memory areas */
        struct rb_root         mm_rb;               /* rb tree of memory areas  */
        struct vm_area_struct  *mmap_cache;         /* last used memory area */
        unsigned long          free_area_cache;     /* first hole */
        pgd_t                  *pgd;                 /* page global directory */
        atomic_t               mm_users;            /* users */
        atomic_t               mm_count;            /* primary usage counter */
        int                    map_count;           /* number of memory areas */
        struct rw_semaphore    mmap_sem;            /* memory area semaphore */
        spinlock_t             page_table_lock;     /* page-table lock */
        struct list_head       mmlist;              /* list of all mm_structs */
        unsigned long          start_code;          /* start of object code */
        unsigned long          end_code;            /* end of object code */
        unsigned long          start_data;          /* initial address of data */
        unsigned long          end_data;            /* final address of data */
        unsigned long          start_brk;           /* initial address of heap */
        unsigned long          brk;                 /* final address of heap */
        unsigned long          start_stack;         /* start of process stack */
        unsigned long          arg_start;           /* start of arguments */
        unsigned long          arg_end;             /* end of arguments */
        unsigned long          env_start;           /* start of environment */
        unsigned long          env_end;             /* end of environment */
        unsigned long          rss;                 /* physical pages */
        unsigned long          total_vm;            /* total number of pages */
        unsigned long          locked_vm;           /* number of locked pages */
        unsigned long          def_flags;           /* default access flags */
        unsigned long          cpu_vm_mask;         /* lazy TLB switch mask */
        unsigned long          swap_address;        /* last scanned address */
        unsigned               dumpable:1;          /* can we core dump? */
        int                    used_hugetlb;        /* have we used hugetlb? */
        mm_context_t           context;             /* arch-specific data */
        int                    core_waiters;        /* thread core dump waiters */
        struct completion      *core_startup_done;  /* dump start completion */
        struct completion      core_done;           /* dump end completion */
        rwlock_t               ioctx_list_lock;     /* AIO I/O list lock */
        struct kioctx          *ioctx_list;         /* AIO I/O list */
        struct kioctx          default_kioctx;      /* AIO default I/O context */
};
```

The mm_users field is the number of processes using this address space. For example, if two threads share this address space, mm_users is equal to two. The mm_count field is the primary reference count for the mm_struct. All mm_users equate to one increment of mm_count. Thus, in the previous example, mm_count is only one. Only when mm_users reaches zero (when both threads exit) is mm_count decremented. When mm_count finally reaches zero, there are no remaining references to this mm_struct and it is freed. Having two counters enables the kernel to differentiate between the main usage counter (mm_count) and the number of processes using the address space (mm_users).

The mmap and mm_rb fields are different data structures that contain the same thing: all the memory areas in this address space. The former stores them in a linked list whereas the latter stores them in a red-black tree. A red-black tree is a type of binary tree; like all binary trees, searching for a given element is an O(log n) operation.

While the kernel would normally avoid the redundancy of using two data structures to organize the same data, the redundancy comes in handy here. The mmap data structure, as a linked list, allows for simple and efficient traversing of all elements. On the other hand, the mm_rb data structure, as a red-black tree, is more suitable to searching for a given element. We will look more closely at memory areas later in this chapter.

All the mm_struct structures are strung together in a doubly linked list via the mmlist field. The initial element in the list is the init_mm memory descriptor, which describes the address space of the idle process. The list is protected from concurrent access via the mmlist_lock, which is defined in kernel/fork.c. The total number of memory descriptors is stored in the mmlist_nr global integer, which is defined in the same place.

Allocating a Memory Descriptor

The memory descriptor associated with a given task is stored in the mm field of the task's process descriptor. Thus, current->mm is the current process's memory descriptor. The copy_mm() function is used to copy a parent's memory descriptor to its child during fork(). The mm_struct structure is allocated from the mm_cachep slab cache via the allocate_mm() macro in kernel/fork.c. Normally, each process receives a unique mm_struct and thus a unique process address space.

Processes may elect to share their address space with their children by means of the CLONE_VM flag to clone(). We then call the process a thread. Recall from Chapter 2, "Process Management," that this is basically the *only* difference between normal processes and so-called threads in Linux; the Linux kernel does not otherwise differentiate between them. Threads are regular processes to the kernel that merely share certain resources.

In the case that `CLONE_VM` is specified, `allocate_mm()` is *not* called and the process's mm field is set to point to the memory descriptor of its parent via this logic in `copy_mm()`:

```
if (clone_flags & CLONE_VM) {
        /*
         * current is the parent process and
         * tsk is the child process during a fork()
         */
        atomic_inc(&current->mm->mm_users);
        tsk->mm = current->mm;
}
```

Destroying a Memory Descriptor

When the process associated with an address space exits, the `exit_mm()` function is invoked. This function performs some housekeeping and updates some statistics. It then calls `mmput()`, which decrements the memory descriptor's `mm_users` user counter. If the user count reaches zero, `mmdrop()` is called to decrement the `mm_count` usage counter. If *that* counter is finally zero, then the `free_mm()` macro is invoked to return the `mm_struct` to the `mm_cachep` slab cache via `kmem_cache_free()`, because the memory descriptor does not have any users.

The `mm_struct` and Kernel Threads

Kernel threads do not have a process address space and, therefore, do not have an associated memory descriptor. Thus, the mm field of a kernel thread's process descriptor is NULL. Basically, this is the *definition* of a kernel thread—they have no user context.

This is fine, because kernel threads do not ever access any user-space memory (whose would they access?). Because kernel threads do not have any pages in user-space, they do not really deserve their own memory descriptor and page tables (page tables are discussed later in the chapter). Despite this, kernel threads need some of the data, such as the page tables, even to access kernel memory. To provide kernel threads the needed data, without wasting memory on a memory descriptor and page tables, or wasting processor cycles to switch to a new address space whenever a kernel thread begins running, kernel threads use the memory descriptor of whatever task ran previously.

Whenever a process is scheduled, the process address space referenced by their mm field is loaded. The `active_mm` field in the process descriptor is then updated to refer to the new address space. Kernel threads do not have an address space and mm is NULL. Therefore, when a kernel thread is scheduled, the kernel notices that mm is NULL and keeps the previous process's address space loaded. The kernel then updates the `active_mm` field of the kernel thread's process descriptor to refer to the previous process's memory descriptor. The kernel thread can then use the previous process's page tables as needed. Because kernel threads do not access user-space memory, they only make use of the information in the address space pertaining to kernel memory, which is the same for all processes.

Memory Areas

Memory areas are represented by a memory area object, which is stored in the `vm_area_struct` structure and defined in `<linux/mm.h>`. Memory areas are often called *virtual memory areas* or *VMA's* in the kernel.

The `vm_area_struct` structure describes a single memory area over a contiguous interval in a given address space. The kernel treats each memory area as a unique memory object. Each memory area shares certain properties, such as permissions and a set of associated operations. In this manner, the single VMA structure can represent multiple types of memory areas—for example, memory-mapped files or the process's user-space stack. This is similar to the object-oriented approach taken by the VFS layer (see Chapter 11, "The Virtual Filesystem"). Let's look at the structure, with comments added describing each field:

```
struct vm_area_struct {
        struct mm_struct        *vm_mm;         /* associated mm_struct */
        unsigned long           vm_start;       /* start of interval */
        unsigned long           vm_end;         /* end of interval */
        struct vm_area_struct   *vm_next;       /* list of VMA's */
        pgprot_t                vm_page_prot;   /* access permissions */
        unsigned long           vm_flags;       /* flags */
        struct rb_node          vm_rb;          /* this VMA's node */
        struct list_head        shared;         /* list of mappings */
        struct vm_operations_struct *vm_ops;    /* operations */
        unsigned long           vm_pgoff;       /* offset within file */
        struct file             *vm_file;       /* mapped file (if any) */
        void                    *vm_private_data; /* private data */
};
```

As discussed, each memory descriptor is associated with a unique interval in the process's address space. The `vm_start` field is the initial (lowest) address in the interval and the `vm_end` field is the final (highest) address in the interval. Thus, `vm_end - vm_start` is the size (length) in bytes of the interval. Intervals in different memory areas in the same address space cannot overlap.

The `vm_mm` field points to this VMA's associated `mm_struct`. Note each VMA is unique to the `mm_struct` to which it is associated. Therefore, even if two separate processes map the same file into their respective address spaces, they each have a unique `vm_area_struct` to identify their unique memory area. Conversely, two threads that share an address space also share all the `vm_area_struct` structures therein.

VMA Flags

The vm_flags field contains bit flags that specify the behavior of and delineate information about the pages contained in the memory area. Unlike permissions associated with a specific physical page, the VMA flags specify behavior that the kernel is responsible for, not the hardware. Furthermore, vm_flags contains information that relates to each page in the memory area, or the memory area as a whole. *Table 13.1* is a listing of the possible vm_flags values.

Table 13.1 **VMA Flags**

Flag	Effect on the VMA and its pages
VM_READ	Pages can be read from
VM_WRITE	Pages can be written to
VM_EXEC	Pages can be executed
VM_SHARED	Pages are shared
VM_MAYREAD	The VM_READ flag can be set
VM_MAYWRITE	The VM_WRITE flag can be set
VM_MAYEXEC	The VM_EXEC flag can be set
VM_MAYSHARE	The VM_SHARE flag can be set
VM_GROWSDOWN	The area can grow downward
VM_GROWSUP	The area can grow upward
VM_SHM	The area is used for shared memory
VM_DENYWRITE	The area maps an unwritable file
VM_EXECUTABLE	The area maps an executable file
VM_LOCKED	The pages in this area are locked
VM_IO	The area maps a device's I/O space
VM_SEQ_READ	The pages seem to be accessed sequentially
VM_RAND_READ	The pages seem to be accessed randomly
VM_DONTCOPY	This area must not be copied on fork()
VM_DONTEXPAND	This area cannot grow via mremap()
VM_RESERVED	This area must not be swapped out
VM_ACCOUNT	This area is an accounted VM object
VM_HUGETLB	This area uses hugetlb pages

Let's look at some of the more important and interesting flags in depth. The VM_READ, VM_WRITE, and VM_EXEC flags specify the usual read, write, and execute permissions for the pages in this memory area. They are combined as needed to form the appropriate access permissions. For example, a mapping of the object code for a process might be mapped with VM_READ and VM_EXEC, but not VM_WRITE. On the other hand, the data section from an executable object would be mapped VM_READ and VM_WRITE, but VM_EXEC would make little sense. Meanwhile, a read-only memory mapped data file would be mapped with only the VM_READ flag.

The VM_SHARED flag specifies whether the memory area contains a mapping that is shared among multiple processes. If the flag is set, we intuitively call this a *shared mapping*. If the flag is not set, only a single process can view this particular mapping, and we call it a *private mapping*.

The VM_IO flag specifies that this memory area contains a mapping of a device's I/O space. This field is typically set by device drivers when performing mmap() on their I/O space. It specifies, among other things, that the memory area must not be included in any process's core dump. The VM_RESERVED flag specifies that the memory region must not be swapped out. It is also used by device driver mappings.

The VM_SEQ_READ flag provides a hint to the kernel that the application is performing sequential (that is, linear and contiguous) reads in this mapping. The kernel can then opt to increase the read-ahead performed on the backing file. The VM_RAND_READ flag specifies just the opposite, that the application is performing relatively random (that is, not sequential) reads in this mapping. The kernel can then opt to decrease or altogether disable read-ahead on the backing file. These flags are set via the madvise() system call with the MADV_SEQUENTIAL and MADV_RANDOM flags, respectively. Read-ahead is the act of reading sequentially ahead of requested data, in hopes that the additional data will be needed soon. Such behavior is beneficial if applications are reading data sequentially. If data access patterns are random, however, read-ahead is not effective.

VMA Operations

The vm_ops field in the vm_area_struct structure points to the table of operations associated with a given memory area, which the kernel can invoke to manipulate the VMA. The vm_area_struct acts as a generic object for representing any type of memory area and the operations table describes the specific methods, which can operate on this particular instance of the object.

The operations table is represented by struct vm_operations_struct and is defined in <linux/mm.h>:

```
struct vm_operations_struct {
        void (*open) (struct vm_area_struct *);
        void (*close) (struct vm_area_struct *);
        struct page * (*nopage) (struct vm_area_struct *, unsigned long, int);
        int (*populate) (struct vm_area_struct *, unsigned long, unsigned long,
                        pgprot_t, unsigned long, int);
};
```

Let's look at each individual method:

- void open(struct vm_area_struct *area)

This function is invoked when the given memory area is added to an address space.

- `void close(struct vm_area_struct *area)`
This function is invoked when the given memory area is removed from an address space.

- `struct page * nopage(struct vm_area_sruct *area,`
                       `unsigned long address,`
                       `int unused)`
This function is invoked by the page fault handler when a page which is not present in physical memory is accessed.

- `int populate(struct vm_area_struct *area,`
           `unsigned long address,`
           `unsigned long len, pgprot_t prot,`
           `unsigned long pgoff, int nonblock)`
This function is invoked by the `remap_pages()` system call to prefault a new mapping.

Lists and Trees of Memory Areas

As discussed, memory areas are accessed via both the `mmap` and the `mm_rb` fields of the memory descriptor. These two data structures independently point to all the memory area objects associated with the memory descriptor. In fact, they both contain pointers to the very same `vm_area_struct` structures, merely linked in different ways.

The first field, `mmap`, links together all the memory area objects in a singly linked list. Each `vm_area_struct` structure is linked into the list via their `vm_next` field. The areas are sorted by ascended address. The first memory area is the `vm_area_struct` structure that `mmap` points to. The last structure points to `NULL`.

The second field, `mm_rb`, links together all the memory area objects in a red-black tree. The root of the red-black tree is `mm_rb` and each `vm_area_struct` structure in this address space is linked to the tree via their `vm_rb` field.

A red-black tree is a type of balanced binary tree. Each element in a red-black tree is called a node. The initial node is called the root of the tree. Most nodes have two children: a left child and a right child. Some nodes have only one child, and the final nodes, called leaves, have no children. For any node, the elements to the left are smaller in value, whereas the elements to the right are larger in value. Furthermore, each node is assigned a color (red or black, hence the name of this tree) according to two rules: The children of a red node are black and every path through the tree from a node to a leaf must contain the same number of black nodes. The root node is always red. Searching of, insertion to, and deletion from the tree is an `O(log(n))` operation.

The linked list is used when every node needs to be traversed. The red-black tree is used when locating a specific memory area in the address space. In this manner, the kernel uses the redundant data structures to provide optimal performance regardless of the operation performed on the memory areas.

Memory Areas in Real Life

Let's look at a particular process's address space and the memory areas inside. For this task, we can use the useful /proc filesystem and pmap(1) utility. Let's consider a very simple user-space program example, which does absolutely nothing of value, except act as our example:

```
int main(int argc, char *argv[])
{
        return 0;
}
```

Let's list a few of the memory areas in this process's address space. Right off the bat, we know there is the text section, data section, and bss. Assuming this process is dynamically linked with the C library, these three memory areas also exist for libc.so and again for ld.so. Finally, there is also the process's stack.

The output from /proc/<pid>/maps lists the memory areas in this process's address space:

```
rml@phantasy:~$ cat /proc/1426/maps
00e80000-00faf000 r-xp 00000000 03:01 208530     /lib/tls/libc-2.3.2.so
00faf000-00fb2000 rw-p 0012f000 03:01 208530     /lib/tls/libc-2.3.2.so
00fb2000-00fb4000 rw-p 00000000 00:00 0
08048000-08049000 r-xp 00000000 03:03 439029     /home/rml/src/example
08049000-0804a000 rw-p 00000000 03:03 439029     /home/rml/src/example
40000000-40015000 r-xp 00000000 03:01 80276      /lib/ld-2.3.2.so
40015000-40016000 rw-p 00015000 03:01 80276      /lib/ld-2.3.2.so
4001e000-4001f000 rw-p 00000000 00:00 0
bfffe000-c0000000 rwxp fffff000 00:00 0
```

The data is in the form:

```
start-end permission   offset   major:minor   inode   file
```

The pmap(1) utility[5] formats this information in a bit more readable manner. Let's look at that, instead:

```
rml@phantasy:~$ pmap 1426
example[1426]
00e80000 (1212 KB)      r-xp (03:01 208530)   /lib/tls/libc-2.3.2.so
00faf000 (12 KB)        rw-p (03:01 208530)   /lib/tls/libc-2.3.2.so
00fb2000 (8 KB)         rw-p (00:00 0)
08048000 (4 KB)         r-xp (03:03 439029)   /home/rml/src/example
08049000 (4 KB)         rw-p (03:03 439029)   /home/rml/src/example
```

---

[5]The pmap(1) utility displays a formatted listing of a process's memory areas. It is a bit more readable than the /proc output, but it is the same information. It is found in newer versions of the procps package, which is available from http://sources.redhat.com/procps/.

```
40000000 (84 KB)        r-xp (03:01 80276)      /lib/ld-2.3.2.so
40015000 (4 KB)         rw-p (03:01 80276)      /lib/ld-2.3.2.so
4001e000 (4 KB)         rw-p (00:00 0)
bfffe000 (8 KB)         rwxp (00:00 0)
mapped: 1340 KB         writable/private: 40 KB     shared: 0 KB
```

The first three rows are the text section, data section, and bss of `libc.so`, the C library. The next two rows are the text and data section of our executable object. The following three rows are the text section, data section, and bss for `ld.so`, the dynamic linker. The last row is the process's stack.

Note how the text sections are all readable and executable, which is what we expect for object code. On the other hand, the data section and bss (which both contain global variables) are marked readable and writable, but not executable.

The entire address space takes up about 1340 KB, but only 40 KB are writable and private. If a memory region is shared or nonwritable, the kernel only keeps one copy of the backing file in memory. This might seem like common sense for shared mappings, but the nonwritable case can come as a bit of a surprise. If you consider the fact that a nonwritable mapping can never be changed (the mapping is only read from), it is clear that it is safe to load the image only once into memory. Therefore, the C library need only occupy 1212 KB in physical memory, and not 1212 KB multiplied by every process using the library. Since this process has access to about 1340 KB worth of data and code, yet only consumes about 40 KB of physical memory, the space savings from such sharing is substantial.

Note the memory areas without a mapped file that are on device `00:00` and inode zero. This is the zero page. The zero page is a mapping that consists of all zeros. By mapping the zero page over a writable memory area, the area is in effect "initialized" to all zeros. This is important as it provides a zeroed memory area, which is expected by the bss.

Each of the memory areas that are associated with the process corresponds to a `vm_area_struct` structure. Because the process was not a thread, it has a unique `mm_struct` structure referenced from its `task_struct`.

Manipulating Memory Areas

The kernel often has to find whether any memory areas in a process address space matches a given criteria, such as whether a given address exists in a memory area. These operations are frequent, and form the basis of the `mmap()` routine, which we will look at in the next section. A handful of helper functions are defined to assist these jobs.

These functions are all declared in `<linux/mm.h>`.

find_vma()

The `find_vma()` function is defined in `mm/mmap.c`.

The function searches the given address space for the first memory area whose `vm_end` field is greater than `addr`. In other words, this function finds the first memory area that contains `addr` or begins at an address greater than `addr`. If no such memory area exists, the function returns NULL. Otherwise, a pointer to the vm_area_struct structure is returned. Note that, because the returned VMA may start at an address greater than addr, the given address does not necessarily lie *inside* of the returned VMA. The result of the find_vma() function is cached in the mmap_cache field of the memory descriptor. Because of the probability of an operation on one VMA being followed by more operations on that same VMA, the cached results have a decent hit rate (about 30-40% in practice). Checking the cached result is quick. If the given address is *not* in the cache, all the memory areas associated with this memory descriptor must be searched. This is done via the red-black tree:

```
struct vm_area_struct * find_vma(struct mm_struct *mm, unsigned long addr)
{
        struct vm_area_struct *vma = NULL;

        if (mm) {
                vma = mm->mmap_cache;
                if (!(vma && vma->vm_end > addr && vma->vm_start <= addr)) {
                        struct rb_node * rb_node;

                        rb_node = mm->mm_rb.rb_node;
                        vma = NULL;
                        while (rb_node) {
                                struct vm_area_struct * vma_tmp;

                                vma_tmp = rb_entry(rb_node,
                                                struct vm_area_struct, vm_rb);
                                if (vma_tmp->vm_end > addr) {
                                        vma = vma_tmp;
                                        if (vma_tmp->vm_start <= addr)
                                                break;
                                        rb_node = rb_node->rb_left;
                                } else
                                        rb_node = rb_node->rb_right;
                        }
                        if (vma)
                                mm->mmap_cache = vma;
                }
        }

        return vma;
}
```

The initial check of mmap_cache tests whether the cached VMA contains the desired address. Note that simply checking if the VMA's vm_end field is bigger than addr would not ensure that this is the first such VMA that is larger than addr. Thus, for the cache to be useful here, the given addr must lie in the VMA—thankfully, this is just the sort of scenario in which consecutive operations on the same VMA would occur.

If the cache does not contain the desired VMA, the function must search the red-black tree. Checking each node of the tree accomplishes this. If the current VMA's vm_end is larger than addr, the function follows the left child; otherwise, it follows the right child. The function terminates as soon as a VMA is found that contains addr. If such a VMA is not found, the function continues traversing the tree and returns the first VMA it found that starts after addr. If no VMA is ever found, NULL is returned.

find_vma_prev()

The find_vma_prev() function works the same as find_vma(), but it also returns the last VMA *before* addr. The function is also defined in mm/mmap.c and declared in <linux/mm.h>:

```
struct vm_area_struct * find_vma_prev(struct mm_struct *mm, unsigned long addr,
                                      struct vm_area_struct **pprev)
```

The pprev argument stores a pointer to the VMA preceding addr.

find_vma_intersection()

The find_vma_intersection() function returns the first VMA that overlaps a given address interval. The function is defined in <linux/mm.h>, because it is inline:

```
static inline struct vm_area_struct * find_vma_intersection(struct mm_struct *mm,
       unsigned long start_addr, unsigned long end_addr)
{
       struct vm_area_struct *vma;

       vma = find_vma(mm,start_addr);
       if (vma && end_addr <= vma->vm_start)
               vma = NULL;
       return vma;
}
```

The first parameter is the address space to search, start_addr is the start of the interval, and end_addr is the end of the interval.

Obviously, if find_vma() returns NULL, so would find_vma_intersection(). If find_vma() returns a valid VMA, however, find_vma_intersection() returns the same VMA only if it does *not* start after the end of the given address range. If the returned memory area does start after the end of the given address range, the function returns NULL.

mmap() and do_mmap(): Creating an Address Interval

The do_mmap() function is used by the kernel to create a new linear address interval. Saying that this function creates a new VMA is not technically correct, because if the created address interval is adjacent to an existing address interval, and if they share the same permissions, the two intervals are merged into one. If this is not possible, a new VMA is created. In any case, do_mmap() is the function used to add an address interval to a process's address space—whether that means expanding an existing memory area or creating a new one.

The do_mmap() function is declared in <linux/mm.h>:

```
unsigned long do_mmap(struct file *file, unsigned long addr,
                      unsigned long len, unsigned long prot,
                      unsigned long flag, unsigned long offset)
```

This function maps the file specified by file at offset offset for length len. The file parameter can be NULL and offset can be zero, in which case a file will not back the mapping. In that case, this is called an *anonymous mapping*. If a file and offset are provided, the mapping is called a *file-backed mapping*.

The addr function optionally specifies the initial address from which to start the search for a free interval.

The prot parameter specifies the access permissions for pages in the memory area. The possible permission flags are defined in <asm/mman.h> and are unique to each supported architecture, although in practice each architecture defines the flags listed in *Table 13.2*.

The flags parameter specifies flags that correspond to the remaining VMA flags. These flags are also defined in <asm/mman.h>. See *Table 13.3*.

Table 13.2   **Page Protection Flags**

Flag	Effect on the pages in the new interval
PROT_READ	Corresponds to VM_READ
PROT_WRITE	Corresponds to VM_WRITE
PROT_EXEC	Corresponds to VM_EXEC
PROT_NONE	Page cannot be accessed

Table 13.3   **Page Protection Flags**

Flag	Effect on the new interval
MAP_SHARED	The mapping can be shared
MAP_PRIVATE	The mapping cannot be shared
MAP_FIXED	The new interval *must* start at the given address addr
MAP_ANONYMOUS	The mapping is not file-backed, but is anonymous
MAP_GROWSDOWN	Corresponds to VM_GROWSDOWN
MAP_DENYWRITE	Corresponds to VM_DENYWRITE
MAP_EXECUTABLE	Corresponds to VM_EXECUTABLE
MAP_LOCKED	Corresponds to VM_LOCKED

Table 13.3 **Continued**

FlagsFlag	Effect on the new interval
MAP_NORESERVE	No need to reserve space for the mapping
MAP_POPULATE	Populate (prefault) page tables
MAP_NONBLOCK	Do not block on I/O

If any of the parameters are invalid, do_mmap() returns a negative value. Otherwise, a suitable interval in virtual memory is located. If possible, the interval is merged with an adjacent memory area. Otherwise, a new vm_area_struct structure is allocated from the vm_area_cachep slab cache, and the new memory area is added to the address space's linked list and red-black tree of memory areas via the vma_link() function. Next, the total_vm field in the memory descriptor is updated. Finally, the function returns the initial address of the newly created address interval.

The mmap() System Call

The do_mmap() functionality is exported to user-space via the mmap() system call. The mmap() system call is defined as

```
void  * mmap2(void *start, size_t length, int prot, int flags, int fd, off_t pgoff)
```

This system call is named mmap2() because it is the second variant of mmap(). The original mmap() took an offset in bytes as the last parameter; the current mmap2() receives the offset in pages. This enables larger files with larger offsets to be mapped. The original mmap(), as specified by POSIX, is available from the C library as mmap() but is no longer implemented in the kernel proper, while the new version is available as mmap2(). Both library calls use the mmap2() system call, with the original mmap() converting the offset from bytes to pages.

munmap() and do_munmap(): Removing an Address Interval

The do_munmap() function removes an address interval from a specified process address space. The function is declared in <linux/mm.h>:

```
int do_munmap(struct mm_struct *mm, unsigned long start, size_t len)
```

The first parameter specifies the address space from which the interval starting at address start of length len bytes is removed. On success, zero is returned. Otherwise, a negative error code is returned.

The munmap() System Call

The munmap() system call is exported to user-space as a means to allow processes to remove address intervals from their address space; it is the complement of the mmap() system call:

```
int munmap(void *start, size_t length)
```

The system call is defined in `mm/mmap.c` and acts as a very simple wrapper to `do_munmap()`:

```
asmlinkage long sys_munmap(unsigned long addr, size_t len)
{
        int ret;
        struct mm_struct *mm;

        mm = current->mm;
        down_write(&mm->mmap_sem);
        ret = do_munmap(mm, addr, len);
        up_write(&mm->mmap_sem);
        return ret;
}
```

Page Tables

Although applications operate on virtual memory that is mapped to physical addresses, processors operate directly on those physical addresses. Consequently, when an application accesses a virtual memory address, it must first be converted to a physical address before the processor can resolve the request. Performing this lookup is done via page tables. Page tables work by splitting the virtual address into chunks. Each chunk is used as an index into a table. The table either points to another table or the associated physical page.

In Linux, the page tables consist of three levels. The multiple levels allow a sparsely populated address space, even on 64-bit machines. If the page tables were implemented as a single static array, their size on even 32-bit architectures would be enormous. Linux uses three levels of page tables even on architectures that do not support three levels in hardware (for example, some hardware uses only two levels or implements a hash in hardware). Using three levels is a sort of "greatest common denominator"—architectures with a less complicated implementation can simplify the kernel page tables as needed with compiler optimizations.

The top-level page table is the page global directory (PGD). The PGD consists of an array of `pgd_t` types. On most architectures, the `pgd_t` type is an `unsigned long`. The entries in the PGD point to entries in the second-level directory, the PMD.

The second-level page table is the page middle directory (PMD). The PMD is an array of `pmd_t` types. The entries in the PMD point to entries in the PTE.

The final level is called simply the page table and consists of page table entries of type `pte_t`. Page table entries point to physical page.

In most architectures, page table lookups are handled (at least to some degree) by hardware. In normal operation, hardware can handle much of the responsibility of using the page tables. The kernel must set things up, however, in such a way that the hardware is happy and can do its thing. Figure 13.1 diagrams the flow of a virtual to physical address lookup using page tables.

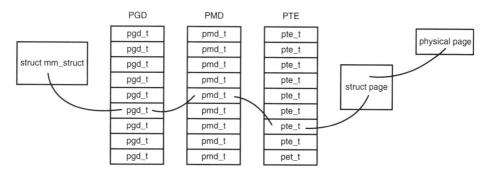

Figure 13.1   Page tables.

Each process has its own page tables (threads share them, of course). The pgd field of the memory descriptor points to the process's page global directory. Manipulating and traversing page tables requires the page_table_lock, which is located inside the associated memory descriptor.

Page table data structures are quite architecture-dependent and thus are defined in <asm/page.h>.

Because nearly every access of a page in virtual memory must be resolved to its corresponding address in physical memory, the performance of the page tables is very critical. Unfortunately, looking up all of these addresses in memory can only be so fast. To facilitate this, most processors implement a *translation lookaside buffer*, or simply *TLB*, which acts as a hardware cache of virtual to physical mappings. When accessing a virtual address, the processor will first check if the mapping is cached in the TLB. If there is a hit, the physical address is immediately returned. Otherwise, if there is a miss, the page tables are consulted for the corresponding physical address.

Nonetheless, page table management is still a critical—and evolving—part of the kernel. Changes to this area in 2.6 include allocating parts of the page table out of high memory. Future possibilities include shared page tables with copy-on-write semantics. In that scheme, page tables would be shared between parent and child across a fork(). When the parent or the child attempted to modify a particular page table entry, a copy would be created and the two processes would no longer share that entry. Sharing page tables would remove the overhead of copying the page table entries on fork().

14

The Page Cache and Page Writeback

T HE LINUX KERNEL IMPLEMENTS ONE PRIMARY DISK cache, known as the page cache. The goal of this cache is to minimize disk I/O by storing in physical memory data that would otherwise be accessed from disk. This chapter deals with the page cache.

Disk caches are beneficial for two reasons. First, disk access is magnitudes slower than memory access. Accessing data from memory instead of the disk is much faster. Second, data accessed once will, with a high likelihood, find itself accessed again in the near future. This principle, that access to a particular piece of data tends to be clustered in time, is called *temporal locality*. Temporal locality ensures that if data is cached on its first access, there is a high probability of a cache hit (access to data that is in the cache) in the near future.

The page cache consists of physical pages in RAM. Each page in the cache corresponds to multiple blocks on the disk. Whenever the kernel begins a page I/O operation (a disk operation in page-size chunks, usually to a regular file), it first checks if the requisite data is in the page cache. If it is, the kernel can forgo accessing the disk and use the data straight from the page cache.

Individual disk blocks can also tie into the page cache, by way of block I/O buffers. Recall from Chapter 12, "The Block I/O Layer," that a buffer is the in-memory representation of a single physical disk block. Buffers act as descriptors that map pages in memory to disk blocks; thus, the page cache also reduces disk access during block I/O operations by both caching disk blocks and buffering block I/O operations until later. This caching is often referred to as the "buffer cache," although in reality it is not a separate cache and is part of the page cache.

Let's look at the sort of operations and data that end up in the page cache. The page cache is primarily populated by page I/O operations, such as `read()` and `write()`. Page I/O operations manipulate entire pages of data at a time; this entails operations on more than one disk block. Consequently, the page cache caches page-size chunks of files.

Block I/O operations manipulate a single disk block at a time. A common block I/O operation is reading and writing inodes. The kernel provides the `bread()` function to perform a low-level read of a single block from disk. Via buffers, disk blocks are mapped to their associated in-memory pages and, thus, cached in the page cache.

For example, when you first open a source file in a text editor, data from the file is read into memory from disk. As you edit the file, more and more pages are read in. When you later compile the file, the kernel can use the pages directly from the page cache; it need not reread the file from disk. Because users tend to read and manipulate the same files repeatedly, the page cache reduces the need for a large number of disk operations.

Page Cache

The page cache, as its name suggests, is a cache of pages. The pages originate from reads and writes of regular filesystem files, block device files, and memory-mapped files. In this manner, the page cache contains entire pages from recently accessed files. Prior to a page I/O operation, such as `read()`[1], the kernel checks if the data resides in the page cache. If the data is in the page cache, the kernel can quickly return the requested page.

The `address_space` Object

A physical page might be composed of multiple noncontiguous physical blocks[2]. Checking the page cache to see if certain data has been cached is rendered more difficult because of the noncontiguous nature of the blocks that can up each page. Because of this, it is not possible to index the data in the page cache using only a device name and block number, which would otherwise be the simplest solution.

Furthermore, the Linux page cache is quite general in what pages it can cache. Indeed, the original page cache introduced in System V Release 4 cached only filesystem data. Consequently, the SVR4 page cache used its equivalent of the file object (called `struct vnode`) to manage the page cache. The Linux page cache aims to cache *any* page-based object, which includes many forms of files and memory mappings.

To remain generic, the Linux page cache uses the `address_space` structure to identify pages in the page cache. This structure is defined in `<linux/fs.h>`:

```
struct address_space {
        struct inode            *host;          /* owning inode */
        struct radix_tree_root  page_tree;      /* radix tree of all pages */
```

---

[1]As we saw in Chapter 11, "The Virtual Filesystem," it is not the read() and write() system calls which perform the actual page I/O operation, but the filesystem-specific methods specified by file->f_op->read() and file->f_op->write().

[2]For example, a physical page is 4KB on the x86 architecture while a disk block on most filesystems can be as small as 512 bytes. Therefore, 8 blocks might fit in a single page. The blocks need not by contiguous because the files themselves might be laid out all over the disk.

```
        spinlock_t              page_lock;     /* lock protecting page_tree */
        struct list_head        clean_pages;   /* list of clean pages */
        struct list_head        dirty_pages;   /* list of dirty pages */
        struct list_head        locked_pages;  /* list of locked pages */
        struct list_head        io_pages;      /* pages under I/O */
        unsigned long           nrpages;       /* total number of pages */
        struct address_space_operations *a_ops; /* operations table */
        struct list_head        i_mmap;        /* list of private mappings */
        struct list_head        i_mmap_shared; /* list of shared mappings */
        struct semaphore        i_shared_sem;  /* protects above two lists */
        unsigned long           dirtied_when;  /* last modification */
        int                     gfp_mask;      /* allocator flag for the pages */
        struct backing_dev_info *backing_dev_info; /* read-ahead information */
        spinlock_t              private_lock;  /* private address_space lock */
        struct list_head        private_list;  /* private address_space list */
        struct address_space    *assoc_mapping; /* associated buffres */
};
```

The fields clean_pages, dirty_pages, and locked_pages are doubly linked lists of all clean, dirty, and locked pages, respectively, that belong to this address_space. Together, these lists contain all the pages associated with this address space. There are a total of nrpages pages among the lists.

The clean_pages doubly linked list contains all the page descriptors associated with this address_space that are neither locked nor dirty. A page is locked if it is currently undergoing disk I/O. A page is dirty if the in-memory page has been updated, but the changes have not yet been written back to disk.

The dirty_pages list contains all the page descriptors associated with this address_space that are not locked, but are dirty. These pages have been updated, but not yet written back to disk. That is, the cached copy of the page is newer than the on-disk copy. Eventually, the copy in the page cache needs to be written back (synchronized) with the copy on the disk. Note that it is never possible that the on-disk copy becomes newer than the cached copy because all page I/O goes through the page cache.

The locked_pages list contains all the page descriptors associated with this address_space that are locked; the contents of these pages are currently being transferred from the disk into the page cache, or vice versa.

The address_space is associated with some kernel object. Normally, this is an inode. If so, the host field points to the associated inode. The host field is NULL if the associated object is not an inode; for example, if the address_space is associated with the swapper.

If the associated kernel object is the inode of a memory-mapped file, the i_mmap and i_mmap_shared fields are used.

The a_ops field points to the address space operations table, in the same manner as the VFS objects and their operations tables. The operations table is represented by struct address_space_operations and is also defined in <linux/fs.h>:

```
struct address_space_operations {
        int (*writepage)(struct page *, struct writeback_control *);
        int (*readpage) (struct file *, struct page *);
        int (*sync_page) (struct page *);
        int (*writepages) (struct address_space *, struct writeback_control *);
        int (*set_page_dirty) (struct page *);
        int (*readpages) (struct file *, struct address_space *,
                          struct list_head *, unsigned);
        int (*prepare_write) (struct file *, struct page *, unsigned, unsigned);
        int (*commit_write) (struct file *, struct page *, unsigned, unsigned);
        sector_t (*bmap)(struct address_space *, sector_t);
        int (*invalidatepage) (struct page *, unsigned long);
        int (*releasepage) (struct page *, int);
        int (*direct_IO) (int, struct kiocb *, const struct iovec *,
                          loff_t, unsigned long);
};
```

The `readpage()` and `writepage()` methods are most important. Let's look at the steps involved in a page read operation.

First, the read method is passed an `address_space` plus offset pair. These values are used to search the page cache for the desired data:

```
page = find_get_page(mapping, index);
```

where `mapping` is the given address space and `index` is the desired position in the file.

If the page does not exist in the cache, a new page is allocated and added to the page cache:

```
struct page *cached_page;
int error;

cached_page = page_cache_alloc_cold(mapping);
if (!cached_page)
        /* error allocating memory */
error = add_to_page_cache_lru(cached_page, mapping, index, GFP_KERNEL);
if (error)
        /* error adding page to page cache */
```

Finally, the requested data can be read from disk, added to the page cache, and returned to the user:

```
error = mapping->a_ops->readpage(file, page);
```

Write operations are a bit different. For file mappings, whenever a page is modified, the VM simply calls

```
SetPageDirty(page);
```

The kernel later writes the page out via the `writepage()` method. Write operations on specific files are more complicated. Basically, the generic write path in `mm/filemap.c` performs the following steps:

```
page = __grab_cache_page(mapping, index, &cached_page, &lru_pvec);
status = a_ops->prepare_write(file, page, offset, offset+bytes);
page_fault = filemap_copy_from_user(page, offset, buf, bytes);
status = a_ops->commit_write(file, page, offset, offset+bytes);
```

First, the page cache is searched for the desired page. If it is not in the cache, an entry is allocated and added. Next, the `prepare_write()` method is called to set up the write request. The data is then copied from user-space into a kernel buffer. Finally, the data is written to disk via the `commit_write()` function.

Because the previous steps are performed during all page I/O operations, all page I/O is guaranteed to go through the page cache. Consequently, the kernel attempts to satisfy all read requests from the page cache. If this fails, the page is read in from disk and added to the page cache. For write operations, the page cache acts as a staging ground for the writes. Therefore, all written pages are also added to the page cache.

Radix Tree

Because the kernel must check for the existence of a page in the page cache before initiating any page I/O, such a check must be quick. Otherwise, the overhead of searching and checking the page cache could nullify any benefits the cache might provide (at least if the cache hit rate is low—the overhead would have to be awful to cancel out the benefit of retrieving the data from memory in lieu of disk).

As we saw in the previous section, the page cache is searched via the `address_space` object plus an offset value. Each `address_space` has a unique radix tree stored as `page_tree`. A radix tree is a type of binary tree. The radix tree allows very quick searching for the desired page, given only the file offset. Page cache searching functions such as `find_get_page()` call `radix_tree_lookup()`, which performs a search on the given tree for the given object.

The core radix tree code is available in generic form in `lib/radix-tree.c`. Users of the radix tree need to include `<linux/radix-tree.h>`.

The Old Page Hash Table

Prior to the 2.6 kernel, the page cache was not searched via radix tree. Instead, a global hash was maintained over all the pages in the system. The hash returned a doubly linked list of entries, which hash to the same given value. If the desired page was in the cache, one of the items in the list was the corresponding page. Otherwise, the page was not in the page cache and the hash function returned NULL.

The global hash had four primary problems:

- A single global lock protected the hash. Lock contention was quite high on even moderately sized machines, and performance suffered as a result.

- The hash was larger than needed because it contained all of the pages in the page cache, whereas only pages pertaining to the current file were relevant.

- Performance when the hash lookup failed (that is, the given page was not in the page cache) was slower than desired, particularly because of having to walk the chains off a given hash value.

- The hash consumed more memory than other possible solutions.

The introduction of a radix tree-based page cache in 2.6 solved these issues.

The Buffer Cache

Linux no longer has a distinct buffer cache. Way back in the 2.2 kernel, there were two separate disk caches: the page cache and the buffer cache. The former cached pages, the latter cached buffers. The two caches were not unified in the least; a disk block could exist in both caches simultaneously. This led to extensive effort in synchronization between the two cached copies—not to mention wasted memory.

This was the case in the 2.2 Linux kernel and earlier, but starting with the 2.4 Linux kernel the two caches were unified. Today, we have one disk cache—the page cache.

The kernel still needs to use buffers, however, to represent disk blocks in memory. Thankfully, the buffers describe the mapping of a block onto a page, which is in the page cache.

The `pdflush` Daemon

Dirty pages that accumulate in memory eventually need to be written back to disk. Dirty page writeback occurs in two situations:

- When free memory shrinks below a specified threshold, the kernel must write dirty data back to disk to free memory.

- When dirty data grows older than a specific threshold, sufficiently old data is written back to disk, to ensure that dirty data does not remain dirty indefinitely.

These two jobs have rather different goals. In fact, in older kernel they were performed by two separate kernel threads (see the following section). In 2.6, however, a gang[3] of kernel threads, the `pdflush` background writeback daemons (or, simply, the `pdflush` threads), performs these jobs. Rumor has it that `pdflush` is short for "dirty page flush." Ignore the confusing name; let's look at each of these goals in more detail.

First, the `pdflush` threads need to flush dirty data to disk when the amount of free memory in the system shrinks beyond a specified level. The goal of this background writeback is to regain memory from dirty pages when available physical memory is low. The specified memory level is configurable by the `dirty_background_ratio` sysctl. When free memory drops below this threshold, the kernel invokes the

---

[3] This is not slang. The term "gang" is commonly used in computer science to denote a group of things that can operate in parallel.

`wakeup_bdflush()`[4] call to wake up a pdflush thread and have it run the `background_writeout()` function to begin writeback of dirty pages. This function takes a lone parameter, which is the number of pages to attempt to writeback. The function continues writing out data until two conditions are true:

- The specified minimum number of pages has been written out.
- The mount of free memory is above the `dirty_background_ratio` threshold.

These conditions ensure that pdflush does its part to relieve low-memory conditions. Writeback stops prior to these conditions only if `pdflush` writes back *all* the dirty pages and there is nothing left to do.

For its second goal, `pdflush` periodically wakes up (unrelated to low memory conditions) and writes out very old dirty pages. This is done to ensure that no dirty pages remain in memory indefinitely. During a system failure, because memory is volatile, dirty pages in memory that have not been written to disk are lost. Consequently, periodically synchronizing the page cache with the disk is important. On system boot, a timer is initialized to wakeup a `pdflush` thread and have it run the `wb_kupdate()` function. This function will then writeback all data that was modified longer than `dirty_expire_centisecs` hundredths of a second ago. The timer is then reinitialized to expire again in `dirty_writeback_centisecs` hundredths of a second. In this manner, the `pdflush` threads periodically wakeup and write to disk all dirty pages that are older than a specified limit.

The system administrator may set these values either in `/proc/sys/vm` or via sysctl. *Table 11.1* is a list of each variable.

Table 11.1   `pdflush` **Settings**

Variable	Description
`dirty_background_ratio`	As a percentage of total memory, the number of pages at which the `pdflush` threads will begin writeback of dirty data.
`dirty_expire_centisecs`	In one hundredths of a second, how old data must be to be written out next time a `pdflush` thread wakes to perform periodic writeback.
`dirty_ratio`	As a percentage of total memory, the number of pages a process will generate before it will begin writeback of dirty data.
`dirty_writeback_centisecs`	In one hundredths of a second, how often the `pdflush` threads wake up to writeback out data.

The pdflush threads live in `mm/pdflush.c` and the write back mechanism lives in `mm/page-writeback.c` and `fs/fs-writeback.c`.

---

[4]Yes, it is misnamed. It should be `wakeup_pdflush()`. See the following section for the heritage of this call.

bdflush **and** kupdated

Prior to the 2.6 kernel, the job of the pdflush threads was met by two other kernel threads, bdflush and kupdated.

The bdflush kernel thread performed background writeback of dirty pages when available memory was low. A set of thresholds were maintained, similar to pdflush, and bdflush was awakened via wakeup_bdflush() whenever free memory dropped below those thresholds.

There are two main differences between bdflush and pdflush. The first, which we look at in the next section, is that there is always only one bdflush daemon, while the number of pdflush threads is dynamic. The second difference is that bdflush was buffer-based; it wrote back dirty buffers. Conversely, pdflush is page-based; it writes back whole pages. Of course, the pages may correspond to buffers, but the actual I/O unit is a full page and not a single buffer. This is beneficial as managing pages is easier than buffers, because pages are a more general and common unit.

Because bdflush only flushes buffers when memory is low or the number of buffers is too large, the kupdated thread was introduced to periodically write back dirty pages. It served an identical purpose to pdflush's wb_kupdate() function.

Both the bdflush and kupdated kernel threads and their functionality was replaced by the pdflush threads.

Congestion Avoidance: Why We Have Multiple Threads

One of the major flaws in the bdflush solution was that bdflush consisted of one thread. This led to possible congestion during heavy page writeback where the single bdflush thread would block on a single congested device queue (the list of I/O requests waiting to submit to disk), while other device queues would sit relatively idle. If the system has multiple disks, and the associated processing power, the kernel should be able to keep each disk busy. Unfortunately, even with plenty of data needing writeback, bdflush can become stuck handling a single queue and fail to keep all disks saturated. This occurs because the throughput of disks is a finite—and unfortunately rather small—number. If only a single thread is performing page writeback, that single thread can easily spend a large portion of time waiting for a single disk, because disk throughput is such a limiting quantity. To mitigate this, the kernel needs to multithread page writeback. In this manner, no single device queue can become a bottleneck.

The 2.6 kernel solves this problem by allowing multiple pdflush threads to exist. Each thread individually flushes dirty pages to disk, allowing different pdflush threads to concentrate on different device queues.

The number of threads changes throughout the uptime of a system, according to a simple algorithm. If all existing pdflush threads are busy for at least one second, a new pdflush thread is created. The total number of threads cannot exceed MAX_PDFLUSH_THREADS, which by default is eight. Conversely, if a pdflush thread was asleep for more than a second, it is terminated. The minimum number of threads is at least MIN_PDFLUSH_THREADS, which by default is two. In this manner, the number of pdflush threads adjusts dynamically depending on the amount of page writeback and congestion. If all existing `pdflush` threads are busy writing back data, a new thread is created. This ensures that a single device queue is not congested while other, less busy, device queues sit around needing data writeback. If the congestion diminishes, however, the number of `pdflush` threads is scaled back to conserve memory.

This is all well and good, but what if each `pdflush` thread gets hung up writing to the same, congested, queue? In that case, the performance of multiple `pdflush` threads would not be much improved over a single thread. The memory wasted, however, would be significantly greater. To mitigate this effect, the `pdflush` threads employ congestion avoidance. They actively try to writeback pages whose queues are not congested. As a result, the `pdflush` threads spread out their work and refrain from merely hammering on the same busy device. When the `pdflush` threads are "busy"—and thus, a new thread is spawned—they are *truly* busy.

Because of the improvements in page writeback, including the introduction of `pdflush`, the 2.6 kernel is capable of keeping many more disks saturated than any earlier kernel. In the face of heavy activity, the `pdflush` threads can maintain high throughput across multiple disks.

15

Debugging

ONE OF THE DEFINING FACTORS THAT SETS kernel development apart from user-space development is the hardship associated with debugging. It is difficult, at least relative to user-space, to debug the kernel. To complicate the matter, a fault in the kernel could bring the whole system down—hard.

Growing successful at debugging the kernel—and ultimately, becoming successful at kernel development as a whole—is largely a function of your experience and understanding of the operating system. Sure, looks and charm help, too—but to successfully debug kernel issues, you need to understand the kernel. We have to start somewhere, however, so in this chapter we will look at approaches to debugging the kernel.

What You Need to Start

So, you're ready to start bug hunting? It might be a long and frustrating journey. Some bugs have perplexed the entire kernel development community for months. Fortunately, for every one of these evil bugs, there is a simple bug with an equally simple fix. With luck, all your bugs will remain simple and trivial. You will not know that, however, until you start investigating. For that, you need

- A bug. It might sound silly, but you need a well-defined and specific bug. It helps if it is reliably reproducible, at least for someone, but unfortunately bugs are not always well-behaved or well-defined.

- A kernel version the bug exists on (presumably in the latest kernel, or who cares?). Even better is if you know the kernel version where the bug first appeared. We will look at how to figure that out if you do not know it.

- Some good luck.

If you cannot reproduce the bug, many of the following approaches become worthless. It is rather crucial that you be able to duplicate the problem. If you cannot, fixing the bug is limited to conceptualizing the problem and finding a flaw in the code. This does often happen (yep, the kernel developers are that good), but chances of success are obviously much more favorable if you can reproduce the problem.

It might seem strange that there is a bug that someone cannot reproduce. In user-space programs, bugs are quite often a lot more straightforward—for example, *doing foo makes me core dump*. The kernel is an entirely different beast. The interactions between the kernel, user-space, and hardware can be quite delicate. Race conditions might rear their ugly head only once in a million iterations of an algorithm. Poorly designed or even miscompiled code can result in acceptable performances on some systems, but terrible performances on others. It is very common for some specific configuration, on some random machine, under some odd workload, to trigger a bug otherwise unseen. The more information you have when tackling a bug, the better. Many times, if you can reliably reproduce the bug, you are more than halfway home.

Bugs in the Kernel

Bugs in the kernel are as varied as bugs in user-space applications. They occur for a myriad of reasons and manifest themselves in just as many forms. Bugs range from clearly incorrect code (for example, not storing the right value in the right place) to synchronization errors (for example, not properly locking a shared variable). They manifest themselves as everything from poor performance to incorrect behavior to corrupt data.

Often, it is a large chain of events that leads from the error in the code to the error witnessed by the user. For example, a shared structure without a reference count might cause a race condition. Without proper accounting, one process might free the structure while another still wants to use it. Later on, the second process may attempt to use the variable. This might result in a NULL pointer dereference, reading of garbage data, or nothing bad at all (if the data was not yet overwritten). The NULL pointer dereference causes an oops while the garbage data leads to corruption (and then bad behavior or an oops). The user reports the oops or incorrect behavior. The kernel developer must then work backward from the error and see that the data was accessed after it was freed, there was a race, and the fix is proper reference counting on the shared structure. It probably needs locking, too.

Debugging the kernel might sound difficult, but in reality the kernel is not unlike any other large software project. The kernel does have unique issues, such as timing constraints and race conditions, which are a consequence of allowing multiple threads of execution inside the kernel. I assure you that with a little effort and understanding, you can debug kernel problems (and perhaps even enjoy the challenge).

printk()

The kernel print function, printk(), behaves almost identically to the C library printf() function. Indeed, throughout this book we have not made use of any real differences. For most intentions, this is fine; printk() is simply the name of the kernel's formatted print function. It does have some differences, however.

The Robustness of `printk()`

One property of `printk()` quickly taken for granted is its robustness. The `printk()` function is callable from just about *anywhere* in the kernel at *anytime*. It can be called from interrupt or process context. It can be called while holding a lock. It can be called simultaneously on multiple processors, yet it does not require the caller to hold a lock.

It is a resilient function. This is important because the usefulness of `printk()` rests on the fact that it is always there and always works.

The Nonrobustness of `printk()`

A hole in the robustness of `printk()` does exist. It is unusable before a certain point in the kernel boot process, prior to console initialization. Indeed, if the console is not initialized, where is the output supposed to go?

This is normally not an issue, unless you are debugging issues very early in the boot process (for example, in `setup_arch()`, which performs architecture-specific initialization). Such debugging is a challenge to begin with—the absence of any sort of print method only compounds the problem.

There is some hope, but not a lot. Hardcore architecture hackers use the hardware that does work (say, a serial port) to communicate with the outside world. Trust me, this is not fun for most people. Some supported architectures do implement a sane solution, however—and others (i386 included) have patches available that also save the day.

The solution is a `printk()` variant that can output to the console very early in the boot process: `early_printk()`. The behavior is the same as `printk()`, only the name and its capability to work earlier are changed. This is not a portable solution, however, because not all supported architectures have such a method implemented. It might become your best friend, though, if it does.

Unless you need to write to the console very early in the boot process, you can rely on `printk()` to always work.

Loglevels

The major difference between `printk()` and `printf()` is the capability of the former to specify a *loglevel*. The kernel uses the loglevel to decide whether to print the message to the console. The kernel displays all messages with a loglevel below a specified value on the console.

You specify a loglevel like this:

```
printk(KERN_WARNING "This is a warning!\n");
printk(KERN_DEBUG "This is a debug notice!\n");
printk("I did not specify a loglevel!\n");
```

The `KERN_WARNING` and `KERN_DEBUG` strings are simple defines found in `<linux/kernel.h>`. They expand to a string such as "`<4>`" or "`<7>`" that is concatenated onto the front of the `printk()` message. The kernel then decides which messages to print on the console based on this specified loglevel and the current console loglevel, `console_loglevel`. *Table 15.1* is a full listing of the available loglevels.

Table 15.1   **Available loglevels**

Loglevel	Description
KERN_EMERG	An emergency condition
KERN_ALERT	A problem that requires immediate attention
KERN_CRIT	A critical condition
KERN_ERR	An error
KERN_WARNING	A warning
KERN_NOTICE	A normal, but perhaps noteworthy, condition
KERN_INFO	An informational message
KERN_DEBUG	A debug message—typically superfluous

If you do not specify a loglevel, it defaults to DEFAULT_MESSAGE_LOGLEVEL, which is currently KERN_WARNING. Because this value might change, you should always specify a loglevel for your messages.

The kernel defines the most important loglevel, KERN_EMERG, as "<0>" and it defines KERN_DEBUG, the least critical loglevel, as "<7>". For example, after the preprocessor is done, our previous examples resemble:

```
printk("<4>This is a warning!\n");
printk("<7>This is a debug notice!\n");
printk("<4>I did not specify a loglevel!\n");
```

The avenue you take with your printk() loglevels is up to you. Of course, normal messages you intend to keep around should have the appropriate loglevel. But the debugging messages you sprinkle everywhere when trying to get a handle on a problem—admit it, we all do it and it works—can have any loglevel you want. One option is to leave your default console loglevel where it is, and make all your debugging messages KERN_CRIT or so. Conversely, you can make the debugging messages KERN_DEBUG and change your console loglevel. Each has pros and cons; you decide.

The Log Buffer

Kernel messages are stored in a circular buffer of size LOG_BUF_LEN. This size is configurable at compile time via the CONFIG_LOG_BUF_SHIFT option. The default for a uniprocessor machine is 16KB. In other words, the kernel can simultaneously store 16KB of kernel messages. If it is at this maximum and it receives another message, it overwrites the oldest message. The log buffer is called *circular* because the reading and writing occurs in a circular pattern.

Using a circular buffer has multiple advantages. Because it is easy to simultaneously write to and read from a circular buffer, even interrupt context can easily use printk(). Furthermore, it makes log maintenance easy. If there are too many messages, new messages simply overwrite the older ones. If there is a problem that results in the generation of many messages, the log simply overwrites itself in lieu of uncontrollably consuming memory. The lone disadvantage of a circular buffer—the possibility of loosing messages—is a small price to pay for the simplicity and robustness it affords.

`syslogd` and `klogd`

On a standard Linux system, the user-space `klogd` daemon retrieves the kernel messages from the log buffer and feeds them into the system log file via the `syslogd` daemon. To read the log, the `klogd` program can either read the `/proc/kmsg` file or call the `syslog()` system call. By default, it uses the `/proc` approach. In either case, `klogd` blocks until there is new kernel messages to read. It then wakes up, reads any new messages, and processes them. By default, it sends the messages to the `syslogd` daemon.

The `syslogd` daemon appends all the messages it receives to a file, which is by default `/var/log/messages`. It is configurable via `/etc/syslog.conf`.

You can have `klogd` change the console loglevel when it loads by specifying the `-c` flag when starting it.

A Note About `printk()` and Kernel Hacking

When you first start developing kernel code, you most likely will often transpose `printf()` for `printk()`. It is only natural because you cannot deny years of experience using `printf()` in user-space programs. Hopefully, this mistake won't last long because the repeated linker errors will eventually grow rather annoying.

Someday, you might find yourself accidentally using `printk()` instead of `printf()` in your user-space code. When that day comes, you can say you are a truc kernel hacker.

Oops

An *oops* is the usual way a kernel says to the user something bad happened. Because the kernel is the supervisor of the entire system, it cannot simply fix itself or kill itself as it can when user-space goes awry. Instead, the kernel issues an oops. This involves printing an error message to the console, dumping the contents of the registers, and providing a back trace. A failure in the kernel is hard to manage, so the kernel must jump through many hoops to issue the oops and clean up after itself. Often, after an oops the kernel is in an inconsistent state. For example, the kernel could have been in the middle of processing important data when the oops occurred. It might have held a lock or been in the middle of talking to hardware. The kernel must gracefully back out of its current context and try to resume control of the system. In many cases, this is not possible. If the oops occurred in interrupt context, the kernel cannot continue and it panics. A panic results in an instant halt of the system. If the oops occurred in the idle task (pid zero) or the init task (pid one), the result is also a panic because the kernel cannot continue without these important processes. If the oops occurs in any other process, however, the kernel kills the process and tries to continue executing.

An oops might occur for multiple reasons, including a memory access violation or an illegal instruction. As a kernel developer, you will often deal with (and undoubtedly cause) oopses.

What follows is an oops example from a PPC machine, in the timer handler of the tulip network interface card:

```
Oops: Exception in kernel mode, sig: 4
Unable to handle kernel NULL pointer dereference at virtual address 00000001

NIP: C013A7F0 LR: C013A7F0 SP: C0685E00 REGS: c0905d10 TRAP: 0700
Not tainted
MSR: 00089037 EE: 1 PR: 0 FP: 0 ME: 1 IR/DR: 11
TASK = c0712530[0] 'swapper' Last syscall: 120
GPR00: C013A7C0 C0295E00 C0231530 0000002F 00000001 C0380CB8 C0291B80 C02D0000
GPR08: 000012A0 00000000 00000000 C0292AA0 4020A088 00000000 00000000 00000000
GPR16: 00000000 00000000 00000000 00000000 00000000 00000000 00000000 00000000
GPR24: 00000000 00000005 00000000 00001032 C3F7C000 00000032 FFFFFFFF C3F7C1C0
Call trace:
[c013ab30] tulip_timer+0x128/0x1c4
[c0020744] run_timer_softirq+0x10c/0x164
[c001b864] do_softirq+0x88/0x104
[c0007e80] timer_interrupt+0x284/0x298
[c00033c4] ret_from_except+0x0/0x34
[c0007b84] default_idle+0x20/0x60
[c0007bf8] cpu_idle+0x34/0x38
[c0003ae8] rest_init+0x24/0x34
```

PC users might marvel at the number of registers (a whopping 32!). An oops on x86, which you might be more familiar with, is a little simpler. The important information, however, is identical for all the architectures: the contents of the registers and the back trace.

The back trace shows the exact function call chain leading up to the problem. In this case, we can see exactly what happened: the machine was idle and executing the idle loop, cpu_idle(), which calls default_idle() in a loop. The timer interrupt occurred, which resulted in the processing of timers. A timer handler, the tulip_timer() function, was executed, which performed a NULL pointer dereference. You can even use the offsets (those numbers like *0x128/0x1c4* to the right of the functions) to find exactly the offending line.

The register contents can be equally useful, although less commonly so. With a decoded copy of the function in assembly, the register values help you recreate the exact events leading to the problem. Seeing an unexpected value in a register might shine some light on the root of the issue. In this case, we can see which registers held NULL (a value of all zeros) and discover which variable in the function had the unexpected value. In situations such as this, the problem is often a race—in this case, between the timer and some other part of this network card. Debugging a race condition is always a challenge.

ksymoops

The previous oops is said to be *decoded* because the memory addresses are translated into the functions they represent. An undecoded version of the previous oops is shown here:

```
NIP: C013A7F0 LR: C013A7F0 SP: C0685E00 REGS: c0905d10 TRAP: 0700
Not tainted
MSR: 00089037 EE: 1 PR: 0 FP: 0 ME: 1 IR/DR: 11
TASK = c0712530[0] 'swapper' Last syscall: 120
GPR00: C013A7C0 C0295E00 C0231530 0000002F 00000001 C0380CB8 C0291B80 C02D0000
GPR08: 000012A0 00000000 00000000 C0292AA0 4020A088 00000000 00000000 00000000
GPR16: 00000000 00000000 00000000 00000000 00000000 00000000 00000000 00000000
GPR24: 00000000 00000005 00000000 00001032 C3F7C000 00000032 FFFFFFFF C3F7C1C0
Call trace: [c013ab30] [c0020744] [c001b864] [c0007e80] [c00061c4]
[c0007b84] [c0007bf8] [c0003ae8]
```

The addresses in the back trace need to be converted into symbolic names. This is done via the `ksymoops` command in conjunction with the `System.map` generated during kernel compile. If you are using modules, you also need some module information. `ksymoops` tries to figure out most of this information, so you can usually invoke it via

```
ksymoops saved_oops.txt
```

The program then spits out a decoded version of the oops. If the default information `ksymoops` uses is unacceptable, or you want to provide alternative locations for the information, the program understands various options. Its manual page has a lot of information that you should read before using.

The `ksymoops` program most likely came with your distribution.

kallsyms

Thankfully, dealing with `ksymoops` is no longer a requirement. This is a big deal, because while developers might have had little problem using it, end users often mismatch `System.map` files or fail to decode oopses altogether.

The 2.5 development kernel introduced the `kallsyms` feature, which is enabled via the `CONFIG_KALLSYMS` configuration option. This option loads the symbolic kernel name of memory address mapping into the kernel image, so the kernel can print predecoded back traces. Consequently, decoding oopses no longer requires `System.map` or `ksymoops`. On the downside, the size of the kernel increases a bit, as the address to symbol mappings must reside in permanently mapped kernel memory. It is worth the memory use, however, at least during development.

Kernel Debugging Options

Multiple configure options that you can set during compile to aid in debugging and testing kernel code are available. These options are in the *Kernel hacking* menu of the

kernel configuration editor. They all depend on CONFIG_DEBUG_KERNEL. When hacking
on the kernel, consider enabling as many of these options as practical.

Some of the options are rather useful, enabling slab layer debugging, high-memory
debugging, I/O mapping debugging, spin-lock debugging, and stack-overflow checking.
One of the most useful settings, however, is the *sleep-inside-spinlock checking*, which actually does much more.

Atomicity Debugging

Starting with 2.5, the kernel has an excellent infrastructure for detecting all sorts of
atomicity violations. Recall from Chapter 7, "Kernel Synchronization Introduction,"
atomic refers to something's capability to execute without division; the code completes
without interruption or it does not complete at all. Code that holds a spin lock or has
disabled kernel preemption is atomic. Code cannot sleep while atomic—sleeping while
holding a lock is a recipe for deadlock.

Thanks to kernel preemption, the kernel has a great atomicity counter. The kernel
can be set such that if a task sleeps while atomic, or even does something that *might*
sleep, the kernel will print a warning and provide a back trace. Potential bugs that are
detectable include calling schedule() while holding a lock, issuing a blocking memory
allocation while holding a lock, or sleeping while holding a reference to per-CPU data.
This debugging infrastructure catches a lot of bugs and is highly recommended.

The following options make the best use of this feature:

```
CONFIG_PREEMPT=y
CONFIG_DEBUG_KERNEL=y
CONFIG_KALLSYMS=y
CONFIG_SPINLOCK_SLEEP=y
```

Causing Bugs and Dumping Information

A number of kernel routines make it easy to flag bugs, provide assertions, and dump
information. Two of the most common are BUG() and BUG_ON(). When called, they
cause an oops, which results in a stack trace and an error message dumped to the kernel.
Why these statements cause an oops is architecture-dependent. Most architectures define
BUG() and BUG_ON() to illegal instructions, which result in the desired oops. You normally use these routines as assertions, to flag situations that should not happen:

```
if (bad_thing)
    BUG();
```

Or, even better,

```
BUG_ON(bad_thing);
```

A more critical error is signaled via panic(). A call to panic() prints an error message
and then halts the kernel. Obviously, you only want to use it in the worst of situations:

```
if (terrible_thing)
   panic("foo is %ld!\n", foo);
```

Sometimes, you just want a simple stack trace issued on the console to help you in debugging. In those cases, `dump_stack()` is used. It simply dumps the contents of the registers and a function back trace to the console:

```
if (!debug_check) {
   printk(KERN_DEBUG "provide some information...\n");
   dump_stack();
}
```

Magic SysRq Key

A possible lifesaver is the Magic SysRq Key, which is enabled via the `CONFIG_MAGIC_SYSRQ` configure option. The `SysRq` (system request) key is a standard key on most keyboards. On i386 and PPC, it is accessible via `ALT-PrintScreen`. When this configure option is enabled, special combinations of keys enable you to communicate with the kernel regardless of what else it is doing. This allows you to perform some useful tasks in the face of a dying system.

In addition to the configure option, there is a sysctl to toggle this feature on and off. To turn it on:

```
echo 1 > /proc/sys/kernel/sysrq
```

From the console, you can hit `SysRq-h` for a list of available options. `SysRq-s` syncs dirty buffers to disk, `SysRq-u` unmounts all file systems, and `SysRq-b` reboots the machine. Issuing these three key combinations in a row is a safer way to reboot a dying machine than simply hitting the machine reset switch.

If the machine is badly locked, it might not respond to any Magic SysRq combinations, or it might fail to complete a given command. With luck, however, these options might save your data or aid in debugging. *Table 15.2* is a listing of the supported SysRq commands.

Table 15.2 **Supporting** `SysRq` **Commands**

Key Command	Description
SysRq-b	Reboot the machine
SysRq-e	Send a `SIGTERM` to all processes except init
SysRq-h	Display SysRq help on the console
SysRq-i	Send a `SIGKILL` to all processes except init
SysRq-k	Secure Access Key: kill all programs on this console
SysRq-l	Send a `SIGKILL` to all processes including init
SysRq-m	Dump memory information to console
SysRq-o	Shutdown the machine

Table 15.2   **Continued**

Key Command	Description
SysRq-p	Dump registers to console
SysRq-r	Turn off keyboard raw mode
SysRq-s	Sync all mounted file systems to disk
SysRq-t	Dump task information to console
SysRq-u	Unmount all mounted file systems

The file `Documentation/sysrq.txt` in the kernel source tree has more information. The actual implementation is in `drivers/char/sysrq.txt`. The Magic `SysRq` Key is a vital tool for aiding in debugging or saving a dying system. Because it provides powerful capabilities to any user on the console, however, you should exercise caution on important machines. For your development machine, however, it is a great help.

The Saga of a Kernel Debugger

Many kernel developers have long demanded an in-kernel debugger. Unfortunately, Linus does not want a debugger in his tree. He believes that debuggers lead to bad fixes by misinformed developers. No one can argue with his logic—a fix derived from real understanding of the code is certainly more likely to be correct. Nonetheless, plenty of kernel developers still want an official in-kernel debugger. Because it is unlikely to happen anytime soon, a number of patches have arisen that add kernel-debugging support to the standard Linux kernel. Despite being external unofficial patches, these tools are quite well featured and powerful. Before we delve into these solutions, let's look at how much help the standard Linux debugger, `gdb`, will give us.

gdb

You can use the standard GNU debugger to glimpse inside a running kernel. Starting the debugger on the kernel is about the same as debugging a running process:

```
gdb vmlinux /proc/kcore
```

The `vmlinux` file is the uncompressed kernel image stored in the root of the build directory, not the compressed `zImage` or `bzImage`.

The optional `/proc/kcore` parameter acts as a core file, to let `gdb` actually peak into the memory of the running kernel. You need to be root to read it.

You can issue just about any of the `gdb` commands for reading information. For example, to print the value of a variable:

```
p global_variable
```

To disassemble a function:

```
disassemble function
```

If you compile the kernel with the `-g` flag (add `-g` to the `CFLAGS` variable in the kernel `Makefile`), `gdb` is able to provide much more information. For example, you can dump the contents of structures and follow pointers. You also get a much larger kernel, so do not routinely compile with debugging information included.

Unfortunately, this is about the limit of what `gdb` can do. It cannot modify kernel data in any way. It is unable to single step through kernel code or set breakpoints. The inability to modify kernel data structures is a large downside. Although it is undoubtedly useful to disassemble functions on occasion, it would be much more useful to modify data, too.

kgdb

`kgdb` is a patch that enables `gdb` to fully debug the kernel remotely over a serial line. It requires two computers. The first runs a kernel patched with `kgdb`. The second debugs the first over the serial line (a null modem cable connecting the two machines) using `gdb`. With `kgdb`, the entire feature set of `gdb` is accessible: reading and writing any variables, settings breakpoints, setting watch points, single stepping, and so on! Special versions of `kgdb` even allow function execution.

Setting up `kgdb` and the serial line is a little tricky, but when complete, debugging is simple. The patch installs plenty of documentation in `Documentation/`—check it out.

Different people maintain the `kgdb` patch for various architectures and kernel releases. Searching online is your best bet for finding a patch for a given kernel.

kdb

An alternative to `kgdb` is `kdb`. Unlike `kgdb`, `kdb` is not a remote debugger. `kdb` is a kernel patch that extensively modifies the kernel to allow direct debugging on the host system. It provides variable modification, breakpoints, and single stepping, among other things. Running the debugger is simple: simply hit the `break` key on the console. The debugger also automatically executes when the kernel oopses. Much documentation is available in `Documentation/kdb`, after the patch is applied.

`kdb` is available at `http://oss.sgi.com/`.

Poking and Probing the System

As you gain experience in kernel debugging, you gain little tricks to help you poke and probe the kernel for answers. Because kernel debugging can prove rather challenging, every little tip and trick helps. Let's look at a couple.

Using UID as a Conditional

If the code you are developing is process-related, sometimes you can develop alternative implementations without breaking the existing code. This is helpful if you are rewriting an important system call and would like a fully functional system with which to debug it. For example, assume you are rewriting the `fork()` algorithm to take advantage of an exciting new feature. Unless you get everything right on the first try, it would not be easy to debug the system, as a nonfunctioning `fork()` system call will certainly result in a nonfunctioning system. As always, there is hope.

Often, it is safe to keep the remaining algorithm in place and construct your replacement on the side. You can achieve this by using the user id (UID) as a conditional with which to decide which algorithm to use:

```
if (current->uid != 7777) {
    /* old algorithm .. */
} else {
    /* new algorithm .. */
}
```

All users except UID 7777 will use the old algorithm. You can create a special user, with UID 7777, for testing the new algorithm. This makes testing critical process-related code much easier.

Using Condition Variables

If the code in question is not in process context, or if you want a more global method of controlling the feature, you can use a condition variable. This approach is even simpler that using the UID. Simply create a global variable and use it as a conditional check in your code. If the variable is zero, you follow one code path. If it is nonzero, you follow another. The variable can be set via an interface you export or a poke from the debugger.

Using Statistics

Sometimes you want to get a feel for how often a specific event is occurring. Sometimes you want to compare multiple events and generate some ratios for comparison. This is easily done by creating statistics and a mechanism to export their values.

For instance, say we want to look at the occurrence of *foo* and the occurrence of *bar*. In a file, ideally the one where these events occur, declare two global variables:

```
unsigned long foo_stat = 0;
unsigned long bar_stat = 0;
```

For each occurrence of these events, increment the appropriate variable. Then, export the data how ever you feel fit. For example, you can create a file in `/proc` with the values or write a system call. Alternatively, simply read them via a debugger.

Note, this approach is not particularly SMP-safe. Ideally, you would use atomic operations. For a trivial one-time debugging statistic, however, you normally do not need such protection.

Rate Limiting Your Debugging

Oftentimes, you want to stick some debugging checks (with some corresponding print statements) in an area to sniff out a problem. In the kernel, however, some functions are called numerous times per second. If you stick a call to `printk()` in such a function, the system is overwhelmed with debugging output and quickly grows unusable.

Two relatively simple tricks exist to prevent this problem. The first is *rate limiting*, which is useful when you want to watch the progression of an event, but the event occurs rather often. To prevent a deluge of debugging output, you only print your debug message (or do whatever you are doing) every few seconds. For example:

```
static unsigned long prev_jiffy = jiffies;    /* rate limiting */

if (time_after(jiffies, prev_jiffy + 2*HZ)) {
    prev_jiffy = jiffies;
    printk(KERN_ERR "blah blah blah\n");
}
```

In this example, the debug message is printed at most every two seconds. This prevents any flood of information on the console and the computer remains usable. You might need the rate limiting to be larger or smaller, depending on your needs.

Another sticky situation arises if you are looking for any occurrence of an event. Unlike the previous example, you do not want to monitor the progress of the kernel, but simply receive a notification when something happens. Perhaps you only want to receive this notice once or twice. This is an especially sticky problem if after the check is triggered once, it is triggered a lot. The solution here is not to rate limit the debugging, but *occurrence limit* it:

```
static unsigned long limit = 0;

if (limit < 5) {
    limit++;
    printk(KERN_ERR "blah blah blah\n");
}
```

This example caps the debugging output to five. After five such messages, the conditional is always false.

In both examples, the variables should be `static` and local to the function, as shown. This enables the variable's values to persist across functions calls.

Neither of these examples are SMP- or preempt-safe, although a quick switch to atomic operators will make them safe. Frankly, however, this is just debugging code, so why go through the trouble?

Binary Searching to Find the Culprit Change

It is usually useful to know when a bug was introduced into the kernel source. If you know a bug occurred in version 2.4.18, but not 2.4.17, then you have a clear picture of the changes that occurred to cause the bug. The bug fix is often as simple as reverting or otherwise fixing the bad change.

Many times, however, you do not know what kernel version introduced the bug. You know the bug is in the *current* kernel, but it seemed to *always* have been in the current kernel. It takes some investigative work, but with a little effort, you can find the offending change. With the change in hand, the bug fix is usually near.

To start, you need a reliably reproducible problem. Preferably, a bug you can verify immediately after boot. Next, you need a known-good kernel. You might already know this. For example, you know a couple months back the kernel worked, so grab a kernel from that period. If you are wrong, try an earlier release. It shouldn't be too hard—unless the bug has existed forever—to find a kernel without the bug.

Next, you need a known-bad kernel. To make things easier, start with the earliest kernel you know to have the bug.

Now, you begin a binary search from the known-bad kernel down to the known-good kernel. Let's look at an example. Assume the latest known-good kernel is 2.4.11 and the earliest known-bad is 2.4.20. Start by picking a kernel in the middle, such as 2.4.15. Test 2.4.15 for the bug. If 2.4.15 works, then you know the problem began in a later kernel, so try a kernel in between 2.4.15 and 2.4.20—say, 2.4.17. On the other hand, if 2.4.15 does not work, then you know the problem is in an earlier kernel, so you might try 2.4.13. Rinse and repeat.

Eventually you should narrow the problem down to two kernels—one of which will have the bug and one of which will not. You then have a clear picture of the changes that caused the bug.

This approach beats looking at every kernel!

When All Else Fails: The Community

Perhaps you have tried everything you know. You have slaved over the keyboard for countless hours—indeed, perhaps countless days—and the solution still escapes you. If the bug is in the mainstream Linux kernel, you can always elicit the help of the other developers in the kernel community.

A brief, but complete, email sent to the kernel mailing list describing the bug and your findings might help aid in discovery of a solution. After all, no one likes bugs.

Chapter 17, "Patches, Hacking, and the Community," specifically addresses the community and its primary forum, the Linux Kernel Mailing List (LKML).

16

Portability

LINUX IS A PORTABLE OPERATING SYSTEM that supports a wide range of computer architectures. *Portability* refers to how easily—if at all—code can move from one system architecture to another. We all know that Linux *is portable* because it has already been *ported* to various systems. But this portability did not occur overnight—it required many design decisions along the way. Consequently, now it is easy (relatively speaking) to bring Linux up on a new system. This chapter discusses how to write portable code—the issues you need to keep in mind when writing core kernel code or device drivers.

Some operating systems are designed with portability as a primary feature. As little code as possible is machine-specific. Assembly is kept to a minimum and interfaces and features are sufficiently general and abstract that they work on a wide range of architectures. The obvious benefit is the relative ease with which a new architecture can be supported. In some cases, highly portable and simple operating systems can be moved to a new architecture with just a few hundred lines of unique code. The downside is that architecture-specific features are not supported and code cannot be hand-tuned for a specific machine. With this design choice, optimal code is traded for portable code. Some examples of highly portable operating systems are Minix, NetBSD, and many research systems.

On the opposite side are operating systems that trade all portability for highly customized optimum code. As much as possible, code is written in assembly or otherwise designed for a specific architecture. Kernel features are designed around specific architectural features. Consequently, moving the operating system to a new architecture is tantamount to writing a kernel from scratch. With this design decision, portable code is traded for optimal code. Such systems are often harder to maintain than more portable systems. Example systems are DOS and Windows 9x. Now, these systems need not be more optimal than a more portable system; they have, however, the ability to hand-tune as much code as possible.

Linux takes the middle road toward portability. As much as practical, interfaces and core code are architecture-independent C code. Where performance is critical, however, kernel features are tuned for each architecture. For example, much fast-path and low-level code is architecture-dependent and often assembly. This approach enables Linux to remain portable without forgoing optimizations. Where portability would hinder performance, performance generally wins. Otherwise, code is kept portable.

Generally, exported kernel interfaces are architecture-independent. If there are any parts of the function that need be unique for each supported architecture (either for performance reasons or as a necessity), that code is implemented in separate functions and called as needed.

A good example is the scheduler. The large majority of the scheduler is written in architecture-independent C and lives in `kernel/sched.c`. A few jobs of the scheduler, such as switching processor state or switching the address space, are very architecture-dependent. Consequently, the C method `context_switch()`, which switches from one process to another, calls the methods `switch_to()` and `switch_mm()`, to switch processor state and switch address space, respectively.

The code for `switch_to()` and `switch_mm()` is uniquely implemented for each architecture Linux supports. When Linux is *ported* to a new architecture, the new architecture simply provides an implementation for these functions.

Architecture-specific files are located in `arch/<architecture>/` and `include/asm-<architecture>/` where `<architecture>` is a short name representing each architecture in Linux. As an example, the Intel x86 architecture is given the short name `i386`. Architecture-specific files for these machines live in `arch/i386` and `include/asm-i386`. The supported architectures in the 2.6 kernel series are `alpha`, `arm`, `cris`, `h8300`, `i386`, `ia64`, `m68k`, `m68knommu`, `mips`, `mips64`, `parisc`, `ppc`, `ppc64`, `s390`, `sh`, `sparc`, `sparc64`, `um`, `v850`, and `x86-64`. A more complete listing of these architectures is in Table 16.1.

History of Portability in Linux

When Linus first unleashed Linux on the unsuspecting world, it ran only on Intel 386 machines. Although the operating system was rather generalized and well written, portability was not a major concern. In fact, Linus even once suggested Linux would never run on anything but the i386 architecture! In 1993, however, work began on porting Linux to the Digital Alpha architecture. The Digital Alpha was a modern high-performance RISC-based architecture with 64-bit memory addressing. This is a stark contrast to Linus's original 386. Nonetheless, the initial port of Linux to the Alpha took about a year and the Alpha became the first officially supported architecture after x86. This port was perhaps rather difficult because it had the unwelcome challenge of being the first. Instead of simply grafting onto the kernel support for the Alpha, pieces of the kernel were rewritten as needed with portability in mind[1]. Although this made for more work overall, the result was much cleaner and future porting was made much easier.

---

[1] This is a common occurrence in kernel development. If something is going to be done at all, it should be done right! Kernel developers are not averse to rewriting large amounts of code in the name of perfection.

Although the first releases of Linux supported only the Intel x86 architecture, the 1.2 kernel series supported Digital Alpha, Intel x86, MIPS, and SPARC—although support was somewhat experimental.

With the release of the 2.0 kernel, Linux officially added support for the Motorola 68k and PowerPC. Additionally, the architectures previously supported in 1.2 became official and stable.

The 2.2 kernel series brought even more architecture support, with the addition of ARM, IBM S/390, and UltraSPARC. A few years later, 2.4 nearly doubled the number of supported architectures to 15, as support was added for the CRIS, IA-64, 64-bit MIPS, HP PA-RISC, 64-bit IBM S/390, and Hitachi SH.

The current kernel, 2.6, brought the number of supported architectures to 20 with the addition of Motorola 68k without MMU, H8/300, IBM POWER, v850, x86-64, and a version of the kernel that runs in a virtual machine under Linux, known as Usermode Linux. The 64-bit s390 port was folded into the 32-bit s390 port, removing the duplication.

It should be noted that each of these architectures supports various chip and machine types. Some supported architectures, such as ARM and PowerPC, each support many different chips and machine types. Therefore, although Linux runs under 20 broad architectures, it runs on many more different machines!

Word Size and Data Types

A *word* is the amount of data that a machine can process at one time. This fits into the document analogy that includes *characters* (eight bits) and *pages* (many words) as other measurements of data. A word is some number of bits—most commonly, 16, 32, or 64. When someone talks about the "n-bits" of a machine, they are generally talking about the machine's *word size*. For example, when people say the Pentium is a 32-bit chip, they are referring to its word size, which is 32-bits, or four bytes.

The size of a processor's general-purpose registers is equal to its word size. Usually, the widths of the components in a given architecture—for example, the memory bus— are at least as wide as the word size. Typically, at least in the architectures Linux supports, the memory address space is equal to the word size[2]. Consequently, the length of a pointer is equal to the word size. Additionally, the size of the C type `long` is equal to the word size, whereas the size of the `int` type is sometimes less than that of the word size. For example, the Alpha has a 64-bit word size. Consequently, registers, pointers, and the `long` type are 64-bits in length. The `int` type, however, is 32-bits long. The Alpha can access and manipulate 64-bits, one word, at a time.

---

[2]However, the actual addressable memory may be less than the word size. For example, while a 64-bit architecture would have 64-bit pointers, only 48-bits may be usable and addressable. In addition, the total physical memory may be larger than the word size, thanks to things like Intel's PAE.

> ### Words, Doublewords, and Confusion
> Some operating systems and processors do not call the standard data size a *word*. Instead, a word is some
> fixed size based on history or arbitrary naming decisions. For example, some systems might partition data
> sizes into bytes (8-bits), words (16-bits), double words (32-bits), and quad words (64-bit) despite the fact
> the system in question may be 32-bit. In this book—and Linux in general—a word is the standard data size
> of the processor, as discussed previously.

Each supported architecture under Linux defines BITS_PER_LONG in <asm/types.h> to
the length of the C long type, which is the system word size. A full listing of all supported architectures and their word size is in *Table 16.1*.

Table 16.1   **Supported Linux Architectures**

Architecture	Description	Word size
alpha	Digital Alpha	64-bit
arm	ARM and StrongARM	32-bit
cris	CRIS	32-bit
h8300	H8/300	32-bit
i386	Intel x86	32-bit
ia64	IA-64	64-bit
m68k	Motorola 68k	32-bit
m68knommu	m68k without MMU	32-bit
mips	MIPS	32-bit
mips64	64-bit MIPS	64-bit
parisc	HP PA-RISC	32-bit or 64-bit
ppc	PowerPC	32-bit
ppc64	POWER	64-bit
s390	IBM S/390	32-bit or 64-bit
sh	Hitachi SH	32-bit
sparc	SPARC	32-bit
sparc64	UltraSPARC	64-bit
um	Usermode Linux	32-bit or 64-bit
v850	v850	32-bit
x86_64	x86-64	64-bit

The C standard explicitly leaves the size of the standard variable types up to implementations[3]. The uncertainty in the standard C types across architectures is both a pro and a
con. On the plus side, the standard C types can take advantage of the word size of various architectures and types need not explicitly specify a size. Under Linux, a long is

---

[3]With the exception of char, which is always 8-bits (one byte).

guaranteed to be the machine's word size. This is not strictly true of ANSI C, but is standard practice in Linux. On the downside, however, code cannot assume the standard C types have any specific size. Furthermore, there is no guarantee that an int is the same size as a long[4].

The situation grows even more confusing because there doesn't need to be a relation between the types in user-space and kernel-space. The sparc64 architecture provides a 32-bit user-space and therefore pointers and both the int and long types are 32-bit. In kernel-space, however, sparc64 has a 32-bit int type and 64-bit pointers and long types. This is not the norm, however.

Some rules to keep in mind:

- As dictated by the ANSI C standard, a char is always 8-bits (1 byte).

- Although there is no rule that the int type be 32-bits, it is on all currently supported architectures.

- The same goes for the short type, which is 16-bits on all current architectures.

- Never assume the size of a pointer or a long, which can be either 32- or 64-bits on currently supported machines.

- Because the size of a long varies on different architectures, *never* assume sizeof(int) == sizeof(long).

- Likewise, do not assume a pointer and an int are the same size.

Opaque Types

Opaque data types do not reveal their internal format or structure. They are about as *black box* as you can get in C. There is not a lot of language support for them. Instead, developers declare a typedef, call it an opaque type, and hope no one typecasts it back to a standard C type. All use is generally through a special set of interfaces the developer creates. An example is the pid_t type, which stores a process identification value. The actual size of this type is not revealed—although anyone can cheat and take a peak and see it is an int. If no code makes explicit use of this type's size, it can be changed without much hassle. Indeed, this was once the case: in older Unix systems, pid_t was declared as a short.

Another example of an opaque type is atomic_t. As discussed in Chapter 8, "Kernel Synchronization Methods," this type holds an integer value that can be manipulated atomically. Although this type is an int, using the opaque type helps ensure the data is used only in the special atomic operation functions. The opaque type also helps hide the size of the type, which is not always the full 32-bits.

---

[4]On the 64-bit architectures supported in Linux, in fact, an int and a long are not the same size; an int is 32-bits and a long is 64-bits. The 32-bit architectures we are all familiar with have both types equal to 32-bits.

Other examples of opaque types in the kernel include dev_t, gid_t, and uid_t. Rules when dealing with opaque types:

- Do not assume the size of the type.

- Do not typecast the type back to a standard C type.

- Write your code so that the actual storage and format of the type can change.

Special Types

Some data in the kernel, despite not being represented by an opaque type, requires a specific data type. Two examples are jiffy counts and the flags parameter used in interrupt control, both of which should always be stored in an unsigned long.

When storing and manipulating specific data, always pay careful attention to the data type that represents the type and use it. It is a common mistake to store one of these values in another type, such as unsigned int. Although this will not result in a problem on 32-bit architectures, 64-bit machines will have trouble.

Explicitly Sized Types

Often, as a programmer, you need explicitly sized data in your code. This is usually to match an external requirement, such as with hardware, networking, or binary files. For example, a sound card might have a 32-bit register, a networking packet might have a 16-bit field, or an executable file might have an 8-bit cookie. In these cases, the data type that represents the data needs to be *exactly* the right size.

The kernel defines these explicitly sized data types in <asm/types.h>, which is included by <linux/types.h>. *Table 16.2* is a complete listing.

Table 16.2   **Explicitly-Sized Data Types**

Type	Description
s8	signed byte
u8	unsigned byte
s16	signed 16-bit integer
u16	unsigned 16-bit integer
s32	signed 32-bit integer
u32	unsigned 32-bit integer
s64	signed 64-bit integer
u64	unsigned 64-bit integer

The signed variants are rarely used.

These explicit types are merely typedefs to standard C types. On a 64-bit machine, they may look like:

```
typedef signed char s8;
typedef unsigned char u8;
typedef signed short s16;
typedef unsigned short u16;
typedef signed int s32;
typedef unsigned int u32;
typedef signed long s64;
typedef unsigned long u64;
```

While on a 32-bit machine, they are probably defined as:

```
typedef signed char s8;
typedef unsigned char u8;
typedef signed short s16;
typedef unsigned short u16;
typedef signed int s32;
typedef unsigned int u32;
typedef signed long long s64;
typedef unsigned long long u64;
```

Signedness of Chars

The C standard says that the char data type can be either signed or unsigned. It is the responsibility of the compiler, the processor, or both to decide what the suitable default for the char type is.

On most architectures, char is signed by default and thus has a range from –128 to 127. On a few other architectures, such as ARM, char is unsigned by default and has a range from 0 to 255.

For example, on systems where a char is by default unsigned, this code ends up storing 255 instead of –1 in i:

```
char i = -1;
```

On other machines, where char is by default signed, this code correctly stores –1 in i. If the programmer's intention is to store –1, the previous code should be

```
signed char i = -1;
```

If you use char in your code, assume it can be *either* a signed char or an unsigned char. If you need it to be explicitly one or the other, declare it as such.

Data Alignment

Alignment refers to a piece of data's location in memory. A variable is said to be *naturally aligned* if it exists at a memory address that is a multiple of its size. For example, a 32-bit type is naturally aligned if it is located in memory at an address that is a multiple of four (that is, its lowest two bits are zero). Thus, a data type with size 2^n bytes must have an address with the n least significant bits set to zero.

Some architectures have very stringent demands for the alignment of data. On some systems, usually RISC-based ones, a load of unaligned data results in a processor trap (a handled error). On other systems, accessing unaligned data works, but results in degradation of performance. When writing portable code, alignment issues must be avoided and all types should be naturally aligned.

Avoiding Alignment Issues

The compiler generally prevents alignment issues by naturally aligning all data types. In fact, alignment issues are normally not major concerns of the kernel developers—the gcc folks have to worry about them. Issues arise, however, when the programmer plays too closely with pointers and accesses data outside of the environment anticipated by the compiler.

Accessing an aligned address with a recast pointer of a larger-aligned address causes an alignment issue (whatever that might mean for a particular architecture). That is, this is bad:

```
char dog[10];
char *p = &dog[1];
unsigned long l = *(unsigned long *)p;
```

This example treats the pointer to a `char` as a pointer to an `unsigned long` which might result in loading the 32-bit `unsigned long` from an address that is not a multiple of four.

If you are thinking, *"when in the world would I do this?"* you are probably right. Nevertheless, it has come up, and it will again, so be careful. The real-world examples might not be so obvious.

Alignment of Nonstandard Types

As mentioned, the aligned address of a standard data type is a multiple of the size of that data type. Nonstandard (complex) C types have the following alignment rules:

- The alignment of an array is the alignment of the base type (and thus, each element is further aligned correctly).
- The alignment of a `union` is the alignment of the largest included type.
- The alignment of a structure is the alignment of the largest included type.

Structures also introduce padding, which introduces other issues.

Structure Padding

Structures are padded so that each element of the structure is naturally aligned. For example, consider this structure on a 32-bit machine:

```
struct foo_struct {
    char dog;          /* 1 byte */
    unsigned long cat;    /* 4 bytes */
```

```
    unsigned short pig;    /* 2 bytes */
    char fox;          /* 1 byte */
};
```

The structure does not look like this in memory because the natural alignment of the members is insufficient. Instead, the compiler creates the structure such that in memory, the struct resembles:

```
struct foo_struct {
    char dog;          /* 1 byte */
    u8 __pad0[3];        /* 3 bytes */
    unsigned long cat;    /* 4 bytes */
    unsigned short pig;   /* 2 bytes */
    char fox;          /* 1 byte */
    u8 __pad1;         /* 1 byte */
};
```

The padding variables exist to ensure proper natural alignment. The first padding provides a 3-byte waste-of-space to place cat on a 4-byte boundary. This automatically aligns the remaining types because they are all smaller than cat. The second and final padding is to pad the size of the struct itself. The extra byte ensures the structure is a multiple of four and thus, each member of an array of this structure is naturally aligned.

Note that sizeof(foo_struct) returns 12 for *either* of these structures on most 32-bit machines. The C compiler automatically adds this padding to ensure proper alignment.

You can often rearrange the order of members in a structure to obviate the need for padding. This gives you properly aligned data without the need for padding, and therefore a smaller structure:

```
struct foo_struct {
    unsigned long cat;    /* 4 bytes */
    unsigned short pig;   /* 2 bytes */
    char dog;          /* 1 byte */
    char fox;          /* 1 byte */
};
```

This structure is only eight bytes in size. It might not always be possible to rearrange structure definitions, however. For example, if this structure was specified as part of a standard or already used in existing code, its order is set in stone. Oftentimes, you might want to use a specific order for other reasons—for example, to best layout variables to optimize cache hit rates. Note that ANSI C specifies that the compiler itself must never change the order of members in a structure[5]—it is always up to you, the programmer.

---

[5]If the compiler could arbitrarily change the order of items in a structure, any existing code using the structure would break. In C, functions calculate the location of variables in a structure simply by adding offsets to the base address of the structure.

Kernel developers need to be aware of structure padding when using structures wholesale—that is, when sending them out over the network or when saving a structure directly to disk because the required padding might differ among various architectures. This is one reason C does not have a native structure comparison operator. The padding in a structure might contain gibberish, and it is not possible to do a byte-by-byte comparison of one structure to another. The C designers (correctly) felt it is best if the programmer write a comparison function for each unique situation, to take advantage of the structure's layout.

Byte Order

Byte ordering is the order of bytes within a word. Processors can either number the bytes in a word such that the least significant bit is the first (left-most) or last (right-most) value in the word. The byte ordering is called *big-endian* if the most significant byte is encoding first with the remaining bytes decreasing in significance. The byte ordering is called *little-endian* if the least significant byte is encoded first with the remaining bytes growing in significance.

Do not ever assume any given byte ordering when writing kernel code (unless you are writing code for a specific architecture, of course). The Linux kernel supports machines of both byte orders—including machines that can select from either ordering upon boot—and generic code must be compatible with either.

Figure 16.1 is an example of a big-endian byte ordering. *Figure 16.2* is an example of a little-endian byte ordering.

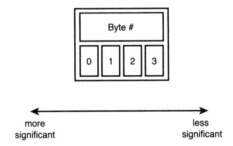

Figure 16.1   Big-endian byte ordering.

The i386 architecture is little-endian. Most other architectures are big-endian.

Let's look at what this encoding means in practice. Consider the number 1027, stored as a four-byte integer in binary:

```
00000000 00000000 00000100 00000011
```

The internal storage in memory is different on big- verses little-endian, as shown in *Table 16.3*.

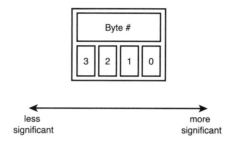

Figure 16.2   Little-endian byte ordering.

Table 16.3   **Explicitly-Sized Data Types**

Address	Big Endian	Little Endian
0	00000000	00000011
1	00000000	00000100
2	00000100	00000000
3	00000011	00000000

Notice how the big-endian architectures store the most significant bytes in its smallest address. This is the exact inverse of little-endian.

As a final example, here is a simple code snippet to test whether a given architecture is big- or little-endian:

```
int x = 1;

if (*(char *)&x == 1)
    /* little endian */
else
    /* big endian */
```

This works either in user-space or inside the kernel.

History of Big and Little Endian

The terms big-endian and little-endian derive from Jonathan Swift's 1726 satirical novel, *Gulliver's Travels*. In the novel, the fictional Lilliputians major political issue is whether eggs should be cracked open on the big side or the little side. Those who favor the big side are big-endians, whereas those who favor the small are little-endians.

The parable to the big-endian versus little-endian debate is that the argument is rooted deeper in politics than technical merits.

Byte Ordering in the Kernel

Each supported architecture in Linux defines one of __BIG_ENDIAN or __LITTLE_ENDIAN in <asm/byteorder.h> in correspondence to the machine's byte order.

This header file also includes a family of macros from include/linux/byteorder/, which help converting to and from the various orderings. The most commonly needed macros are

```
u23 __cpu_to_be32(u32);    /* convert cpu's byte order to big-endian */
u32 __cpu_to_le32(u32);    /* convert cpu's byte order to little-endian */
u32 __be32_to_cpu(u32);    /* convert big-endian to cpu's byte order */
u32 __le32_to_cpus(u32);   /* convert little-endian to cpu's byte order */
```

These convert from one byte order to another. In the case that the orders are the same (for example, if converting from native ordering to big-endian, and the processor is big-endian), the macros do nothing. Otherwise, they return the converted value.

Time

Never assume the frequency of the timer interrupt and thus, the number of jiffies per second. Instead, always use HZ to scale your units of time correctly. This is very important because not only can the timer frequency differ among the various architectures, but it can also change on a given architecture from one kernel release to the next.

For example, HZ is 1000 on the x86 platforms. That is, the timer interrupt occurs 1000 times per second, or every millisecond. Before 2.6, however, HZ was 100 on x86. On other architectures, the value differs: Alpha has HZ equal to 1024 and ARM has it equal to 100.

Never simply compare jiffies to a number such as 1000 and assume that always means the same thing. To scale time appropriately, multiply or divide by HZ. For example:

```
HZ           /* one second */
(2*HZ)       /* two seconds */
(HZ/2)       /* half a second */
(HZ/100)     /* 10 ms */
(2*HZ/100)   /* 20 ms */
```

HZ is defined in <asm/param.h>. This is discussed further in Chapter 9, "Timers and Time Management."

Page Size

When working with pages of memory never assume the page size. It is a common mistake for x86 programmers to assume the page size is 4KB. Although this is true on x86 machines, other architectures have different sizes. Some architectures support multiple page sizes, in fact! *Table 16.4* lists each support architecture's valid page size(s).

When working with pages of memory, use PAGE_SIZE as the size of a page, in bytes. The value PAGE_SHIFT is the number of bits to left shift an address to get its page number. For example, on x86 with 4KB pages, `PAGE_SIZE` is 4096 and `PAGE_SHIFT` is 12. These vales are defined in `<asm/page.h>`.

Table 16.4 **Architecture page size(s)**

Architecture	PAGE_SHIFT	PAGE_SIZE
alpha	13	8KB
arm	12, 14, 15	4KB, 16KB, 32KB
cris	13	8KB
h8300	12	4KB
i386	12	4KB
ia64	12, 13, 14, 16	4KB, 8KB, 16KB, 64KB
m68k	12, 13	4KB, 8KB
m68knommu	12	4KB
mips	12	4KB
mips64	12	4KB
parisc	12	4KB
ppc	12	4KB
ppc64	12	4KB
s390	12	4KB
sh	12	4KB
sparc	12, 13	4KB, 8KB
sparc64	13	8KB
v850	12	4KB
x86_64	12	4KB

Processor Ordering

Recall from Chapter 8, "Kernel Synchronization Methods," that architectures have varying degrees of processor ordering. Some have very strict ordering constraints where all loads and stores occur in the order prescribed by the code. Other chips have very weak ordering and loads and stores are reordered as the processor sees fit.

In your code, if you depend on data ordering, ensure even the weakest ordered processor commits your load and stores in the right order by using the appropriate barriers, such as `rmb()` and `wmb()`. Chapter 8, "Kernel Synchronization Methods," has more information.

SMP, Kernel Preemption, and High Memory

It might seem somewhat incorrect to include symmetrical multiprocessing, kernel preemption, and high memory in a discussion of portability. After all, these are not machine characteristics that affect an operating system but instead they are features of the Linux kernel that are indeed somewhat architecture-agnostic. They represent, however, important configuration options that you should always assume are available in your code. That is, always program for an SMP/preempt/highmem system and you will always be safe, in any configuration. In addition to following the previous portability rules:

- Always assume your code will run on an SMP system and use appropriate locking.

- Always assume your code will run with kernel preemption enabled and use appropriate locking and kernel preemption statements.

- Always assume your code will run on a system with high memory (nonpermanently mapped memory) and use kmap() as needed.

Portability Is Fun

In short, writing portable, clean, proper code has two major implications:

- Always code for the highest common factor: assume anything can happen and any potential constraint is in place.

- Always assume only the lowest common denominator is available: do not assume any given kernel feature is available and only require the minimum architectural features.

Writing portable code requires adherence to many issues: wordsize, data type size, alignment, byte order, page size, processor ordering, and so on. In the large majority of kernel programming, your primary concern is most likely only ensuring that data types are used correctly. Nonetheless, one day an archaic architecture issue will arise—it is important to understand portability issues and always write clean, portable code inside the kernel.

17

Patches, Hacking, and the Community

ONE OF THE GREATEST BENEFITS OF LINUX is the large community of users and developers that surround it. The community provides eyes to check your code and users to test and report issues. Additionally, the community ultimately decides what code is accepted into the kernel. Understanding how everything works is very important.

The Community

If the Linux kernel community had to exist somewhere physically, it would call the *Linux Kernel Mailing List* home. The Linux Kernel Mailing List (or, as the regulars abbreviate it, just *lkml*) is the location of the majority of the discussions, debates, and flame wars over the kernel. New features are discussed and most code is posted to the list before any action is taken. The list sees upward of 300 messages a day, so it is not for the faint of heart. Subscribing (or at least reading a digest or the archives) is recommended for anyone interested in serious kernel development. You can learn a lot simply by watching the wizards at work.

You can subscribe by sending the message:

```
subscribe linux-kernel <your@email.address>
```

in plain text to `majordomo@vger.kernel.org`. More information can be had at `http://vger.kernel.org/` and a FAQ is available at `http://www.tux.org/lkml/`.

Numerous Web sites and other mailing lists pertain to the kernel specifically and Linux in general. An excellent resource for beginning kernel hackers is `http://www.kernelnewbies.org/`—a Web site that, of all things, caters to those cutting their teeth on the kernel. Two other excellent sources of kernel information include `http://www.lwn.net/`, Linux Weekly News, which has a great kernel news section, and `http://www.kerneltraffic.org`, Kernel Traffic, which includes a summary of the previous week's lkml emails with insightful commentary.

Linux Coding Style

The Linux Kernel, like any large software project, has a defined coding style that stipulates the formatting, style, and layout of your code. This is done not because the Linux kernel style is superior (although it is) or because your style is illegible (although it might well be), but because *consistency* of coding style is crucial to *productivity* in coding. Yet, it is often argued that coding style is irrelevant because it does not affect the compiled object code. In a large project, such as the kernel, in which many developers are involved, consistency of coding style is crucial. Consistency implies familiarity, which leads to ease of reading, lack of confusion, and further expectations that code will continue to follow a given style. This increases the number of developers who can read your code, and the amount of code in which you can read. In an open-source project, the more eyes the better.

It is not so important *what* style is chosen as long as one is indeed selected and used exclusively. Fortunately, Linus long ago laid out the style we should use and most code sticks to it. The majority of the style is covered in Linus's usual humor in `Documentation/CodingStyle`.

Indention

The kernel style for indention is to use tabs that are eight characters in length. This does not mean it is okay to use eight spaces for indention or four spaces or anything else. It means each level of indention is a tab from the previous, and a tab is eight characters. For an unknown reason, this rule is one of the most commonly broken, despite its very high impact on readability. Eight-character tabs make clearly identifying indention of different code blocks magnitudes easier after hours of hacking.

If eight-character tabs seem too long, stop indenting so much. Why are your functions nested five levels deep, anyhow? Fix the code, not the indention.

Braces

Brace placement is personal, and few technical reasons exist for one convention over the other, but we have to agree on something. The accepted kernel style is to put the opening brace on the first line, at the end of the statement. The closing brace goes on a new line as the first character. Example:

```
if (fox) {
    dog();
    cat();
}
```

Note the closing brace is not on a line by itself when the following token is a continuation of the same statement. For example:

```
if (fox) {
    ant();
```

```
    pig();
} else {
    dog();
    cat();
}
```

And,

```
do {
    dog();
    cat();
} while(fox);
```

This rule is broken for functions, because functions cannot nest inside of functions:
```
unsigned long func(void)
```

```
{
   /* .. */
}
```

Finally, statements that do not *need* braces can omit them. For example, the following is acceptable:

```
if (foo)
  bar();
```

The logic behind all this is *K&R.*[1]

Naming

No name should have mixed case. Calling a local variable `idx` or even just `i` is perfectly fine if it is clear what it does. A cute name such as `theLoopIndex` is unacceptable. Hungarian notation (encoding the variable type in the variable name) is evil and should never ever be used—this is C not Java, and Unix not Windows.

Nonetheless, global variables and functions should have very descriptive names. Calling a global function `atty()` is confusing; something like `get_active_tty()` is much more acceptable. This is Linux, not BSD.

Functions

As a rule of thumb, functions should not exceed one or two screens of text and should have less than ten local variables. A function should do one thing and do it well. There is no harm in breaking a function into a series of smaller functions. If you are worried about function call overhead, use `inline`.

[1]The C Programming Language by Brian Kernighan and Dennis Ritchie (Prentice Hall, ISBN# 0-13-11-362-8), nicknamed K&R, is the bible of C, written by C's author and his colleague.

Comments

Commenting your code is very important, but the commenting must be done correctly. Generally, you want to describe *what* and *why* your code is doing what it is doing, not *how* it is doing it. The *how* should be apparent from the code itself. If not, maybe you need to rethink what you wrote. Additionally, comments should not include who wrote a function, the modification date, or other trivial nonsense. Such information is generally acceptable at the top of the source file, however.

The kernel uses C-style comments, even though gcc supports C++-style comments, too. The general style of a comment in the kernel resembles:

```
/*
 * get_foo() - return the current value of foo
 * We need this to calculate the bar ratio. This can sleep,
 * so do not call while holding a lock.
 */
```

Comments inside of functions are rare, and should be reserved for special needs, such as documenting a bug or an important assumption. In comments, important notes are often prefixed with "xxx:", and bugs are often prefixed with "FIXME:" like so:

```
/*
 * FIXME: We assume dog == cat which may not be true in the future
 */
```

The kernel has a facility for self-generating documentation. It is based on GNOME-doc, but slightly modified and renamed Kernel-doc. To create the standalone documentation in HTML format, run:

```
make htmldocs
```

Or, for postscript,

```
make psdocs
```

You can document your functions using the system by following a special format for your comments:

```
/**
 * calculate_fox - calculate the fox quotient
 * @dog - the current dog value
 * @cat - the current cat value
 *
 * Must call while holding the fox_lock.
 */
void calculate_fox(int dog, int cat)
{
  /* .. */
}
```

For more information, see Documentation/kernel-doc-nano-HOWTO.txt.

Typedefs

For various reasons, the kernel developers have a certain hatred for `typedef` that almost defies explanation. Their rationale is

- `typedef` hides the real type of data structures.
- Because the type is hidden, code is more prone to do bad things, such as pass a structure by value on the stack.
- `typedef` is just being lazy.

Therefore, to avoid ridicule, avoid `typedef`.

Of course, there are a few good uses of `typedef`s: hiding an architecture-specific implementation of a variable or providing forward-compatibility when a type may change. Decide carefully whether the `typedef` is truly needed or exists just to reduce the number of characters you need to type.

Using What Is Already Provided

Do not reinvent the wheel. The kernel provides string manipulation functions, compression routines, and a linked list interface, so use them.

Do not wrap existing interfaces in generic interfaces. Often you see code that was obviously ported from one operating system to Linux, and various kernel interfaces are wrapped in some gross glue function. No one likes this, so just use the provided interfaces directly.

No `ifdefs` in the Source

Putting `ifdef` preprocessor directives directly in the C source is frowned upon. You should never do something like the following in your functions:

```
    ...
#ifdef CONFIG_FOO
    foo();
#endif
    ...
```

Instead, define `foo()` to nothing if `CONFIG_FOO` is not set:

```
#ifdef CONFIG_FOO
static int foo(void)
{
    /* .. */
}
#else
static inline int foo(void) { }
#endif
```

Then, you can unconditionally call `foo()`. Let the compiler do the work for you.

Structure Initializers

Structures need to be initialized using labeled identifiers. This is good because it prevents structure changes from resulting in incorrect initialization. It also enables values to be omitted. Unfortunately, C99 adopted quite an ugly format for labeled identifiers, and gcc is deprecating usage of the previous GNU-style labeled identifier, which was rather handsome. Consequently, kernel code needs to use the new C99 labeled identifier format, however ugly it is

```
struct foo my_foo = {
        .a    = INITIAL_A,
        .b    = INITIAL_B,
};
```

where a and b are members of struct foo and INITIAL_A and INITIAL_B are their initialized values, respectively. If a field is not set, it is set to its default value per ANSI C (for example, pointers are NULL, integers are zero, and floats are 0.0). For example, if struct foo also has int c as a member, the previous statement would initialize c to zero.

Yes, it is ugly. No, we do not have a choice.

Fixing Code Up *Ex Post Facto*

If a pile of code falls into your lap that fails to even mildly resemble the Linux kernel coding style, do not fret. A little elbow grease and the indent utility will make everything perfect. The indent program, an excellent GNU utility found on most Linux systems, formats source according to given rules. The default settings are for the GNU coding style, which is not too pretty. To get the utility to follow the Linux kernel style, do

```
indent -kr -i8 -ts8 -sob -l80 -ss -bs -psl <file>
```

This instructs the utility to format the code according to the kernel coding style. Alternatively, the script scripts/Lindent automatically invokes indent with the desired options.

Chain of Command

Kernel hackers are the developers who work on the kernel. Some do it for pay, some as a hobby, but nearly all for fun. Kernel hackers with many significant contributions are listed in the CREDITS file in the root of the kernel source tree.

Most parts of the kernel have an associated *maintainer*. The maintainer is the individual or individuals who are in charge of specific parts of the kernel. For example, each individual driver has an associated maintainer. Each kernel subsystem—for example, networking—also has an associated maintainer. The maintainer for a specific driver or subsystem is usually listed in the file MAINTAINERS which is also located in the root of the kernel source tree.

There is a special type of maintainer, known as the kernel maintainer. This individual actually maintains the kernel tree itself. Historically, Linus maintains the development kernel (where the real fun is) and the stable kernel for some period after development ends. Shortly after a development kernel becomes a stable kernel, Linus passes the torch to one of the top kernel developers. They continue to maintain the tree while Linus begins work on the new development tree. In this fashion, the 2.0, 2.2, and 2.4 kernels are still actively maintained.

Despite the rumors, there is no *cabal*. Really.

Submitting Bug Reports

If you encounter a bug, the best course of action is to write a fix, create a patch, test it, and submit it as discussed in the following sections. Of course, you can also report the problem and get someone to fix it for you.

The most important part of submitting a bug report is fully describing the problem. Describe the symptoms, any system output, and a fully decoded oops (if there is an oops). More importantly, if you can, provide steps to reliably reproduce the problem, and a brief description of your hardware.

Determining who to send the bug report to is the next step. The file MAINTAINERS lists the individuals associated with each driver and subsystem—they should receive any issues related to the code they maintain. If you cannot find an interested party, send the report to the Linux Kernel Mailing List at linux-kernel@vger.kernel.org. Even if you do find a maintainer, carbon copying the kernel mailing list never hurts.

The files REPORTING-BUGS and Documentation/oops-tracing.txt provide more information.

Generating Patches

All changes to the Linux kernel are distributed in the form of patches, which are the output of the GNU diff(1) program in a form that is readable by the patch(1) program. The simplest way to generate a patch is to have two source trees, one that is the vanilla stock kernel and another that is the stock tree with your modifications. A common scheme is to name the stock tree linux-x.y.z (which is what the source tarball extracts to, initially) and to name your modified tree simply linux. Then, to generate a patch of the two trees, issue the command

```
diff -urN linux-x.y.z/ linux/ > my-patch
```

from one directory below your trees. This is typically done somewhere in your home, and not /usr/src/linux, so you don't need to be root. The -u flag specifies that the unified diff format should be used. Without this, the patch is ugly and not very readable by humans. The -r flag specifies to recursively diff all directories, and the -N flag specifies that new files in the modified tree should be included in the diff. Alternatively, if you need to diff only a single file, you can do

```
diff -u linux-x.y.z/some/file linux/some/file > my-patch
```

Note, it is important to always diff the trees from one directory below your source trees. This creates a patch that is very usable by others, even if their directory names differ. To apply a patch made in this format, do

```
patch -p1 < ../my-patch
```

from the root of your source tree. In this example, the patch is named my_patch and is created one directory below the current. The -p1 flag specifies to strip the first directory name from the patch. This enables you to apply a patch regardless of the directory-naming convention used by the patch maker.

A useful utility is diffstat, which generates a histogram of a patch's changes (line additions and removals). To generate the output on one of your patches, do

```
diffstat -p1 my-patch
```

It is often useful to include this output when you post a patch to lkml. Because the patch(1) program ignores all lines until a diff is detected, you can even include a short description at the top of the patch itself.

Submitting Patches

Patches should be generated as described in the previous section. If the patch touches a specific driver or subsystem, the patch should be sent to the maintainer listed in MAINTAINER. Either way, the Linux Kernel Mailing List at linux-kernel@vger. kernel.org should be carbon copied. The patch should only be sent to the kernel maintainer (for example, Linus) after extensive discussion, or if the patch is trivial and clearly correct.

Typically, the subject line of the email containing the patch is of the form "[PATCH] brief description." The body of the email describes in technical detail the changes your patch makes and the rationale behind them. Be as specific as possible. Somewhere in the email, note the kernel version the patch was created against.

Most kernel developers want to be able to read your patch inline with your email and optionally save the whole thing to a single file. Consequently, it is best to insert the patch directly inline in the email, at the end of your message. Be aware that some evil email clients might wrap lines or otherwise change formatting; this will break the patch and annoy developers. If your email client does this, see if it has an "Insert Inline" or similar feature. Otherwise, attaching the patch as plain text without encoding works, too.

If your patch is large or contains several logical changes, you should break the patch into chunks, with each chunk representing a logical change. For example, if you both introduce a new API and change a handful of drivers to use it, you can break that into two patches (the new API and then the driver changeover) and two emails. If any chunk requires a previous patch, explicitly state that.

After posting, remain patient and wait for a reply. Do not be discouraged by any negative response—at least you got a response! Discuss the issues and provide updated patches as needed. If you fail to receive *any* response, try to discover what was wrong and resolve the issues. Solicit additional comments from the mailing list and maintainer. With luck, you may see your changes in the next kernel release—congratulations!

A

Linked Lists

A *linked list* is a data structure that allows the storage and manipulation of a variable number of *elements* (often called *nodes*) of data. Unlike a static array, the elements in a linked list are dynamically created. This enables the creation of a variable number of elements that are unknown at compile time. Because the elements are created at different times, they do not necessarily occupy contiguous regions in memory. Therefore, the elements need to be *linked* together, so each element contains a pointer to the *next* element. As elements are added or removed from the list, the pointer to the next node is simply adjusted. *Figure A.1* is a linked list.

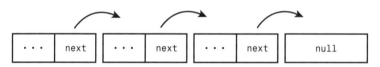

Figure A.1   A singly linked list.

In some linked lists, each element also contains a pointer to the *previous* element. These lists are called *doubly linked lists* because they are linked both forward and backward. Linked lists, similar to the one in *Figure A.1*, that do not have a pointer to the previous element are called *singly linked lists*. *Figure A.2* is a doubly linked list.

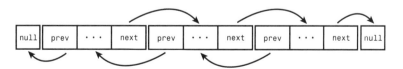

Figure A.2   A doubly linked list.

Circular Linked Lists

Normally, because the last element in a linked list has no next element, it is usually set to point to a special value, usually NULL, to indicate it is the last element in the list. In some linked lists, the last element does *not* point to a special value. Instead, it points back to the first value. This linked list is called a *circular linked list* because the links follow a circle. Circular linked lists can come in both doubly and singly linked versions. In a circular doubly linked list, the first node's 'previous' pointer points to the last node. *Figures A.3* and *A.4* are singly and doubly circular linked list, respectively.

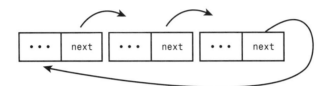

Figure A.3   A circular singly linked list.

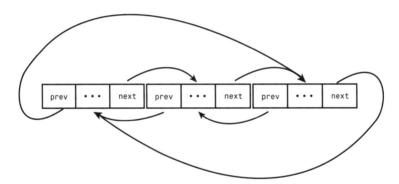

Figure A.4   A circular doubly linked list.

The Linux kernel's standard linked list implementation is a *circular doubly linked list*. Going with this type of linked list provides the greatest flexibility.

Moving Through a Linked List

Movement through a linked list occurs linearly. You visit one element, follow the next pointer, and visit the next element. Rinse and repeat. This is the easiest method of moving through a linked list, and the one by which linked lists are best suited. Linked lists are usually not used when random access is an important goal. Instead, you use linked lists when iterating over the whole list *is* important and the dynamic addition and removal of elements is required.

Oftentimes, the first element is represented by a special pointer—called the *head*—that makes it quick and easy to find. In a noncircular-linked list, the last element is delineated by its next pointer being NULL. In a circular-linked list, the last element is delineated by the fact that it points to the head element. Traversing the list, therefore, occurs linearly through each element from the first to the last. In a doubly linked list, movement can also occur backward, linearly from the last element to the first. Of course, given a specific element in the list, you can go back and forth any number of elements, too. You need not traverse the whole list.

The Linux Kernel's Implementation

The Linux kernel has a unique approach to traversing linked lists. When traversing a linked list, unless ordering is important, it does not matter if you start at the head element, in fact, it doesn't matter *where* you start at all! All that matters is that you visit each and every node. Indeed, we do not even need the concept of a first and last node. If a circular linked list simply contains a collection of unordered data, *any* element can be the head element. To traverse the list, simply pick an element and follow the pointers until you get back to the original element. This removes the need for a special head pointer. Additionally, the routines for manipulating a linked list are simplified. Each routine simply needs a pointer to a single element in the list—*any* element. The kernel hackers are particularly proud of this clever implementation.

Linked lists in the kernel, as with any complex program, are common. For example, the kernel uses a linked list to store the task list (each process's task_struct is an element in the linked list).

The Linked-List Structure

In the old days, there were multiple implementations of linked lists in the kernel. A single, powerful linked list implementation was needed to remove duplicate code. During the 2.1 kernel development series, the official kernel linked-list implementation was introduced. All existing uses of linked lists are now using the official implementation and *all new users must use the existing interface and not reinvent the wheel.*

The linked-list code is declared in <linux/list.h> and the data structure is simple:

```
struct list_head {
  struct list_head *next, *prev;
};
```

Note the curious name, list_head. The name takes a cue from the fact that there is no head node. Instead, because the list can be traversed starting with any given element, each element is in effect a head. Thus, the individual nodes are all called *list heads*. The next pointer points to the next element in the list and the prev pointer points to the previous element. If this is the last element in the list, the next pointer points to the first node. Likewise, if this is the first element in the list, the prev pointer points to the last node. However, thanks to the kernel's elegant list implementation with no concept of list heads, we can ignore any concept of *first* and *last* element. Consider the list a big cycle with no start or finish.

A `list_head` by itself is worthless; it is normally embedded inside your own structure:

```
struct my_struct {
  struct list_head list;
  unsigned long dog;
  void *cat;
};
```

The list needs to be initialized before it can be used. Because most of the elements are created dynamically (probably why you need a linked list), the most common way of initializing the linked list is at runtime:

```
struct my_struct *p;
/* allocate my_struct .. */
p->dog = 0;
p->cat = NULL;
INIT_LIST_HEAD(&p->list);
```

If the structure is statically created at compile time, and you have a direct reference to it, then you can simply do:

```
struct my_struct mine = {
  .list = LIST_HEAD_INIT(mine.list),
  .dog  = 0,
  .cat  = NULL
};
```

To declare and initialize a static list directly:

```
static LIST_HEAD(fox);
```

This will declare and initialize a static list named fox.

You should never actually need to play with the internal members of the linked list. Instead, just embed the structure in your data, and you can make use of the linked list interface to easily manipulate and traverse your data.

Manipulating Linked Lists

A family of functions is provided to manipulate linked lists. All of them take pointers to one or more `list_head` structures. All the functions are implemented as inline functions in generic C and can be found in `include/linux/list.h`.

Interestingly, all these functions are $O(1)$ [1]. This means they execute in *constant time* regardless of the size of the list or any other inputs. For example, it takes the same

---

[1] See Appendix D for an overview of algorithmic complexity.

amount of time to add or remove an entry to or from a list whether that list has 3 or 3,000 entries. This is perhaps not surprising, but still good to know.

`list_add(struct list_head *new, struct list_head *head)`

This function adds the `new` node to the given list immediately *after* the `head` node. Because the list is circular and generally has no concept of *first* or *last* nodes, you can pass any element for `head`. If you do pass the last element, however, this function can be used to implement a stack.

`list_add_tail(struct list_head *new, struct list_head *head)`

This function adds the `new` node to the given list immediately *before* the `head` node. As with `list_add()` because the lists are circular you can generally pass any element for `head`. This function can be used to implement a queue, however, if you do indeed pass the first element.

`list_del(struct list_head *entry)`

This function removes the element `entry` from the list. Note, it does not free any memory belonging to `entry` or the data structure it is embedded in; this function merely removes the element from the list. After calling this, you would typically destroy your data structure and the `list_head` inside it.

`list_del_init(struct list_head *entry)`

This function is the same as `list_del()` except it also reinitializes the given `list_head` with the rationale that you no longer want the entry in the list, but you can reuse the data structure itself.

`list_move(struct list_head *list, struct list_head *head)`

This function removes the `list` entry from its linked list and adds it to the given list *after* the `head` element.

`list_move_tail(struct list_head *list, struct list_head *head)`

This function does the same as `list_move()`, but inserts the `list` element *before* the head entry.

`list_empty(struct list_head *head)`

This returns nonzero if the given list is empty, otherwise it returns zero.

`list_splice(struct list_head *list, struct list_head *head)`

This one splices together two lists by inserting the list pointed to by `list` to the given list after the element `head`.

`list_splice_init(struct list_head *list, struct list_head *head)`

This function works the same as `list_splice()`, except that the emptied list pointed to by `list` is reinitialized.

> **Saving a couple dereferences**
>
> If you happen to already have the next and prev pointers available, you can save a couple cycles (specifically, the dereferences to get the pointers) by calling the internal list functions directly. Every previously discussed function actually does nothing except find the next and prev pointers and call the internal functions. The internal functions generally have the same name as their wrappers, except they are prefixed by double underscores. For example, instead of calling list_del(list) you can call __list_del(prev, next). This is only useful if the next and previous pointers are *already* dereferenced. Otherwise, you are just writing ugly code. See include/linux/list.h for the exact interfaces.

Traversing Linked Lists

Now you know how to declare, initialize, and manipulate a linked list in the kernel. This is all very well and good, but it is meaningless if you have no way to access your data! The linked lists are just a container that holds your important data; we need a way to use the list to move around and access the actual structures that contain our data. Thankfully, the kernel provides a very nice set of interfaces for traversing linked lists and referencing the data structures that include them.

Note that, unlike the list manipulation routines, iterating over a linked list is clearly an O(n) deal, for *n* entries in the list.

The simplest way to iterate over a list is with the list_for_each() macro. The macro takes two parameters, both list_head structures. The first is a pointer used to point to the current entry. The second is a list_head in the list you want to traverse. On each iteration of the loop, the first parameter points to the next entry in the list, until each entry has been visited. Usage:

```
struct list_head *p;

list_for_each(p, list) {
  /* p points to an entry in the list */
}
```

Well, that is still worthless! A pointer to the list structure is usually no good, what we need is a pointer to the structure that contains the list. For example, with our previous my_struct example, we want a pointer to each my_struct, not a pointer to the list member in the structure. The macro list_entry() is provided, which returns the structure that contains a given list_head. It takes three parameters: a pointer to the given element, the type of structure the list is embedded in, and the member name of the list within that structure.

Example:

```
struct list_head *p;
struct my_struct *my;

list_for_each(p, mine->list) {
```

```
    my = list_entry(p, struct my_struct, list);
    /*
     * my points to each structure that list is
     * embedded in
     */
}
```

The `list_for_each()` macro expands to a simple `for` loop. For example, the previous use expands to

```
for (p = mine->list->next; p != mine->list; p = p->next)
```

With the exception that the `list_for_each()` macro also uses processor prefetching, if the processor supports such a feature, to prefetch subsequent entries into memory. To *not* perform prefetching, the macro `__list_for_each()` works just like this `for` loop. Unless you know the list is very small or empty, you should always use the prefetching version. You should never hand code the loop; always use the provided macros.

If you need to iterate through the list backward, you can use `list_for_each_prev()`, which follows the `prev` pointers instead of the `next` pointer.

Note, nothing prevents removal of list entries from the list while you are traversing it. Normally, the list needs some sort of lock to prevent concurrent access. The macro `list_for_each_safe()`, however, uses temporary storage to make traversing the list safe from removals:

```
struct list_head *p, *n;
struct my_struct *my;
list_for_each_safe(p, n, mine->list) {
  my = list_entry(p, struct my_struct, list);
  /* my points to each my_struct in the list */
}
```

Note, this macro *only* provides protection from removals. You might additionally require some locking protection to prevent concurrent manipulation of the actual list data.

B

The Per-CPU Interface

MODERN SMP-CAPABLE OPERATING SYSTEMS USE per-CPU data—data that is unique to a given processor—extensively. Typically, per-CPU data is stored in an array. Each item in the array corresponds to a possible processor on the system. The current processor number indexes this array, which is how the 2.4 kernel handles per-CPU data. Nothing is wrong with this approach, so plenty of 2.6 kernel code still uses it. You declare the data as

```
unsigned long my_percpu[NR_CPUS];
```

Then you access it as

```
int cpu;

cpu = get_cpu(); /* get current processor index and disable kernel preemption */
my_percpu[cpu]++;
printk("my_percpu on cpu=%d is %ld\n", cpu, my_percpu[cpu]);
put_cpu();                 /* enable kernel preemption */
```

Note, no lock is required because this data is unique to the current processor. As long as no processor touches this data except the current, no concurrency concerns exist, and the current processor can safely access the data without lock.

Kernel preemption is the only concern with per-CPU data. Kernel preemption poses two problems, listed here:

- If our code is preempted and reschedules on another processor, the cpu variable is no longer valid because it points to the wrong processor. (In general, code cannot sleep after obtaining the current processor.)

- If another task preempts our code, it can concurrently access my_percpu on the *same* processor, which is a race condition.

Any fears are unwarranted, however, because the call get_cpu(), on top of returning the current processor number, also disables kernel preemption. The corresponding call to put_cpu() enables kernel preemption. Note, if you use a call to `smp_processor_id()` to get the current processor number, kernel preemption is not disabled——always use the aforementioned methods to remain safe.

The New `percpu` Interface

The 2.6 kernel introduced a new interface, known as *percpu*, for creating and manipulating per-CPU data. This interface generalizes the previous example. Creation and manipulation of per-CPU data is simplified with this new approach.

The previously discussed method of creating and accessing per-CPU data is still valid and accepted. This new interface, however, grew out of the needs for a simpler and more powerful method for manipulating per-CPU data on large symmetrical multiprocessing computers.

The header `<linux/percpu.h>` declares all the routines. You can find the actual definitions there, in `mm/slab.c`, and in `<asm/percpu.h>`.

Per-CPU Data at Compile-Time

Defining a per-CPU variable at compile-time is quite easy:

```
DEFINE_PER_CPU(type, name);
```

This creates an instance of a variable of type `type`, named `name`, for each processor on the system. If you need a declaration of the variable elsewhere, to avoid compile warnings, the following macro is your friend:

```
DECLARE_PER_CPU(type, name);
```

You can manipulate the variables with the `get_cpu_var()` and `put_cpu_var()` routines. A call to `get_cpu_var()` returns an l-value for the given variable on the current processor. It also disables preemption, which `put_cpu_var()` correspondingly enables.

```
get_cpu_var(name)++;    /* increment name on this processor */
put_cpu_var();        /* done; enable kernel preemption */
```

You can obtain the value of *another* processor's per-CPU data, too:

```
per_cpu(name, cpu)++;    /* increment name on the given processor */
```

You need to be careful with this approach because `per_cpu()` neither disables kernel preemption nor provides any sort of locking mechanism. The lockless nature of per-CPU data only exists if the current processor is the only manipulator of the data. If other processors touch other processor's data, you need locks. Be careful. Chapter 7, "Kernel Synchronization Introduction," and Chapter 8, "Kernel Synchronization Methods," discuss locking.

Another subtle note, these compile-time per-CPU examples do not work for modules because the linker actually creates them in a unique executable section (for the curious, `.data.percpu`). If you need to access per-CPU data from modules, or if you need to create such data dynamically, there is hope.

Per-CPU Data at Run-Time

The kernel implements a dynamic allocator, similar to `kmalloc()`, for creating per-CPU data. This routine creates an instance of the requested memory for each processor on the systems. The prototypes are in `<linux/percpu.h>`:

```
void *kmalloc_percpu(size_t size, int flags);
void kfree_percpu(const void *);
```

The `kmalloc_percpu()` function allocates one instance of an object of the given size for every processor on the system. The `flags` parameters works the same way as the flags for `kmalloc()`, as discussed in Chapter 10, "Memory Management and Addressing." See *Table B.1*.

Table B.1   `kmalloc_percpu()` **Flags**

Flags	Description
GFP_ATOMIC	Allocate memory atomically; it will not sleep
GFP_KERNEL	Allocate normal kernel memory; it might sleep
GFP_USER	Allocate memory on behalf of the user; it might sleep

A corresponding call to `kfree_percpu()` will free the data, on all processors.

A call to `kmalloc_percpu()` returns a pointer, which is used to indirectly reference the dynamically created per-CPU data. The kernel provides two macros to make this easy:

```
get_cpu_ptr(ptr);  /* return a void pointer to this processor's copy of ptr */
put_cpu_ptr(ptr);  /* done; enable kernel preemption */
```

The `get_cpu_ptr()` macro returns a pointer to the specific instance of the current processor's data. It also disables kernel preemption, which a call to `put_cpu_ptr()` then enables.

Let's look at a full example of using these functions. Of course, this example is a bit silly because you would normally allocate the memory once (perhaps in some initialization function), use it in various places, and free it once (perhaps in some shutdown function). Nevertheless, this example should make usage quite clear:

```
void *percpu_ptr;
unsigned long *foo;

percpu_ptr = kmalloc_percpu(sizeof(unsigned long), GFP_KERNEL);
if (!ptr)
    /* error allocating memory .. */

foo = get_cpu_ptr(percpu_ptr);
/* manipulate foo .. */
put_cpu_ptr(percpu_ptr);
```

Finally, the function `per_cpu_ptr()` returns a given processor's unique data:

```
per_cpu_ptr(ptr, cpu);
```

Again, it does not disable kernel preemption and—if you touch another processor's data—keep in mind you probably need to implement locking.

Reasons for Using Per-CPU Data

There are a couple benefits to using per-CPU data. The first is the reduction in locking requirements. Depending on the semantics by which processors access the per-CPU data, you might not need any locking at all. Keep in mind the *"only this processor accesses this data"* rule is only a programming convention. You need to ensure that the local processor only accesses its unique data. Nothing stops you from cheating.

Second, per-CPU data greatly reduces cache invalidation. This occurs as processors try to keep their caches in sync. If one processor manipulates data held in another processor's cache, that processor must flush or otherwise update its cache. Constant cache invalidation is called *thrashing the cache* and wrecks havoc on system performance. The use of per-CPU data keeps cache effects to a minimum because processors ideally only access their own data.

Consequently, the use of per-CPU data often removes (or at least minimizes) the need for locking. The only safety requirement for their use is disabling kernel preemption, which is much cheaper than locking and the interface does so automatically. Per-CPU data can safely be used from either interrupt or process context. Note, however, you cannot sleep in the middle of accessing per-CPU data (or else you might end up on a different processor).

No one is currently required to use the new per-CPU interface. Doing things manually (with an array as originally discussed) is fine, as long as you disable kernel preemption. The new interface, however, is much easier to use and might gain additional optimizations in the future. If you do decide to use per-CPU data in your kernel code, consider the new interface. One caveat *against* its use is that it is not backward compatible with earlier kernels.

C

Kernel Random Number Generator

THE KERNEL IMPLEMENTS A STRONG *RANDOM NUMBER GENERATOR* that is theoretically capable of generating *true random numbers*. The random-number generator gathers environmental noise from device drivers into an *entropy pool*. This pool is accessible from within the kernel and from user processes as a source of data that is not only random but also non-deterministic to an outside attacker. Such numbers are of use in various applications, most notably cryptography.

True random numbers differ from the pseudo-random numbers generated by functions such as those found in the C library. Pseudo random numbers are created by a *deterministic* function. Although the function might generate a sequence of numbers that exhibit some properties of a true random number, they are only statistically random. Pseudo random numbers are deterministic—knowing one number in the sequence provides information about the rest of the sequence. In fact, knowing the initial value of the sequence (known as the *seed*) usually determines the entire sequence. For applications that need truly random and nondeterministic numbers, such as cryptography, a pseudo-random number is usually unacceptable.

As opposed to a pseudo-random number, a true random is produced independently of its generating function. Furthermore, knowing some value in a sequence of truly random numbers does not allow an external party to deduce future values from the generator—the generator is nondeterministic.

From physics, *entropy* is a measurement of disorder and randomness in a system. Entropy is measured in energy-per-unit temperature (Joules/Kelvin). When Claude Shannon[1], the founder of information theory, looked for a term to represent randomness

---

[1] Claude E. Shannon (April 30, 1916—February 24, 2001) was an engineer at Bell Labs whose most famous work, *A Mathematical Theory of Communication*, published in 1948, introduced the concept of information theory and Shannon entropy. Shannon also enjoyed riding his unicycle.

in information, the great mathematician John von Neumann[2] supposedly suggested he use the term entropy because no one really understood what that meant anyhow. Shannon agreed, and today the term is sometimes called *Shannon entropy*. In hindsight, some scientists find the dual use confusing, and prefer simply the term *uncertainty* when discussing information. Kernel hackers, on the other hand, think entropy sounds cool and encourage its use.

In discussions of random-number generators, Shannon entropy is an important property. It is measured in bits per symbol; high entropy implies there is little useful information (but lots of random junk) in a sequence of characters. The kernel maintains an entropy pool that is fed data obtained from nondeterministic device events. Ideally, this pool is entirely random. To help keep track of the entropy in the pool, the kernel keeps a measurement of the uncertainty of the data in the pool. As the kernel feeds data into the pool, it estimates the amount of randomness in the data it is adding. Conversely, the kernel reduces the estimate of entropy as data is removed from the pool. This measurement is called the *entropy estimate*. Optionally, the kernel can refuse a request for a random number if the entropy estimate is zero.

The kernel random-number generator was introduced in kernel version 1.3.30 and lives at `drivers/char/random.c` in the kernel source.

Design and Implementation

Computers are predictable devices. Indeed, it is hard to find randomness in a system whose behavior is entirely programmed. The environment of the machine, however, is full of *noise* that is accessible and nondeterministic. Such sources include the timing of various hardware devices and user interaction with the computer. For example, the time between key presses, the movement of the mouse, the timing between certain interrupts, and the time taken to complete a block I/O request are all both nondeterministic and not measurable by an outside attacker. Randomness from these values is taken and fed into the entropy pool. The pool grows to become a random and unpredictable mixture of noise. As the values are added to the pool, an estimate of the randomness is calculated and a tally is kept. This enables the kernel to keep track of the entropy in the pool. *Figure C.1* is a diagram of the flow of entropy into and out of the pool.

The kernel provides a set of interfaces to allow access to the entropy pool, both from within the kernel and from user-space processes. When the interfaces are accessed, the kernel first takes the *SHA* hash of the pool. SHA (Secure Hash Algorithm) is a message

---

[2] John von Neumann (December 28, 1903—February 8, 1957) was a member of the Institute for Advanced Study at Princeton. In his life, he gave the world numerous contributions to mathematics, economics, and computer science. Some of his most important contributions were game theory, Neumann algebras, and the von Neumann bottleneck.

digest algorithm developed by the National Security Agency and made a United States Federal standard by NIST (via FIPS 186). A message digest is an algorithm that takes a variable-sized input (small or large) and outputs a fixed-size hash value (typically 128 or 160-bits) that is a digest of the original input. From the outputted hash value, the input cannot be reconstructed. Furthermore, trivial manipulations to the input (for example, changing one character) result in a radically different hash value. Message digest algorithms have various uses, including data verification and fingerprinting. Other message digest algorithms include MD4 and MD5. The SHA hash, not the raw contents of the pool, is returned to the user—the contents of the entropy pool are never directly accessible. It is assumed impossible to derive any information about the state of the pool from the SHA hash. Therefore, knowing some values from the pool does not lend any knowledge to past or future values. Nonetheless, the kernel can use the entropy estimate to refuse to return data if the pool has zero entropy. As entropy is read from the pool, the entropy estimate is decreased in response to how much information is now known about the pool.

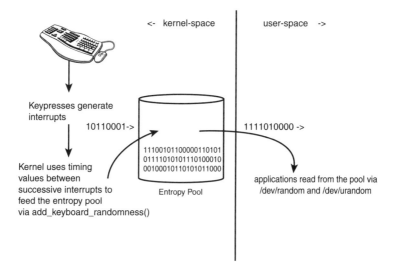

Figure C.1   The flow of entropy into and out of the kernel entropy pool.

When the estimate reaches zero, the kernel can still return random numbers. Theoretically, however, an attacker is then capable of inferring future output given prior output. This requires that the attacker have nearly all the prior outputs from the entropy pool, and that the attacker successfully perform cryptanalysis on SHA. Because SHA is believed to be secure, this possibility is infeasible. To high security cryptography users who accept no risk, however, the entropy estimate ensures the strength of the random numbers. To the vast majority of users this extra assurance is not needed.

Why is this done in the kernel?

A criterion for a kernel feature in Linux is that they cannot also be easily implemented in user space. Tossing things in the kernel because we can is not acceptable. At first glance, a random-number generator and entropy pool has no place in the kernel. Three conditions, however, all but require that they live in the kernel. First, the random-number generator needs access to system timings, such as interrupts and user input. It is not possible for user space to access such timings without forcing the kernel to export various interfaces and hooks to notify user space of these events. Even if the data were exported, retrieving it would be neither clean nor fast. Second, the random-number generator must be secure. Although the system could run as *root* and institute various security measures, the kernel provides a much safer home for the entropy pool. Finally, the kernel itself makes use of the random data. It is neither practical nor clean for the kernel to have to obtain the values from a user space agent. Therefore, the random-number generator lives happily in the kernel.

The Dilemma of System Startup

When the kernel first boots, it completes a series of actions that are almost entirely predictable. Consequently, an attacker can infer much about the state of the entropy pool at boot. Worse, each boot is largely similar to the next, and the pool initializes to largely the same contents on each boot. This reduces the accuracy of the entropy estimate, which has no way of knowing the entropy contributed during the boot sequence is less predictable than entropy contributed at other times.

To offset this problem, most Linux systems save some information from the entropy pool across system shutdowns. They do this by saving the contents of the entropy pool on each shutdown. When the system boots, the data is read and fed into the entropy pool. This effectively loads the previous contents of the pool into the current pool, without increasing the entropy estimate.

Therefore, an attacker cannot predict the state of the entropy pool without knowledge of both the current state of the system and the *previous* state of the system.

Interfaces to Input Entropy

The kernel exports a family of interfaces to facilitate feeding data into the entropy pool that are called by the appropriate kernel subsystems or drivers. They are

```
void add_interrupt_randomness(int irq)
void add_keyboard_randomness(unsigned char scancode)
void add_mouse_randomness(__u32 mouse_data)
```

`add_interrupt_randomness()` is called by the interrupt system whenever an interrupt is received whose handler was registered with SA_SAMPLE_RANDOM. The parameter irq is the interrupt number. The random-number generator uses the timing between interrupts as a source of noise. Note, not all devices are suitable for this; if the device generates interrupts deterministically (for example, the timer interrupt) or might be influenced by an outside attacker (for example, a network device) it should not feed the pool. An acceptable device is a hard disk, which generates interrupts at an unpredictable rate.

`add_keyboard_randomness()` uses the scancode and the timing between successive key presses to feed the entropy pool. Interestingly, the routine is smart enough to ignore *autorepeat* (when the user holds a key down) because both the scancode and timing interval are then constant, contributing little entropy. The sole parameter is the scancode of the pressed key.

`add_mouse_randomness()` uses the mouse position as well as the timing between interrupts to feed the pool. The parameter `mouse_data` is the hardware-reported position of the mouse.

All three of these routines add the supplied data to the entropy pool, calculate an estimate of the entropy of the given data, and increment the entropy estimate by this amount.

All these exported interfaces use the internal function `add_timer_randomness()` to feed the pool. This function calculates the timing between successive events of the same type and adds the delay to the pool. For example, the timing between two successive disk interrupts is largely random—especially when measured very precisely. Often, the low order bits are electrical noise. After this function feeds the pool, it calculates how much randomness was present in the data. It does this by calculating the first, second, and third order deltas from the previous timing, along with the first and second order deltas. The greatest of these deltas, rounded down to 12 bits, is used as the entropy estimate.

Interfaces to Output Entropy

The kernel exports one interface for obtaining random data from within the kernel:

```
void get_random_bytes(void *buf, int nbytes)
```

This function stores `nbytes` worth of random data in the buffer pointed to by `buf`. The function returns the values regardless of whether the entropy estimate is zero. This is less of a concern to the kernel than user space cryptography applications. The random data is suitable for a handful of kernel tasks, most notably networking, where it is used to seed the initial TCP sequence number in a connection.

Kernel code can do the following to receive a word-size helping of randomness:

```
unsigned long rand;

get_random_bytes(&rand, sizeof(rand));
```

For user-space processes, the kernel provides two character devices: `/dev/random` and `/dev/urandom`. The first, `/dev/random` is suitable when very strong random numbers are desired, as in high-security cryptographic applications. It only returns up to the maximum number of bits of random data noted by the entropy estimate. When the entropy estimate reaches zero, `/dev/random` blocks and will not return the remaining data until the entropy estimate is sufficiently positive. Conversely, the device `/dev/urandom` does *not* have this feature but is generally just as secure. Both devices return numbers from the same pool.

Reading from either file is simple. Here is an example of a user space function that an application can use to extract a word of entropy:

```
unsigned long get_random(void)
{
    unsigned long seed = 0;
    int fd;

    fd = open("/dev/urandom", O_RDONLY);
    if (fd == -1) {
        perror("open");
        return 0;
    }
    if (read (fd, &seed, sizeof(seed)) < 0) {
        perror("read");
        seed = 0;
    }
    if (close(fd))
        perror("close");

    return seed;
}
```

Alternatively, you can easily read $bytes bytes into the file $file using the dd program:

```
dd if=/dev/urandom of=$file count=1 bs=$bytes
```

D

Algorithmic Complexity

OFTEN, IN COMPUTER SCIENCE AND RELATED DISCIPLINES, it is useful to express the algorithmic complexity—or *scalability*—of algorithms as a meaningful value (as opposed to less descriptive terms, like *gross*). Various methods for representing scalability exist. One common technique is to study the *asymptotic behavior* of the algorithm. This is the behavior of the algorithm as its inputs grow exceedingly large or *approach infinity*. Asymptotic behavior shows how well an algorithm scales as its input grows larger and larger. Studying an algorithm's scalability—how it performs as the size of its input increases—enables us to model the algorithm against a benchmark and better understand its behavior.

Algorithms

An algorithm is a series of instructions, possibly one or more inputs, and ultimately a result or output. For example, the steps to count the number of people in the room are an algorithm, with the people being the input and the count being the output. In the Linux kernel, both page eviction and the process scheduler are examples of algorithms. Mathematically, an algorithm is like a function (or at least, we may model it as one). For example, if we call the people counting algorithm f and the number of people to count x, we can write:

    y = f(x)   people counting function

Where y is the time required to count the x people.

Big-O Notation

One useful asymptotic notation is the upper bound—a function whose behavior is always greater than the one we are studying. It is said that the upper bound grows faster than the function in question. A special notation, big-o (pronounced *big oh*) notation, is used to describe this growth. It is written f(x) is O(g(x)) and is read f is big-oh of g. The formal mathematical definition is

```
If f(x) is O(g(x)), then
∃c, x' such that f(x) ≤ c·g(x), ∀x > x'
```

In English, the time to complete f(x) is always less than the time to complete g(x) multiplied by some arbitrary constant (at least, it is less as long as the input x is larger than some initial value x').

Essentially, we are looking for a function whose behavior is as bad as or worse than our algorithm. We can then look at the result of very large inputs to the function and obtain an understanding of the bound of our algorithm.

Big Theta Notation

When most people talk about big-oh notation they are more accurately referring to what Donald Knuth describes as big-theta notation. Technically, big-oh notation refers to an upper bound. For example, seven is an upper bound of six; so are 9, 12, and 65. Subsequently, when most people discuss function growth they talk about the *least upper bound,* or a function that models both the upper and lower bounds[1]. Professor Knuth describes this as big-theta notation and gives the following definition:

```
If f(x) is big-theta of g(x), then
g(x) is both an upper bound and a
lower bound for f(x).
```

Then, we can also say f(x) is of *order* g(x). The order, or big-theta, of an algorithm is one of the most important mathematical tools for understanding algorithms in the kernel.

Consequently, when people refer to big-o notation they are more often talking about the least such big-o, the big-theta. You really do not have to worry about this, unless you want to make Professor Knuth really happy.

Putting It All Together

For example, consider again having to count the number of people in a room. Pretend you can count one person per second. Then, if there are seven people in the room, it will take seven seconds to count them. Obviously, given n people it will take n seconds to count everyone. Thus, we can say this algorithm is O(n). What if the task was to dance in front of everyone in the room? Because it would take the same amount of time to dance whether there were five or five thousand people in the room, this task is O(1). See Table D.1 for other common complexities.

---

[1]If curious, the lower bound is modeled by big-omega notation. The definition is the same as big-o, except g(x) is always less than or equal to f(x).

Table D.1   **Table of Time Complexity Values**

O(g(x))	Name
1	constant (perfect scalability)
log n	logarithmic
n	linear
n^2	quadratic
n^3	cubic
2^n	exponential (evil)
n!	factorial (pure evil)

What is the complexity of introducing everyone in the room to everyone else? What is a possible function that models this algorithm? If it took thirty seconds to introduce each person, how long would it take to introduce 10 people to each other? What about one hundred people to each other?

Perils of Time Complexity

Obviously, it is wise to avoid complexities such as O(n!) or O(2^n). Likewise, it is usually an improvement to replace an O(n) algorithm with a functionally-equivalent O(1) algorithm. This is not always the case, however, and a blind assumption should not be made based solely on big-o notation. Recall that, given O(g(x)), there is a constant, c, multiplied by g(x). Therefore, it is possible an O(1) algorithm takes three hours to complete. Sure, it is *always* three hours, regardless of how large the input, but that can still be a long time compared to an O(n) algorithm with few inputs. The typical input size should always be taken into account when comparing algorithms. Do not optimize blindly for some random case!

Bibliography and Reading List

This bibliography is sorted by subject and contains some of the more interesting and useful books on subjects similar or complimentary to those in this book.

All of these books have proved themselves quite useful over time. Some of them represent "sacred tomes" in their respective subjects, whereas others I have simply found interesting, insightful, or entertaining in some capacity. I hope that they can assist you, as well.

Note that the absolute best reference or "additional reading" to compliment this book is the kernel source. Working on Linux, we are all gifted with full and unrestricted access to the source code for an entire modern operating system. Do not take that for granted! Dive in!

Books on Operating System Design

These books cover OS Design, as discussed in an undergraduate course. They all tackle the concepts, algorithms, problems, and solutions involved in designing a functional operating system.

Tanenbaum, Andrew. *Operating Systems: Design and Implementation*. Prentice Hall, 1997. A great introductory work on both the design and implementation of a Unix-like system, Minix.

Tanenbaum, Andrew. *Modern Operating Systems*. Prentice Hall, 2001. A strong overview of the standard operating system design issues plus discussion on many of the concepts used in today's modern operating systems, such as Unix and Windows.

A. Silberschatz, P. Galvin, and G. Gagne. *Operating System Concepts*. John Wiley and Sons, 2001. Also known as the Dinosaur book, for the seemingly irrelevant dinosaurs on the cover. A great introduction to OS design. The book has frequent revisions; any of them should do fine.

Books on Unix Kernels

These books tackle the design and implementation of Unix kernels. The first three discuss a specific flavor of Unix, and the later two focus on issues common to all Unix variants.

Bach, Maurice. *The Design of the Unix Operating System*. Prentice Hall, 1986. A good discussion on the design of Unix System V Release 2.

M. McKusick, K. Bostic, M. Karels, and J. Quarterman. *The Design and Implementation of the 4.4BSD Operating System*. Addison-Wesley, 1996. A good discussion on the design of the 4.4BSD system by the system designers themselves.

J. Mauro and R. McDougall. *Solaris Internals: Core Kernel Architecture*. Prentice Hall, 2000. An interesting discussion on the core subsystems and algorithms in the Solaris kernel.

Vahalia, Uresh. *Unix Internals: The New Frontiers*. Prentice Hall, 1995. A superb book on very modern Unix features, such as thread management and kernel preemption.

Schimmel, Curt. *UNIX Systems for Modern Architectures: Symmetric Multiprocessing and Caching for Kernel Programmers*. Addison-Wesley, 1994. A superb book on the perils of supporting a modern Unix on a modern architecture.

Books on Linux Kernels

These books, like this one, discuss the Linux kernel.

A. Rubini and J. Corbet. *Linux Device Drivers*. O'Reilly and Associates, 2001. An excellent discussion on how to write device drivers for the 2.4 kernel.

D. Bovet and M. Cesati. *Understanding the Linux Kernel*. O'Reilly and Associates, 2002. A good discussion of the internal algorithms of the 2.4 Linux kernel. It focuses on the underlying design of the kernel.

D. Mosberger and S. Eranian. *IA-64 Linux Kernel: Design and Implementation*. Prentice Hall, 2002. An excellent look at the Intel Itanium architecture and its port of the Linux 2.4 kernel.

Books on Other Kernels

Understanding your enemies—err, competitors—never hurts. These books discuss the design and implementation of operating systems other than Linux. See what they got right and what they got wrong.

M. Kogan and H. Deitel. *The Design of OS/2*. Addison-Wesley, 1996. An interesting look at OS/2 2.0.

D. Solomon and M. Russinovich. *Inside Windows 2000*. Microsoft Press, 2000. An interesting look at a very non-Unix operating system.

Richter, Jeff. *Advanced Windows*. Microsoft Press, 1997. A thorough discussion of low-level and systems programming in Windows.

Books on the Unix API

In-depth discussions of the Unix system and its API are important not only for writing powerful user-space programs, but also understanding the responsibilities of the kernel.

Stevens, W. Richard. *Advanced Programming in the UNIX Environment*. Addison-Wesley, 1992. An excellent, if not definitive, discussion on the Unix system call interface.

Stevens, W. Richard. *UNIX Network Programming, Volume 1*. Prentice Hall, 1998. A classic text on the sockets API used by Unix systems.

M. Johnson and E. Troan. *Linux Application Development*. Addison-Wesley, 1998. A general overview of the Linux system and Linux-specific interfaces.

Other Works

A collection of other books not strictly related to operating systems, but which undoubtedly affect them.

Knuth, Donald. *The Art of Computer Programming, Volume 1*. Addison-Wesley, 1997. A priceless tour de force in the fundamental algorithms of computer science, including best- and worst-fit algorithms used in memory management.

B. Kernighan and D. Ritchie. *The C Programming Language*. Prentice Hall, 1988. The definitive book on the C programming language.

Hofstadter, Douglas. *Gödel, Escher, Bach: An Eternal Golden Braid*. Basic Books, 1999. A profound and indispensable look at human thought that delves wildly into multiple subjects, including computer science.

Web Sites

These Web sites provide up-to-date news and downloads related to Linux and our beloved kernel.

http://www.kerneltraffic.org/ *Kernel Traffic*. An excellent summary of the previous week's traffic on the Linux kernel mailing list (lkml). Also highly recommended.

http://www.lwn.net/ *Linux Weekly News*. A great news site with an excellent commentary on the week's kernel happenings. Highly recommended.

http://www.kernelnewbies.org/ *Kernel Newbies*. Kernel Newbies is a community project to provide information and help to aspiring kernel hackers.

http://www.kernel.org/ *Kernel.org*. The official repository of the kernel source. It is also home to a large number of the core kernel hacker's patches.

Index

G

H

KERN_NOTICE, 256

KERN_WARNING, 256

printk() function, 255-256

M

macros

EXPIRED_STARVING(), 43

TASK_INTERACTIVE(), 43

user_mode(), 151

Magic SysRq Key, 261-262

mailing list, 8, 281

maintainers, 286

MAINTAINERS file, 286

mapping memory, 182-184, 238

mb() function, 137-139

mdelay() function, 159-160

memory

address intervals, 237-240

addressing, 165-167, 225-226

allocating, 163, 167-170, 174-176, 179-182, 184, 228-229

allocation, 163

areas, 225-226, 230-237

flags, 231-232

free lists, 176

freeing, 167-169, 174-176

gfp_mask flags, 170-174

kernel threads, 229-230

mapping, 238

mappings, 182-184

memory descriptor, 226-229

page tables, 240-241

pages, 163-165

process address space, 225

protection, 11

slab allocator interface, 179-181

slab layer, 176-181

stack, 181-182

virtual memory areas (VMAs), 230-233

zones, 165-167

metadata, 187

methods. *See* functions

mmap() function, 239

mod_timer() function, 156

modifying timers, 156

module setting, 13

mount flags, 207-208

mount points, 187

Multics, 1

multiple threads of execution

contention, 115

critical regions, 108-110

deadlocks, 113-115

defined, 107

granularity of locking, 115

locking, 109-110, 112-113, 116

race conditions, 108-110

multitasking operating systems

cooperative multitasking, 31

preemptive multitasking, 31, 34

munmap() function, 239-240

mutex semaphores, 128

N

namespace, 187

namespace structure (VFS), 209-210

naming conventions (coding style), 283

navigating linked lists, 292-293, 296-297

nice() function, 51

notation

big-o notation, 309-310

big-theta notation, 310

O

O(1) scheduler, 32

objects (VFS)

dentry, 188, 198-202

directory, 188

file, 188, 202-206

inode, 188, 193-198

operations, 189

superblock, 188-193

Q-R

Your Guide to Computer Technology

www.informit.com